IMMIGRATION LAW AND PROCEDURE

IN A NUTSHELL

FOURTH EDITION

By

DAVID WEISSBRODT
Fredrikson & Byron Professor of Law
University of Minnesota Law School

WEST
GROUP

ST. PAUL, MINN.
1998

COPYRIGHT © 1984, 1989, 1992 WEST PUBLISHING CO.
COPYRIGHT © 1998 By WEST GROUP
                          610 Opperman Drive
                          P.O. Box 64526
                          St. Paul, MN 55164–0526
                          1–800–328–9352

Library of Congress Cataloging-in-Publication Data

Weissbrodt, David S.
   Immigration law and procedure in a nutshell / by David Weissbrodt.
  — 4th ed.
    p.   cm. — (Nutshell series)
   Includes index.
   ISBN 0–314–23208–7 (softcover)
   1. Emigration and immigration law—United States. I. Title.
II. Series.
KF4819.3.W4   1998
342.73'082—dc21   98–17903
                                   CIP

ISBN 0–314–23208–7

PREFACE

This brief text is designed to assist students in obtaining an overview of the material which might be expected to be found in a course on immigration law and procedure.

When the first edition of this Nutshell was written, there did not yet exist a standard casebook on immigration law and it was unclear what substance belonged in a course on immigration law and procedure. At that time only a few law schools considered immigration law worthy of a course. Since then many major law schools have decided to offer immigration law courses and three principal coursebooks have been published: Thomas Alexander Aleinikoff et al., Immigration and Citizenship: Process and Policy (4th ed. 1998); Richard Boswell, Immigration and Nationality Law: Cases and Materials (3d ed. 1997); and Stephen Legomsky, Immigration Law: Cases, Materials and Problems (2d ed. 1997). It was gratifying to see that several parts of this Nutshell were reprinted in two of those coursebooks.

This Nutshell presents the information which a student should want to know about the immigration process as it functions in the United States. With the enactment of the Antiterrorism and Effective Death Penalty Act of 1996 (AEDPA) and the Illegal Immigration Reform and Immigrant Responsibility Act of 1996 (IIRIRA), immigration law and procedures have undergone significant change. In addition to those legislative changes, political upheaval throughout the world has made immigration a far more visible and controversial issue—leading, in turn, to a constantly evolving body of laws, regulations, decisions, and policies. The fourth edition of this text is organized in six parts to reflect these changes and make them as comprehensible and accessible as possible.

The *first* part—chapters 1 through 4—provides a general overview of the history, constitutional source, and institutional structure of immigration law. In addition to tracing the evolution of immigration law and history in the U.S., the first part discusses the increasing recognition of the federal power to regulate immigration and describes the federal agencies and congressional committees responsible for the formulation and implementation of immigration law.

The *second* part—chapters 5 through 7—covers the various standards and application procedures for immigrant, nonimmigrant, and student visas. It should be noted, however, that this Nutshell does not attempt to serve as a manual for practitioners or potential immigrants.

In part *three*, chapters 8 and 9 explain the grounds for requiring an alien to depart from the United States and the procedures for removal and denial of admission.

In the fourth part, chapters 10 and 11 discuss refugee and asylum issues and summarize international law as it relates to immigration.

Because immigration law is ultimately founded upon the relationship between the individual and the state, part five—chapters 12 and 13—focuses on citizenship and the rights of aliens in the United States.

Part six—chapters 14 through 17—identifies several ethical issues which immigration lawyers confront and which may help to clarify for students the nature of the immigration process. Chapters 16 and 17 contain a brief conclusion and a bibliography.

The author wishes to thank several present and former law students who assisted in the preparation of this Nutshell. The students who assisted with the first, second, and third editions are identified in those respective editions. The author wishes to thank Lucie Bendova and Chris Rediehs for their help in revising all chapters of the present fourth edition. Meredith McQuaid, Assistant Dean, and Seema Shah, a former student, contributed their comments on immigration concerns specific to international students in chapter 7. Marci Hoffman provided very helpful bibliographical assistance—especially on the last chapter. Ann Browning did excellent secretarial work to make the fourth edition possible.

I am also very grateful to Laura Danielson who practices immigration law in Minneapolis and co-teaches the immigration law course at the University of Minnesota, for contributing her valuable time and expertise in reviewing the manuscript. Joan Fitzpatrick, a colleague at the University of Washington Law School, was also very helpful in providing her comments. H. Sam Myers, an immigration lawyer in Minneapolis and the 1991–1992 President of the American Immigration Lawyers Association, generously took time from his busy law practice to review the manuscript and to give much assistance. In addition, Michelle A. Egan, District Adjudication Officer, Immigration and Naturalization Service in the St. Paul District Office, gave me very useful comments on the citizenship issues in chapter 12. The author, of course, must take ultimate responsibility for what remains in this book and what the Nutshell format required to be deleted.

DAVID WEISSBRODT

Minneapolis, Minnesota
June, 1998

EXPLANATORY NOTES

I have attempted to follow the format of other Nutshell volumes. Accordingly, cases have been cited only where they represent relatively significant landmarks or where they clarify significant issues. The text ordinarily contains only the name of the case, the court of decision, and the date. The student will find the full citation in the Table of Authorities, which follows the Outline. Due to limitations of space and format, some cases are omitted where they would have supported statements in the text and one case is often cited where many others would have been usable as authority.

Immigration law is considerably based upon statutes and regulations. Hence, the text contains frequent references to the principal statutes and regulations, but for reasons of space the citations have been abbreviated in the text. Where both a statute and regulation appear relevant, only the statute is cited. The Table of Authorities contains fuller references to cases, statutes, regulations, and other relevant material.

Because the Nutshell format does not admit footnotes, this volume often omits references to secondary material and other sources, even where such citations clearly exist. The bibliography in the last chapter attempts to redress this problem by listing at least most of the principal sources for the use of the serious student who may want to read more.

*

OUTLINE

OUTLINE

*

Contents

TABLE OF CASES

References are to Pages

TABLE OF CASES

*

TABLE OF OTHER AUTHORITIES

UNITED STATES

UNITED STATES CONSTITUTION

TABLE OF OTHER AUTHORITIES

UNITED STATES CONSTITUTION

UNITED STATES CODE ANNOTATED

7 U.S.C.A.—Agriculture

8 U.S.C.A.—Aliens and Nationality

TABLE OF OTHER AUTHORITIES

UNITED STATES CODE ANNOTATED
8 U.S.C.A.—Aliens and Nationality

18 U.S.C.A.—Crimes and Criminal Procedure

21 U.S.C.A.—Food and Drugs

22 U.S.C.A.—Foreign Relations and Intercourse

UNITED STATES CODE ANNOTATED
26 U.S.C.A.—Internal Revenue Code

28 U.S.C.A.—Judiciary and Judicial Procedure

30 U.S.C.A.—Mineral Lands and Mining

42 U.S.C.A.—The Public Health and Welfare

TABLE OF OTHER AUTHORITIES

UNITED STATES CODE ANNOTATED
43 U.S.C.A.—Public Lands

50 U.S.C.A.—War and National Defense

50 U.S.C.A.App.—War and National Defense

STATUTES AT LARGE

STATUTES AT LARGE

STATUTES AT LARGE

TABLE OF OTHER AUTHORITIES

STATUTES AT LARGE

POPULAR NAME ACTS

ILLEGAL IMMIGRATION REFORM AND IMMIGRANT RESPONSIBILITY ACT OF 1996

IMMIGRATION ACT OF 1990

IMMIGRATION AND NATIONALITY ACT

TABLE OF OTHER AUTHORITIES

IMMIGRATION AND NATIONALITY ACT

TABLE OF OTHER AUTHORITIES

IMMIGRATION AND NATIONALITY ACT

TABLE OF OTHER AUTHORITIES

IMMIGRATION AND NATIONALITY ACT

TABLE OF OTHER AUTHORITIES

IMMIGRATION AND NATIONALITY ACT

TABLE OF OTHER AUTHORITIES

IMMIGRATION AND NATIONALITY ACT

TABLE OF OTHER AUTHORITIES

IMMIGRATION AND NATIONALITY ACT

TABLE OF OTHER AUTHORITIES

IMMIGRATION AND NATIONALITY ACT

TABLE OF OTHER AUTHORITIES

IMMIGRATION AND NATIONALITY ACT

TABLE OF OTHER AUTHORITIES

IMMIGRATION AND NATIONALITY ACT

TABLE OF OTHER AUTHORITIES

IMMIGRATION AND NATIONALITY ACT

TABLE OF OTHER AUTHORITIES

IMMIGRATION AND NATIONALITY ACT

TABLE OF OTHER AUTHORITIES

IMMIGRATION AND NATIONALITY ACT

TABLE OF OTHER AUTHORITIES

IMMIGRATION AND NATIONALITY ACT

TABLE OF OTHER AUTHORITIES

IMMIGRATION AND NATIONALITY ACT

TABLE OF OTHER AUTHORITIES

IMMIGRATION AND NATIONALITY ACT

IMMIGRATION REFORM AND CONTROL ACT

NATIONALITY ACT OF 1952

NATIONALITY ACT OF 1940

SELECTIVE SERVICE ACT OF 1940

TABLE OF OTHER AUTHORITIES

CODE OF FEDERAL REGULATIONS

TABLE OF OTHER AUTHORITIES

CODE OF FEDERAL REGULATIONS

TABLE OF OTHER AUTHORITIES

CODE OF FEDERAL REGULATIONS

TABLE OF OTHER AUTHORITIES

CODE OF FEDERAL REGULATIONS

FEDERAL REGISTER

TABLE OF OTHER AUTHORITIES

FEDERAL REGISTER

EXECUTIVE ORDERS

OPERATING INSTRUCTIONS

INTERNATIONAL INSTRUMENTS

AFRICAN CHARTER ON HUMAN AND PEOPLE'S RIGHTS

AMERICAN CONVENTION ON HUMAN RIGHTS

CONVENTION AGAINST TORTURE

TABLE OF OTHER AUTHORITIES

CONVENTION RELATING TO THE STATUS OF STATELESS PERSONS

EUROPEAN CONVENTION ON HUMAN RIGHTS

INTERNATIONAL COVENANT ON CIVIL AND POLITICAL RIGHTS

REFUGEE CONVENTION OF 1951

UNITED NATIONS CONVENTION

TABLE OF OTHER AUTHORITIES

MODEL RULES OF PROFESSIONAL CONDUCT

OPINION OF THE ATTORNEY GENERAL

*

IMMIGRATION LAW AND PROCEDURE

IN A NUTSHELL

FOURTH EDITION

*

CHAPTER 1

HISTORY OF U.S. IMMIGRA-
TION LAW AND POLICY

§ 1–1 COLONIAL IMMIGRATION

Because an immigrant is defined by *Black's Law Dictionary* as one who leaves a country to settle permanently in another to live, one tends to think of United States immigration as dating from the nation's inception. Most anthropologists, however, believe that the first newcomers to the region that is now the United States entered from Asia over 20,000 years ago across the land bridge where the Bering Strait now lies. These people first settled the western regions, and distinct cultural groups lived in areas spanning to the Atlantic Ocean before any European explorers or later settlers arrived.

In settling the English colonies, immigrants arrived freely and were at first welcomed by other Europeans already settled. Immigration was limited principally by the cost of travel, diseases, and conflict with indigenous inhabitants. Yet by 1640, the population of the colonies had reached approximately 25,000. Population records can only suggest the rate of increase because no immigration records were kept.

The newcomers to the colonies in the years before the American Revolution came from many places and for diverse reasons. Most Europeans—English, French, German, Dutch, Spanish, and Portuguese—came for economic reasons or to avoid religious persecution in their homelands.

Unfortunately, some of these immigrants began to encounter that same hostility and persecution in the colonies. The Quakers set themselves apart in Pennsylvania and the Scotch–Irish Presbyterians moved west to settle the Mississippi frontier when they received a cold reception in the East. Others, like the French Huguenots, assimilated more easily. Some religious restrictions were adopted by individual colonies attempting to exclude Quakers and Catholics or to subject them to discriminatory taxes. The colonial restrictions were somewhat effective in discouraging immigrants.

Others came involuntarily as punishment or under servitude. Slaves from Africa were forcibly brought. Children were kidnapped from English slums and sold for American labor. English judges were empowered to send both vagrants and felons to the colonies as punishment. These groups also met with disfavor and colonial restrictions; colonies began legislating to exclude "paupers" and "criminals" as early as 1639. Those restrictions excluding "public charges" embraced not only people sent by English courts but also the poor and the diseased who came voluntarily. Southern colonies especially tried to restrict criminals, because that region had received the greatest influx of the 50,000 sent under penal sanction during the fifty years before the Revolution.

These restrictions illustrate the hostility felt toward newcomers by colonists who had just arrived themselves. Although aimed primarily at those banished from England and at public charges who would be added to relief rolls, these restrictions were also a product of religious and national rivalries imported from Europe. The colonies were generally unable to check the influx of migrants, for they lacked both legal authority and a centralized administrative structure. In addition, immigration was still favored to the extent that the colonies needed more people for labor and security. To outsiders, the New World held great promise. Accordingly, by the year 1776, the population of the colonies stood at about 2,500,000, or 100 times the 1640 figure.

The colonial immigration restrictions may have influenced the later legislation of the United States on this subject. In fashioning its laws, the federal government eventually excluded the same general classes of immigrants as did the colonies. The federal legislation also used certain colonial sanctions on immigrants, such as head taxes on individuals and deportation of undesirable aliens.

§ 1–2 EARLY U.S. IMMIGRATION POLICY

Although colonial attitudes continued after the American Revolution, extensive federal legislation dealing with immigration was not enacted for some time, primarily for two reasons. First, for almost a hundred years, it was unclear whether the federal government was even intended by the Constitution to have power to regulate immigration. Second, the United States officially favored unrestricted immigration for about the same period of time after the nation's birth.

The locus of power over the subject of immigration was not definitively identified in any early proclamation of the new government. Under the Articles of Confederation, each state apparently determined its own immigration policy, but there was confusion over the status of prior colonial enactments. The United States Constitution, adopted in 1789, granted Congress broad power to regulate foreign commerce in Article I, section 8, but it was not clear whether foreign commerce included immigration. Not until 1875 did the U.S. Supreme Court in *Henderson v. City of New York* (Sup.Ct.1875) declare state restrictions on immigration to be unconstitutional, as an infringement on the federal power over foreign commerce.

During this long period of uncertainty, Congress did not generally attempt to invoke its power to regulate immigration, but principally passed a series of acts regulating naturalization and a few other nonrestrictive pieces of legislation. Congress adopted the first such law in 1790, liberally granting citizenship to immigrants. Subsequent legislation, however, required increasingly longer periods of residency as well as the renunciation of former allegiances and titles of nobility. In 1798 Congress authorized the President to expel "dangerous" aliens in the Alien Friends Act and the Alien Enemies Act, but the Alien Friends Act expired without extension after two years. A new Naturalization Act in 1802 reestablished the provisions of a 1795 act, creating a five-year residency requirement for citizenship. In addition, the "passenger acts" of 1819, 1847, 1848, and 1855 set certain minimum space and provisions standards for overseas vessels. Further, the Constitution specifically permitted the adoption of a law forbidding the importation of slaves after 1808 and such a law came into effect that year.

Apart from piecemeal legislation, the first one hundred years of the nation's existence can be characterized as a period of unrestricted immigration. The spacious frontier and the need for labor were the primary reasons for this unrestrictive policy. No official records were kept of immigration until 1820, but it is estimated that 250,000 immigrants arrived in the United States between 1790 and 1820. From 1820 to 1880, while the issue of power over immigration was being debated, over 10 million people arrived.

Discontent with the open immigration policy increased with the rate of immigration and with change in the composition of immigrants. Between 1820 and 1880, political conditions and economic devastation brought over 2.8 million Irish immigrants to the United States. German Catholic immigrants came in large numbers during the European depressions of the 1840's. In a predominantly Protestant country, the Catholic Irish and Germans were not well accepted. The anti-Catholicism that had prevailed in colonial days resurfaced. Several groups and overlapping political parties, including social reformers, Protestant Evangelicals, the Nativists, the Order of the Star–Spangled Banner, and the Know–Nothing Party, campaigned for legislation halting immigration and prohibiting even naturalized immigrants from participating in the nation's political process. These groups were somewhat successful at the state level, but failed at the federal level because the Irish and Germans constituted a large voting block. Politicians at the national level actively sought the vote of these and other newly arrived groups. Hence, federal policy, and apparently the majority of the nation, continued to favor immigration.

Eventually, the Civil War drowned the protests of groups like the Know–Nothings. The need for labor in both North and South was magnified during these war years; an 1864 Act even facilitated immigration by validating contracts pledging future wages in payment for overseas passage.

§ 1–3 RESTRICTION BEGINS: EXCLUDING THE UNWANTED

After the Civil War, federal law began to reflect the growing desire to restrict the immigration of certain groups. The facilitating act of 1864 was repealed in 1868, and in 1875 Congress passed the first restrictive statute. That statute, borrowing from earlier colonial legislation, barred convicts and prostitutes from admission. These limits were the first of many "quality control" exclusions based on the nature of the immigrants themselves. The list of unacceptable types of immigrants would continue to grow in subsequent enactments.

The 1875 Act also attempted to solve the new problem faced by the western states. Westward expansion demanded huge numbers of laborers for work in the mines and on the railroads. Imported Chinese labor had been used since about 1850, and tension between the Chinese workers and the settlers of European descent ran high. Chinese labor depressed wage scales and some Chinese women were being imported as prostitutes. The Chinese did not assimilate and the European groups would not tolerate the cultural differences. In response, Congress adopted a law outlawing so-called "coolie labor" contracts and immigration for lewd and immoral purposes. Many Chinese, however, continued to immigrate voluntarily or were routed through Canada. Hence, in 1882 Congress took stronger action in the Chinese Exclusion Act, the nation's first racist, restrictive immigration law, and one of several acts in the 1880's aimed at stemming the tide of Chinese immigration. The act suspended all immigration of Chinese laborers for ten years and forbade any court to admit Chinese to citizenship. The act was extended in 1902 and later made permanent. (Not until 1943 was it finally repealed so that Chinese could become citizens.)

Congress had finally decided by the 1880's that immigration was fully appropriate for federal control. The Act of 1882 may be considered the first general federal immigration act. It continued to base restrictions on quality controls; in addition to the 1875 exclusions of "convicts" and "prostitutes," it barred "lunatics," "idiots," and those "likely to become public charges." The act also for the first time imposed a head tax on every arriving immigrant. The tax served the express function of raising revenues to defray administrative expenses. Congress did not want the poor of other nations to be added to the government relief rolls; the tax served the underlying function of deterring the immigration of people unable to pay. In several subsequent statutes, the head tax was raised from fifty cents to two dollars, making the barrier relatively substantial at that time.

Despite these limits, over 5.2 million immigrant aliens arrived in the 1880's. Immigration was seen as a threat to the U.S. economy, and Congress began expanding the list of "undesirable classes," hoping both to upgrade the type of immigrants and to limit overall entry. An 1891 act added the "diseased," "paupers," and "polygamists" to the list of excludable persons. It also forbade advertising in foreign countries that encouraged immigration to America. In addition, immigrants were required to take medical examinations to determine whether they were "diseased." A few years later, special boards of inquiry were established to decide other questions of admissibility under the "quality" restrictions. The 1891 law established the Bureau of Immigration, the forerunner of the present Immigration and Naturalization Service (INS). The Bureau was responsible for inspecting entrants at the 24 ports of entry to the U.S.

Immigration did abate somewhat in the 1890's, totaling 3.6 million—a reduction of over 1.5 million from the previous decade. There was a sharp increase in immigration, however, at the turn of the century, and Congress tried to stem the flow by excluding more classes of immigrants. In 1903, a new law excluded epileptics, the "insane," "beggars," and "anarchists." In 1907 the "feebleminded," the tubercular, and those persons with a mental or physical defect that "may affect" their ability to earn a living were added to the list. During this period, Japanese immigration was restricted by a 1907 agreement negotiated between the United States and Japan. Although the cumulative list was long, these quality controls were not easily enforced. Moreover, at that time the Bureau of Immigration and Naturalization had only 1,200 employees in the U.S. to process arriving immigrants and enforce the entry restrictions. Nonetheless, almost 8.8 million immigrants were admitted by the Bureau in the first decade of the 1900's.

More than the huge numbers concerned Congress, however. The type of person immigrating was changing. In the 1880's, 72% of immigrants to the U.S. came from northern and western Europe. In contrast, during the 1900–10 decade, 71% came from countries in southern or eastern Europe. These "new immigrants" were Latins, Slavs, and Jews, who were considered "inferior" by the predominantly Anglo–Saxon population. Much like the Chinese who preceded them by several decades, the "new immigrants" were slow to assimilate, living together in urban ethnic neighborhoods. The Anglo–Saxons feared that their predominance was threatened and pressured Congress for more restrictive measures.

Because the earlier "quality control" exclusions did little to stem the flow of immigrants, those groups favoring restrictions on immigration began to advocate literacy as an entrance requirement. In 1907, after several failed attempts to pass a literacy bill, Congress established a joint congressional-presidential commission to study the impact of immigration on the United States. In 1911 the Commission published its findings. It concluded that twentieth century immigration to the U.S. was significantly different from earlier immigration and that the new immigration was dominated by the so-called "inferior" and "less desirable" groups. As a result, the Commission concluded that the United States no longer benefited from a liberal immigration policy and should impose further entry restrictions. The Commission recommended a literacy test as one such restriction.

In 1917, over President Wilson's veto, Congress responded. The 1917 Act was clearly aimed at restricting immigration of various nationalities. One important purpose of the act was to limit immigration from southern and eastern Europe, which was accomplished by barring people unable to read. Because the new immigrants were largely illiterate, the impact of literacy tests limited that region's immigration more than any other. The act also raised the head tax to eight dollars, providing yet another obstacle.

In addition, Congress addressed the growing concern over foreign "anarchists" in the 1917 Act. This group had been excluded by an earlier law of 1903 that had been enacted in response to President McKinley's assassination. In 1917, Congress apparently focused on the anti-alien mood prevalent during World War I. This sentiment led to subsequent enactment of the Anarchist Act of 1918, which more specifically defined "anarchists."

The last major exclusion of the 1917 Act prohibited all immigration of Asians from countries within specified latitudes and longitudes. Many similar racist exclusions had been proposed in Congress that year, and the Asiatic Barred Zone survived as an undebated amendment to the 1917 Act. Congressional attempts to prevent blacks from immigrating to the U.S. were defeated, however, due in large part to intensive lobbying by the NAACP.

The literacy entrance requirement and the nervousness surrounding World War I about the ability to assimilate foreign born persons resulted in an Americanization movement. Beginning in 1919, many states established Americanization programs to ensure that immigrants would learn English. Industry joined the movement by establishing similar programs for workers. By 1923, the Bureau of Naturalization reported 252,808 immigrants in 6,632 programs across the country.

§ 1–4 THE QUOTA LAWS

World War I naturally limited immigration by making shipping less available, but after its end, immigration began to grow. The country favored an isolationist policy and wanted to protect its own labor force from the anticipated postwar flood of European refugees. Dissatisfied with its latest set of quality exclusions, Congress implemented numerical controls. Enacted first as a temporary measure, the 1921 Quota Law marked a major shift in the U.S. approach to immigration control. The law limited immigration of each nation to 3% of the number of foreign-born persons of that nationality residing in the U.S. as of the 1910 census. The total quota was 357,000, but because few foreign-born persons from the South and East of Europe lived in the U.S. in 1910, that region's total quota was 45,000 less than that from the North and West of Europe. The effect of the quota allotments was to restrict immigration from the disfavored regions; the northern and western countries of Europe did not even fill their quotas under this law. Fortunately for the restricted group, Congress established certain "non-quota" exceptions. For example, the law permitted a person to be admitted to the United States as an immigrant if the individual had lived in the Western Hemisphere for one year (later changed to five years). Hence, by temporarily living in a Western Hemisphere country, many avoided the quotas.

In 1924, Congress further restricted immigration by reducing the immigration quota from 3% of foreign-born persons under the 1910 census to 2% of the foreign-born under the 1890 census. This change cut the total quota to 164,667 and made the southern and eastern quotas proportionately even smaller than before. Again, people from those regions had to use the non-quota provisions to enter the U.S. Although under the 1924 Act only Western Hemisphere natives were non-quota, Europeans and others used another provision exempting spouses of U.S. citizens from the quotas.

Despite the restrictive 1924 Act, immigration from the southern and eastern countries of Europe equaled entries from the northern and western countries, thereby defeating the restrictive purposes of Congress. The quota and quality restrictions resulted in increased surreptitious border crossing. Moreover, although Europe was the targeted region, immigration from the Western Hemisphere began to climb in the 1920's, presenting border control problems. In response, the Bureau created the Border Patrol in 1924, hiring 45 men to guard the country's 8,000 miles of land and sea borders. Total immigration in the years 1924–29 reached 1.5 million.

In 1929, as provided by the 1924 Act, a new quota took effect. The "national origins formula" used the ethnic background of the entire U.S. population, rather than the first generation immigrant population, as its base for calculating national quotas. Because the U.S. population was still predominantly Anglo–Saxon, the national origins quota restricted the newer immigrant groups more severely than the foreign-born formula of the previous quota laws. The national origins quota allotted 85% of the total quota of 150,000 to countries from the North and West of Europe, while the South and East received only 15% of that total quota.

The effect of the national origins formula, however, cannot accurately be measured. Soon after it took effect, the U.S. economy collapsed. The Great Depression limited immigration; only one-half million immigrated to the U.S. during the 1930's. In 1932, at the height of the Great Depression, emigration far exceeded legal immigration. Only 35,576 entered the country in that year, while over 100,000 left. The potential for immigration increased during those years, however, with the growth of highways and increased airplane traffic. By 1938, there were 186 ports of entry into the U.S. On June 14, 1940, the INS was transferred from the Department of Labor to the Department of Justice.

One of the most tragic consequences of the U.S. restrictive immigration policy fell upon refugees trying to flee Europe before World War II. In 1939, Congress defeated a bill that would have accommodated 20,000 children fleeing from Nazi Germany—despite the availability of willing sponsor families—because the number of children would have exceeded the quota allocated to German nationals. In 1940 the State Department did permit consuls outside Germany to issue visas to German refugees when the German quota was unfilled, but this and other measures were inadequate to help the vast majority of victims of Nazi persecution.

World War II brought an economic upswing, and immigration increased in response, bringing the total of entrants in the 1940's to one million. The United States again needed labor from abroad and negotiated with Mexico for a temporary worker program to satisfy the country's wartime employment needs. Congress also repealed the ban on Chinese immigration, largely due to the wartime alliance of the United States with China. Congress established a small quota for Chinese immigrants and also permitted Chinese immigrants to be naturalized as U.S. Citizens.

As the United States became painfully aware of the Nazi atrocities and the fate of the refugees it had refused, there was a short period of liberalization of the strict quota laws. President Truman issued a directive in 1945, admitting 40,000 war refugees. Under the War Brides Act of 1945 and the Fiancees Act of 1946, about

123,000 alien spouses, children, and fiancées of WW II military personnel were admitted to the U.S. The Displaced Persons Act of 1948 admitted 400,000 war refugees from Austria, Germany, and Italy to the U.S., but these admissions "mortgaged" their countries' quotas, sometimes limiting or closing off all immigration from a country for several years thereafter.

The work of the INS had burgeoned by the late 1940's. By 1949, the U.S. had 416 ports of entry by land, sea, and air at which the INS annually made about 90 million inspections of immigrants, nonimmigrants, and returning citizens for compliance with entry requirements. The Border Patrol force remained stable at about 1,100, yet its total apprehensions of deportable aliens tripled in three years from 100,000 in 1946 to 300,000 in 1949.

In contrast to its liberalizing legislation, Congress soon afterwards acted to restrict another group. Anti–Communism rose after WW II and particularly during the war in Korea. As a result, national security legislation received high priority in Congress. The Internal Security Act of 1950 amended the 1918 Anarchists Act. The exclusions, however, were expressly directed this time at Communists; the act broadly defined the excluded group, barring anyone "likely to" engage in "subversive activity."

At the same time, however, Congress continued to legislate in the area of refugee admissions. In 1953 Congress passed the Refugee Relief Act, which admitted an additional 214,000 refugees. Although designed primarily to facilitate the admission of refugees fleeing from Eastern European countries dominated by the Soviet Union, the act also included provisions to prevent the admission of undesirable aliens. Similar measures were passed in 1956 and 1957 to assist the entry of Hungarians and others fleeing from Communism as well as persons fleeing from countries in the Middle East. The 1960 Refugee Fair Share Law established a temporary admission and assistance program for those World War II refugees and displaced persons who remained in camps under the mandate of the United Nations High Commissioner for Refugees.

§ 1–5 THE 1952 ACT AND LATER AMENDMENTS

The Immigration and Nationality Act of 1952 (INA) consolidated previous immigration laws into one coordinated statute. As amended, the 1952 Act provides the foundation for immigration law in effect today.

In the 1952 Act Congress retained, over President Truman's veto, the controversial national origins quota. The 1952 quota was calculated differently than the original national origins quota and established a 150,000 person limit on immigration from the Eastern Hemisphere. Congress exempted the Asia–Pacific Triangle from this quota, because so few people from that region lived in the U.S. as a consequence of the Barred Zone law of 1917; the quota would have been grossly inequitable in that respect. Instead, a modest quota of 2,000 was established for that area. Congress also retained the detailed "quality control" exclusions found in earlier legislation and added several new ones. Within the quota system, four types of entrance preferences were established. First preference was given those entrants with skills or experience needed by the U.S. economy. Those persons with close family relations to U.S. citizens or resident aliens received lower preferences. This ordering was changed by amendment in 1965, but it should be noted that spouses of U.S. citizens were not and are still not subject to the quota or preference system.

Several aspects of the 1952 Act drew heavy criticism. The national origins quota, based on the 1920 census, was a blatant form of racial and ethnic discrimination. Also, despite some increased procedural safeguards for aliens, the 1952 Act did not provide them procedural due process.

The 1952 Act presented the INS with new and complex laws to enforce, yet Congress did not supply the Service with increased personnel or appropriations to perform its new work. Moreover, the early 1950's saw a large increase in deportable alien apprehensions aimed at the expulsion of Mexicans from the U.S. The Border Patrol, still about 1,000 strong, apprehended 800,000 deportable aliens in 1952; in 1954, that number increased to one million. Because of "Operation Wetback" 90% of those apprehended came from Mexico. It is believed that this expulsion included U.S. citizens of Mexican descent who were not given an opportunity to establish their claim to citizenship.

During the 1950's, Congress made several minor revisions in the 1952 Act, and over 2.5 million immigrated to the U.S. The number of people entering the U.S. increased in the 1960's, reflecting the growing availability of all means of travel. To facilitate the necessary inspections, in 1963 the INS consolidated duties at ports of entry with several agencies. Hence, one officer performed the duties of the INS, Customs, U.S. Public Health Service, and the Bureau of Plant Quarantine at the Mexican border. This joint approach eased the workload somewhat, for in 1964 the INS made 178 million inspections, almost twice the 1949 figure, yet total INS personnel had only increased from 6,900 to 7,058. In 1966, 200 million persons—immigrants, non-immigrants, and returning citizens—were inspected at over 400 ports of entry. Total immigration for the 1960's was 3.3 million.

The criticized national origins formula was not abolished until 1965 when President Johnson successfully urged enactment of former President Kennedy's program of immigration reform. The 1965 amendments replaced the national origins formula with a limit of 20,000 on each country in the Eastern Hemisphere and an overall limit of 170,000 for that hemisphere. The law established a quota of 120,000 for the Western Hemisphere, without preferences or country limits—to take effect in 1968.

The 1965 amendments abolished the old four-preference system and established in its place a seven-preference system for close relatives and those immigrants with needed occupational skills from the Eastern Hemisphere. Again, spouses of U.S. citizens were permitted to immigrate without reference to the quota or preference system. Under the preference system, unmarried children of U.S. citizens received highest preference; second preference was granted to spouses and unmarried children of permanent resident aliens. The preference for immigrants of "exceptional ability" and those in "the professions" was changed from first to third. Other relatives of citizens and aliens received the fourth and fifth preferences. Sixth preference was given to needed workers. Seventh preference was allocated to refugees.

The abolition of the national origins formula was in large part the result of a pervasive attitudinal change. Anti–Catholic, –Asian, and –Semitic sentiment decreased as the civil rights movement stimulated an increased tolerance of racial and ethnic differences. Unfortunately, there remained strong prejudice against people of color. After World War II, the proportion of Spanish-speaking immigrants increased, and much prejudice was directed toward these newcomers from Mexico as well as Central and South America. Although the 1952 Act did not place a numerical limit on immigration from these areas, Congress included the Western Hemisphere quota of 120,000 in the 1965 amendments as a compromise for abolishing the national origins system. As a result, there was a steadily growing backlog of Latin American applicants forced to wait several years for a visa.

In 1976, a new law was passed which applied the Eastern Hemisphere preference system to the Western Hemisphere. Hence, both hemispheres were subject to the 20,000 per country limit and the seven preference system. The law, however, did retain separate annual limits—120,000 for the Western and 170,000 for the Eastern Hemisphere—and a special 600 visa ceiling for colonies and dependencies.

A 1978 amendment established a world-wide quota of 290,000 and applied the same per country limits and seven preference system to both hemispheres. This worldwide ceiling eliminated the hemisphere consideration and allowed visas to go where the need was greatest. The 20,000 per country limit, however, was a serious restraint on immigration from a few countries such as Mexico.

Meanwhile, the INS staff became increasingly overworked. The number of deportable aliens, which fell in the 1950's, climbed rapidly in the 1960's and 1970's, as did the number of total entries. In 1972, one half million deportable aliens were apprehended. By 1977, that annual figure had doubled. The Border Patrol had grown to a force of 2,400, still too few to guard the borders properly. The Immigration Service estimated that, between undetected border crossings and violations of legal entry conditions, millions of undocumented aliens were living in the U.S. in 1974. In 1973, 250 million persons were inspected at about 1,000 ports of entry. By 1979, 274 million were inspected annually, and the Border Patrol apprehended one million deportable aliens. That year, the INS employed almost 11,000 personnel under a 300 million dollar budget.

In March 1980 Congress dealt with the issue of refugees. The 1980 Refugee Act broadened the definition of refugees to accord with the international definition in the Convention and Protocol relating to the Status of Refugees. Further, the Refugee Act set an annual maximum of 50,000 refugees through the year 1982, but permitted the Administration, in consultation with Congress, to set the number of refugees to be admitted each year after 1982. The initial numerical limits in the Refugee Act were undermined, however, by the deluge of Cuban refugees soon after its enactment. More than 100,000 Cubans arrived in the U.S. in the spring of 1980—mostly via the port of Mariel. Eventually, the Carter Administration concluded that the influx of "Mariel" Cubans was not within the contemplation of the Refugee Act and asked for special legislation to deal with the problem. The 1980 Act reduced the worldwide immigrant quota from 290,000 to 270,000 to offset partially the separate allocation for refugees.

In 1981 Congress adopted another series of amendments to the immigration law, which *inter alia,* eliminated the permanent exclusion of aliens who had been deported and permitted these deportees to return without permission five years after deportation. Also, a person convicted of a single minor marihuana offense could obtain a waiver of excludability. There were a number of other amendments concerning foreign medical graduates, congressional reporting requirements as to visas issued, exchange visitors, and treaty investors. But these minor changes did not address the national perception that the U.S. had lost control of its borders and required a much more thorough revision of immigration law.

The Immigration Marriage Fraud Amendments of 1986 amended the INA to deter immigration-related marriage fraud. The 1986 Fraud Amendments imposed a two-year conditional residency requirement on alien spouses and children or "sons and daughters" before they could obtain permanent resident status on the basis of a "qualifying marriage" to a U.S. citizen or permanent resident alien. *See* § 5–3.1, *infra* for a discussion of the distinction between the term "children" and "sons and daughters." To obtain permanent status, the couple must have filed a petition within the last 90 days of the conditional status period. The INS could then interview the couple to ascertain that (a) the "qualifying marriage" was not entered into "for the purpose of procuring an alien's entry as an immigrant"; (b) the marriage had not been judicially annulled or terminated, other than through the death of a spouse; or (c) a fee or other consideration other than attorney's fees was not given for the filing of the alien's petition. If these conditions were not met, the alien spouse could have the conditional basis removed from the permanent residence status. In 1990 Congress amended those provisions to permit waiver for cases of battered spouses or children as well as other hardships.

The 1986 Fraud Amendments also imposed criminal penalties for immigration-related marriage fraud of not more than five years and/or not more than $250,000 in fines. In addition, the 1986 Fraud Amendments explicitly made marriage fraud an additional ground for deportation as well as a perpetual bar to future immigration. Furthermore, the Fraud Amendments restricted adjustment of the alien's status based on a marriage undertaken while exclusion or deportation proceedings were pending. The Fraud Amendments required that an alien, who seeks immigration status based upon a marriage to a U.S. citizen or lawful permanent resident initiated after the commencement of deportation or exclusion proceedings, must have resided for a period of two years outside the United States before being eligible to acquire legal status based upon the marriage. The 1990 Act, however, allowed the alien to avoid the foreign residence requirement if s/he establishes by clear and convincing evidence that the marriage was entered in good faith, in accordance with the laws of the place where the marriage took place, and not for the purpose of procuring the alien's admission as an immigrant. INA § 245(e)(3).

§ 1–6   THE 1986 IMMIGRATION REFORM AND CONTROL ACT (IRCA)

In 1980 the United States Census Bureau counted 2,047,000 undocumented aliens in the country. Based on the Bureau of Census' experience in miscounting other segments of the population, the Bureau had estimated that there were 5,965,000 undocumented aliens in the country on census day April 1, 1980. As the INS attempted to confront these problems with inadequate resources,

it was criticized for inefficient internal operations, misconduct, and a general inability to control the flow of
undocumented immigration.

Thirty-four years had passed since the enactment of
the last major immigration reform, when Congress finally adopted in 1986 the Immigration Reform and Control
Act (IRCA). IRCA was not easily adopted, having been
unsuccessfully attempted in three previous congressional
sessions. It represented a political compromise between
four interests—(1) those people seeking to deter illegal
immigration by discouraging unauthorized employment
in the U.S.; (2) those seeking a one-time amnesty for
aliens who, for years, had been locked out as illegal
immigrants; (3) those who wanted to insure continued
access to low-cost agricultural labor without elaborate
federal regulation; and (4) those who wished to insure
that penalizing employers for illegally hiring aliens would
not encourage discriminatory employment practices. Ultimately, the act that was adopted focused almost exclusively on illegal immigration. The act was a partial
response to the 1981 recommendations of the Select
Committee on Immigration and Refugee Policy chaired
by (Rev.) Theodore M. Hesbergh, then President of the
University of Notre Dame. IRCA dealt with the major
problem of undocumented aliens by imposing sanctions
on employers, and at the same time legalizing the status
of undocumented entrants who had arrived prior to
January 1, 1982. Because Congress was concerned that
employer sanctions would result in discrimination in the
workplace, IRCA included provisions prohibiting discrimination on the basis of national origin or citizenship
status. IRCA also provided the INS with significant new
resources to enforce the immigration laws. Furthermore,
in response to the demand for foreign agricultural labor,

IRCA created a program that grants temporary and permanent resident status to qualified agricultural workers. Despite these major provisions and a number of less important ones, IRCA did not substantially restructure the immigration law as it pertains to immigrant and nonimmigrant visas.

The employer sanction provisions of the act penalized a "person or other entity" who hires, recruits, or refers for a fee for employment in the United States an alien, knowing the alien is unauthorized, or who employs any individual without complying with the act's employment verification system. Employers would also be sanctioned, if after lawfully hiring an alien, the employer continues to employ the alien knowing the alien has since become unauthorized. Those sanctions, however, did not apply to employees hired, recruited, or referred before November 6, 1986. Violating employers were subject to civil fines, injunctive relief, and criminal penalties of up to $3,000 and/or six months' imprisonment for a pattern or practice of violations. Civil fines, which were imposed per illegal alien, ranged from $250 to $2,000 for the first offense and increased in severity for subsequent offenses. Employers were forbidden from shifting their liability for fines to employees, even illegally employed aliens. In a reversal of previous law, the felony of "harboring" an illegal alien was made applicable to circumstances involving employment. IRCA explicitly preempted all state criminal statutes concerning the employment of illegal aliens, leaving unaffected only areas such as licensing or laws regarding "fitness to do business." Interestingly, to this day there are no sanctions against aliens who illegally accept employment other than the threat of deportation (now "removal") and penalties for document fraud. *See* chapter 14.

A significant obstacle to earlier immigration reform was the concern that employer sanctions would result in widespread discrimination against persons who looked or sounded "foreign." IRCA attempted to resolve this potential problem by prohibiting employment discrimination on the basis of national origin or citizenship status. IRCA stated that it is an unfair immigration-related employment practice for a person or other entity employing four or more persons to discriminate against any individual other than an unauthorized alien, with respect to employment or discharge, on the basis of the individual's national origin or citizenship status. President Reagan addressed employer concerns about their inability to verify an employee's identity, authorization, and national origin without appearing to discriminate in their hiring practices, by announcing that these anti-discrimination provisions would be interpreted to require actual discriminatory intent and not simply a disparate impact resulting from employment practices.

Improvement of enforcement and services was a corresponding major goal of IRCA. The act asserted that essential elements of the program of immigration control: (1) increased border patrol as well as other enforcement activities of the INS to deter unlawful entry of aliens into the U.S. and (2) increased the examinations and other service activities of the INS to ensure prompt, efficient adjudication of petitions and applications. To facilitate achievement of these goals, the act increased appropriations for the INS and the Executive Office for Immigration Review (EOIR), increased community outreach programs and in-service training programs, increased the Border Patrol for fiscal years 1987 and 1988 by fifty percent or more from the 1986 level, and sought to improve other immigration and naturalization services.

In exchange for the increased enforcement provisions of IRCA, Congress offered a broad amnesty for many undocumented aliens already present in the country. IRCA directed the Attorney General to grant lawful temporary resident status to qualified aliens. Those persons who qualified as temporary resident aliens could then become lawful permanent residents. Since the legalization provisions were intended as a one-time, limited opportunity for aliens to receive amnesty, however, they provided for stringent application deadlines.

Aliens must have applied for legalization within one year from May 5, 1987. The alien must have established that s/he entered the United States before January 1, 1982, and that s/he resided unlawfully and continuously in the United States from that date through the date the application was filed. If the alien entered the United States as a nonimmigrant before January 1, 1982, the alien must have established that her/his authorized stay expired before that date or that the alien's unlawful status was known to the government as of that date. On March 30, 1988, a U.S. District Court held that the phrase "known to the Government" meant known to the U.S. government, not just to the INS, as the INS had maintained. The U.S. Court of Appeals, however, vacated this judgment for lack of jurisdiction and ripeness. *Ayuda, Inc. v. Thornburgh* (D.C.Cir.1989).

Legalization applicants also must have established that they had been continuously physically present in the United States since November 6, 1986, except for "brief, casual, and innocent" absences. In *Gutierrez v. Ilchert* (N.D.Cal.1988), the court struck down the provisions of 8

C.F.R. § 245a.1(g) defining the phrase "brief, casual, and innocent" as meaning only an absence authorized in advance by the INS. Applicants must furthermore have established that they: (1) meet most of the requirements of immigrant admissibility to the United States; (2) have not been convicted of any felony or of three or more misdemeanors committed in the United States; (3) have not assisted in any form of persecution; and (4) are registered or registering for the draft, if required to do so.

If an alien succeeded in establishing the above qualifications, s/he should have been granted temporary residence. After 18 months of temporary residence, the alien must then have applied for adjustment to permanent resident status during the one year period beginning with the 19th month of temporary resident status. If the alien failed to apply during this period, the alien lost temporary resident status and once again became undocumented. To qualify for permanent resident status, the alien must have established that s/he had continuously resided in the United States since the date temporary resident status was granted (except for certain authorized absences). Applicants must again meet most of the grounds of admissibility to the United States, must not have been convicted of any felony or of three or more misdemeanors committed in the United States, and must also meet minimal English and civics requirements.

IRCA required strict confidentiality in the legalization program. The act provided for "qualified designated entities"—voluntary organizations experienced in preparing applications for adjustment of status—to receive and forward legalization applications to the INS, but also permitted the alien to apply directly to the INS. Information contained in the files and records of the "qualified designated entity" relating to an alien's application was confidential. The INS could have access to such information only with consent of the alien. The INS could use information contained in a legalization application only for making a determination on the application or for imposing penalties for false statements. INS access to this information was also limited to INS officers with no deportation responsibilities, thereby allowing nonqualifying applicants to avoid the risk of deportation. The act prescribed criminal penalties for both (1) misuse of such information and (2) the filing of an application with false information.

Adverse financial impact upon the states was a substantial concern in adopting IRCA. For this reason, IRCA included extensive provisions disqualifying newly legalized aliens (except Cuban/Haitian entrants) from receiving most federal public welfare assistance for five years. Appropriations were also included to compensate state and local governments for other public assistance and medical benefits conferred upon newly legalized aliens, as well as for the costs of incarcerating undocumented aliens and "Mariel" Cubans.

IRCA also established a separate program for granting temporary and permanent status to qualified agricultural workers. This program was the result of agribusiness pressure for greater availability of such farm workers. The act sought to provide a one time supplement to the supply of available agricultural workers by granting temporary legal resident status to workers who had worked at least 90 days between May 1, 1985, and May 1, 1986. Adjustment to permanent resident status was then permitted for qualified temporary workers. The act, however, also allowed for a replenishment of workers for four years (1990–1993) if the secretaries of agriculture and labor determine that there was a shortage of agricultural workers, based on anticipated need minus the supply of workers for that year.

Beginning in 1986, Congress began to act on growing constituent concern over the difficulty of immigration from Eastern Hemisphere countries, most notably, Ireland and Italy. This situation was generally thought to have arisen with the repeal of the Western Hemisphere quota in 1965 accompanied by a steady increase in immigration from Asia, Africa, and the Middle East. In Section 314 of IRCA and in Section 3 of P.L. 100–658 (the Immigration Amendments of 1988), Congress created what came to be known as the NP–5 and the OP–1 programs respectively.

The NP–5 program created a "first-come-first-served" worldwide mail registration program benefiting aliens from 36 countries whose immigrant visa availability were adversely affected by the unification of the worldwide quota system in 1965. This program, in effect, "gave away" 30,000 immigrant visas, between fiscal years 1987 and 1988, to earliest-registered aliens and their immediate families, requiring them only to meet the nationality, health, and morals qualifications of immigration laws. This program was extended to cover 30,000 more NP–5 registrants over fiscal years 1989 and 1990.

The OP–1 program was a pure lottery based on a one-time registration program without the facets of early or multiple filings that were characteristic of the NP–5 program. It benefited natives of 162 countries which used less than 25 percent of their maximum quota entitlement in fiscal year 1988.

The significance of these programs was their underlying policy of expanding immigration to countries other than the Eastern Hemisphere sources which have increasingly affected our immigration over the past several decades.

Other less important IRCA provisions increased the quotas for colonies (most significantly Hong Kong) from 600 to 5,000 immigrant visas annually; provided for adjustment of status to special immigrant status for certain G–4 nonimmigrants (officers and employees of international organizations and their family members) who have resided in the U.S. for certain periods; established a three-year pilot program for waiving tourist visas for nationals from certain countries; authorized a number of additional nonpreference visas for fiscal years 1987 and 1988; required reports to Congress on certain provisions of the act; authorized the promulgation of rules to implement the act; established the Commission for the Study of International Migration and Cooperative Economic Development; and established federal responsibility for deportable and excludable aliens convicted of crimes.

It may be useful to examine the success of IRCA's major provisions, (1) imposing employer sanctions, (2) including anti-discrimination provisions, and (3) establishing an amnesty program for the legalization of many undocumented aliens.

The implementation of the employer sanction provisions of IRCA received mixed reviews. Surveys taken by the General Accounting Office in the three years following IRCA's passage offered inconsistent evidence as to whether employers were aware of and complying with their obligations under the new law. *See* INA

§ 274A(j)(1). While one survey reported that the vast majority of responding employers had learned of their obligations under the new law, others reported that a large percentage or even a majority believed that the INS had not adequately informed employers of their obligations and that most businesses did not understand their responsibilities. Social service agencies responded that about nine percent of their clients had unjustly lost their jobs because their employers were inadequately informed of the law.

The majority of survey respondents stated that they would comply with the act's employment verification system; but of this group intending to comply, a majority had not actually done so. A small percentage indicated that they did not intend to comply with the act.

IRCA's anti-discrimination provisions did not succeed in eradicating concern about discrimination in the workplace. The majority of respondents believed that IRCA had already resulted in discrimination against workers with a foreign appearance. Almost one-third of large companies surveyed predicted that requiring new employees to provide race, nationality, and age information would result in more discrimination in the future. Reports indicate that discrimination against Hispanics and Asians has been particularly severe.

IRCA's legalization program received a relatively disappointing response. The INS had originally estimated that between two and four million aliens would apply for amnesty. By early 1988, less than 1.2 million applications had been filed. In response, the INS sought innovative means to encourage aliens to apply for amnesty, such as inserting 80,000 amnesty program reminders into tortilla packages in Texas. The INS sent letters to aliens granted temporary resident status, asking them to encourage and help their friends, relatives, and neighbors to apply for amnesty. In a last-minute attempt to encourage applications before the May 4, 1988, deadline, the INS liberalized the legalization process. Beginning April 4, amnesty applicants could file a completed I–687 form and filing fee, and provide supporting documentation or medical information up to 60 days later.

Significant barriers to broader participation in the amnesty program included the aliens' fear of the INS, the high application fee, family unity problems, problems of obtaining required documentation, and sluggish INS program implementation and publicity efforts.

In April 1988, the House of Representatives narrowly approved an extension of the May 4, 1988, deadline for aliens to apply for legalization. Proponents argued that extension was necessary because of the delayed implementation of the amnesty program, the many changes in requirements that resulted in confusion, and the continuing fear of the INS among undocumented aliens. The Senate, however, ended any hope of extension by failing to pass a motion to close debate on the extension proposal, thereby preventing the Senate from voting it. Opponents of extension argued that amnesty had gone far enough and that extension would give the wrong impression. They claimed that extension would encourage millions of aliens to cross the border illegally in the future, on the assumption that the U.S. could not enforce its immigration laws. By the May 4, 1988, deadline, 1.4 million people had applied for amnesty through the general legalization program and 479,000 people through the legalization program for special agricultural workers. 65 Interpr.Rel.481 (1988).

§ 1–7　THE IMMIGRATION
ACT OF 1990

In 1990, Congress passed a series of amendments to the Immigration and Nationality Act, collectively referred to as the Immigration Act of 1990 ("1990 Act" also known as "IMMACT 90"). Like the INA of 1952, the 1965 Amendments, and IRCA, IMMACT 90 was a landmark in immigration legislation. The statute significantly modified many of the INA's provisions, and left virtually no area of the previous law untouched. Primarily, IMMACT 90 reformed the rules pertaining to the *legal* entry of foreign nationals. It augmented the regulations enacted by IRCA (see § 1–6), which focused primarily on illegal immigration. Because of the breadth of IMMACT 90's provisions, specific changes are treated in their proper context throughout this book. This section presents a synopsis of the most prominent changes enacted in the 1990 Act and the less important Immigration Technical Amendments Act of 1991.

§ 1–7.1　Overall Increase in Worldwide Immigration

The most visible feature of IMMACT 90 was the increase by approximately 35% in the numerical limitation system, or overall immigration allowed. IMMACT 90 established an annual limit for worldwide immigration of 700,000 for three years, after which it decreased to 675,000. Because other provisions of the 1990 Act allowed immigration of groups not counted in the 700,000, and a separate law permitted as many as 125,000 refugees to be legally admitted, the actual worldwide immigration limit was closer to 800,000.

The groups benefiting from this increase illustrate congressional priorities, and reflect a moderately optimistic belief in the country's capacity to absorb new immigrants. The 1990 Act increased the allocation for both family-related and employee-related immigration. In addition, the new law created a separate basis by which "diversity" immigrants, that is, nationals of countries previously under-represented by visa issuance since 1965, could gain entry. The 1990 Act eliminated the nonpreference category that had been unavailable due to excessive visa demand since late 1976. All-in-all, of the 700,000 annual allotment, 465,000 were made available to family-sponsored immigrants, 140,000 for employment-based immigrants, and 55,000 for diversity visas.

a. Family–Sponsored Immigration

Beginning October 1, 1991, all family-sponsored immigration was limited to approximately 480,000 annually for two years, after which the yearly limit dropped to 465,000. The relatively large percentage of the overall limit allocated to family-related immigration reflected the continued commitment to family unity as a primary goal of immigration policy. The 1990 Act did not dramatically increase the total number of visas for family-sponsored immigration, however. After adoption of the 1990 Act, family-preference visas were allocated to 216,-000 persons, while 200,000 visas not figured in the quota were granted to immediate relatives (*i.e.*, spouses, minor children, and parents of U.S. citizens).

The 1990 Act accounted for both family-preference visas and immediate relatives of U.S. citizens in the new limit; hence, the new law increased potential family-related immigration by approximately 65,000 annually.

It was anticipated that visas for immediate relatives of U.S. citizens would continue to increase. The 1990 Act provided, however, that the other family-preferences were guaranteed a minimum of 226,000 visas annually, irrespective of the demand for visas to immediate relatives. In addition, the "cap" of 480,000 discussed above may be "pierced" as the result of provisions of the 1990 act that permitted this figure to be supplemented by any visas from the employment-related categories which may have been unused in a previous fiscal year. *See* INA § 201(c)(ii). The four family-preference categories in the previous law remained essentially unchanged. In addition, the 1990 Act codified a "family fairness" policy that gave work authorization and indefinite stay of deportation for the spouses and minor children of aliens granted amnesty under IRCA.

b. Employment–Related Immigration

Responding to fears concerning the U.S. work force's ability to compete in the global economy, the 1990 Act significantly changed the allotments of employment-related visas. The 1990 law replaced the previous third and sixth preferences (which distinguished between professional and skilled employees) with five new classifications totaling 140,000 visas per year. The first employment-based preference category allocated 28.6% of the total number of employment-based visas (currently 40,000) for "priority workers," that is, aliens with an extraordinary potential for contribution to their fields. This category included noted professors, researchers, and multinational executives, as well as individuals who have attained widespread acclaim.

The second employment-based preference category allocated another 28.6% of the employment-based visas for professionals with advanced degrees or aliens with exceptional ability in science, the arts, or business. Hence, the new second preference largely covered the old third preference for professionals. The new third employment-based preference class allotted 28.6% for skilled workers or professionals with baccalaureate degrees, as well as other unskilled workers. The new category combined the balance of the old third preference with the old sixth preference that included "other unskilled workers." The 1990 Act allowed a maximum of 10,000 visas for this group. The fourth employment-related category allocated 10,000 visas for certain religious workers and employees of the U.S. mission in Hong Kong.

The "Employment Creation" fifth preference encouraged the immigration of aliens who invest at least $1 million in a business that benefits the U.S. economy and employs at least 10 U.S. citizen workers or current permanent residents. This preference provided for up to 10,000 visas. Unused visas "spill up" to the first priority category with further visas "spilling down" to the second and third categories. The Attorney General was authorized to lower the required investment to $500,000 if the business is located in an area of high unemployment, or raise it up to $3 million if the business is located in an area of high employment. The present regulations contain an upper limit of $1 million on the investment and a lower limit of $500,000 for areas of high unemployment. The investor is granted a conditional permanent residence for two years, after which s/he can petition for the condition's removal. This provision was criticized for allowing wealthy foreign nationals to "buy their way in." Its supporters contended, however, that the previous law curtailed foreign investment by impeding a company's principal investor from gaining Labor Department certification and pointed to the employment creation facet of the new status as of considerable benefit to the U.S. economy.

The new employment-based preference system placed a high priority on educational attainment, or excellence in a profession. To illustrate: an outstanding offer of employment and labor certification were not required for applicants with extraordinary ability (first preference class). Multinational managers and executives were also exempt from the certification requirement. Because employers have often been unwilling to wait for labor certification to employ low-skilled workers, and because of the low allocation of 10,000 visas, the 1990 Act offered limited opportunities for individuals without skills or the benefit of formal education.

The 1990 Act did not substantially change the Labor Department's certification process which requires showing that no qualified U.S. workers are available to work in the position sought. One revision required that notice of filing for labor certification be given to the union representative of the affected employees in the potential place of employment. The act also replaced the Schedules A & B with a pilot program in which the Labor Department was to determine whether labor shortages or surpluses exist in ten occupations. The pilot program, however, has expired and the Schedules A & B prevailed.

(1) DIVERSITY VISAS

Because the families of immigrants who arrived in the U.S. two or more generations ago no longer qualified for family-related visas (see § 1–2), several of the countries which figured most prominently in this nation's immigration history were considered "under-represented."

Section 132 of the 1990 Act established a mail-in lottery, known as the AA–1 program to address the problem of under-representation by allocating 40,000 "diversity" visas (55,000 beginning in 1994) to nationals from "adversely affected" countries. Of the visas made available in this category, 40% were designated for natives of Ireland. Significantly, this allotment created the first visas by which foreign nationals could immigrate without an immediate relative to sponsor them and without a job for which there is a labor shortage. Because applicants would be selected on a random basis, the diversity visa became an unpredictable way for a foreign national to gain entry.

(2) INHABITANTS OF HONG KONG

Motivated by the then impending return of Hong Kong to the People's Republic of China, the 1990 Act allowed for separate means of aiding Hong Kong residents who wanted to immigrate to the U.S. The provision increased the allocation for immigration from Hong Kong to 10,000 (from 5,000) for the first three years of the act, after which the level rose to 20,000. Other provisions benefit employees of certain U.S. businesses in Hong Kong, and employees of the U.S. mission there. In addition, the new law extended visas issued to Hong Kong residents until January 1, 2002, allowing them to immigrate if conditions after 1997 so dictate, while providing them with the security to stay in the meantime.

(3) REFUGEES AND TEMPORARY STATUS

The 1990 Act altered the process of attaining permanent residence for refugees. One year after an alien has been granted asylum in the U.S., s/he can apply for permanent residence. The 1990 Act increased the number of refugees who may become permanent residents to

10,000 annually (from 5,000); moreover, aliens who had previously qualified were granted permanent residence by a special provision. The 1990 law also offered "Temporary Protected Status" (TPS) to aliens prevented from returning to their home countries because of war, disaster, or other unstable circumstances. In the interim, the Attorney General was required to provide employment authorization for those aliens. The Attorney General was authorized to determine which countries are "protected." El Salvador received designated TPS status from the statute itself. Other countries have also been given TPS designation, including Bosnia–Herzegovina (1991), Kuwait (1991), Lebanon (1991), Liberia (1991), Somalia (1991), Rwanda (1994), Burundi (1997), Montserrat (1997), Sierra Leone (1997), and Sudan (1997).

§ 1–7.2 Nonimmigrant Provisions

The 1990 Act modified some of the INA's provisions pertaining to aliens who seek entry for a temporary period of time or for a limited purpose. The 1990 law added four categories of nonimmigrants to the previous 14 visas. Hence, the 1990 Act defined 18 nonimmigrant categories, identified as A through R visas. The visa waiver pilot program benefiting foreign travelers, previously applicable to eight countries, was extended to any country designated by the Attorney General and Secretary of State. The 1990 law also modified visa categories for crewmembers (D), traders (E), temporary workers (H), and intracompany transferees (L).

The 1990 Act established four new nonimmigrant categories. Category O nonimmigrants must have attained great achievements or possess extraordinary ability in the arts, sciences, education, business, or athletics, provided the alien seeks entry to work within their field of expertise. Category P included aliens who perform as athletes or entertainers, or are members of a performance group, again provided the alien seeks entry to perform within this discipline. Category Q provided for international cultural exchange programs and participants, while category R granted entry to aliens within certain religious occupations.

§ 1–7.3 Naturalization

Until the 1990 Act, the federal district court had the ultimate responsibility for naturalization upon a recommendation by the INS and for administration of the oath of allegiance to new U.S. citizens. Under the 1990 Act, the INS made the actual determination on naturalization and the district director administered the oath. The Immigration Technical Amendments Act of 1991, however, left the naturalization decision with the INS, but returned most oaths of allegiance to the federal district court. The courts were considered more conveniently located for the administration of oaths and better able to handle the problems of changing names which often occur with acquisition of U.S. citizenship.

The 1990 Act also provided that an alien denied naturalization by the INS may seek *de novo* judicial review. In addition, the 1990 Act effectively overruled three Supreme Court determinations denying naturalization to Philippine veterans of World War II (see *INS v. Hibi* (Sup.Ct.1973); *United States v. Mendoza* (Sup.Ct.1984); *INS v. Pangilinan* (Sup.Ct.1988)), thus naturalizing Filipinos who performed honorably in World War II.

§ 1–7.4 Grounds for Exclusion

Prior to the 1990 Act, there were more than 34 separate grounds for exclusion, many of which had complex rules and subdivisions. Some of these provisions were considered obsolete. For example, as a result of the McCarran–Walter Act of 1952, individuals could be excluded for beliefs or party membership, rather than a specific act. The 1990 Act attempted to address this problem, but by no means enacted provisions that will significantly narrow the grounds for exclusion.

a. Health–Related Exclusion

The health-related provisions were modified to exclude only aliens with communicable diseases that threatened public health. This determination would be made by the Secretary for Health and Human Services. Moreover, the 1990 Act attempted to bring the health-related grounds for exclusion up to date with modern medical knowledge and procedure. A meaningful illustration of the 1990 Act's reforms was the elimination of the exclusion of gay men and lesbians. Further, the waiver for close relatives was expanded, thus diminishing the number of family-sponsored aliens excluded for health reasons.

b. Crime–Related Exclusion

The substantive rules of criminal exclusion were not significantly modified by the 1990 Act. For aliens under 18 years of age, minor criminal conduct was not considered a ground for exclusion, provided the alien was convicted at least five years prior to her/his application. One significant revision reduced the number of discretionary waivers by requiring the criminal conviction to have occurred at least 15 years prior to application.

c. Security as a Grounds for Exclusion

The 1990 Act barred any alien who had engaged in terrorist activities, adding this ground for exclusion to espionage, sabotage, or violent overthrow of the U.S. government. Further, the Secretary of State was authorized to bar any alien who would adversely affect the foreign policy of the United States. Critics of these provisions contended that the new law places too much discretion with the Secretary of State. Moreover, they feared that the term "terrorism" would be construed broadly or for political reasons.

d. Communists

The 1990 Act limited the exclusion of members of the Communist or another totalitarian party. This exclusion would no longer be applicable to nonimmigrants, and involuntary membership was excused. In addition, membership was excused if it was terminated at least two years prior to application (five years if the country was still controlled by a totalitarian dictatorship, *e.g.,* China). Again, a discretionary waiver was permitted for close relatives and if the waiver is in the public interest.

e. Exclusion for Misrepresentation

The 1990 Act retained the exclusion for misrepresentation (extended by the Immigration Marriage Fraud Act) with two modifications. First, the waiver for close relatives was expanded by changing the term "child" to "son or daughter," which included adult married children. Second, if the misrepresentation occurred more than 10 years prior to the application, waiver was permitted. Unfortunately, a ten year bar may still be excessive.

§ 1–7.5   Grounds for Deportation

a. Marriage Fraud

The 1990 Act substantially modified three provisions of the Immigration Marriage Fraud Act. First, and most significant, the new law recognized marriages entered into while deportation or exclusion proceedings are pending. The law, however, required "clear and convincing evidence" that the marriage was undertaken in good faith and not for the purposes of evading immigration laws. Second, when a marriage was terminated within two years of the conditional grant of residence, the alien spouse could petition for removal of the condition, regardless of who initiated the divorce. Third, discretionary waiver of the conditional residence requirement was made available if the alien spouse or her/his child was the victim of battery or abuse.

b. *National Security Concerns*

The 1990 Act eliminated the provision for deporting members of the Communist party or other "subversive" organizations. Like the related ground for exclusion, the act prescribed deportation for aliens who have engaged in terrorist activity or who would pose a threat to national security. Again, the Secretary of State was given considerable discretion in determining whether an alien threatens foreign relations.

§ 1–7.6 Summary of Technical Amendments of 1991

The Immigration Technical Corrections Act of 1991 clarified, defined, and modified various provisions in the 1990 Act. Although all relevant corrections will be treated in their proper context in this book, some significant modifications should be mentioned here. For example, the 1991 Act translated numerical allocations of employment-related visas to percentages for determining visas remaining from other categories that have not been exhausted.

The considerable political battle fought over restricting the H–1B status continued in the Technical Amendments. The procedural requirements for prospective U.S. employers of H–1B workers were loosened somewhat and foreign-educated medical doctors' ability to be employed in the U.S. under the authority of H–1B visa status was clarified and defined.

Several other corrections clarified whether relatives of the principal alien would be charged against the numerical limits of various categories through which that alien sought entry. The diversity program and application process were changed significantly to become more of a pure lottery. Temporary Protected Status was modified, for example, to cover stateless residents of the countries selected. As to immigration enforcement, murder was made a permanent bar to a finding of good moral character; the INS no longer was required to stay the deportation of an alien convicted of an aggravated felony pending the determination of a petition for review; and no security grounds could be waived for legalization applicants.

The technical corrections returned to the federal district courts and state courts the authority to administer oaths of allegiance for the purposes of naturalization provided that the oath is administered within 45 days from INS approval of the naturalization application. These provisions were adopted under the heading, "Judicial Naturalization Ceremonies Amendments of 1991." The technical corrections filled in several of the gaps that the 1990 Act left ambiguous. Again, the corrections are better understood in the context of the provisions they modify.

§ 1–7.7   Further Reform

The 1990 Act established a commission to examine how immigration affects our society, how immigration laws function, and how to assess the demographics of the immigrant population. The commission, chaired by former Congresswoman Barbara Jordan, issued its first report in 1994 acknowledging that IRCA's mechanisms for prohibiting illegal employment "have proved less effective than anticipated" and recommending a pilot program using on-line verification of employment authorization. President Clinton, however, instead established a pilot program that allows employers to verify work authorization by telephoning a centralized computer database. The Clinton Administration accepted the Jordan Commission recommendations for strengthening border enforcement, for example, by erecting new fencing on the southern border and employing additional Border Patrol personnel. The Jordan Commission's 1995 report stated that an agriculture guest worker program is not in the national interest. The Commission on Immigration Reform has also considered whether the INS should be limited to its service, *i.e.*, visa-issuing function, while another agency is established to perform its law enforcement function.

§ 1–8   THE ACTS OF 1996
(AEDPA AND IIRIRA)

Congress responded to perceived anti-immigration sentiment in the 1990's with three new acts, each of which was signed by President Bill Clinton in 1996. The first of these acts was the Antiterrorism and Effective Death Penalty Act (AEDPA), which became law on April 24, 1996. The second was the Personal Responsibility and

Work Opportunity Reconciliation Act (Welfare Act), which became law on August 22, 1996. The third was the Illegal Immigration Reform and Immigrant Responsibility Act (IIRIRA), which became law on September 30, 1996. While the Welfare Act removed many federal services for non-citizens, AEDPA and IIRIRA focussed on enforcement of immigration laws by, for example, adding Border Patrol agents and reducing the procedures that were previously required to remove aliens from the U.S. *See* § 13–4.4 for additional information on the Welfare Act.

Although both AEDPA and IIRIRA were examples of a similar immigration policy direction, IIRIRA, which was signed latest, went furthest and replaced many of AEDPA's provisions. For example, IIRIRA's summary removal procedure replaced AEDPA's procedure. Under IIRIRA, an alien arriving without documents, or with invalid or fraudulent documents, can be removed without a hearing or review unless the alien expresses a desire to apply for asylum or a fear of persecution. Also, while AEDPA restricted judicial review for aliens, IIRIRA restricted judicial review even further. Except for asylum decisions, judicial review was barred under IIRIRA for any decision reached by the Attorney General that required an exercise of discretion.

The pre-IIRIRA discretionary relief that was available to deportable aliens was included by IIRIRA in cancellation of removal. Prior to IIRIRA, the applicant for certain forms of discretionary relief was required to show hardship to the alien or her/his family. Under IIRIRA, an applicant must generally show "exceptional and extremely unusual hardship" to her/his "citizen or permanent resident spouse, parent, or child." INA § 240A(b)(1). If an alien does not have a spouse, parent, or child who is a citizen or permanent resident, cancellation of removal is generally not available. IIRIRA provided an exception, however, for battered spouses and children.

Both AEDPA and IIRIRA enlarged the definition of "aggravated felony." AEDPA added felonies such as those relating to gambling and passport fraud. IIRIRA expanded the definition further to include, for example, crimes carrying sentences of one year or more, even if the alien was not sentenced to prison. Formerly, aggravated felonies included crimes with sentences of five years or more. This expanded definition increased the number of aliens ineligible for cancellation of removal. Also, because AEDPA and IIRIRA provided for mandatory detention of aliens subject to removal for aggravated felonies, more aliens must be detained. IIRIRA also provided for increasing detention space.

The previous distinction between exclusion and deportation changed with IIRIRA. Before IIRIRA, aliens who entered the U.S., even if they had avoided inspection, were subject to deportation proceedings. Aliens who had not entered the U.S., including aliens who were paroled into the U.S., were subject to exclusion proceedings. Under IIRIRA, all aliens who have not been inspected and admitted to the U.S. were subjected to the grounds for inadmissibility (formerly "grounds for exclusion"). The grounds of inadmissibility were also expanded beyond the former grounds for exclusion to include aliens who are unlawfully present in the U.S., as when for example aliens overstay nonimmigrant visas. Aliens subject to grounds for deportation are similarly removable. Removal proceedings replaced the formerly separate exclusion and deportation proceedings.

The IIRIRA also stiffened the requirement for affidavits of support for immigrants entering on the basis of their relationship to U.S. citizens or permanent residents. A sponsor must agree in the affidavit to provide support for the alien at an annual income that is not less than 125% of the federal poverty standard. Also, the sponsor must reimburse the government if the alien receives means-tested public benefits within ten years of admission.

It is uncertain how Congress will continue to respond to perceptions about immigrants or to periods of recession and increased unemployment by cutting immigration. It is also unclear how establishing a free trade zone with Canada, Mexico, and eventually other countries in the Western Hemisphere will continue to affect U.S. immigration policy.

§ 1–9 MORAL AND POLICY ISSUES OF IMMIGRATION

Immigration transforms the demographic profile of the U.S. population, particularly in large cities. Fears of overcrowding, unemployment, scarcity of resources, and fears of cultural fragmentation make the politics of immigration extremely complex. Immigration law is the principal means by which the country not only determines who will gain access to the limited resources and opportunities in the U.S., but also what will be the national and cultural identity of the U.S.

The argument in favor of free immigration—that is, an "open-door" policy of admission—asserts that fears are greatly exaggerated that the U.S. national and cultural identity will be destroyed by immigration. The United

States functions best as a heterogeneous, diverse population, and is expansive enough to absorb many new immigrants. Contrary to fears about job security, immigration is a necessary ingredient in plans for future U.S. economic growth and an enlarged workforce. In fact, even the influx of unskilled workers—often the group most feared for the potential to sap the country's social programs and resources—aid U.S. economic growth by filling jobs that many U.S. citizens and permanent residents do not want.

There is a moral component to the argument in favor of free immigration as well. Given the U.S. tradition as a country of immigrants, it is difficult to comprehend how current citizens—almost all of whom have benefited from immigration—can claim any right to exclude future immigrants. Also, family reunification is the core of much of our immigration policy and is based upon a fundamental respect for the right to be with one's loved ones. Moreover, immigration law is only as effective as its enforcement. Weak enforcement and illegal immigration mock the actual numerical limits that are enacted. Some scholars argue that the U.S. should adopt an immigration policy commensurate with the country's capacity for enforcement, or at least, legally recognize the actual number of aliens who enter the U.S.

The arguments against free immigration—that is, for maintaining a restrictive immigration policy—have figured prominently in the history of U.S. immigration law. These reasons are often based upon a fear that increased immigration will compromise the U.S. standard of living. It is argued that the very reasons immigrants have historically been attracted to the United States—*e.g.*, the "American Dream"—are weakened if the country becomes overcrowded.

Specifically, the arguments against a free or even more lenient immigration are as follows: First, xenophobia plays a strong role in persons who seek to protect the cultural identity of the U.S.; the English-only movement is one example. Second, individuals who oppose freer immigration argue that there are finite resources and jobs; accordingly, U.S. citizens and lawful permanent residents should not have to compete with immigrants for them. Third, advocates of a restrictive immigration policy argue that there must be limits somewhere— certainly, the U.S. cannot allow the whole world to come here. Once the need for some limits is recognized, the U.S. ought to structure those limits in a realistic and pragmatic way that will be most advantageous to the future of the U.S. Fourth, some scholars argue that the U.S. should commit its resources to helping countries in need so that potential immigrants will be encouraged to remain in their developing countries. This perspective contends that immigration is a drain on other countries' human resources. All countries would benefit if these potential immigrants remained in their country of origin.

The tension throughout the debate comes from the fact that the U.S. is largely a nation of immigrants who did not inherit this land by divine right, but rather, by an open immigration policy and by taking the land from the indigenous inhabitants. It appears to be an act of selfishness, if not moral ingratitude, to bar future groups seeking to immigrate. In addition, U.S. citizens like to believe that our nation helps the world's needy, sharing the plentiful resources that this country enjoys. U.S. immigration policy turns on this moral inquiry: what is the U.S. obligation to those people in need of a better place to live, and where should the lines be drawn?

Some political forces have played upon the nation's fears that open borders will exacerbate domestic problems such as crime, drugs, urban violence, unemployment, and homelessness. They remain unconvinced that freer immigration is a pragmatically or morally persuasive policy.

The 1996 acts, like the 1990 Act and most immigration legislation, constitute a compromise; this middle-ground appears to be the destination for our immigration policy. These acts recognize that immigration policy is a tool to help the United States compete internationally. The immigrants who principally benefit are those who are perceived to help the U.S. economically, as immigrants have throughout the nation's history. IIRIRA also seeks to immunize the U.S. against the burden of providing means-tested public benefits to recent immigrants. The minimum income necessary for sponsorship disqualifies many economically disadvantaged persons from bringing their family members into the United States. This selectivity illustrates the unanswered, if not unaddressed, moral and policy issues regarding the right to exclude others.

CHAPTER 2

THE SOURCE AND SCOPE OF THE FEDERAL POWER TO REGULATE IMMIGRATION AND NATURALIZATION

The broad power of the federal government to regulate the admission, removal, and naturalization of aliens has its roots in the early history of the United States. Modern statutes, Supreme Court decisions, and federal agency regulations attest to the plenary nature of this power. This chapter examines the source of the power over immigration, the limits such federal power impose on state attempts to regulate aliens, and the allocation of this power among the three branches of the federal government—Congress, the courts, and executive agencies.

§ 2-1 THE SOURCE OF THE FEDERAL POWER

Throughout the history of the United States the Supreme Court has upheld all manner of federal statutes regulating immigration. By contrast, Supreme Court decisions preclude states from passing legislation that directly impinges on this area of federal dominion. The Supreme Court's basis for action is clear when the area regulated is naturalization. Article 1, § 8, clause 4, of the United States Constitution specifically grants Congress the power to establish a "uniform Rule of Naturaliza-

51

tion." By expressly allocating this power to Congress, the Constitution prevents the confusion that would result if individual states could bestow citizenship. The Constitution does not, however, explicitly provide that the power to deny admission or remove aliens rests with the federal as opposed to state governments. Hence, in the early immigration cases the Supreme Court faced the problem of identifying the source of the federal government's exclusive and plenary power over immigration. Later cases found the plenary power to be an inherent sovereign power.

§ 2–1.1 The Commerce Clause

In the earliest cases, the Court looked to the federal power over foreign commerce. The Commerce Clause in Article I, § 8, clause 3, of the United States Constitution provides Congress with the power "to regulate Commerce with foreign Nations, and among the several States." The Supreme Court in the *Passenger Cases* (Sup.Ct.1849) invoked the Commerce Clause to ban the levy of fees upon foreigners wishing to disembark at state ports. The Court invalidated state immigration fees even though Congress had yet to implement any relevant federal regulations. The Court reasoned that foreign affairs and foreign commerce were exclusively controlled by Congress even when the power had not been exercised. In the *Head Money Cases* (Sup.Ct.1884), the Court upheld a federally imposed tax on foreign immigrants, again with direct citation to the commerce power. As congressional action began to reach beyond taxation to other forms of regulation, however, the Court sought a broader ground for decision.

§ 2–1.2   Other Constitutional Provisions

Early cases also cite other specific constitutional provisions to support the inference that the federal government possesses complete power over international relations, arguably including immigration matters. In addition to citing the foreign commerce power, the Supreme Court in *Nishimura Ekiu v. United States* (Sup. Ct.1892) also cites the power to establish a uniform rule of naturalization; the power to declare war and provide and maintain armies and navies; and the power to make all laws necessary and proper. The *Fong Yue Ting v. United States* (Sup.Ct.1893) case adds the power to define and punish piracies, felonies committed on the high seas, and offenses against the law of nations; as well as the presidential power to make treaties, to appoint ambassadors, and to select other public ministers and consuls.

The Migration and Importation Clause in Article I, § 9, clause 1 of the Constitution has also been considered a potential grant of power to Congress. This clause provides: "The Migration or Importation of such Persons as any of the States now existing shall think proper to admit, shall not be prohibited by the Congress prior to the year one thousand eight hundred and eight." The specific limit on congressional power before 1808 could be construed to imply that after 1808, Congress would have power over migration and importation. The prevailing interpretation, however, is that this clause was simply intended to bar any attempts by Congress to stop the slave trade before 1808.

The War Power, found in Article I, § 8, clause 11, could be cited as a potential source of federal control over immigration. The War Power gives Congress the authority to "declare war." The War Power authorized the exclusion and expulsion of enemy aliens. In the Alien and Sedition Acts, for example, Congress granted this power to the President. The Supreme Court upheld the constitutionality of such provisions in *Ludecke v. Watkins* (Sup.Ct.1948), but it is difficult to stretch this rationale to cover the myriad of immigration provisions not apparently related to national security.

The Naturalization Clause, at Article I, § 8, clause 4, has served as an argument for federal control over immigration. The dissent in the *Passenger Cases* rejected this argument. *Passenger Cases* (Sup.Ct.1849). As mentioned earlier, the Naturalization Clause's granting of power to "establish an uniform Rule of Naturalization" concerns decisions about citizenship rather than immigration generally.

Another way of looking at the possible constitutional provisions that provide specific federal power is to view them as indicative of an original intent to give the federal government power over all immigration. Under this view, the Commerce, War, and Naturalization Clauses together imply a federal right to regulate aliens. Later cases clarified, however, that such constitutional provisions are not the source of an implied right of the federal government to regulate aliens, but only show that the federal government is the national government and therefore the keeper of the inherent sovereign power to regulate international affairs.

§ 2–1.3 National Sovereignty

The Court eventually found the source of the federal power to regulate immigration in a combination of international and constitutional legal principles. *The Chinese*

Exclusion Case (Sup.Ct.1889) was the first case to hold that the federal power to exclude aliens is an incident of national sovereignty. The Court reasoned that every national government has the inherent authority to protect the national public interest. Immigration is a matter of vital national concern. Furthermore, it is the role of the federal government to oversee matters of national concern, while it is the province of the states to govern local matters. Therefore, the Court found that the inherent sovereign power to regulate immigration clearly resides in the federal government. Subsequent cases reinforced national sovereignty as the source of federal power to control immigration and consistently reasserted the plenary and unqualified scope of this power. *Fong Yue Ting v. United States* (Sup.Ct.1893) explicitly held that the power to deport (now "remove") aliens rests upon the same ground as the exclusion power and is equally "absolute and unqualified."

§ 2–1.4 Delegated Versus Inherent Power

In *United States v. Curtiss–Wright Export Corp.* (Sup. Ct.1936), the Court clearly distinguished between powers delegated to the federal government in the Constitution and inherent sovereign powers. Delegated powers were carved from the general mass of legislative powers previously governed by the states. The inherent sovereign powers were, however, transferred from Great Britain to the union of states when the U.S. declared its independence. These powers were thus vested in the national government before the Constitution was written and exist without regard to any constitutional grant. It has been suggested that the apparently limitless scope of federal authority over immigration results from this undefined and undefinable source. The Supreme Court has upheld every exercise of this power and has consistently termed it "plenary and unqualified."

Other theorists suggest sources of federal immigration power that lie somewhere between the explicitly delegated powers of the Constitution and the inherent powers. The "Rule of Necessity," for instance, suggests that because federal power over immigration is *necessary* to the successful operation of the Constitution, this power may be interpolated into the Constitution.

Structural arguments have also been used to justify the exclusive federal immigration power. These arguments draw an inference of power from the structure of the Constitution as a whole, rather than from individual clauses. The Constitution's primary goal is to create a system of government for the nation, and a process through which its citizens establish the rules governing people within the territory. Under this premise, two structural arguments emerge.

First, the power to regulate immigration is essential to a nation's self-preservation. To be a sovereign nation, a people must have control over its territory. Without such control, a nation would be unable to govern itself and its borders effectively, and as a result, would be subject to the sovereignty of other nations. The power to regulate immigration is therefore inherent in the Constitution's creation of a sovereign nation.

Second, the power to regulate immigration is essential to the process of national "self-definition." Through the governmental process, a nation's citizens determine the values espoused by the nation, and hence, formulate the nation's identity. By determining who will comprise the nation and participate in creating the nation's identity, immigration laws constitute the process of self-definition itself. Decisions about who may enter a country say much about a nation. Although the process of national self-definition may be characterized as racist, discriminatory against outsiders, and otherwise unjust, it is an essential characteristic of a sovereign nation. These theories of self-preservation and self-definition mandate broad federal powers over immigration.

In addition, scholars have cited the constitutionally "implied" power of the executive over foreign affairs to authorize federal control over immigration. In *The Chinese Exclusion Case* (Sup.Ct.1889) (see § 2–1.3, *supra.*), Justice Field stated that the Foreign Affairs Power is the foundation for all federal control over immigration. Moreover, this power has been cited as a basis for invalidating state statutes that attempt to regulate immigration. *See, e.g., Chy Lung v. Freeman* (Sup.Ct.1875).

Today the source of the federal government's power to control international affairs generally, and immigration in particular, is accepted without question. For example, during the Iranian hostage ordeal of 1979–81, the U.S. Court of Appeals for the D.C. Circuit upheld the Attorney General's authority to order all Iranian students in the United States to report to INS offices and demonstrate the lawfulness of their presence in the country. *Narenji v. Civiletti* (D.C.Cir.1979). Many cases refer to these powers as constitutional when, in fact, the powers are drawn from a more ancient foundation. The practically unlimited scope of the federal power over aliens may possibly be traced back to the undefined nature of its source.

§ 2–2 THE SCOPE OF THE FEDERAL POWER

§ 2–2.1 Plenary Congressional Power

To date there have been no successful challenges to federal legislation that refuses admission to classes of aliens or removes resident aliens. Federal immigration power thus appears limitless. Indeed, the Supreme Court has stated: "[O]ver no conceivable subject is the legislative power of Congress more complete." *Fiallo v. Bell* (Sup.Ct.1977), *Kleindienst v. Mandel,* (Sup.Ct.1972), and *Oceanic Steam Nav. Co. v. Stranahan* (Sup.Ct.1909). Extreme judicial deference bears witness to the truth of this statement.

Both the Constitution and the U.N. Charter have been dismissed as grounds for opposing federal immigration power. The federal courts and immigration authorities have without much consideration rejected an assertion in *Hitai v. INS* (2d Cir.1965), *Vlissidis v. Anadell* (7th Cir.1959), and *Matter of Laurenzano* (BIA 1970) that the immigration quota system is inconsistent with the U.N. Charter. The Supreme Court has upheld the constitutionality of federal statutes that exclude aliens on the basis of race (*Chinese Exclusion Case* (S.Ct.1889)) and political belief (*Kleindienst v. Mandel* (Sup.Ct.1972)). Moreover, excluded aliens have no constitutional right to a hearing. *Shaughnessy v. Mezei* (Sup.Ct.1953).

Even where the First Amendment and Equal Protection rights of U.S. citizens were jeopardized, in *Mandel,* the Supreme Court refused to look behind the Executive's negative exercise of discretion on the basis of a "facially legitimate and bona fide reason" in refusing entry to a Belgian Communist. One district court, found that aliens have First Amendment rights not to be deported (now "removed") for political activity. The U.S. Court of Appeals reversed for lack of standing and ripeness *American–Arab Anti–Discrimination Committee v. Thornburgh* (9th Cir.1991), amended (9th Cir.1991), but later affirmed an injunction against deportation of the aliens. *American–Arab Anti–Discrimination Committee v. Reno* (9th Cir. 1997). *See* § 13–4.5, *infra.*

Federal courts have sustained the detention of aliens convicted of aggravated felonies without the opportunity for a pre-detention hearing under the Fifth and Eighth Amendments. The Supreme Court also refused to reach the issue of whether the Equal Protection principles inherent in the Due Process Clause of the Fifth Amendment protected a class of undocumented Haitians detained without parole. Instead, the Court ruled that the aliens' claims were to be judged under nondiscriminatory federal statutes and regulations. *Jean v. Nelson* (Sup.Ct. 1985). In *Fernandez–Roque v. Smith* (11th Cir.1984), however, the U.S. Court of Appeals for the Eleventh Circuit held that Cuban nationals found excludable had no constitutionally-based liberty interest in challenging denial or revocation of parole. In *Garcia–Mir v. Meese* (11th Cir.1986), the same court further held that unadmitted Mariel Cuban parolees did not have any other Due Process liberty interest entitling them to parole revocation hearings, nor were they entitled to such hearings on the basis of international law. Similarly, deportation (now "removal") orders are consistently upheld despite a myriad of conceivable constitutional challenges. Courts inclined to limit Due Process restrictions have cited *Mathews v. Diaz* (Sup.Ct.1976).

In *McNary v. Haitian Refugee Center* (Sup.Ct.1991), the Supreme Court held that challenges to the constitutionality of the practices, procedures, and policies of the INS were proper subjects for judicial review. In that case Congress had required aliens to seek judicial review of individual denials of special agricultural worker (SAW) status only in the context of exclusion or deportation. Since the Haitian Refugee Center was not challenging an individual determination but the entire process, because of the presumption in favor of review of administrative actions, and because constitutional issues were at stake, the court found jurisdiction. In 1992, the U.S. Court of Appeals held in *Haitian Refugee Center v. Baker* (11th Cir.1991) that aliens who were detained on the high seas and, therefore, had never presented themselves at a U.S. border, had no right to judicial review of INS decisions under the Administrative Procedure Act. Moreover, the court held that these aliens had no individual right of action, unless they qualified for refugee status. Further, the court held that the refugee center and their attorneys had no First Amendment claim for gaining access to those detained aliens. The Supreme Court denied certiorari over the objections of Justice Blackmun, who complained that this challenge to the U.S. procedures for determining whether a group faces political persecution should not go unheard by the Court. In *Sale v. Haitian Centers Council, Inc.* (Sup.Ct.1993), the Court upheld summary return of Haitians intercepted on the high seas without considering their asylum claims. The interdiction agreement ceased to exist in 1994, when Haitian President Aristide withdrew his government's consent. *See* §§ 8–3.1, 9–2.4, *infra*.

Federal legislative decisions not to admit or remove an alien are subject to a very limited scope of judicial scrutiny. Cases sustaining the broad authority of Congress over immigration have relied upon *Fiallo v. Bell*

(Sup.Ct.1977). Thus far, the courts have largely resisted prodding by scholars and litigants to encourage the courts to scrutinize federal power over this subject matter. Also, Congress has restricted the availability of judicial review over immigration decisions. *See* § 8–4.1, *infra*.

Some scholars have argued that the plenary power Congress enjoys is susceptible to abuse, often at the expense of fundamental human rights. These critics argue that Congress' current plenary power over immigration is an outdated manifestation of repression arising from racism, past wars, and cold war tensions.

§ 2–2.2 Permissible and Impermissible State Regulations

States may not usurp the federal power over immigration. State attempts to regulate concurrently in a field already occupied by a federal statute have been struck down under the doctrine of preemption. In *Hines v. Davidowitz* (1941), for example, the Court held that the Federal Alien Registration Act preempted the Pennsylvania alien registration provisions. Under the preemption doctrine, federal law in a specific area may preclude even consistent state regulations.

The courts will also invalidate state statutes that conflict with federal policy. This ground has been coupled with the Equal Protection Clause to invalidate state discrimination against aliens. In the nineteenth and early twentieth centuries, the Supreme Court allowed states to pass laws discriminating against aliens. In 1915, however, the case of *Truax v. Raich* (Sup.Ct.1915) reversed this trend. *Truax* rested on the dual ground of equal protection and exclusive federal control over immigration. The Court overturned an Arizona statute restricting alien employment. Besides being a denial of equal protection, the statute ran contrary to the implied intent of Congress that aliens allowed into the country under federal immigration laws would be free to pursue a livelihood. Similarly, the Court rejected state laws restricting fishing rights of aliens denied naturalization in *Takahashi v. Fish and Game Com'n* (Sup.Ct.1948), and length of residency requirements for aliens seeking welfare in *Graham v. Richardson* (Sup.Ct.1971). In each of these cases, the Court perceived a conflict between the burdensome state regulation and the decision by federal authorities to grant residency privileges to the affected aliens.

In a somewhat different vein, the Court in *Nyquist v. Mauclet* (Sup.Ct.1977) invalidated a New York law that made commencing naturalization procedures a prerequisite to receiving financial assistance for higher education. Although the *Mauclet* case relied heavily on the Equal Protection Clause for its outcome, the Court noted that encouraging naturalization is an illegitimate purpose for discrimination in light of federal dominion over that field. It seems then that even where state statutes do not directly conflict with federal policy covering the same subject, the state statute may still be struck down if it meddles in immigration policy.

The mere existence of the federal immigration power does not, however, automatically preclude state regulations affecting aliens. The Supreme Court so held in *De Canas v. Bica* (Sup.Ct.1976). In *De Canas* the Court upheld a California statute prohibiting an employer from knowingly employing an alien who is not entitled to lawful residence in the U.S. if such employment would have an adverse effect on lawful resident workers. Writing for the majority, Justice Blackmun stated "the Court has never held that every state enactment which in any way deals with aliens is a regulation of immigration and thus per se preempted by this constitutional immigration power, whether latent or exercised."

In finding that the Immigration and Nationality Act (INA) did not preempt the California statute, the Court noted that the nature of the subject matter does not compel a conclusion of exclusive federal control. Furthermore, the INA does not show a congressional intent to occupy the field totally. The Court distinguished previous preemption cases in the immigration field on four grounds. First, the California statute did not cover ground specifically addressed by the INA. (Such a federal statute, however, was adopted in 1986.) Second, Congress seemed at that time to authorize concurrent state legislation in the area regulated by the state law. Third, the federal interest is not as predominant in a "situation in which state law is fashioned to remedy local problems, and operates only on local employers and only with respect to individuals whom the federal government has already declared cannot work in this country." Fourth, the previous cases overturned statutes that "imposed burdens on aliens lawfully within the country that created conflicts with various federal laws." *De Canas* indicates that states may fill gaps in the federal regulatory scheme governing aliens so long as the state regulations do not run afoul of federal policy. Lower courts have thus upheld state and local regulation in certain areas such as enforcement of the criminal provisions of federal immigration law. *Gonzales v. City of Peoria* (9th Cir.1983). The Immigration Reform and Control Act of 1986, as well as the Immigration Act of 1990, indicates federal preemption of a far broader range of immigration-related activity, including state laws regulating the employment of aliens.

In a related area the Supreme Court also has upheld state probate laws that incidentally and indirectly affect foreign relations. *Clark v. Allen* (Sup.Ct.1947) called into question a state statute that conditioned a nonresident alien's right to inherit property upon the existence of a reciprocal right of U.S. citizens to inherit property in the alien's nation. The statute's opponents claimed it was an incursion into an area of exclusive federal control. The Court labeled that claim "far fetched" and held that such laws are valid unless they conflict with a federal law or statute.

Of course, if states use their probate laws to implement foreign policy, they enter a forbidden field. Hence, in *Zschernig v. Miller* (Sup.Ct.1968) the Court struck down an Oregon statute requiring an alien entitled to inherit property to show that her/his government would allow the receipt of such property without confiscation. The provision necessarily mandated judicial inquiry into the current status of political rights in foreign countries. Such inquiries are the exclusive responsibility of the federal government. A state may not cross the line between incidental and direct effects on either immigration or foreign policy. For example, the U.S. District Court for California's Central District held in *League of United Latin American Citizens v. Wilson* (C.D.Cal.1995) that California's Proposition 187 inappropriately invaded federal authority in purporting to deny primary/secondary education and federally-funded benefits to undocumented aliens. The court said that federal law preempts Proposition 187's requirement that state agents discover, report, and initiate the removal of aliens who are unlawfully present according to state-created criteria. The District Court, however, found that California could limit post-secondary education, state-funded benefits, and even some cooperative state-federal benefits to lawful U.S. residents.

It is clear that the scope of federal immigration power is not so broad as to preclude all state statutes touching the field. While state statutes may be preempted, the *De Canas* case holds that the unexercised federal power over immigration is not by itself a bar to state regulations which single out aliens. State statutes that do not discriminate against resident aliens should be analyzed under the preemption doctrine to determine if they conflict with congressional intent or govern an area already exclusively covered by federal law.

Somewhat related issues of federalism were raised by Arizona and California in seeking federal reimbursement for state expenditures incurred by reason of the federal government's failure to control immigration. The U.S. Court of Appeals in *Arizona v. United States* (9th Cir. 1997) and *California v. United States* (9th Cir.1997) held that the states' claims presented non-justiciable political questions and should be dismissed. The U.S. Supreme Court denied review.

§ 2–3 THE FUNCTIONS OF THE THREE BRANCHES OF THE FEDERAL GOVERNMENT IN REGULATING IMMIGRATION

§ 2–3.1 The Legislature

The plenary and unqualified power of the federal government to regulate immigration, naturalization, and related foreign policy belongs to Congress. The possible international consequences of decisions in this area have made the federal judiciary extremely reluctant to substitute its judgment for the legislature's. Justice Jackson articulated the Court's position in *Harisiades v. Shaughnessy* (Sup.Ct.1952): "[A]ny policy towards aliens is vitally and intricately interwoven with contemporaneous policies in regard to the conduct of foreign relations, the war power, and the maintenance of a republican form of government. Such matters are so exclusively entrusted to the political branches of government as to be largely immune from judicial inquiry or interference." Subsequent decisions echo this sentiment. Since the judiciary poses no obstacle, Congress has been historically free to "exclude aliens altogether or prescribe the terms and conditions upon which they may enter and stay in this country." *Lapina v. Williams* (Sup.Ct.1914). For example, Congress exercised its plenary authority in the Illegal Immigration Reform and Immigrant Responsibility Act of 1996 that facilitated the removal of aliens. Accordingly, it appears the legislative branch wields the full measure of the federal plenary power over immigration.

§ 2–3.2 The Judiciary

The Supreme Court has stopped short of abdicating all responsibility for immigration law. The Court has reserved a narrow ground for review that is worth examining for hints of possible future trends.

a. Decisions Relating to Exclusion (Now "Inadmissibility")

Aliens who are outside the national boundaries of the United States have no constitutional rights and as a practical matter have absolutely no basis for challenging their exclusion (now "inadmissibility") from this country. Although the Supreme Court has not quite deemed exclusion cases non-justiciable under the political question doctrine, the extreme degree of deference the Court gives to legislative determinations on this issue make the ground of review so narrow as to be practically nonexistent. Indeed, earlier cases show a complete "hands off" attitude by the courts. Later cases refer to a narrow ground of review.

Fiallo v. Bell (Sup.Ct.1977) illustrates the Court's gingerly approach to exclusion (now "inadmissibility") cases. A federal statute governing immigration preferences made it more difficult for illegitimate children and fathers to be reunited in this country than illegitimate children and mothers. *See* § 5—2.1, *infra*. U.S. citizens and resident aliens disadvantaged by the statute challenged it on equal protection grounds. In a footnote, Justice Blackmun, for the majority, explicitly rejected the government's contention that admission of aliens is not an appropriate subject for review: "our cases reflect acceptance of limited judicial responsibility under the Constitution even with respect to the power of Congress to regulate the admission and exclusion of aliens.... " Having once established the reviewability of this type of case, however, Blackmun applied a standard of review that is, as dissenter Justice Marshall noted, "toothless." The Court acknowledged that the statute discriminates on the basis of sex and that the fathers have no opportunity to prove a close relationship in order to overcome the statutory presumption. Blackmun flatly stated, "[T]he decision nonetheless remains one solely for the responsibility of the Congress and wholly outside the power of this Court to control." After the Court's decision, Congress did resolve the problem raised in this case by providing that illegitimate children can obtain the same immigration benefits from the natural father as from the natural mother "if the father has or had a bona fide parent-child relationship." INA § 101(b)(1)(D). The Supreme Court in *Miller v. Albright* (Sup.Ct.1998) rejected a child's challenge to the statute's distinction between illegitimate children born abroad of U.S. citizen mothers and "illegitimate" children born abroad of U.S. citizen fathers. The Supreme Court hinted, however, that it might sustain a father's challenge to the requirement that he demonstrate a "bona fide parent-child relationship" even though a mother need not make such a showing.

Federal courts have reserved a narrow ground of review in a few cases: *Hill v. INS* (9th Cir.1983) (although the power of Congress is plenary, exclusion of homosexuals is improper without a medical certificate of psychopathic personality, sexual deviation, or mental defect); *Allende v. Shultz* (1st Cir.1988) (government impermissibly denied visa to widow of former Chilean president invited to speak in U.S. on the basis of general harm to foreign policy created by her presence); *Abourezk v. Reagan* (D.C.Cir.1986) (when alien is a member of Communist or anarchist organization, government may exclude alien based on projected engagement in activities prejudicial to public interest, only if reason for threat to public interest is independent of membership in proscribed organization); and *Harvard Law School Forum v. Shultz* (D.Mass.1986) (Law School forum entitled to preliminary injunction prohibiting Secretary of State from refusing travel permission to a Palestine Liberation Organization member without a "facially legitimate and bona fide reason" for the INS decision). These court decisions presaged legislative actions in 1990 that removed restrictions on the immigration of homosexuals and eased issuance of nonimmigrant visas to members of the Communist Party and other controversial visitors.

b. Resident Alien Cases

Resident aliens possess recognized constitutional rights. When pitted against the federal power to regulate immigration, however, these rights provide little protection. Deportation proceedings (now "removal proceedings") must observe procedural Due Process. *Japanese Immigrant Case* (Sup.Ct.1903). The Court does not, however, examine the adequacy of the fair hearing Congress prescribes. *Id.* Although in early deportation cases the Court refused to recognize substantive Due Process guarantees, recent cases indicate this practice may change. In *Galvan v. Press* (Sup.Ct.1954) the Court at least looked at the congressional classification making Communists deportable and found "it was not so baseless as to be violative of due process and therefore beyond the power of Congress." Similarly, in *Mathews v. Diaz* (Sup.Ct. 1976) the Court implicitly applied equal protection analysis to a federal statute that discriminated between two classes of aliens. The Court upheld the classification as rational. Instead of declaring a harsh provision unconstitutional, the U.S. Court of Appeals for the Second Circuit in *Francis v. INS* (2d Cir.1976) construed a deportation statute very broadly to give relief to aliens who had lived in the United States for at least seven years. *See* § 8–4.1.d(2)(g), *infra*. In *Fernandez-Santander v. Thornburgh* (D.C.Me.1990) and *Kellman v. District Director, INS* (S.D.N.Y.1990) federal trial courts required that aliens in certain situations have an opportunity to apply for bail. Although these cases provide no direct precedent for questioning the plenary authority of Congress over immigration matters, they do suggest that congressional power in this area may some day fail to support a completely arbitrary act or classification.

In fact, the Supreme Court has more than once expressed in dicta regret in not being able to afford some measure of protection to resident aliens. For example, in *Galvan v. Press* (Sup.Ct.1954), Justice Frankfurter remarked:

"[C]onsidering what it means to deport an alien who legally became a part of the American community, and the extent to which, since he is a 'person' an alien has the same protection for his life, liberty and property under the Due Process Clause as is afforded to a citizen, deportation without permitting the alien to prove that he was unaware of the Communist Party's advocacy of violence strikes one with a sense of harsh incongruity. If due process bars Congress from enactments which shock the sense of fair play—which is the essence of due process—one is entitled to ask whether it is not beyond the power of Congress to deport an alien who was duped into joining the Communist Party, particularly when his conduct antedated the enactment of the legislation under which his deportation is sought. And this is because deportation may ... deprive a man 'of all that makes life worth living.' "

The weight of authority backing the government's plenary power to deport was too great to push aside with the mere invocation of "fair play," however, and the Court held Due Process was satisfied in this case. These judicial rumblings may yet produce results.

Deportation (now "removal") is not a criminal penalty. Therefore, deportation orders cannot be challenged as a violation of the *ex post facto* clause when past conduct that was not illegal when committed, is the basis for a deportation order (*Mahler v. Eby* (Sup.Ct.1924); *Harisiades v. Shaughnessy* (Sup.Ct.1952)). For the same reason denial of bail (*Carlson v. Landon* (Sup.Ct.1952)), double jeopardy (*United States v. Ramirez–Aguilar* (9th Cir.1972)), speedy trial (*Argiz v. INS* (7th Cir.1983)), and cruel and unusual punishment (*Fong Yue Ting v. United States* (Sup.Ct.1893)) challenges are of no use.

c. Naturalization Cases

As with exclusion and deportation (now "inadmissibility" and "removal"), the Supreme Court accords great deference to the naturalization guidelines set by Congress. In *United States v. Ginsberg* (1917) the Court stated, "An alien who seeks political rights as a member of this nation can rightfully obtain them only upon the terms and conditions specified by Congress. Courts are without authority to sanction changes or modifications; their duty is rigidly to enforce the legislative will. . . . " In cases involving classifications in the naturalization process, the Court has given a near absolute presumption of validity to distinctions drawn by Congress.

As discussed above, all phases of immigration, including the regulation of resident aliens and naturalization, are guided by the legislative branch. In all cases the judiciary has refused to second guess federal legislation, although the courts retain the power of review. *See* chapter 4, *infra*.

d. Asylum Cases

The Supreme Court also defers to Congress on issues involving asylum. The problem has been reconciling the nation's commitments under the Protocol relating to the Status of Refugees with Congress' expressions of substantive and procedural rights under the Refugee Act of 1980. In *INS v. Cardoza–Fonseca* (Sup.Ct.1987) the Supreme Court used its power of review to determine the standard to be applied in granting asylum. Specifically, the Court held that a refugee seeking asylum pursuant to § 208(a) of the INA must show only a "well-founded fear of persecution" in her/his country of origin, and not a "clear probability" of persecution, as was required for withholding of deportation under § 243(h)(now § 241(b)(3)) of the INA. *See* § 10–2.3, *infra*. The Court had earlier decided in *INS v. Stevic* (Sup.Ct.1984) that the "well-founded fear" standard did not govern § 243(h) applications for withholding of deportation.

In rejecting the "clear probability" test, Justice Stevens made it clear that the Court was within its boundaries. He wrote,

"... courts must respect the interpretation of the agency to which Congress has delegated the responsibility for administering the statutory program.... But our task today is much narrower, and is well within the province of the judiciary. We do not attempt to set forth a detailed description of how the well-founded fear test should be applied. Instead, we merely hold that the Immigration Judge and the BIA were incorrect in holding that the two standards are identical."

Therefore, while generally deferring to Congress, the Court will take an indirect role in shaping immigration policy by ruling on issues of statutory interpretation, including whether INS regulations are consistent with the intent of legislation.

Critics have also charged that persons seeking asylum are victims of discrimination on the basis of their nationality. In particular, persons from El Salvador and Guatemala have alleged that they have not been given fair adjudications of their asylum claims. In a significant settlement, the Department of Justice agreed to re-adjudicate up to 150,000 asylum claims; further, all Salvadorans who had arrived to this country by September 19, 1990 and Guatemalans who had arrived by October 1, 1990 were for a period of time protected from deportation (now "removal") and received work authorization. *American Baptist Churches v. Thornburgh* (N.D.Cal. 1991). As many as half a million people might have been affected by the settlement.

§ 2–3.3 The Executive

As in other areas of the law, the function of executive agencies in the field of immigration is to enforce the legislation passed by Congress. The structure of the federal executive agencies that administer and enforce the immigration laws is discussed in chapter 3. Once Congress determines which classes of aliens will be denied admission or removed, the executive decides who fits within each class. Since the executive has no inherent power over immigration, it must stay within the grant of authority defined by the statute. Any unauthorized executive decisions are illegal and the courts may overturn them. *Mahler v. Eby* (Sup.Ct.1924).

Congress need not give the agencies detailed direction. The courts have not hesitated to uphold broad delegations of power to the enforcement agency. *Jay v. Boyd* (Sup.Ct.1956). In general, Congress need only delineate basic policy. Agencies then have relatively free rein in creating procedures to implement, administer, and enforce the immigration laws. Congress also may make the executive decisions final, thereby precluding review by the courts of agency factual findings. IIRIRA, for example, stripped the courts of jurisdiction to review any individual determination which arose from or is related to summary removal under INA § 235(b)(1). INA § 242(a)(2)(A)(i). The courts are precluded from reviewing any decision by the Attorney General to invoke the summary removal provisions. INA § 242(a)(2)(A)(ii). The application of summary removal to individual aliens, including the determination of an alien's credible fear, is also not subject to judicial review. INA § 242(a)(2)(A)(iii). In addition, IIRIRA bars judicial review of procedures and policies adopted by the

Attorney General to implement the summary removal provisions of INA § 235(b)(1). INA § 242(a)(2)(A)(iv). Those limitations on judicial review are being challenged. *See* § 8–4.1.d(1), *infra*.

In 1983, an issue surfaced concerning the division of power between the executive and legislative branches that pertained to deportation procedures. Congress had reserved the power of one house of Congress to veto any individual decision by the INS to suspend deportation (now "cancel removal"). *See* § 8–4.1.d(2)(b), *infra* for a discussion of cancellation of removal. The House of Representatives exercised this veto in the case of an East Indian from Kenya and the alien, who was thus to be deported, challenged the congressional action as a violation of constitutional separation of powers. The Supreme Court held in the landmark decision of *INS v. Chadha* (Sup.Ct.1983) that such legislative veto provisions violated the constitutional requirement that, before becoming law, all bills must pass both the House and the Senate, and be presented to and signed by the President.

Finally, Congress may not give the executive the power to impose punishment for crimes. The courts alone may exercise this power and the procedures must comply with the constitutional requirements for all criminal prosecutions. Deportation (now "removal") is not considered criminal punishment, however, even when triggered by illegal acts.

CHAPTER 3

ADMINISTRATIVE STRUCTURE OF IMMIGRATION LAW

There are five major departments of the executive branch of the federal government involved in the immigration process: the Department of State, the Department of Justice, the Department of Labor, the Department of Health and Human Services, and the United States Information Agency. Congress has a role in the immigration process discussed in chapter 4.

§ 3–1 THE DEPARTMENT OF STATE

For most aliens the immigration process begins abroad in the over 200 U.S. consulates and embassies, which are a part of the Department of State. To obtain the visa necessary to travel to this country, an alien must file an application at the U.S. consulate in her/his country of last residence. A common example is the B–2 tourist visa, which is usually obtained abroad. In contrast, for example, if an alien wishes to enter the U.S. as an immediate relative or fiancé(e) of a U.S. citizen, or under almost all employment-sponsored temporary visa statuses, a petition must first be filed by the sponsoring relative or employer for such classification with the Immigration and Naturalization Service (INS) in the United States. A U.S. citizen or permanent resident residing abroad may also file family petitions at INS offices abroad. If the INS grants the petition, it notifies the U.S. embassy or consulate in the alien's country of last residence, and the visa is sought by the alien following a separate application process.

Consular officers make the decision whether to grant or refuse a visa and this decision is subject to very limited review. Although the Immigration and Nationality Act (INA) delegates general visa documentation responsibility to the Department of State, it excludes from the Secretary of State's broad authority "those powers, duties, and functions conferred upon the consular officers relating to the granting or refusal of visas." INA § 104(a)(1). The Department of State, however, conducts a highly discretionary informal review system in which each visa refusal is reviewed by a second consular officer. The second consular officer may disagree with the first officer's decision and issue the visa, but s/he cannot mandate that the visa be granted by the first officer. If a dispute does arise between consular officers, the matter may be referred to the Visa Office of the Department of State in Washington, D.C. The Visa Office will issue an advisory opinion. Although technically only binding as to legal questions, the Visa Office advisory opinion is usually followed.

Consular decisions denying visas to aliens not yet present in the United States are generally held to be neither administratively nor judicially reviewable. *See, e.g., Li Hing of Hong Kong, Inc. v. Levin* (9th Cir.1986); *Ventura–Escamilla v. INS* (9th Cir.1981). Several courts, however, have asserted a narrow ground of review in visa denial cases. *See Abourezk v. Reagan* (D.C.Cir.1986) (plaintiffs were entitled under the Administrative Procedure Act to judicial review of agency action denying a visa, due to the absence of "clear and convincing evidence" of congressional intent to the contrary) and *Allende v. Shultz* (D.Mass.1985) (U.S. citizens claiming that the denial of a visa for the Chilean speaker violated their First Amendment rights of free speech and association were entitled to judicial review because "[t]he exercise of judicial review, though necessarily limited in scope, is particularly appropriate in cases ... which involve fundamental rights of U.S. citizens").

Even receipt of a visa, however, does not ensure admission to the United States. The immigration officer at the U.S. border or port of entry (referred to as an "inspector") may either disagree with the consular officer and hold the alien for a removal hearing or conclude that the alien has given false information to the consular officer and subject the alien to a summary removal. Fortunately, such situations seldom occur. An interesting illustration of INS efforts to avoid removal hearings at the border for entering aliens can be seen in the "preinspection" procedures or "interdiction" programs where INS officials examine aliens either in their country of departure or on the high seas.

The Department of State's role extends beyond issuing visas. The Department of State supervises embassy adjudications of citizenship questions when a person outside the U.S. claims to be a U.S. citizen. It issues advisory opinions on refugee and asylum petitions, and supervises consular actions in other matters that might affect the relationship of the U.S. government with other countries. The Department of State also provides consular services for U.S. citizens abroad, such as for persons with lost passports or a need for other documents, as well as for U.S. citizens arrested in a foreign country.

§ 3–2   THE DEPARTMENT OF JUSTICE

The Attorney General has the power of administering and enforcing the INA, and "all other laws relating to the immigration and naturalization of aliens." INA § 103(a). This power does not include those duties expressly delegated to other officials or agencies, such as the Department of State. *Id.* The Attorney General is authorized to delegate his responsibilities to agencies within the Department of Justice, such as the INS and the Executive Office for Immigration Review. INA § 103.

§ 3–2.1   The Immigration and Naturalization Service

Although the INA does not state specifically which duties are to be delegated to a particular agency, the Attorney General delegates most duties to the Immigration and Naturalization Service (INS). The INS, which has general jurisdiction over aliens in the U.S., handles visa petitions, adjustments from nonimmigrant to immigrant status, citizenship adjudications, and removals for aliens present in this country. As previously mentioned, the INS also inspects aliens at the border before entry into the U.S. and does not allow entry to persons who are inadmissible.

The Commissioner of Immigration and Naturalization heads the INS. The Commissioner is appointed by the President, normally on the recommendation of the Attorney General, and with the consent of the Senate. INA § 103(b). Four Associate Commissioners and the General Counsel assist the Commissioner; all are located in the INS central office in Washington, D.C.

The central office deals almost exclusively with administrative matters, such as budgeting and policy formulation. Given this administrative function, an attorney handling an immigration case involving an individual alien would not normally deal with the central office. In some instances, however, such as when the attorney believes that a district office is not complying with national policy, the central office may be contacted for assistance and even advisory opinions. For example, there is a division called the Administrative Appeals Unit that handles administrative appeals from certain decisions of lower adjudicatory officers.

There are three INS regional offices, which are located in Burlington, Vermont; Laguna Nigel, California; and Dallas, Texas. These three regional offices constitute the intermediate administrative level of the INS. Each region has a Regional Commissioner. Like the central office, the regional offices are concerned primarily with administrative issues. The regional offices provide administrative coordination for the 33 domestic district offices. There are also several district offices abroad, which have a very limited scope of responsibility.

The level of the INS primarily responsible for implementing the immigration laws is the district office. Each district office has a district director and several assistant directors. District offices are divided into units that focus on investigation, examination, removal, administration, and records/information. The district counsel advises the district and acts as their advocate. The investigative division in each district includes officers who enforce the immigration law in the interior of the country by locating undocumented aliens, investigating fraud and smuggling operations, and engaging in other enforcement activities. The examination unit is comprised of officers who engage in border inspections and adjudications. The officers responsible for inspections examine documents presented by entering citizens and aliens at the approximately 200 ports of entry within the U.S.

The Border Patrol prevents illegal entries into the U.S. and detains or expels undocumented aliens already present. The Patrol's officers report to the central office and are not under the supervision of the district directors. In § 101 of the Illegal Immigration Reform and Immigrant Responsibility Act of 1996 (IIRIRA), the number of border patrol agents is to increase from approximately 5,700 in 1996 by at least one thousand each year until the year 2001.

The adjudication division of each INS district office reviews petitions for adjustment of status, visa extension, immigrant visas for overseas relatives, and for various other benefits under the INA. Immigration officers have broad discretion in deciding whether an application is complete, accurate, credible, and in compliance with statutory and regulatory requirements. The district director has the authority to initiate investigations, removals, notices to appear, and arrest warrants, as well as to set bail in connection with removal hearings.

For the past several years, the INS has embarked upon an intensive program to centralize its adjudication functions into what are known as Regional Service Centers. The INS hopes that eventually almost all adjudications will be handled at those regional centers. A large number of petitions for immigrant and nonimmigrant status are sent to one of the four Regional Service Centers, where a high-volume of applications can be decided without any personal contact with the applicant. The centers are located in St. Albans, Vermont; Lincoln, Nebraska; Laguna Nigel, California; and Dallas, Texas. In most regions, the applicant sends her/his petition directly to the appropriate center. INS officers at these centers decide the cases almost in a "vacuum." They are very difficult to be reach by phone, but will respond to written inquiries. This approach renders the application process highly documentary and less susceptible to personal advocacy.

§ 3–2.2 The Executive Office for Immigration Review

The INS does not have complete control over every alien's fate. The immigration courts and the Board of Immigration Appeals are independent from the INS. Together they constitute the Executive Office for Immigration Review (EOIR). The EOIR is an administrative body, not a court under Article 1 or 3 of the Constitution.

a. The Immigration Courts

Immigration judges preside primarily over removal hearings. They may also participate in other adjudications such as proceedings to rescind adjustments of status under INA § 246, hearings to withdraw approval of schools for attendance by nonimmigrant students, 8 C.F.R. § 214.4, and challenges brought by aliens ordered to remain in the country under the provisions of 8 C.F.R. §§ 215, 215.4, 215.5. Decisions made by immigration judges are final unless appealed to the Board of Immigration Appeals. 8 C.F.R. §§ 3.36, 3.37.

Until 1983, immigration judges were a part of the INS. These judges were senior immigration officers who held hearings in addition to their enforcement responsibilities. Concerns about the neutrality of judges with enforcement responsibilities prompted Due Process challenges to these hearings. In 1950, the Supreme Court ruled that the Administrative Procedure Act (APA) demands a separation of functions between immigration judges and enforcement officials. *Wong Yang Sung v. McGrath* (Sup. Ct.1950). Shortly thereafter, Congress passed a provision exempting immigration adjudications from the APA separation-of-functions requirements. Under the INA, Congress again expressly provided that immigration judges could also serve as enforcement officials. INA § 242(b). The act, however, did prohibit an immigration judge from presiding over a case on which s/he had previously acted as prosecutor or investigator. *Id.* The Supreme Court found no Due Process violation under these new provisions. *Marcello v. Bonds* (Sup.Ct.1955).

While Due Process arguments failed, the desire for professionalism within the INS and the need for more predictable, rational adjudication resulted in changes. Beginning in 1956, the INS required immigration judges to have law degrees. In 1962, the INS began to employ a staff of trial attorneys to present the government's case; it became standard practice for a trial attorney (now "service counsel") or other INS officer to appear in almost every deportation and exclusion proceeding (now "removal proceeding").

Despite these reforms, immigration judges remained dependent on INS district directors for budgeting and administrative matters. In 1983, the Department of Justice resolved this problem by removing immigration judges from the INS and placing them under the direct supervision of the Associate Attorney General in the newly created Executive Office for Immigration Review. *See* 8 C.F.R. § 3.

b. *The Board of Immigration Appeals*

Unlike the immigration courts, the Board of Immigration Appeals (BIA) has never been a part of the INS and has always been directly accountable to the Attorney General. In fact, the BIA was not created by the INA, but pursuant to regulations promulgated by the Attorney General. For many years, the Board consisted of five permanent members appointed by the Attorney General. During 1994–1995, the Board expanded from nine to twelve permanent members. In December 1996, the Executive Office for Immigration Review further enlarged the Board's membership to 15 members. The expansion was necessary to handle the heavy workload and allows the Board to sit in five permanent panels comprised of three members. The Board may still hear important matters sitting *en banc.*

Most appeals to the Board are from immigration judges' decisions on removal. *See* 8 C.F.R. § 242.21 and 8 C.F.R. § 3.1(b)(1), (2). The Board also hears appeals from other decisions of immigration judges, for example, relating to bonds, parole, or detention of an alien; the imposition of fines and penalties on carriers; and rescission of adjustment of status. The Board also reviews certain decisions of INS district directors, including determinations made on immigrant visa petitions based on family relationship. 8 C.F.R. § 3.1(b). The Attorney General may review certain decisions of the Board that the Chair or a majority of the Board believe should be referred to the Attorney General for review, as well as those decisions which the Commissioner of the INS requests be referred for review, and those decisions that the Attorney General directs the Board to refer to her/him. 8 C.F.R. § 3.1(h). Such referrals are, however, very rare.

c. The Administrative Appeals Unit

Most decisions made by immigration judges are reviewable by the BIA. Most decisions issued by district offices and Regional Service Centers, however, can be appealed to the Administrative Appeals Unit (AAU), a group of appellate examiners located within the office of the Associate Commissioner for Examinations in Washington, D.C. There are exceptions to these usual routes of appeal; for example, the AAU also has limited authority to hear appeals from immigration judge decisions. Hence, a practitioner is advised to consult the regulations to determine which route of appeal—the BIA or AAU—is appropriate. *See* 8 C.F.R. §§ 3.1(b), 103.1(f).

§ 3–2.3 Asylum Adjudication

In 1990, the INS issued regulations creating a new system for processing asylum applications and authorizing the installation of a documentation center to collect and disseminate information on worldwide human rights conditions.

Under this system, a corps of asylum officers reports directly to the INS Central Office for Refugees, Asylum, and Parole (CORAP) in Washington, D.C., rather than to the INS district offices. Therefore, the asylum officers have been separated from INS enforcement functions. Under the regulations, the asylum officers are trained in international relations and international law, and receive briefings about human rights from the new documentation center. 8 C.F.R. § 208.1(b).

Asylum officers adjudicate affirmative applications for asylum, *i.e.* applications filed by an alien who is not yet the subject of removal proceedings. (Affirmative applications should be distinguished from defensive applications for asylum which are filed with the immigration judge by aliens in removal proceedings. If an alien fails to obtain asylum from an immigration judge, s/he may appeal the decision to the BIA and further to the federal court of appeals). An alien seeking asylum, not arising out of a removal proceeding, applies to the district director, who then forwards the application to an asylum officer. After a nonadversarial interview and an examination of supporting documents, the asylum officer determines whether the applicant has established asylum status.

The 1994 asylum regulations and 1996 statutory reforms changed the nature of the asylum officer's decision. Before 1994, the asylum officer granted or denied the application for asylum stating the reasons for denial. There was no right of appeal from a decision of an asylum officer, though an unsuccessful applicant could renew the asylum petition at such time as removal proceedings were commenced. Under the 1996 regulations, the INS officer may grant asylum or, if the alien appears to be removable, refer her/his application to an immigration judge for adjudication in removal proceedings. 8 C.F.R. § 208.14(b)(2). The 1996 Act attempted to simplify the asylum application process and to address long delays in disposing of asylum cases. *See* chapter 10, *infra*, for a more complete discussion of asylum procedures.

§ 3–2.4 Other Units

Passage of the Immigration Reform and Control Act of 1986 (IRCA) led to the creation of two additional units dealing with employment discrimination within the Department of Justice. The first, the Office of Chief Administrative Hearing Officer (OCAHO), hears allegations of employer violations—particularly the employment of certain unlawful aliens and employer discrimination on the basis of national origin or citizenship status. The second unit, the Office of Special Counsel for Immigration–

Related Unfair Employment Practices is empowered to investigate and bring charges under the employer sanctions provisions of IRCA.

§ 3–2.5 States

In 1996, IIRIRA provided the Attorney General with the authority to enter into agreements with states and subdivisions of states to implement the administration and enforcement of federal immigration laws. INA § 103(a). With the appropriate agreements, for example, states can receive federal funds to construct and rehabilitate space for detention and confinement. *Id.* The Commissioner may also enter into agreements with law enforcement agencies at the state and local levels to enforce immigration laws. *Id.*

§ 3–3 THE DEPARTMENT OF LABOR

Most aliens wishing to immigrate to the U.S. based upon an offer of permanent employment by a U.S. employer must first obtain certification from the Department of Labor that the employment can not be performed by a qualified, willing U.S. worker and that it will not adversely affect U.S. wages or working conditions. The labor certification program is a stark reminder that one of Congress' aims in controlling immigration is to protect the U.S. labor force. Under the 1990 Act, labor certification is required for immigrants in the second employment-related preference class (members of the professions holding advanced degrees and aliens of exceptional ability), the third (skilled workers, professionals, and other workers), as well as for H–2 nonimmigrant visas. The Department of Labor will grant certification if it determines that there are insufficient qualified and willing U.S. workers available where the alien will be employed and that the alien's employment will not have an adverse impact on wages or working conditions of similarly employed U.S. workers. INA § 212(a)(14). For a further discussion of the procedure to obtain a labor certificate, see § 5–5.1, *infra*.

While the Department of Labor ultimately grants the labor certification, the state employment service office where the job will be located is substantially involved in the procedure. 20 C.F.R. § 656.21(a). In Minnesota, for example, the Minnesota Department of Economic Security makes the initial review as to the local prevailing wage rate for the job, considers the availability of persons within the geographic area for the type of job being sought, and takes into account other factors. A prospective employer must follow a supervised recruitment procedure. The employer must advertise for the position, including a detailed job description stating the prevailing wage and hours. In addition, the 1990 Act requires a showing by the applicant-employer that notice of the individual application for labor certification has been given to the union or bargaining representatives. Where no union exists, the employer must post the notice at the workplace. If the Department of Economic Security is satisfied that there are no qualified, willing U.S. workers for the position and that employing the alien will not adversely affect U.S. labor, the labor certification is sent to the regional office of the Department of Labor for final review. The Department of Labor then examines the certification to ensure that all statutory and regulatory provisions are met. Once all applicable provisions are met, the Labor Department grants certification. Denials of labor certification may occur for a number of reasons including position requirements that are not normal to the occupation or justified by business necessity, improper recruitment procedures, or bad faith of the employer in reviewing U.S. worker applicants. Denials may be appealed by the prospective employer to the Board of Alien Labor Certification Appeals (BALCA), an appellate process that can last two years.

For some occupations the Department of Labor does not make an independent decision on each application for labor certification. Instead, it uses two schedules of occupations. Schedule A contains a list of occupations for which the Department has determined that there are insufficient workers and for which the employment of aliens would not adversely affect wages or working conditions. Examples of Schedule A occupations include physical therapists and professional nurses. 20 C.F.R. § 656.10. In addition, immigrants within the first employment-related preference class ("priority workers") are exempt from the certification requirement.

In contrast, Schedule B occupations are those jobs for which the Department has determined that there are sufficient U.S. citizens and permanent resident workers, upon which alien employment would have an adverse impact. This group mainly includes unskilled workers such as janitors, salespeople, and drivers. 20 C.F.R. § 656.11.

Schedule A applications may be submitted directly to the INS or to a U.S. consular office abroad. 20 C.F.R. § 656.22. Certification is granted without further processing if the INS determines that the alien does, indeed, have a Schedule A occupation. No certification is available for Schedule B occupations unless a rare special waiver is obtained. 20 C.F.R. §§ 656.11, 656.23.

The 1990 Act created a pilot program in which the Secretary of Labor was requested to publish a list of ten occupations with labor shortages or surpluses. This program was supposed to replace the two Schedules A and B, and reflected a congressional interest in relying upon scheduled occupations to a greater extent in order to stem the increasing number of individual labor certifications. It, however, was not implemented and the schedules have been maintained.

§ 3–4 THE DEPARTMENT OF HEALTH AND HUMAN SERVICES

The Department of Health and Human Services also plays a role in the administration of immigration law. The Department's Public Health Service has doctors abroad and at ports of entry to give medical exams before visas are issued and to arriving aliens. These doctors play a significant role in the immigrant process by determining whether an alien's physical or mental condition is within the grounds for inadmissibility.

§ 3–5 THE UNITED STATES INFORMATION AGENCY

The United States Information Agency (USIA) is responsible for cultural and educational exchange programs, sending U.S. citizens to other countries, and encouraging thousands of foreign nationals to visit the U.S. Those aliens enter the U.S. under the nonimmigrant status for "exchange visitors" (J–1). Unlike most of the other nonimmigrant visas, aliens entering the U.S. on a J nonimmigrant visa must generally meet a two-year foreign residency requirement before they seek immigration status.

The Fulbright program is one example of an exchange arrangement overseen by the USIA. The USIA (formerly the International Communications Agency) promulgates all of the regulations concerning exchange visitor programs, including employment-related provisions. *See* § 6–10, *infra* for a detailed discussion of J nonimmigrant visas. In the future, the USIA may become part of the Department of State.

CHAPTER 4

THE CONGRESSIONAL ROLE IN THE IMMIGRATION PROCESS

§ 4–1 INTRODUCTION

Members of the U.S. Senate and House of Representatives are important actors in the formation of immigration law and policy. They draft and approve legislation that, with Presidential signature, becomes the foundation of U.S. immigration law. But Congress performs other vital immigration functions as well. In cases of extreme hardship, private legislation may be passed providing lawful permanent residence or even citizenship for an individual alien. Senators and Representatives are available to take up the case of an alien who may be having administrative problems with the Immigration and Naturalization Service (INS). Both houses of Congress hold oversight hearings in which they examine the internal workings of the INS and other agencies. Furthermore, particularly in the area of refugees, the executive branch must regularly consult with Congress.

This chapter will address each of these congressional immigration activities. While all of them are important, private legislation receives the most extensive treatment, primarily because of the distinctive technical rules governing that process.

§ 4–2 LEGISLATION

The most obvious responsibility of Congress in the immigration area is considering public legislation. Congress took virtually no action in this regard until passing its first general immigration statute in 1882. Over the next 70 years, Congress passed a variety of restrictive immigration laws. In large part these laws were aimed at excluding Asians, criminals, and the diseased from the U.S.

In 1952 Congress passed, over President Truman's veto, the Immigration and Nationality Act of 1952 (also known as the Walter–McCarran Act). This legislation consolidated and revised many earlier immigration statutes. To this day the Walter–McCarran Act remains the foundation of U.S. immigration law.

That view does not indicate that Congress has failed to pass significant immigration legislation since 1952. Major reforms occurred in 1965, 1980, 1986 (the Immigration Reform and Control Act), the Immigration Act of 1990, and most recently, the Illegal Immigration Reform and Immigrant Responsibility Act of 1996. The Immigration Reform and Control Act of 1986 offers an example of congressional action to establish an amnesty program for some of the hundreds of thousands of undocumented aliens in the U.S., to impose criminal sanctions on employers of aliens not eligible for legalization, and to provide for stricter border control in the future. The 1990 Act was an example of an attempt by Congress to update family immigration quotas in light of increasing demand, modernize grounds of exclusion (now "inadmissibility"), toughen laws related to alien criminal offenses, and to create a more globally competitive workforce while trying to protect the U.S. labor market. The 1996

Act, manifests the capacity of Congress to make radical changes in immigration legislation, especially in enforcement, grounds for inadmissibility and removal, restrictions of benefits for aliens, and procedures for seeking asylum.

§ 4–3 PRIVATE LEGISLATION

§ 4–3.1 The Theory

Private legislation provides another way for Congress to contribute in the immigration area. Private legislation, through a private bill, may be introduced specifically to benefit an individual alien or group of aliens. These bills most often provide relief for adopted children and foreign medical graduates. In effect, through this process, an alien is asking that he or she be exempted from the general immigration laws. In conjunction with this request, Congress acts as a tribunal of last resort—primarily through the House Subcommittee on Immigration and Claims and the Senate Subcommittee on Immigration. Congress is hesitant to provide many exceptions to the general immigration laws, however, believing that to do so would undermine their effectiveness. Former House Subcommittee Chairman Mazzoli, in introducing the House procedures and policy for private bills in the 99th Congress, spoke to this practice: "Since the Subcommittee acts as a court of equity in deciding whether to grant special relief in private immigration cases, it must reserve affirmative action to those of extraordinary merit and posing heavy hardship."

The constitutional rationale for private bills has never been adequately developed. Some members of Congress view this process as one in which individuals are able to use the First Amendment to petition for a redress of grievances. Complaints that private bills violate the separation of powers were rejected in *Paramino Lumber Co. v. Marshall* (Sup.Ct.1940), in which the Supreme Court found that such measures did not intrude into judicial matters.

§ 4–3.2 The History of Private Legislation

Private immigration bills have traditionally served a number of useful purposes. As mentioned already, they are a way for Congress to provide some flexibility in situations where the strict application of immigration law would produce harsh or unjust results. Also, a number of private bills pertaining to similarly situated aliens may lead to legislation amending the immigration law from which hardship is emanating. For example, before the Immigration and Nationality Act of 1952, the number of Asian spouses of U.S. citizens allowed to enter the country was restricted by quota. When U.S. servicemen were stationed in the Far East, marriages between the servicemen and Asian spouses resulted in a multitude of private bills granting non-quota status to the individual Asian spouse. The increased number of private bills relating to Asian spouses of U.S. servicemen led to public legislation that granted non-quota status to spouses of U.S. servicemen irrespective of ancestry. This public legislation in turn was incorporated into the Immigration and Nationality Act of 1952, which treats equally all spouses of U.S. citizens.

This transformation from private bill exceptions to immigration law is justified on the theory that "it is unfair and improper to extend the benefit of legislative relief solely to a few selected individuals who are in a position to reach the Congress for redress of their grievances. It is felt that that humanitarian approach should be extended to an entire defined class of aliens rather than to selected individuals." House Report No. 1199, 85th Congress, 1st Session.

In a similar manner, private legislation is occasionally amended to create a public law during congressional deliberations. For example, a private bill in 1978 to exempt an elderly alien from the English literacy requirement of INA § 312 for naturalization was passed by the Senate. The House amended the private bill to provide for a waiver of the requirement for all aliens over fifty years of age who have been living in the United States for periods totaling at least twenty years after lawful admission for permanent residence. The Senate concurred in the amendment, the President signed the bill, and again, the exception became law.

While keeping these benefits in mind, it is important to understand that very few privately introduced immigration bills ever gain congressional approval. For example, in the 77th Congress (1941–42), 22 of 430 private immigration bills were passed, in the 98th Congress (1983–84) 33 of 454 bills were passed, and in the 104th Congress (1995–96), that number was 2 of 14. Given these statistics, one may question the feasibility of a private bill for most aliens seeking relief from removal (formerly "deportation") or other benefits. There may be an increase in requests for private bills as a result of the severe hardships caused by the 1996 Illegal Immigration Reform and Immigrant Responsibility Act (IIRIRA).

In the past, however, the introduction of these bills was almost as important as their passage. Formerly, the mere introduction of a private immigration bill would automatically cause the INS to halt deportation activity during the bill's pendency. *See United States ex rel.*

Knauff v. McGrath (2d Cir.1950). After a private bill was introduced, the House or Senate Judiciary Committee would request a report from the INS on the alien who was the subject of the bill. According to Operations Instruction 107.1c, a stay of deportation would be generally authorized by the INS when it received a committee's report request. If a bill is introduced early in a session of Congress, it could effectively gain the alien a stay of deportation for the remainder of the session (up to two years) with no further action being taken. Also, it was not uncommon for a Representative or Senator to reintroduce an expired private bill at the beginning of the next Congress, thereby continuing the stay of deportation.

As the effectiveness of these tactics in delaying removal became apparent, private legislation grew in popularity. By the 90th Congress (1967–68), 7,293 private immigration bills were introduced; 218 were enacted. Because of this volume, 4,896 of these private bills were still pending at the end of that Congress. These numbers led the House of Representatives to tighten considerably the requirements for the introduction and consideration of private bills. Most significantly, the previously commonplace requests for INS reports on aliens after private bill introduction were restricted to cases involving extreme hardship. An earlier decision, *Roumeliotis v. INS* (7th Cir.1962), had established that there was no right to a stay of deportation without such a request for a report from the INS.

For a time, the Senate refused to follow the House of Representatives' lead, making the Senate more attractive for those seeking introduction of a private bill. The Senate continued automatically to request an INS report on an alien who was the subject of the private bill, thus producing a stay of deportation. Finally in 1981, the Senate approved rules similar to those enacted by the House of Representatives. These rules were a significant factor in bringing the number of private bills introduced down to 14 in the 104th Congress (1995–96).

§ 4–3.3 How Private Legislation Works Today

a. An Overview

The process begins when a Senator or Representative is persuaded to offer a private bill on behalf of an alien. The bill is introduced on the floor of the House of Representatives or Senate and is then referred to the applicable Judiciary Committee. From there it is referred to either the Senate Subcommittee on Immigration or the House Subcommittee on Immigration and Claims. At this stage the author of the bill normally provides the respective Subcommittee with information on the alien's case and requests that a report be requested from the INS (to stay deportation).

If the Subcommittee approves the private bill, it will then return to the Senate or House Judiciary Committee from which it came. Favorable consideration at the Committee level will send the private bill back to the Senate or House floor. After an affirmative vote, which almost always occurs after Committee and Subcommittee approval, the bill will be referred to the other house of Congress for its review. Normally, this step involves referral to its Judiciary Committee, Subcommittee, and so forth. The exception to this procedure is the case in which the latter body has also taken some action on a similar or identical bill, in which instance its approval may be expedited. After both houses of Congress have approved the private bill, it is sent to the President for signature. Because of the extensive screening and investigation done by Congress on each of these bills, Presidential approval is usually only a pro forma requirement.

As can be seen by this overview, the key to a private immigration bill's passage lies in the action taken by the subcommittees. Meeting their requirements and gaining their approval will often insure favorable consideration by subsequent actors. It is important, therefore, to explore what the subcommittees seek in a private bill.

b. The House Subcommittee on Immigration and Claims

It is appropriate to concentrate on the House Subcommittee since the greater number of private immigration bills originate in the House of Representatives. Also, the House Subcommittee's rules were enacted first and serve as the basis for those now employed in the Senate.

Rule 1 sets forth the facts and documents that the author of a private bill must submit to the Subcommittee Chairperson before the Subcommittee takes action. While these necessary supporting items are too numerous to mention here, the rule generally requires the author of the private bill to establish the necessary hardship caused by strict application of the immigration law. The Subcommittee staff is available to offer advice on obtaining necessary materials. The Subcommittee also renders advisory opinions on fact situations that might offer the basis for future private bills. Rule 2 specifies that those aliens having private bills passed on their behalf must thereafter apply for the appropriate relief within two years. Rule 3 provides that all administrative and judicial remedies must be exhausted before the Subcommittee will consider a private bill.

Rule 4 states that the Subcommittee will not intervene in deportation (now "removal") proceedings and will not request stays of deportation (now "stays of removal") on behalf of beneficiaries of private bills, except as indicated in Rule 5. Rule 5, the Subcommittee rule most often cited, provides that the Subcommittee may consider requesting a departmental report (*i.e.,* from the INS) on a beneficiary of a private bill. The rule further states that when a report is requested from the INS, the INS *may* stay deportation (now "stay removal") until final action is taken on the private bill. The INS, however, customarily grants a stay of removal on receipt of such a request. The INS previously made a recommendation on a private bill when submitting the report to the Subcommittee, but no longer does so. Rule 5 has substantially curtailed requests for INS reports and the resulting stays of removal. The last portion of Rule 5 provides that a Subcommittee report request will only be made to prevent extreme hardship to the beneficiary (when the beneficiary is in this country) or to a U.S. citizen spouse, parent, or child.

Rule 6 states that the Subcommittee may request reports on private bills from appropriate federal agencies and/or departments and should await receipt of such reports before taking final action. Rule 7 limits testimony at private bill hearings to that of the bill's author. Rule 8 forbids the deferral of an action on a private bill more than once due to the failure of the author to appear and testify at a duly noticed hearing. Rule 9 establishes that the Subcommittee should take no further action on a private bill that has been tabled by the full Judiciary

Committee. Rule 10 provides that consideration of certain private bills is open to objection unless two-thirds of the Subcommittee approves consideration.

Accompanying these rules is the Subcommittee Statement of Policy, which emphasizes that exceptions to the immigration law are to be granted only in extraordinary cases. The statement outlines various situations in which immigration relief has been sought in the past and the current prospects that each has for success. Included are situations involving adoption, doctors and nurses, drugs and criminal activity, medical cases, deferred action and parole cases, waivers of exclusion (now "inadmissibility"), naturalization, and bills tabled in a previous Congress.

§ 4–4 MEMBERS OF CONGRESS AS OMBUDSMEN

Senators and Representatives are often asked to help ensure that the various government agencies are responsive to the needs and requests of constituents. Members of Congress typically have staff working solely on helping constituents in dealing with bureaucratic procedures and/or obstacles. In essence, the member of Congress is the liaison between the constituent and the government agency, often becoming an advocate for the interests of the constituent. Politically, this casework service for constituents is often viewed as vital to the Congressperson's reelection.

Casework in the immigration area often involves the interests of a U.S. citizen who has filed a petition on behalf of an alien relative or prospective employee. A complaint to a Senator or Representative that the INS is giving inadequate treatment to a citizen's petition will normally lead to immediate communication from the Member of Congress or the congressional staff to INS officials. Such communication is often helpful in relieving excessive delays and ensures that the INS is enforcing immigration laws in accordance with congressional intent. Members of Congress may, and often do, request a status report on an INS petition, or request INS review of a particular case. Sometimes, the Congressperson will also write a letter in support of an alien, either to the INS directly or to a U.S. embassy abroad. To ensure that a letter of support is warranted, however, the Congressperson will often require extensive information on the status of the alien. A Senator or Representative will also be reluctant to take action that might place an alien applying for an immigrant visa ahead of other deserving applicants.

Finally, another important aspect of the casework process is its function in educating a legislator about the bureaucratic workings of the INS. Consistent problems in particular areas may lead to congressional hearings and investigations. The result of such hearings and investigations may be legislation that solves the problem.

§ 4–5 OVERSIGHT OF THE INS

Related to, and sometimes a direct result of, constituent casework, is the oversight function of Congress. Under the Legislative Reorganization Act of 1946, oversight is intended to ensure that the various administrative agencies execute the laws related to them in the manner prescribed by Congress. The oversight task is shared by the standing committees and applicable subcommittees. For the INS, oversight is performed by the

Judiciary Committees of the Senate and House of Representatives with their respective House Subcommittee on Immigration and Claims and the Senate Subcommittee on Immigration.

There are three principal aspects of oversight: investigations, hearings, and reporting requirements. Pursuant to the Legislative Reorganization Act of 1946, Congress investigates how well the laws are being executed and whether administrators are performing effectively. Specific agency investigations, however, are not frequently undertaken.

The focal point of oversight is the hearing process. Hearings are always held to determine the necessary yearly appropriations for the INS. At that time committee members are able to question INS and Department of Justice officials about the operation of their programs. Hearings are also held when new immigration legislation is being considered. For instance, an extensive number of hearings were held over the years leading to enactment of the Immigration Reform and Control Act of 1986. These hearings provide an excellent opportunity for members of Congress to question INS officials about future implementation of the legislation and also to receive information from groups that would be potentially affected.

The oversight process also involves reporting. Legislation often requires the President or the Attorney General to report to the Congress on the progress of certain INS programs. For example, section 402 of the Immigration Reform and Control Act of 1986 required annual Presidential reports to Congress on the implementation of § 274A of the Immigration and Nationality Act (relating to unlawful employment of aliens) during the first three years after its implementation. This requirement was meant to facilitate congressional oversight of the newly established employee verification system.

§ 4–6 EXECUTIVE CONSULTATION WITH CONGRESS

§ 4–6.1 Refugees

The President and Congress have attempted to deal with problems involving refugees several times after refugee issues came to the forefront after World War II. In 1948, Congress adopted the Displaced Persons Act that allowed for the admission into the U.S. of some 400,000 aliens. Congress has passed several other measures facilitating refugee admission.

Despite this congressional action, the requests for relief coming from many other refugees were overwhelming. Two notable examples were the demands of Hungarians and Cubans in 1956 and 1960, respectively. The Attorney General paroled these groups to the United States, pursuant to INA § 212(d)(5)(A). This provision gave the Attorney General discretion to parole into the United States temporarily for emergency reasons or for reasons deemed strictly in the public interest any alien applying for admission. As a matter of practice, the Attorney General regularly consults the relevant Committees about the use of the parole provision—particularly where large groups are involved. Under IIRIRA, the amended version of INA § 212(d)(A) requires the Attorney General's discretion to be used on a "case-by-case basis for urgent humanitarian reasons or significant public benefit."

Wary of the use of parole, particularly as far as it bypassed legislative participation, Congress created a seventh preference category for refugees as part of the Immigration and Nationality Act Amendments of 1965. This preference category, however, only was open to aliens fleeing persecution in a Communist-dominated country or a country in the Middle East. Six percent of the Eastern Hemisphere immigration quota could be filled by such refugees. In 1976 this preference was also opened to Western Hemisphere refugees, and in 1978 the refugee quota was set at a flat 17,400 aliens per year.

Despite this new preference category, the parole power was used extensively in the late 1960's and 1970's. The primary beneficiaries were hundreds of thousands of Cubans and Southeast Asians. Recognizing that the seventh preference provision was inadequate to meet refugee demand, Congress passed the Refugee Act of 1980. That legislation, codified at INA § 207, repealed the seventh preference provision and required extensive Presidential consultation with Congress in conjunction with setting the yearly refugee quotas. Specifically, a Cabinet-level representative of the President must review the refugee situation with members of the House and Senate Judiciary Committees. The administration must provide the Committee members:

(1) a Description of the Nature of the Refugee Situation.

(2) a Description of the Number and Allocation of the Refugees to Be Admitted and an Analysis of Conditions Within the Countries From Which They Come.

(3) a Description of the Proposed Plans for Their Movement and Resettlement and the Estimated Cost of Their Movement and Resettlement.

(4) an Analysis of the Anticipated Social, Economic, and Demographic Impact of Their Admission to the United States.

(5) a Description of the Extent to Which Other Countries Will Admit and Assist in the Resettlement of Such Refugees.

(6) an Analysis of the Impact of the Participation of the United States in the Resettlement of Such Refugees on the Foreign Policy Interests of the United States.

(7) Such Additional Information as May Be Appropriate or Requested by Such Members.

For fiscal years 1980–82, the Refugee Act authorized a 50,000-refugee quota unless the President determined after congressional consultation that a larger number was justified by humanitarian concerns or was otherwise in the national interest. INA § 207(a)(1). Since 1982, the refugee quota has been determined entirely through presidential-congressional consultation. The Presidential Determination for 1997, which followed consultation with Congress, allowed for the admission of 78,000 refugees. That figure was a decrease in recent ceilings that allowed, for example, 90,000 refugees in 1996 and 125,000 in 1990. In the event of an "unforeseen emergency refugee situation," the President may still, after appropriate congressional consultation, expand the admissible number of refugees if such action is justified by "grave humanitarian concerns or is otherwise in the national interest." INA § 207(b). For example, the President expanded the original ceilings of 72,500 for 1988 and 94,000 for 1989, by 15,000 and 22,500 respectively, to help accommodate refugees from Eastern Europe and the Soviet Union.

While the Refugee Act of 1980 has provided a more realistic framework for congressional involvement in the refugee area, it has experienced problems. Soon after its passage in 1980, the Mariel boatlift brought over 100,000 Cubans to the U.S. During the same period thousands of Haitian boat people came to this country. The Carter Administration eventually again resorted to the parole process to handle this influx, later asking for special authorizing legislation from Congress. Section 202 of the Immigration Reform and Control Act of 1986 provided eligibility for permanent resident status for certain Cuban and Haitian entrants who had continuously resided in the United States since before January 1, 1982.

§ 4-6.2   Cancellation of Removal (Formerly "Suspension of Deportation")

Until the mid-1980's, Congress was also a key actor in suspension of deportation proceedings. Pursuant to INA § 244, the Attorney General had the discretion to suspend deportation of an alien and adjust his or her status to that of an alien lawfully admitted for permanent residence in situations where the alien is of good moral character, has been continuously present in the U.S. for a requisite period, and where deportation would cause extreme hardship. The Attorney General was required to report to Congress on the first day of each calendar month in which it is in session with a complete and detailed statement of the facts and pertinent provisions of law in the case.

Before *INS v. Chadha* (Sup.Ct.1983), Congress was authorized to revoke the suspension of deportation through either a resolution or concurrent resolution, depending on the statutory section used for suspension of deportation by the Attorney General. Congress had until the end of the succeeding legislative session to take such action. In *Chadha,* the Supreme Court found this legislative veto provision to be unconstitutional as a violation of the separation of powers doctrine. The legislative veto provision violated specific constitutional process because it did not require action by both houses of Congress or presentment of the action for consideration by the President. In the aftermath of *Chadha,* the Immigration and Technical Corrections Act of 1988 repealed the statute that provided a possible congressional veto for suspension of deportation decisions which are now included in the second prong of the cancellation of removal.

CHAPTER 5

IMMIGRANT VISAS

§ 5–1 INTRODUCTION

All aliens admitted to the United States fall into one of two categories: (1) persons who seek admission for a limited period of time and usually for a limited purpose (known as "nonimmigrants") and (2) persons who want to become permanent residents of the U.S. (known as "immigrants"). The Immigration and Nationality Act (INA) defines a series of nonimmigrant and immigrant classifications by which aliens may be admitted into the U.S. The INA also provides separate grounds for barring admission (grounds for "inadmissibility," formerly "grounds for exclusion") and grounds for removing aliens who have been admitted (formerly "grounds for deportation") along with the associated procedures for seeking admission, admission, and removal.

Any alien desiring to be admitted to the United States is presumed to be an immigrant and therefore must qualify for one of the classes of immigrant visas or demonstrate that s/he is a nonimmigrant. INA § 101(a)(15). Immigrant visas are divided into two categories: visas subject to numerical limitations and visas which are not. Visas not subject to numerical limitations are granted to immediate relatives (spouses and children) of U.S. citizens, resident aliens returning from temporary visits abroad, and former U.S. citizens (discussed in § 5–4, *infra*). INA § 201(b). Visas subject to numerical limita-

109

tions are granted to persons who qualify for family-sponsored, employment-related, or diversity immigrant visas. It is presumed that every person seeking admission to the U.S. is an immigrant, whose visa is subject to numerical limitations, unless the person can establish entitlement to another classification. INA § 203(f).

In order to qualify for an immigrant visa, a person must ordinarily demonstrate that s/he has the intent to live indefinitely in the United States and qualifies for one of the family-sponsored, employment-related, or diversity visas.

§ 5–2 VISAS NOT SUBJECT TO NUMERICAL LIMITATIONS

§ 5–2.1 Immediate Relatives of U.S. Citizens

The 1990 Act authorized the issuance of 226,000 family-sponsored preference visas, as well as 254,000 visas granted to immediate relatives. If more than 254,000 immediate relatives apply, however, the total family-sponsored immigration will exceed the 480,000 numerical limit established from fiscal year 1995. The law does allow "piercing" the 480,000 ceiling in the following fiscal year if the volume of immediate relatives so requires. The piercing of the ceiling thus guarantees a floor for the family-sponsored preference visas of at least 226,-000 admissions every year. INA § 201(c).

An alien may receive a visa as an immediate relative of a U.S. citizen if the person is a child, spouse, or parent of the citizen. INA § 201(b). To qualify as a "child" of a U.S. citizen, the person must be unmarried, under 21 years of age, and either a legitimate child, stepchild, illegitimate child, adopted child, an orphan adopted abroad, or an orphan coming to the United States to be adopted. INA § 101(b)(1). The legitimate child category includes those children born out of wedlock who were later legitimated (granted full legal status) under the laws of either the child's or the father's residence or domicile. The child must have been under 18 and in legal custody of the legitimating parent or parents at the time of legitimation. Children are most often legitimated through marriage of the child's natural parents. The INS interpreted "legitimated" to include a child born out of wedlock who has been accorded legal rights identical to a child born in wedlock. In *De Los Santos v. INS* (2d Cir.1982), the Court of Appeals upheld this interpretation as consistent with the language and purpose of the INA. The stepchild must have been less than 18 years of age at the time of the marriage creating the relationship. Before 1986, an illegitimate child could qualify for a visa only through the relation to its natural mother, and not through its father. The Supreme Court upheld the constitutionality of this discrimination, affirming the government's broad power to expel or exclude aliens. *Fiallo v. Bell* (Sup.Ct.1977). The Immigration Reform and Control Act of 1986, however, provided that an illegitimate child may qualify for a visa through the relation to its natural mother, or to its natural father "if the father has or had a bona fide parent-child relationship with the person." INA § 101(b)(1)(D).

An adopted child may receive a visa if the child was under 16 years of age at the time of adoption and has resided with the adopting parents for two or more years. A child qualifies as an orphan if both parents have died, disappeared, or abandoned the child, or if the sole or surviving parent is incapable of providing proper care and has in writing irrevocably released the child for emigration and adoption. The orphan must be adopted or be coming to the United States to be adopted by a U.S. citizen and spouse jointly, or by an unmarried U.S. citizen at least 25 years of age. If adopted abroad by an unmarried U.S. citizen, that citizen must have personally observed the child prior to or during the adoption proceedings.

A parent who has any of the relationships described under the definition of "child" meets the statutory definition of a "parent," INA § 101(b)(2), provided the sponsoring citizen child is at least 21 years old. INA § 201(b). If the child is a citizen by reason of adoption by U.S. citizens, or if the child qualifies as an orphan, the child's natural parents are barred from claiming any rights to a visa because of the child's citizenship. INA § 101(b)(1)(E) & (F).

In order to receive a visa as the spouse of a U.S. citizen, the alien must have a "valid and subsisting marriage" with that citizen. The validity of the marriage is generally determined by the laws of the country where the marriage took place. The INA defines the term "spouse" in the negative by identifying who cannot qualify as a spouse. INA § 101(a)(35). A spousal relationship cannot be created through a proxy marriage unless the marriage has been consummated. Marriages adverse to public health and morals, such as incestuous or polygamous marriages, cannot create the necessary relationship. The Court of Appeals in *Adams v. Howerton* (9th Cir.1982) denied immediate relative classification to a homosexual spouse. The court reasoned that Congress did not intend for homosexual marriages to confer spouse status under INA § 201(b).

Sham marriages, that is, marriages motivated by a desire to confer an immigration benefit, do not provide the requisite relationship, regardless of their validity in the country where the marriage took place. The INS and the Board of Immigration Appeals originally denied spousal petitions when it determined that the parties "did not intend to establish a life together at the time they were married" (*Bark v. INS* (9th Cir.1975)) or that the marriage was "factually dead" or nonviable at the time of petitioning. The Court of Appeals in *Dabaghian v. Civiletti* (9th Cir.1979), however, rejected the "factually dead" test and held that if the marriage is not a sham or fraudulent from its inception, it is valid for adjustment of status purposes until legally dissolved. Subsequent separation of the spouses alone, therefore, should not be the sole basis for denying a spousal petition.

The Immigration Marriage Fraud Amendments of 1986 attempted to deter immigration-related marriage fraud. The Fraud Amendments impose a two-year conditional residency requirement on alien spouses and "sons and daughters" before they may obtain permanent resident status on the basis of a "qualifying marriage" to a U.S. citizen or permanent resident alien, if the marriage is less than two years old at the time of obtaining such status. To obtain permanent status, the couple must file a petition within the last 90 days of the conditional status period. The INS will then interview the couple to ascertain that (a) the "qualifying marriage" was not entered into "for the purpose of procuring an alien's admission as an immigrant"; (b) the marriage had not been judicially annulled or terminated, other than through the death of a spouse; or (c) a fee or other consideration other than attorney's fees was not given for the filing of the alien's petition. INA § 216.

If the Attorney General makes a favorable determination, conditional status is removed and lawful permanent resident status granted. If the Attorney General makes an unfavorable determination, or if the couple fails to file a petition without good cause shown, the conditional resident status is terminated. The alien spouse and children are then subject to removal. The Attorney General, however, may allow a hardship waiver and grant permanent resident status if the alien demonstrates that extreme hardship would result if s/he were removed. A waiver is also available if the alien can prove that her/his terminated marriage was undertaken in good faith, and that the alien was not at fault for failing to file a proper petition to have the conditional status removed. In addition, the Attorney General may grant a waiver if a good faith marriage resulted in the battery of or "extreme cruelty" to the alien spouse or the couple's child, again assuming the alien was not at fault for failing to file the required petition or appear for a personal interview. INA § 216(c)(4). This provision was designed to remove the incentive for an alien to stay in an abusive relationship in order to maintain an immigration status. Concern, however, was expressed that this waiver provision would be susceptible to fraud. Hence, the alien must provide evidence, including professional evaluations, to support a waiver petition. 56 Fed.Reg. 22635–01.

The Marriage Fraud Amendments seem to suggest that if an alien and U.S. citizen or permanent resident spouse married with the intention of establishing a life together, as required by the pre–1986 standard, but also married, in part, "for the purpose of procuring [the] alien's entry as an immigrant," that alien might be subject to removal. The words "the purpose" may, however, be read to mean "the sole purpose" in which case the alien would not be subject to removal.

An alien who marries while in removal proceedings may not obtain immediate relative or preference status by reason of that marriage until the alien has resided outside the United States for two years following the marriage date. INA § 204(h). An exception to this foreign residency requirement applies if the alien establishes by "clear and convincing evidence" that the marriage was undertaken in good faith and not for the purpose of evading immigration laws, and further, that no fee was paid in consideration of the petition. INA § 245(e). The Fraud Amendments impose criminal penalties for immigration-related marriage fraud of not more than five years and/or not more than $250,000 in fines, and make marriage fraud an additional ground for removal as well as a perpetual bar to permanent residence. INA § 275(b).

§ 5–3 VISAS SUBJECT TO NU-MERICAL LIMITATIONS

Prior to the 1990 Act, visas subject to numerical limitations were divided into six preference and one nonpreference categories. Any visas remaining after all preference visas were granted were allocated to nonpreference immigrants. Because no nonpreference visas had been issued since 1978, the 1990 Act eliminated the nonpreference category altogether. 1990 Act § 162, *amending* INA § 203.

The 1990 Act increased worldwide immigration levels to 700,000 per year for three years, after which the limit decreased to 675,000 annually. Visas subject to numerical limitations were divided among family-sponsored, employment-related, and, in 1995, diversity immigrants. INA § 201(a). Additional visas used to be available to the spouses and children of formerly undocumented aliens who benefited from IRCA's amnesty program; this provision was effective through 1994. More visas also are available for certain employees of U.S. businesses operating in Hong Kong, their spouse, and their children. 1990 Act §§ 112, 124, *amending* INA § 203.

Family-sponsored and employment-related immigrant visas are also subject to per-country numerical caps; the 1990 Act created a series of calculations necessary to determine these limits. *See* INA § 202. Generally, the per-country ceiling is at least 25,000, and does not count visas granted to immediate relatives. In an attempt to ease the backlog of second preference admissions (spouses and minor children of permanent resident aliens), particularly from Mexico, the 1990 Act exempted 75% of the second preference limitation for Mexico from the per-country limits.

Visas are charged to a country based on the alien's country of birth—even if the alien has become a citizen of another country. INA § 202(b). If charging the alien's visa number to the country of birth would result in separation of the family, in the case of a spouse or child, the visa may be charged to the country of the accompanying spouse or parent. This cross-chargeability rule, however, does not apply to aliens born in a country other than the parent's country of residence, or to aliens born in the U.S. The former are charged to the country of their parents' birth and the latter are charged to their country of citizenship or if none, to the country of parental residence. The U.S. Department of State, Bureau of Consular Affairs, publishes a monthly visa bulletin that summarizes the availability of visas subject to numerical limitations, and lists any countries which have filled their allotments.

§ 5–3.1 Preference Visas

Prior to the 1990 Act, visas subject to numerical limitations were divided into six preference categories. The 1990 Act separated family-sponsored immigrant visas from employment-related visas and created new, though often only slightly modified, categories for each. Family-sponsored immigrants are allotted 226,000 annually with a somewhat flexible maximum of 480,000, while employment-related visas are allocated 140,000 per year.

In an effort to avoid separation of nuclear families seeking to immigrate, the law provides that if the spouse or child of an alien granted a family-sponsored, employment-related, or diversity immigrant visa, cannot otherwise gain an immigrant visa, the spouse or child is admitted in the same preference category and the same priority as the principal alien. To obtain this derivative status, however, the spouse or child must be "accompanying" or "following to join" the principal alien. INA § 203(d). A spouse or child acquired after the principal alien obtains permanent resident status, however, is not given this derivative status and must apply under the second preference family-sponsored class, discussed below.

a. Family–Sponsored Preferences

In addition to the minimum of 226,000 family-sponsored immigrant visas, any unused employment-related visas from the previous fiscal year are available in this

category. The four family-sponsored preference categories are as follows:

First Preference—Unmarried sons and daughters of
U.S. citizens—23,400 visas plus any unused visas from
the other family-sponsored preference classes.

Second Preference—Spouses, children, and unmarried sons and daughters of lawful permanent resident
aliens—minimum of 114,200 visas. Separate numerical
limits exist for:

A.   Spouses and children—87,934 (77% of the visas
under this preference);

B.   Unmarried sons and daughters (at least 21 years
old)—26,266 (23% of the visas issued under this preference).

Third Preference—Married sons and daughters of
U.S. citizens—23,400 plus any unused visas from the
first and second family-sponsored preference categories.

Fourth Preference—Brothers and sisters of U.S. citizens, if the citizen is at least 21 years old—65,000 plus
any unused visas from the first, second, and third family-
sponsored preference categories.

The use of the term "sons and daughters" in the
family-sponsored preference classes is designed to avoid
the statute's definition of "child," since "children" of
U.S. citizens are exempt from numerical limitations as
immediate relatives. Hence, a son or daughter is a
"child" of the petitioner who has passed the age limits
for the definition of child. The term "unmarried" used in
the first and second preference classes is defined as the
marital state of the alien at the time of the visa issuance,
regardless of any previous marriage. INA § 101(a)(39).
The term "brothers and sisters" used in the fourth

family-sponsored class is undefined, but may be derived from the defined term "children" from common "parents."

b. *Employment–Related Preferences*

The 1990 Act allocated 140,000 visas, plus any unused family-sponsored visas, to employment-related immigration. Prior to the 1990 Act, only 54,000 employment-related visas were available. Hence, the 1990 Act dramatically increased the visas available for employment-related immigration, and allocated them among the following five preference categories:

First Preference—Priority Workers—28.6% (40,000 at present) of the total worldwide level plus any unused visas from the fourth and fifth employment-related preference categories. INA § 101(a)(44). Priority workers consist of:

  A. Persons of "extraordinary ability" in the sciences, arts, education, business, or athletics;

  B. Outstanding professors and researchers;

  C. Certain multinational executives and managers.

Second Preference—Professionals holding advanced degrees, or persons of exceptional ability in the sciences, arts, or business—28.6% (40,000 at present) of the total worldwide level plus any unused visas from the first preference category. Unless waived by the Attorney General, an alien seeking admission to the U.S. under a second employment-related visa must have proof of a job offer.

Third Preference—Skilled workers in short supply, professionals holding baccalaureate degrees, and other workers in short supply—28.6% (40,000 at present) of the total worldwide level plus any unused visas from the first and second employment-related preference categories; not more than 10,000 visas can go to "other workers" from this preference category.

Fourth Preference—Certain Special Immigrants— 7.1% (10,000 at present) of the total worldwide level. This category includes the special immigrants detailed in § 5–4, *infra*. Principally, this preference category is comprised of religious workers, as well as former employees of the U.S. government and international organizations. The numerical allotment for special immigrants is expected to be sufficient for the next several years. INA § 101(a)(27)(C) through (J).

Fifth Preference—Employment Creation Visas— 7.1% (10,000 at present) of the total worldwide level. This preference category is comprised of investors who will create at least ten U.S. jobs by investing in a new commercial enterprise benefiting the U.S. economy. The minimum required investment is $1 million, though it may be as little as $500,000 if the investment is in a rural area, or an area of high unemployment. If the commercial enterprise is located in an area of low unemployment, the required investment may be raised by the INS to $3 million. The INS has issued regulations setting the required investment at $1 million. To avoid fraud, investors are accorded only conditional permanent resident status for two years, after which a review of the investment will be undertaken.

"Extraordinary ability" is defined as a "level of expertise indicating that the individual is one of that small percentage who have risen to the very top of the field of endeavor." 56 Fed.Reg. 60897–01. The 1990 Act requires that the alien's extraordinary ability be reflected through "sustained national or international acclaim" and extensive documentation of the alien's contribution to her/his field. INA § 203(b)(1). The phrase "members of professions" lacks statutory definition, so case law and the regulations must be consulted for any particular profession.

The employment-related preference categories instead focus on the educational attainment of the alien. A profession is generally an occupation which requires a high level of specialization. Likewise, "exceptional ability" means a degree of expertise significantly above that ordinarily encountered in the arts, sciences, or business. For example, an average musician is not included, but one with national recognition is. *Cf. Dong Yup Lee v. INS* (9th Cir.1969). The possession of a degree, diploma, certificate, or license to practice a particular profession is not, by itself, sufficient evidence of exceptional ability. INA § 203(b)(2).

c. Diversity Immigrants

The 1990 Act attempted to regain the flexibility that the nonpreference categories were intended to create under the INA, while at the same time, reverse the drastic reductions in immigration from European countries, particularly Ireland. The 1986 Immigration Reform and Control Act established the NP–5 pilot lottery program, through which persons from "adversely affected" countries, that is, countries contributing disproportionately few immigrants, could gain immigrant visas. Approximately 1.3 million people applied for these 10,000 visas. In 1988, Congress increased the allotment from 10,000 over two years, to 20,000—again in an effort to assist the admission of aliens from "underrepresented" countries.

The 1990 Act established a permanent diversity immigration program, which began in 1995 (now known as the DV–1 program). The 1990 Act used a complicated formula to determine whether in the previous five years, the alien's country of origin was a "low-admission" country. If so, the alien is eligible for one of the 55,000 visas annually allocated to diversity immigrants. These countries were previously identified under the NP–5 program; under the 1990 Act, aliens seeking admission applied under the AA–1 program. The actual selection process is still a random lottery, and the alien may file only one petition per year. Hence, it is a highly uncertain way to seek an immigrant visa. Furthermore, an alien seeking a diversity visa must have attained a high school education or its equivalent, or have at least two years of work experience in an occupation which requires at least two years of training or experience.

d. Inhabitants of Hong Kong

The 1990 Act also contained several specific provisions aimed at addressing a particular group's needs. One such group is Hong Kong residents who may want to immigrate to the U.S. after the return of Hong Kong to the People's Republic of China. The 1990 Act increased the allocation for immigration from Hong Kong to 10,000 (from 5,000) for the first three years of the act, after which the level rose to 20,000. 1990 Act § 103. These provisions are also aimed at benefitting employees of the U.S. government and certain U.S. businesses in Hong Kong. 1990 Act § 152. In addition, the 1990 Act extended visas issued to Hong Kong residents until January 1, 2002, allowing them to immigrate if conditions after July 1, 1997, so dictate, while providing them with the security to stay in the meantime.

§ 5–4 SPECIAL IMMIGRANTS

Special immigrant visas are available to resident aliens returning from temporary trips abroad; former U.S. citizens; ministers of recognized religious denominations, their spouse, and their children; certain religious workers other than ministers seeking admission to the U.S. before October 1994, their spouse, and their children; employees of the U.S. government abroad with 15 or more years of service; certain employees of the Panama Canal Company or Canal Zone government, their spouse, and their children; certain officers and employees of international organizations, their spouse, and their children; graduates of foreign medical schools who are fully licensed to practice in a state and have been practicing in such state since January 1978 or earlier, their spouse, and their children; and certain aliens declared dependent on a juvenile court in the U.S. and deemed eligible for foster care. INA § 101(a)(27).

Until the 1990 Act, immigrant visas issued to special immigrants were not subject to numerical limitations. The 1990 Act, however, maintained only those special immigrant visas issued to resident aliens returning from temporary trips abroad and to former U.S. citizens free from numerical limits. INA §§ 201(b)(1), 203(b)(4). The remaining special immigrants are limited to 10,000 visas per year. Aside from the several hundred thousand lawful permanent residents returning from temporary trips abroad, special immigrants use approximately six thousand visas annually. The special immigrant group is the subject of frequent legislative modifications, so the possible inclusion or exclusion of any particular alien must regularly be checked against the statutory language.

Commuter aliens, or "green card commuters," are an interesting group included in the special immigrant category. Commuter aliens are those aliens who reside in Mexico or Canada, but who are admitted into the U.S. as immigrants on a daily or seasonal basis for employment. These aliens are placed under the special immigrant category of resident aliens returning from temporary trips abroad. The great majority of these workers commute from Mexico. 8 C.F.R. § 211.5.

§ 5–5 PROCEDURAL REQUIREMENTS

§ 5–5.1 Petitions and Certification

Before a consular officer can issue a visa based on immediate relative status or on one of the family-sponsored or employment-related preference categories, that officer must have received a petition, approved by the INS, on behalf of the applying alien. INA §§ 201(f), 204. For the immediate relative visa and for the family-sponsored preference visas, the petition is filed by the U.S. citizen or resident alien, who claims the requisite relation to the prospective immigrant, on Form I–130 or, for an adopted orphan, on Form I–600. One exception is the Amerasian children provision of the INA, which allows the alien or any person on behalf of the alien to file the petition. Any person fathered by a U.S. citizen, who was born after 1950 and before October 22, 1982, in Korea, Vietnam, Laos, Cambodia, or Thailand, may file or have filed on her/his behalf a visa petition under the immediate relative or first or third family-sponsored preference categories. INA § 204(f).

Form I–130 is submitted by the relative of the alien to the INS office or Regional Processing Center having jurisdiction over the relative's residence. 8 C.F.R.

§ 204.1(a)(3)(I). For example, the wife of an alien might submit Form I–130 on behalf of her husband. If the relative resides outside of the U.S., the nearest consulate must be consulted to determine the proper place to file the petition. 8 C.F.R. § 204.1(a)(3)(ii). The petition must be accompanied by proof of the petitioner's U.S. citizenship or permanent resident status and by documents which prove the petitioner's relationship to the alien (*e.g.*, a marriage certificate in the case of a spouse). 8 C.F.R. § 204.2.

The date on which an approvable Form I–130 visa petition is filed with the Attorney General for a family-sponsored or employment-related preference visa is the petitioner's priority date. This date determines when the alien will be considered for visa issuance in relation to others in the same preference category and from the same country. Depending on their preference category, residents from some countries may have to wait over 10 years. Others may not need to wait at all. If an alien's temporary immigration status changes during the waiting period or even if the alien has no temporary immigration status, the alien may keep his original priority date as long as s/he still meets the criteria of the approved petition.

The 1986 Immigration Fraud Amendments attempted to eliminate benefits gained through a second preference petition as a result of a prior sham marriage. A permanent resident spouse who immigrated through marriage to a prior spouse is prohibited from petitioning on behalf of a new alien spouse for five years after attaining permanent resident status. This condition is eliminated if the marriage was terminated because the prior spouse died or the permanent resident can meet the burden of proving that the prior marriage was not fraudulent. INA § 204(a)(2).

If an adopted orphan seeks admission, petition Form I–600 is used and the documents previously mentioned must be submitted along with proof that the child is an orphan. This petition must also include a home study, conducted by an authorized or licensed public adoption agency, recommending that the proposed place of residence is a suitable environment for the orphan. 8 C.F.R. § 204.2.

For employment-related preference categories, the alien or an employer must file a petition on behalf of the alien on Form I–140, before the status will be granted. For aliens with extraordinary ability, the alien or any person on behalf of the alien may file the petition. INA § 204(a)(1)(E). Similarly, diversity immigrants and aliens in the fourth and fifth employment-related preference categories may file their own petitions. INA § 204(a)(1)(E) through (G). An employer must generally file the petition for an alien seeking immigrant status under second and third employment-related preference categories. INA § 204(a)(1)(D). The Attorney General may waive the job offer requirement for aliens in the second category if the waiver is deemed to be within the national interest. An approved labor certification is usually required before a second or third employment-related preference petition can be filed with the INS.

The Form I–140 petition is submitted to the INS office in the district where the alien will be employed or to the INS office where the alien will reside. 8 C.F.R. § 204.1(d)(1). This petition must be submitted with an approved labor certification, unless the alien is the beneficiary of a Schedule A filing or is pre-certified. 8 C.F.R.

§ 204.2(I)(4). A second employment-related preference petition must also include documents that prove the beneficiary's special ability, such as diplomas and licenses or records of national or international recognition, including any recognized prizes or awards received. 8 C.F.R. § 204.2(I)(1).

An approved labor certification is generally required for second and third employment-related preference classes. INA § 212(a)(5). The labor certification will not be issued unless the Secretary of Labor determines that: (a) there are not sufficient qualified workers available at the place where the alien will be employed; and (b) that employment of the alien will not adversely affect wages or working conditions of similarly employed U.S. workers. The labor certification application is initiated on Form ETA 750, which requires a statement from the employer describing the job, qualifications, and wages as well as a statement from the alien of her/his qualifications. The application for labor certification is initially handled by a local state job service office that acts on behalf of the Department of Labor.

The Department of Labor has simplified the certification process by issuing two lists of occupations in 20 C.F.R. § 656.10, Schedule A (as of 1997, including only physical therapists, professional nurses, and aliens of "exceptional ability in the sciences or arts") and in 20 C.F.R. § 656.11, Schedule B (including unskilled labor such as clerks, janitors, drivers, etc.). If the alien's occupation is included in Schedule A, Form ETA 750 may be submitted directly to the INS or the U.S. consular office abroad along with the preference petition. 20 C.F.R. § 656.22(a). When the INS determines that the occupation is on Schedule A, certification is granted without further process. The determination of the alien's qualification for Schedule A is final; review is not available. If the alien's occupation is included in Schedule B, no certification is available, unless a special waiver is obtained from the Department of Labor Regional Certifying Office. 20 C.F.R. § 656.23. Such waivers are very rare.

For occupations not listed on either schedule, Form ETA 750 must be submitted to the local state job service office where the alien will be employed. 20 C.F.R. § 656.21. Along with Form ETA 750, the employer must include documents showing the employer's unsuccessful attempts to find a U.S. worker for the job. The employer must have advertised the job, describing the job with particularity, and offering the prevailing wage rate, working conditions, and requirements for the occupation in the region of intended employment. The employer must also have offered wages and employment terms and conditions as favorable as those offered to the alien. 20 C.F.R. § 656. The validity of these regulations was upheld in *Production Tool Corp. v. Employment and Training Administration* (7th Cir.1982) and *Industrial Holographics, Inc. v. Donovan* (7th Cir.1983). Furthermore, the employer must document that all U.S. applicants for the job were rejected solely for lawful, job-related reasons. 20 C.F.R. § 656.21(b)(7).

The local state job service office will process the application and forward it to the certifying officer of the Regional Office of the Department of Labor for final determination. If the certifying officer decides to issue a certification, Form ETA 750 will be returned to the employer with an official certification stamp. 20 C.F.R. § 656.28. The INS will then examine the employer's actual visa application. Despite labor certification, the

INS may still deny a visa petition because of fraud or misrepresentation by the employer or alien, the alien's inadequate qualifications for the job, or the employer's inability to pay the offered wage.

If the certifying officer decides that the employer's petition does not meet all the requirements, s/he will issue a Notice of Findings, which is a preliminary denial of certification. 20 C.F.R. § 656.24(b). The employer then has 35 days to comply with the requirements or to submit a written argument rebutting the bases of the negative determination. 20 C.F.R. § 656.25(c). If unsuccessful, the certifying officer will issue a Final Determination, denying certification. 20 C.F.R. § 656.25(g). The employer is entitled to a review of the denial by the Board of Alien Labor Certification Appeals, which may take about two years. 20 C.F.R. § 656.26. If the administrative appeal is unsuccessful, judicial review in federal district court is available under the Administrative Procedure Act.

In considering labor certification, the certifying officer has substantial discretion to determine what is required for the "basic job" that the employer wishes to fill and whether the requirements listed in the employer's job description are excessive. For example, the Court of Appeals for the D.C. Circuit in *Pesikoff v. Secretary of Labor* (D.C.Cir.1974) found no abuse of discretion in denying labor certification to a live-in maid, even though there were no maids available in the area who were willing to live in. The Court held that the employer's live-in requirement was an irrelevant personal preference and that it was "well within the Secretary's discretion to ignore employer specifications which he deems ... irrelevant to the basic job which the employer desires performed." The Department of Labor has issued a Dictionary of Occupational Titles which provides the principal source of information for determining the requirements for jobs which may be the subject of labor certification.

Labor certification will be denied if an alien is self-employed or if the employer's application for certification does not clearly show that the job opportunity has been and is clearly open to any qualified U.S. worker. 20 C.F.R. § 656. In *Hall v. McLaughlin* (D.C.Cir.1989), the U.S. Court of Appeals held that no genuine employment relationship exists where the alien and the corporation were inseparable and the alien was indispensable. The court followed a two-part test for determining whether a genuine employment relationship exists. First, the court considered whether the arrangement was a "sham" and inquired whether the corporation was established for the sole purpose of obtaining labor certification for the alien. Second, the court considered the "inseparability" question: "Whether the corporation, even if legitimately established, relies so heavily on the pervasive presence and personal attributes of the alien that it would be unlikely to continue in operation without him." The court reasoned that if the alien is inseparable from the corporation, the corporation will not truly consider hiring a U.S. worker.

The employment position for which the employer seeks labor certification must also be permanent in nature. There is, however, no guarantee that aliens seeking admission under second or third employment-related preference visas will not later change occupations and compete with U.S. workers. In *Yui Sing Tse v. INS* (9th

Cir.1979), labor certification was upheld despite evidence of the alien's intent to change his occupation eventually.

All visa petitions are made under oath (INA § 204(a)(1)) and the burden of proof is always on the applicant. INA § 291. The petition may be voluntarily withdrawn at any time. Approval of a petition may be revoked if there is a change in either party's status, such as death, divorce, or loss of the job offer, prior to final decision on an application for permanent residency. 8 C.F.R. § 205.

§ 5–5.2 Visa Application for Aliens Outside the U.S.

After approval of the labor certification and preference petition, the actual visa application process begins for an alien who resides outside the United States. This process takes place at the appropriate U.S. consulate, usually in the consular district where the alien resides. 22 C.F.R. § 42.61. For the consul's initial inquiry, the applicant submits a completed Form OF–222, which is used to determine prima facie eligibility and any need for registration on a waiting list, should the visa class applied for be oversubscribed. 22 C.F.R. § 42.63. If the alien appears ineligible, the consul will inform the alien of any deficiencies in the visa application (*e.g.*, lack of labor certification) so that appropriate steps may be taken to cure the defects.

If the consular officer determines that the applicant is eligible, the consul sends the applicant a notice to assemble and submit the documents required to make the final visa determination (Form OF–169). These documents include biographic data; police, court, prison, and military records; birth and marriage certificates; passports; photographs; and evidence that the alien will not become a public charge while in the U.S. INA § 212(a)(4). When all of this information is assembled, the applicant informs the consulate and is then given the formal visa application, Form OF–230, and a scheduled appointment for the required personal appearance. 22 C.F.R. §§ 42.62–.63. The applicant completes Form OF–230 and brings it, along with all of the assembled documents and the results of a medical examination (22 C.F.R. § 42.66) to the consul at the appointed time. The consular officer reviews the documents, may fingerprint the alien (22 C.F.R. § 42.67), conducts a personal interview, and if all is in order, has the applicant sign the formal application under oath.

The consul then rules on the application, usually the same day. The authority to pass on the eligibility of an applicant belongs exclusively to the consul. INA §§ 104(a), 221(a). The principal consular officer must review any refusal to issue a visa, but there is no formal review available after that. 22 C.F.R. § 42.81. The consulate must inform the applicant of the provision of law or regulation upon which the refusal was based. 22 C.F.R. § 42.81(b). The Department of State may also review a visa denial but, other than in matters of·interpretation of law, its opinion to the consul is only advisory. 22 C.F.R. § 42.81(d). The applicant has one year to overcome the objection to the visa on which the refusal was based or else the entire visa application process must be started anew. 22 C.F.R. § 42.81(e). The burden of proof is always on the applicant to establish eligibility. INA § 291.

§ 5–5.3 Visa Issuance and Admission

If the consul rules in favor of the visa applicant, the consul issues a visa from the consular office outside of the U.S. INA § 101(a)(16). The visa consists of a Form

OF–155, showing the consul's approval, the applicant's completed Form OF–230, and any documents necessary in determining the applicant's identity, classification, and eligibility. 22 C.F.R. § 42.73(b). The visa is valid for a period of four months (3 years for an adopted child) and may not be extended beyond that time. 22 C.F.R. § 42.72(a) & (b). A new immigrant visa, however, may be issued to immigrants not subject to numerical limitations if they are unable to travel to the U.S. during the four month period, provided they remain qualified for the visa. 22 C.F.R. § 42.74. An immigrant subject to numerical limitations may receive a "replace" visa if the immigrant was unable to travel to the U.S. during the four month period, but only if the replacement visa is issued in the same fiscal year as the original visa and the immigrant's number was not returned to the Department of State for reissuance. 22 C.F.R. § 42.74(b). A special provision of the 1990 Act allows residents of Hong Kong to defer use of their visas until any time before January 1, 2002.

Once the immigrant actually arrives in the U.S., an immigration officer again independently examines the alien's visa eligibility. If the inspecting immigration officer finds the immigrant to be inadmissible, the officer may commence removal of the alien, in spite of the visa. INA § 221(h). In that case, the alien may be temporarily detained, either aboard the vessel of arrival or in the U.S. while further determination is made. 8 C.F.R. § 235.3. If the immigration officer finds the visa to be in order and the alien to be admissible, the visa is retained by the INS as a permanent record of admission. INA § 240(a). The alien is then issued a Form I–151 (green card) and becomes a permanent resident alien. 8 C.F.R. § 264(1)(b). "Green cards" are now pink in color, but the older green ones remain valid. Although it is most often thought of as an employment permit, the green card was originally designed to serve as evidence of the alien's status as a permanent resident of the United States.

§ 5–5.4 Permanent Resident Procedures for Aliens Already Inside the U.S.

Aliens who want to immigrate are ordinarily expected to remain outside the United States until their immigrant visas are available. Nonetheless, many aliens are admitted to this country as nonimmigrants and then apply to adjust to immigrant visa status. *See* INA § 245. In recent years, adjustments of status have accounted for over twenty percent of all numerically limited immigrant visas. The procedures for the visa petitions and labor certificates are precisely the same for aliens in or outside the U.S. If the alien is immediately eligible for an immigrant visa, the alien may apply to the INS office where s/he resides for the preference status and then for adjustment of status from nonimmigrant to immigrant. For several years it was the practice of the INS that if the alien was entitled to be classified under a preference category and to adjustment of status, both applications could be presented in person to the INS office. The alien was entitled to an expedited "one-step visa processing," in which the preference petition was processed immediately, and the adjustment application was processed later. The concurrent processing is not presently available. Under the present procedure, the INS may need several months to adjudicate the visa petition, after which the adjustment of status application may be processed. The procedures for adjustment of status applications are discussed in the last section of chapter 6 on nonimmigrant visas *infra*.

CHAPTER 6

NONIMMIGRANT VISAS

Nonimmigrant visas constitute the largest category of all visas issued by more than seventeen to one. For example, in 1994 the INS admitted 21,955,916 nonimmigrants to the United States. Most nonimmigrant visas were issued to tourists (17.1 million) and to temporary business visitors (3.1 million). Nonimmigrant visas are divided into nineteen main categories, and one special purpose category for NATO personnel, which will not be considered further. The main categories are given letter designations corresponding fairly closely with the alphabetical and numerical subdivisions of their enabling legislation, INA § 101(a)(15) and 8 C.F.R. § 214.2. Most nonimmigrant visas are not subject to numerical limitation. A significant issue with respect to each nonimmigrant category is whether the nonimmigrant may engage in employment in the U.S. without violating the terms of the visa status.

The 1990 Act changed several of the existing nonimmigrant provisions and added several more. The act created separate nonimmigrant visa status for "aliens with exceptional ability" (category O) and for athletes, artists, and entertainers (categories P, Q, R). The 1990 Act also established nonimmigrant visas for cooperative/coproduction defense workers and for aliens participating in special education training programs for disabled children.

The 1990 Act imposed numerical limitations on a number of categories that were previously unlimited. For example, the law limits temporary visas for professionals to 65,000 (H–1B category); temporary agricultural workers to 66,000 (H–2B); and performing athletes, artists, and entertainers to 25,000 (P–1). The technical amendments of 1991 deleted the numerical limitation for the P–1 classification. These numerical limitations apply only to the principal alien, not to their spouse or children. The nineteen main categories of nonimmigrants are as follows: A, career diplomats; B, temporary visitors for business and pleasure; C, aliens in transit; D, crewmembers; E, treaty traders and investors; F, students; G, international organization representatives; H, temporary workers; I, foreign media representatives; J, exchange program visitors; K, fiancé(e)s or children of U.S. citizens; L, intracompany transferees; M, students in non-academic institutions; N, parents and children of special immigrants; O, aliens with extraordinary abilities; P, entertainers; Q, cultural exchange program participants; R, religious workers; and TN, for NAFTA professionals. Each is treated in greater depth below.

§ 6–1 DIPLOMATIC PERSONNEL

A–1 visas are issued to ambassadors, public ministers, career diplomatic, or consular officers, and members of their immediate families. A–2 visas are issued to other foreign government employees and officials as well as their family members. A–3 visas are for personal employees, attendants, and servants of persons holding A–1 and A–2 visas. 22 C.F.R. §§ 41.12, 41.20. A–1 and A–2 visas are valid as long as the Secretary of State extends recognition to the holder. A–3 visas are valid for not more than three years and may be extended in increments of not more than two years. 8 C.F.R. § 214.2(a). Both A–1 and A–2 visa holders may accept employment if permission is granted after submitting Form I–566. 8 C.F.R. § 214.2(a).

§ 6–2 TEMPORARY VISITORS

B–1 visas cover visitors for business purposes and B–2 visas deal with visitors for pleasure. For example, tourists, prospective F–1 students coming to the U.S. to select a school, and visitors entering the U.S. for medical treatment would receive B–2 visas. Frequently, visitors are issued a multiple purpose B–1/B–2 visa. Both B–1 and B–2 visas are valid for one year and are renewable in six month increments. 8 C.F.R. § 214.2(b). Neither B–1 nor B–2 visa holders may accept employment in the U.S. 8 C.F.R. § 214.1. What constitutes "employment" in violation of the B–1 or B–2 status is sometimes a difficult issue to determine. See, *e.g., Matter of Neil* (BIA 1975).

The Immigration Reform and Control Act of 1986 authorized the development of a three year pilot program to waive B–2 tourist visas for nationals from eight countries which extend reciprocal privileges and have low visa-abuse rates. INA § 217. Aliens entering the U.S. under this program receive a Form I–94W, may remain in the country no longer than 90 days, and are prohibited from adjusting their status to that of immigrant (except as immediate relatives) or to that of any other nonimmigrant classification. INA §§ 245(c), 248(4). Such aliens also waive any right to review or appeal an immigration officer's admissibility determination, or to contest, other than on the basis of an application for asylum, any action for removal against the alien. INA § 217. The visa waiver program has been extended to the present and has been applied to twenty-five countries, including Andorra, Argentina, Australia, Austria, Belgium, Brunei, Denmark, Finland, France, Germany, Iceland, Ireland, Italy, Japan, Liechtenstein, Luxembourg, Monaco, Netherlands, New Zealand, Norway, San Marino, Spain, Sweden, Switzerland, and United Kingdom.

The B–1 visa is often issued when the alien does not fit any of the other nonimmigrant business categories. For the alien, the B–1 is often an easier route to entry than the other categories. Labor certification is not required for B–1 visas and the alien need not file a petition with the INS. In *International Union of Bricklayers and Allied Craftsmen v. Meese* (N.D.Cal.1985), the court held that the INS practice of issuing B–1 visas to skilled and unskilled workers "contravenes both the language and legislative intent of the Act." Those skilled and unskilled workers are explicitly excluded from B–1 eligibility; they must apply instead for H category visas. Hence, in practice, the B–1 visa will not help most workers avoid the labor certification requirement.

§ 6–3 VISITORS IN TRANSIT

The C–1 visa is for continuous travel through the U.S. which involves a layover of eight hours maximum (or the next available transport) and no more than two transfers. C–2 visas are for persons who have a right of transit to the United Nations. The C–3 visa includes foreign government officials in transit. 8 C.F.R. § 214.2(c). Both C–2 and C–3 visas are valid for 29 days maximum and all C visas are nonrenewable. Holders of C visas may not adjust their status to any other nonimmigrant visa classification. 8 C.F.R. § 248.2(b). No employment is permitted under this visa class. 8 C.F.R. § 214.1(e).

§ 6–4   CREW MEMBERS

The D visa classification is for crewmembers serving in a capacity required for normal operation on board a vessel. The D–1 visa is issued to employees remaining with their vessel; the D–2 is issued to discharged employees who intend to work on another vessel. 8 C.F.R. § 252. D visa holders are prohibited, with few exceptions, from engaging in longshore work in the ports or coastal waters of the U.S.

D visa holders cannot be admitted into the U.S. during a strike or lockout involving the alien's employer. The Attorney General, however, may parole an alien into the U.S. if the entry is in the interest of national security. The alien may also be admitted if s/he worked for the employer throughout the year preceding the labor dispute. Both the D–1 and D–2 visas are valid for a maximum of 29 days and are nonrenewable. 8 C.F.R. § 252.1(d). Holders of this visa are not allowed to adjust their status to any other visa. INA § 248.

§ 6–5   TREATY TRADERS AND INVESTORS

E–1 visas are for treaty traders and their spouses and children, while E–2 visas are for treaty investors and their spouses and children. These nonimmigrants are entitled to enter the U.S. pursuant to treaties of commerce existing between the U.S. and the alien's country. Under the 1990 Act, aliens from countries lacking a treaty with the U.S. are still eligible for E treaty alien status if that country grants reciprocal benefits to U.S. nationals. This visa is somewhat unusual in that it does not require a petition to be filed with the INS before application is made at the embassy or consulate.

Certain managers, executives, or employees possessing essential skills who work for organizations, individual investors/traders, or companies (otherwise meeting the requirements for E classification) may also be admitted as E–1 and E–2 visa holders, with their families. They must be entering the U.S. either to engage in substantial trade in goods or services (E–1) including trade in services or trade in technology, or to develop an enterprise involving substantial amounts of capital. INA § 101(a)(15)(E). "Substantial" trade refers to both the volume of trade in goods or services conducted and the monetary value of the transactions. "Substantial" trade is defined as trading activities with the U.S. that comprise more than 50% of the alien's total business transactions in the U.S., and proof of a continued course of international trade. 56 Fed.Reg. 50349–02. Proof of numerous transactions, although each is of small monetary value, might establish the requisite continuing course of international trade. 9 Foreign Affairs Manual of State Department § 41.51 n. 4.2 (1988). *Matter of Walsh and Pollard* (BIA 1988) held that no minimum dollar amount of investment is required to meet the substantiality requirement for E–2 Treaty Investor status. *Nice v. Turnage* (9th Cir.1985) established that the INS could deny E–2 Treaty Investor status when a petitioner fails to prove that he was the source of funds used to make the investment. Applicants have strengthened their case for this visa by showing that the investment will lead to the employment of several U.S. citizens and permanent residents. Under the 1990 Act, employment creation *immi-*

grant visas are available to individuals who invest at least $1 million and create ten U.S. jobs. Hence, the threshold for an E–2 most likely will be consistent with this amount. E–2 status is generally denied if the expected return on the alien's investment will provide a living only for the alien and her/his family. E–1 and E–2 visa holders are permitted employment authorization consistent with the purposes for which they were admitted. Although family members of E visa holders are not permitted to be employed, in a unique policy, this rule will not be enforced if they work without authorization, as would be the case with family members of most other nonimmigrants. Both E–1 and E–2 visas are valid for one year and are renewable indefinitely, as long as the alien continues in the same capacity for which the visa was granted. 8 C.F.R. § 214.2(e).

§ 6–6 ACADEMIC STUDENTS

An F–1 visa is for an academic student, who temporarily enters the U.S. solely to pursue a full course of study at an established academic high school, college, university, seminary, conservatory, or language school. F–2 visas are for the spouse and children of the student. INA § 101(a)(15)(F). Both visas are normally granted for the duration of status as a student or for the time necessary to complete the course of study. 8 C.F.R. § 214.2(f)(5). IIRIRA, however, bars the use of an F–1 visa to attend a public secondary school for a student whose aggregate period of attendance exceeds 12 months and who does not reimburse the school for the full, unsubsidized per capita cost of providing education at the school. INA § 241. An alien who wishes to study at a public secondary school for an aggregate period longer than 12 months, therefore, may wish to request another type of student visa (*e.g.,* J–1 visa).

Students who have been in academic status for eight consecutive academic years or who have remained in one educational level for an extended period of time must apply for an extension of stay to continue studies beyond this time. 8 C.F.R. § 214.2(f)(7). *See* chapter 7 for a more complete discussion of student visas.

§ 6–7 INTERNATIONAL ORGANIZATION REPRESENTATIVES

This class of visas is subdivided into five separate groups. G–1 is for principal representatives of governments, recognized *de jure* by the U.S., to an international organization, their staff, and their family members. G–2 covers other accredited representatives of foreign governments to international organizations, their staff, and their family members. G–3 includes aliens who would qualify for G–1 or G–2, except that their government is not recognized *de jure* by the U.S.; G–3 also includes their family members. G–4 visas are for officers and employees of international organizations and their family members, and G–5 is for the attendants, servants, and personal employees of G–1, G–2, G–3, and G–4 visa holders, as well as members of their immediate families. INA § 101(a)(15)(G). All G visas are normally issued for one year and are renewable. Only family members of the G–4 class may accept employment in the U.S. subject to approval of the INS. 8 C.F.R. § 214.2(g)(2). The Immigration Reform and Control Act of 1986 authorized the adjustment to special immigrant status for certain G–4 nonimmigrants who had resided and been physically present in the U.S. for specified periods of time, including: unmarried sons and daughters of officers or employees of international organizations, retired employees of international organizations and their spouses, and surviving spouses of deceased employees of such organizations. INA § 101(a)(27)(I). The 1986 Act affords nonimmigrant status under a N–visa category to certain parents and children of aliens given special immigrant status. INA § 101(a)(15)(N). *See* § 6–14.

§ 6–8 TEMPORARY WORKERS

H nonimmigrant visas are designed principally to help employers meet an immediate and temporary need for labor. The 1990 Act made a number of changes to this nonimmigrant visa category.

Aliens entering the U.S. temporarily to perform services as registered nurses are classified as H–1A nonimmigrants. Each alien seeking H–1A status must have the Secretary of Labor certify that an unexpired attestation is on file as to each facility, other than a private household worksite, for which the alien will work as a nurse. INA § 101(a)(15)(H)(I).

Prior to the 1990 Act, the H–1B category consisted of professionals and persons of exceptional ability in the sciences and arts. Under the 1990 Act, however, the H–1B classification was redefined to include aliens working in "specialty occupations." To qualify as a member of a specialty occupation, the alien's job must require theoretical and practical application of a highly specialized body of knowledge. In addition, to satisfy credential requirements, an alien seeking an H–1B nonimmigrant visa must either:

(1) obtain a state license to practice in the occupation, if such a license is required to practice;

(2) have attained a bachelor's or higher degree in the specific specialty; or

(3) have attained experience in the specialty equivalent to the completion of the bachelor's degree, as well as positions of expertise which demonstrate specialty.

The 1990 Act's allowance of experience as a substitute for a formal degree is the culmination of an earlier trend within the INS which discouraged such equivalencies. *Compare Matter of Portugues do Atlantico Information Bureau, Inc.* (BIA 1984) with 8 C.F.R. § 214.2.

The 1990 Act for the first time subjects H–1B visas to a numerical limit of 65,000 annually. In a requirement somewhat similar to the nurse (H–1A) classification, H–1B visa holders are also required to have a Labor Condition application filed with the Secretary of Labor by the proposed employer. The application consists of assertions of the employer that the wages to be paid equal or exceed the prevailing average for the occupation, that the position's working conditions will not have an adverse effect on similarly situated U.S. workers, and that no labor dispute or lockout exists at the place of employment. A copy of this application must be conspicuously posted at the principal place of business. A complaint procedure exists to permit adversely affected parties to challenge these assertions. Civil penalties, backpay awards, and debarment from filing other immigration petitions may be assessed for successful complaints. An H–1B visa holder's admission is limited to three years. The authorized stay may be extended to a maximum of six years.

Often, aliens seeking H visa status (and other nonimmigrant categories) wish to immigrate to the U.S. Because most nonimmigrant visas require an intention to return to the alien's home country (sometimes referred to as "nonimmigrant intent"), many aliens have had either to hide their intent, or postpone their plans. The 1990 Act recognizes the propriety of this "dual intent" for H and L visa holders. First, the act removes the requirement that H visa holders have a foreign residence with no intent to abandon. INA § 101(a)(15)(H). Second, aliens seeking H–1B visa status are exempted from the presumption of immigrant intent that usually accompanies the application process. INA § 214(b). Third, the act explicitly allows the H nonimmigrant to seek permanent resident status, without affecting the terms of the H visa. INA § 214(h).

H–1 visa holders are admissible for an initial period of not more than three years. H–2 visa classification covers any alien coming to the U.S. temporarily for work of a temporary nature and includes seasonal workers of all types. The Immigration Reform and Control Act of 1986 (IRCA) created a "H–2A" nonimmigrant visa classification for temporary agricultural workers. Perishable crop growers complained that the procedures for obtaining H–2 workers were too slow and unpredictable for their industry. They feared that, because of their dependence upon undocumented alien workers, implementation of the employer sanction provisions of IRCA would put an end to some of their operations. In response, IRCA provided for expedited procedures for approving grower requests for foreign agricultural workers and for review of denied applications. The employer, however, must still first make an effort to recruit domestic workers. INA § 216.

The H–2B nonimmigrant visa category is specifically for aliens entering temporarily to fill a *temporary* nonagricultural position. *Matter of Artee Corporation* (BIA 1982) held that the test of the temporary need for the position lies in the examination of the short-term requirement for the service, rather than the brief needs of customers. H–2B temporary workers are limited to 66,000 per fiscal year. INA §§ 214(g)(1)(B), (g)(2). The employer must attain a temporary labor certification which is an abbreviated form of the procedure described at § 5–5.1, *supra*.

The 1990 Act authorizes the Attorney General to provide nonimmigrant status to an alien who enters the U.S. to participate in a special education training program. This program must provide practical training and experience in educating children with physical, mental, or emotional disabilities. INA § 223(a)(2). The alien must not have the intent to immigrate and the visa is valid for a maximum of eighteen months. No more than fifty aliens per fiscal year may enter the U.S. under this classification.

The H–3 visa covers trainees coming to the U.S. for up to two years to receive training not available in the alien's own country, except graduate medical training and training programs designed to provide employment are excluded. H–3 visas include aliens coming to the U.S. to receive training in the education of children with physical, mental, or emotional disabilities. 56 Fed.Reg. 50349–02. H–4 visas are issued to the spouse and children of H–1, H–2, and H–3 visa-holders. Subject to regulatory time limitations, H visas are valid for the duration of the employment period specified by the employer in its approved petition. This period may be extended if required. H–4 aliens may not accept employment in the U.S. unless they are specifically included in the employer's petition (Form I–129B). INA § 101(a)(15)(H); 8 C.F.R. § 214.2(h).

§ 6–9 INFORMATION MEDIA REPRESENTATIVES

This single class visa category (I) includes any representative of foreign press, radio, film, television, or other media provided that U.S. citizens are granted reciprocal privileges by the alien's government. Spouses and children of the representative are included in this visa. I visas authorize admission for the duration of employment. INA § 101(a)(15)(I). 8 C.F.R. § 214.2(I).

§ 6–10 EXCHANGE VISITORS

J–1 visas are issued to aliens accepted to participate in exchange visitor programs designated by the United States Information Agency (USIA). 22 C.F.R. § 41.65(a)(1). J–1 nonimmigrants include students, scholars, trainees, teachers, professors, research assistants, specialists, or leaders in a field of specialized knowledge or skill. INA § 101(a)(15)(J). J–2 visas are for the alien's spouse and children. These visas are valid for various periods of time depending upon the underlying program duration. J–1 status holders may engage in employment within the U.S. J–2 visa holders may obtain permission from the INS to accept approved employment, but only for their own support and not for the support of the J–1 recipient. 8 C.F.R. § 214.2(j)(1). Certain J visa holders must reside in their own country for two years after completion of their program before they are eligible to apply for permanent resident status, an immigrant visa, or for nonimmigrant visas H and L. This two-year foreign residence requirement applies to J–1 holders who: (1) participated in a program which received financing from the U.S. government or from the alien's government; (2) are nationals or residents of countries designated by the United States Information Agency as clearly requiring the services of persons engaged in the alien's field of specialized knowledge or skill (such specializations are published in the form of a skills list); or (3) came to the United States or obtained a J visa in order to receive graduate medical training. INA § 212(e). J visa holders who have received graduate medical training are ineligible to change their status to that of any other nonimmigrant classification. Other J visa holders subject to the two-year foreign residency requirement may not change their visa to any other nonimmigrant visa except A or G before complying with the requirement. INA § 248. Waivers of this requirement may be sought in cases where (1) a hardship can be demonstrated to a U.S. citizen or permanent resident spouse, parent, or child of the status holder; (2) fear of persecution on account of nationality, race, religion, political opinion, or membership in a particular social group; or (3) where the alien's home country does not object to the grant of a waiver. The J–1 visa holder may apply for a waiver of the two-year foreign residency requirement through the USIA. In case of hardship or fear of persecution, the application for a waiver should be supported by the request of an interested U.S. governmental agency or of the Commissioner of Immigration and Naturalization that the waiver be granted. INA § 212(e).

§ 6–11   FIANCÉE OR FIANCÉ OF U.S. CITIZEN

The K (fiancé or fiancée) visa is a special, short term visa, valid for ninety days, for an alien who is coming to the U.S. solely to conclude a valid marriage with a U.S. citizen. The U.S. citizen must first file a petition, Form I–129F, with the INS in the district where the citizen resides. 8 C.F.R. § 214.2(k). The approved petition is forwarded to the U.S. consulate where the alien applies for the K visa. Before the visa is approved, the alien must submit to a medical examination. 22 C.F.R. § 41.113. This is the only nonimmigrant visa for which a medical examination is required. The K visa is treated as if it were an immigrant visa, since the alien will generally become a permanent resident alien. The K–1 visa is issued to the principal alien and the K–2 visa is for any accompanying children. The K visa does authorize employment during the ninety day period. If the alien fails to marry the U.S. citizen within ninety days of entry, s/he must depart the U.S. INA § 214(d). Holders of a K visa may not adjust their status to any other nonimmigrant visa classification.

The Immigration Marriage Fraud Amendments of 1986 sought to prevent marriage fraud with respect to K nonimmigrants by requiring the alien fiancé(e) and the U.S. citizen to "have previously met in person within 2 years before the date of filing the petition, [and] have a bona fide intention to marry.... " INA § 214(d). The Attorney General, however, may waive the personal meeting requirement. *Id.* The Fraud Amendments also prohibit adjustment to permanent resident status of K nonimmigrants prior to their marriage, when they become eligible for immediate relative status. INA § 245(d).

§ 6–12 INTRA–COMPANY TRANSFEREES

This classification was intended to help multinational corporations facilitate employee transfers. This visa allows companies to transfer employees temporarily to the U.S. in order to aid or initiate business operations in the U.S. The employer must first submit a petition, Form I–129L, to the INS district where the alien will be employed. 8 C.F.R. § 214.2(*l*)(2). The alien must have been employed for at least one year by the firm outside the U.S. and must be employed in a managerial or executive capacity, or have specialized knowledge of the company's product or procedures in international business markets. INA § 101(a)(15)(L). *Karmali v. INS* (9th Cir.1983) denied a petition for entry into the US as an intra-company transferee because Karmali did not meet the requirement of one-year continuous employment abroad prior to seeking entry into the U.S. The qualifying person receives an L–1 during the period for which the petition is filed—up to a maximum of seven years for managers and executives and five years for individuals with specialized knowledge. Employers may file a blanket petition for intended employees rather than filing individual petitions. Moreover, the L visa holder may possess the dual intent to seek permanent residency while maintaining nonimmigrant status. *See* § 6–8, *supra*. The L visa is renewable. The spouse and children may be granted L–2 visas, but are not authorized to engage in any employment.

§ 6-13   VOCATIONAL STUDENTS

M–1 visas are for vocational or nonacademic students, who enter the U.S. temporarily to pursue a full course of study at an established or recognized vocational or other nonacademic institution. INA § 101(a)(15)(M). M–2 visas are for the spouse and children of the M–1 student. Both visas are normally granted for the period of time necessary to complete the course of study plus thirty days, or for one year, whichever is less, and are renewable. 8 C.F.R. § 214.2(m). M–2 visa holders may not accept employment during their stay in the U.S. Temporary employment for practical training may be authorized for M–1 students after completion of studies. The student's school must certify that the proposed employment is recommended for the purpose of practical training, is related to the student's course of study, and is unavailable to the student in her/his home country. 8 C.F.R. § 214.2(m)(14).

§ 6-14   RELATIVES OF EMPLOYEES OF INTERNATIONAL ORGANIZATIONS

The Immigration Reform and Control Act of 1986 created the N visa category for certain relatives of G–4 employees of international organizations. INA § 101(a)(15)(N). N visas are given to the parents of G–4 aliens accorded special immigrant status under INA §§ 101(a)(27)(I)(i), but only if and while the alien is a child. The children of these parents granted N visas and of G–4 aliens accorded special immigrant status under INA §§ 101(a)(27)(I)(ii), (iii), and (iv) are also given N visas.

§ 6–15 ALIENS WITH EXTRAORDINARY ABILITY

Created by the 1990 Act, O–1 visas are for aliens with "extraordinary ability," as demonstrated by sustained national or international acclaim, in the sciences, arts, education, business, or athletics. This visa is a variation of a class of aliens formerly included within the H–1B category. Moreover, O–1 visas are issued to aliens who have an extensively documented record of extraordinary achievement in motion pictures or television. The alien must seek entry to work in her/his area of expertise and the Attorney General must determine that the alien's entry will result in substantial prospective benefit to the United States.

O–2 visas are for aliens seeking entry solely to accompany and assist the artistic or athletic performance of an admitted O–1 visa holder. An alien seeking an O–2 visa must be an integral part of the performance and have a foreign residence with no intent to abandon it.

An O–3 visa is issued to the spouse and children of an alien with either an O–1 or O–2 visa, provided they are accompanying or following to join the principal alien. O visas are valid for the period specified by the Attorney General, usually the duration of the event for which the alien is admitted.

§ 6–16 INTERNATIONALLY RECOGNIZED ATHLETES AND ARTISTS, ETC.

The 1990 Act also established the P nonimmigrant category to cover a former subclass of H–1B workers. P–1 visas are for athletes who perform or compete at an internationally recognized level, or are members of an internationally recognized entertainment group. The alien must have had a sustained and substantial relationship for at least one year with such a group, and must provide functions integral to the group's performance to qualify for a P–1 visa.

P–2 visas are issued to aliens who perform as artists, entertainers, or as an integral part of an entertainment group associated with an exchange program between a U.S. organization and an organization in a foreign state. INA § 101(a)(15)(P)(iii). P–3 visas are for artists or entertainers performing in a "culturally unique" program. The principal alien entering under P visa status may be accompanied or followed by her/his spouse and children, who receive P–4 visas.

P visas are valid for as long as the Attorney General specifies, but usually last for the duration of the competition, event, or performance for which the alien is admitted. Individual athletes may enter for an initial period of up to five years, which may then be extended for another five years. Under the 1990 Act, P–1 and P–3 visas were subject to a numerical limit of 25,000 annually for each category. That numerical limit, however, was deleted by the technical amendments of 1991.

The 1990 Act also established Q nonimmigrant visas for participants in international exchange programs and R visas for religious workers and their children.

§ 6–17 CANADIAN AND MEXICAN BUSINESS TRAVELERS AND THEIR FAMILIES

The North American Free Trade Agreement, ratified in 1994, establishes special provisions for the temporary admission of Canadian and Mexican business visitors, traders and investors, intra-company transferees, professionals, and their families wishing to enter the United States. U.S. citizens traveling to Canada and Mexico receive reciprocal rights of entry. The agreement, and the occupational schedules which have been promulgated to implement it, facilitate entry by expediting the admission of particular occupational groups. The legislation created a new "TN" visa category for "NAFTA professionals." Their spouses and children are eligible for "TB" visas. The procedure for "TN" applicants is similar to that for the H–1B category. Canadian citizens, however, do not have to file a Labor Condition application or a preliminary petition with the INS. "TN" professionals are not subject to the same 65,000 limitation as the H–1B visas, but the regulations impose a 5,500 annual limit on Mexican "TN" nonimmigrants.

§ 6–18 PROCEDURAL REQUIREMENTS FOR NONIMMIGRANT VISAS

Any alien desiring a nonimmigrant visa must apply using the specific procedures for the particular visa sought. Those procedures may be broadly divided into three classes: (1) Applications which require no prior contact with anyone in the U.S. (visas A, B, C, D, E, G, I, and O); (2) applications which require proof of acceptance in an authorized program (visas F, J, M, Q, and visas for special education trainees); and (3) applications which require approved petitions that provide the basis for the alien's presence in the U.S. (visas H, K, L, P, R, and TN for Mexican citizens only).

In the first class, where no prior U.S. contact is needed, the alien begins the application process by submitting Form OF-156 to the U.S. consular office where the alien resides. The consular officer has the discretion to accept applications from aliens who do not reside in the consular district, but are physically present there. 22 C.F.R. § 41.110. In such cases, the consular officer may examine the alien's reasons for not applying to the consulate where the alien resides. The application is normally made in person, although the consular officer may waive this requirement. 22 C.F.R. § 41.114. The consular officer may also require additional documents to verify the alien's purpose in requesting the visa. Supporting documents will usually concern the alien's eligibility to enter the U.S. and the alien's intention to depart at the end of the intended stay. 22 C.F.R. § 41.111. The alien's intention to depart from the U.S. and return is usually established by the alien's job, residence, and/or family in the alien's country. If the application is for a temporary visitor (B) or a student (F or M) visa, the consul may also require that a bond be posted to insure the alien's departure from the U.S. INA § 221(g). The visa is usually issued on the same day application is made and is in the form of a stamp in the alien's passport. 22 C.F.R. § 41.124.

If the visa desired is in the second class (F, J, and M visas), the alien must also present an acceptance form from the school or program. For the student (F and M) visa, Form I-20 is executed by an accredited school where the student will study. 22 C.F.R. § 41.45; 8 C.F.R. § 214.2(f)(1). The exchange visitor must present Form IAP–66, executed by the program sponsor, indicating the applicant's participation in an approved program. 22 C.F.R. § 41.65. If the consulate is satisfied that the applicant has sufficient funds to cover expenses while in the U.S. and that the applicant has the necessary knowledge of the English language, a visa will be granted. 22 C.F.R. §§ 41.45(a) & 41.65(a).

Visas in the third class (H, K, L, P, R, and TN for Mexican citizens only) require that the applicant be a beneficiary of an approved petition Form I–129 submitted by the prospective employer for the H and TN visas, by the prospective employer for the L visa, and by the prospective spouse for the K visa. Certain prospective employers of L visa applications may file a blanket petition rather than separate, individual petitions. If the consular officer finds the supporting documents in order and the alien eligible in all other respects, the visa will be granted.

The consular officer may require additional proof of the applicant's eligibility for any visa if the officer is not satisfied with the initial application or knows or has reason to believe that the applicant is ineligible for such visa. If the added proof is still deemed insufficient after review, the consulate may deny the visa application, informing the applicant of the grounds for refusal. 22 C.F.R. § 41.130. The Department of State cannot overrule the consulate's decision so long as the decision was based on the application of law to facts. INA §§ 104A & 221(a). Although there is generally no judicial review available, several courts have reserved a narrow ground of review in visa denial cases. *See, e.g., Abourezk v.*

Reagan (D.C.Cir.1986), *Allende v. Shultz* (D.Mass.1985).
See also § 3–1, *supra.*

Upon entry to the U.S., the alien holding any nonimmigrant visa will be subject to inspection by an immigration officer and will receive a Form I–94 indicating the length and terms of their stay.

§ 6–19 ADJUSTMENT OF STATUS
TO IMMIGRANT

Generally, all nonimmigrant visa holders who are in the U.S. may apply to have their visa status adjusted to permanent residence status, with the exception of crew member (D) visa holders and most beneficiaries of the (B) visa waiver program. *See* § 6–2, *infra.* INA § 245. In order to receive an adjustment of status, the alien must file an adjustment of status (Form I–485) with the INS district office where the alien resides. 8 C.F.R. § 245.2. The alien must have been inspected and admitted or paroled into the U.S., must meet standard eligibility requirements for an immigrant visa, and an immigrant visa must be immediately available at the time the application is filed. INA § 245(a). Additionally, the alien must not have either (1) been in an unlawful status anytime after November 6, 1986, since entering the U.S., or (2) on or after January 1, 1977, accepted any unauthorized employment while present in the U.S. as a nonimmigrant, unless the alien is an immediate relative of a U.S. citizen, the alien is a graduate of a foreign medical school licensed to practice in the U.S. since 1978, or unless the violation was technical in nature and not the fault of the alien. INA § 245(c). Aliens who entered the U.S. without being admitted (formerly "entrants without inspection" (EWIs)) or aliens who remained in the U.S. without legal status after the expiration of their visas or violated the terms of their visas ("overstays") were able to apply for adjustment of status upon the payment of $1,000. INA § 245(i). After several temporary extensions, Congress eliminated Section 245(i) in November 1997, but allowed aliens who filed visa petitions or labor certification applications by January 14, 1998, to continue to file applications for adjustment. P.L. 105–119 (Nov. 26, 1997); *see* § 9–1.4, *infra* for further discussion of the validity of INA § 245(i). Now that the provision has expired, overstays and entrants without inspection will no longer be able to adjust and will be subject to the three year and ten years bars on inadmissibility if they depart from the U.S.

CHAPTER 7
NONIMMIGRANT VISAS: STUDENTS

§ 7–1 INTRODUCTION

The F–1 visa is for the academic student, who must be entering the U.S. temporarily and solely to pursue a full course of study at an established academic high school, college, university, seminary, conservatory, or language school. An F–1 visa does not apply to a student who wishes to attend a vocational or nonacademic program. A student who intends to enroll in such a program may enter only on an M visa. Some students also reach the United States as exchange visitors with a J–1 visa. *See* § 6–10, *supra*.

Unlike many of the other nonimmigrant visas, an F visa frequently entails a stay in the United States which spans a number of years. The regulations for F visas, at 8 C.F.R. § 214.2(f), address some of the issues which are likely to arise during a student's stay in the United States.

§ 7–2 APPLYING FOR THE F–1 VISA

Once the student has been accepted into an academic program, the institution in which s/he will enroll completes a Certificate of Eligibility for Nonimmigrant (F–1) Student Status, Form I–20 A–B/I–20 ID and sends it to the student. (The Form I–20 A–B includes a School Copy and an I–20 ID Student Copy.) The student applies for the F–1 visa by presenting the I–20 A–B and a nonimmigrant visa application to a United States consulate in the student's home country. The student should also be prepared to present documentation which will show: (a) that the student will have sufficient funds available to support her-or himself during the entire proposed course of study; and (b) that the student is maintaining a residence abroad to which the student intends to return on completion of her/his studies in the United States. Moreover, the student must provide persuasive documentation showing the student's intention to return to her/his home country. A job offer or proof of demand for the student's skills usually suffices. Once the visa is issued, the student may apply at a port of entry for admission to the United States. When the student reaches a port of entry, s/he presents her/his passport with the F–1 visa stamp and the complete Form I–20 A–B. The inspecting officer will transcribe the student's admission number on the Form I–20 A–B and return the I–20 ID (Student Copy) to the student. The officer will send the I–20 (School Copy) to the school as a notice of the student's admission to the country. Universities and other schools generally require that the student present their stamped I–20 (Student Copy) to the registrar before starting classes.

§ 7–3 FAMILY OF THE STUDENT

F–2 visas are for the spouse and minor children of the student. The spouse and children may accompany the student into the United States or they may follow to join the student. If family members are accompanying the student, they do not need an I–20 A–B of their own to apply for the F–2 visa, because they are included on the student's I–20 A–B. If the family members are following the student, s/he normally sends them a duplicate Form I–20 A–B to facilitate their application for F–2 visas and entry into the United States. 8 C.F.R. § 214.2(f)(3). The F–2 spouse and children of an F–1 student may not, under any circumstances, accept employment. 8 C.F.R. § 214.2(f)(15).

§ 7–4   DURATION OF STATUS

Persons holding F–1 and F–2 visas are generally admitted for the "duration of status" as a student. "Duration of status" is defined as the period during which the student is pursuing a full course of study in any educational program or is receiving authorized practical training, plus sixty days within which to depart from the United States. 8 C.F.R. § 214.2(f)(5). An F–1 student who continues from one educational level to another, from one educational program to another, and/or from one school to another, remains in status as long as the proper procedures are followed. 8 C.F.R. § 214.2(f)(5).

There are limitations to the flexibility allowed the student. When a student begins an educational program, the school must state when the student is expected to complete the particular program of study. The student remains in status as long as s/he is making normal progress toward completing her/his educational objective. 8 C.F.R. § 214.2(f)(7). If a student wishes to transfer to another school but has not pursued a full course of study at the school which s/he was last authorized to attend, the student must apply to the INS for reinstatement to student status. If the student is granted reinstatement, s/he may attend the new school assuming admission is granted. 8 C.F.R. § 214.2(f)(8).

If a student is unable to complete her/his degree objective by the date on her/his I–20, s/he must apply to the school for an extension of stay. 8 C.F.R. § 214.2(f)(7). The school may grant an extension to a student who has maintained student status and whose inability to complete by the date on the I–20 is caused by "compelling academic or medical reasons." 8 C.F.R. § 214.2(f)(7)(iii). Examples of legitimate academic reasons are change of college major and unexpected research difficulties; illnesses must be documented. Delays caused by academic problems (academic probation, suspension) are not acceptable reasons for extension. The school notifies the INS of the extension on a Form I–538, submitted with a new I–20 A–B/I–20 ID showing the new completion date.

An F–1 student is considered to be in status during summer vacation if the student is eligible and intends to register for the upcoming term. If the school operates on the trimester or quarter system, the student may take any term as a vacation, as long as the student takes only one term a year, is eligible and intends to register for the next term, and has completed the equivalent of a complete academic year before taking the vacation. A student remains in status if s/he is forced to interrupt or reduce her/his course of study because of illness or other medical condition, provided the student returns to a full course of study upon recovery. A student will also retain F–1 status for sixty days after completion of her/his last academic program. Upon expiration of this sixty day period, the student must leave the United States. 8 C.F.R. § 214.2(f)(5).

§ 7-5 FULL COURSE OF STUDY

The conditions necessary to satisfy the full course of study requirement vary depending on the academic program involved. For postgraduate or postdoctoral study, research at a college or university, or undergraduate or postgraduate study at a night school, conservatory, or religious seminary, full course of study is a program certified as such by the school. 8 C.F.R. § 214.2(f)(6)(i). An undergraduate student must generally take twelve semester or quarter hours per term, unless fewer hours are required for the student to complete the course of study in the current term. 8 C.F.R. § 214.2(f)(6)(ii). A primary or high school student must take at least the minimum number of hours per week required by the school for normal progress toward graduation. 8 C.F.R. § 214.2(f)(6)(v).

A student may drop below the required number of hours for a full course of study if advised to do so by a designated school official for valid academic reasons. Valid academic reasons include: (a) English language difficulties; (b) unfamiliarity with U.S. teaching methods or reading requirements; and (c) improper course level placement. The designated school official's advice to drop below a full course of study is subject to review by the INS. 8 C.F.R. § 214.2(f)(6). In practice, however, school officials exercise discretion in finding valid academic reasons based on other circumstances such as health problems or the fact that the student is working on a thesis.

§ 7-6 EMPLOYMENT

The 1990 Act significantly modified employment options previously available to F-1 students. An F-1 student may work on-campus up to 20 hours per week while school is in session and while enrolled as a full-time student. A student must be in F–1 student status for nine consecutive months before seeking off-campus employment authorization.

§ 7–6.1 On–campus Employment

An F–1 student pursuing a full course of study is also permitted to engage in on-campus employment as long as the employment will not displace a United States resident. The student may not engage in any on-campus employment for more than twenty hours per week, except when school is not in session, during the annual vacation or after the course of study has been completed and the on-campus employment is part of the optional practical training. "On campus" includes employment by commercial firms which provide services for students on campus, such as a bookstore or food service company. 8 C.F.R. § 214.2(f)(9).

The 1990 Act expanded the definition of on-campus employment to include off-campus locations which are affiliated with the school. 8 C.F.R. § 214.2(f)(9). This arrangement was designed to permit graduate students to conduct research at off-campus locations under the supervision of their professors. The INS requires that employment by an organization whose affiliation with the school is based on a contract be an integral part of the student's educational program and be commensurate with the level of study. 8 C.F.R. § 214.2(f)(9). Employment with on-campus commercial firms (such as a company constructing a school building) which do not provide direct student services are classified as off-campus employment.

On-campus employment pursuant to the terms of a scholarship, fellowship, or assistantship is permitted and is deemed a part of the academic program of a student otherwise taking a full course of study. Hence, students assigned teaching or research responsibilities pursuant to the terms of a scholarship or fellowship may carry a reduced course load. Note, however, that the student's total employment may never exceed 20 hours per week while school is in session.

§ 7–6.2 Off–campus Employment

The F–1 student must apply to the INS for permission to engage in off-campus employment, unless the employment is pursuant to the student's alternate work/study program. The INS may grant a student an off-campus employment authorization based on severe economic hardship. The employment authorization may be granted in one year intervals up to the expected date of completion of the student's current course of study. 8 C.F.R. § 214.2(f)(9). To be eligible, the student must demonstrate that s/he needs to work because of "severe economic hardship caused by unforseen circumstances beyond the student's control." The rules define the unforseen circumstances as follows: (1) loss of financial aid or on-campus employment without fault on the part of the student; (2) substantial fluctuations in the value of currency or exchange rate; (3) inordinate increases in tuition or living costs; (4) unexpected changes in the financial condition of the student's source of support; or (5) medical bills or other substantial and unexpected expenses. 8 C.F.R. § 214.2(f)(9).

The rules also require that the student: (1) have completed one full academic year (nine months) in F–1 status; (2) be in good academic standing as determined by his or her foreign student advisor; (3) obtain a recommendation from the foreign student advisor in favor of work authorization; (4) obtain an employment authorization document from the INS; and (5) work no more than twenty hours per week when school is in session (full-time work is permissible during vacation periods). 8 C.F.R. § 214.2(f)(9).

The work authorization based on economic necessity is now the only available off-campus work authorization aside from practical training. The pilot program, under which the Attorney General allowed students to work off-campus for an employer who complied with Department of Labor regulations, has expired.

§ 7–7 PRACTICAL TRAINING

Practical training is an authorized period of temporary employment which allows the student to obtain work experience related to the student's course of study. A student who is engaged in authorized practical training remains in status for the duration of the training. There are two types of practical training available: curricular and optional. Practical training is available to F–1 students who have been lawfully enrolled on a full-time basis for a minimum of nine consecutive months. 8 C.F.R. § 214.2(f)(10). Exceptions to the nine months requirement are provided for students enrolled in graduate studies which require immediate participation in curricular practical training. 8 C.F.R. § 214.2(f)(10).

§ 7–7.1 Curricular Practical Training

Curricular practical training is employment prior to completion of studies, and is only permitted if the institution requires an internship or other field experience, for a particular degree in that field. 8 C.F.R. § 214.2(f)(10). The 1990 Act does not consider curricular practical training to include unsponsored employment directly related to the student's area of study.

The school may authorize the student for employment if satisfied that the work qualifies as curricular practical training and must then notify the INS by filing a Form I–538 with the data processing center in Kentucky. In practice, many foreign student advisors interpret the concept of "internship" liberally to permit foreign students an opportunity to gain work experience. A student who receives one year or more of full-time curricular practical training is ineligible for optional practical training. "Full-time" includes both employment off-campus and on-campus.

§ 7–7.2 Optional Practical Training

INS regulations provide that a student is eligible to apply for 12 months of optional practical training directly related to the student's major area of study. 8 C.F.R. § 214.2(f)(10). Temporary employment for optional practical training can be authorized only by the INS, upon recommendation of the school.

A student who has been in status for one full academic year is eligible to apply. All optional practical training must be completed within a fourteen-month period following the completion of study. 8 C.F.R. § 214.2(f)(10). The total periods of authorization for optional practical training shall not exceed a maximum of twelve months. 8 C.F.R. § 214.2 (f)(11).

Optional practical training includes training: (1) during the student's annual vacation and at other times when school is not in session, if the student is eligible to register for the next term or semester (and intends to do so); (2) during the school year, provided that employment does not exceed twenty hours per week while school is in session; (3) when the student is in a bachelor's, master's, or doctoral program and has completed all course requirements for the degree (excluding a thesis or its equivalent); and (4) when the student has completed his or her course of study. 8 C.F.R. § 214.2(f)(10).

A student must apply to the INS for an Employment Authorization Document during a period 60 to 90 days prior to graduation plus the 60–day period after graduation (during which the student may stay in the U.S. without being considered unlawfully present). Within this same 120–to 150–day period the designated school official is authorized to recommend practical training. The student may not accept employment until s/he has been issued an Employment Authorization Document. 8 C.F.R. § 214.2 (f)(11).

§ 7–8 CHANGE TO OR FROM F–1 NON–IMMIGRANT STATUS

Generally, nonimmigrant visa holders may change their status to that of an F–1 student. The change to F–1 status is granted to persons who show they qualify as students and have a valid I–20 A–B Certificate of Eligibility for Nonimmigrant (F–1) Student Status from the school the student wishes to attend.

A special situation is presented by a change from B–2 visitor for pleasure to F–1 status. The intending student must give a convincing explanation of why s/he did not apply for an F–1 visa at the consulate abroad. Because the B–2 visitor visa is believed to be easier to acquire than the F–1 visa, the INS is skeptical of applications for change from visitor status to student status-particularly during the first 60 days after arrival. The INS tends to suspect that the individual applying for such a change planned all along to study in the United States. It is possible but not easy, however, to get a B–2 visitor visa as a "prospective student." The intent to visit educational institutions and to seek admission must be clearly explained to the consulate abroad and should be marked on the B–2 visa. A consular officer may require prospective student to show that s/he would eventually be eligible for an F–1 visa (*e.g.*, ability to pay tuition). In this case, the INS will be more liberal in granting a change to F–1 status. The nonimmigrant seeking F–1 student status will also need the supporting documentation required of any applicant for an F–1 visa, including proof of financial resources and of the bona fide intent to return home on completion of studies.

An F–1 nonimmigrant student may qualify to obtain a work-related H–1B visa after completing her/his studies in F–1 status. The F–1 students are not barred from seeking the H–1B status by a two-year foreign residency requirement for many J–1 student visas holders. The student applying for H–1B classification must demonstrate that s/he is qualified to work in a speciality occupation. An employer seeking to hire the student must file a Labor Condition application with the Secretary of Labor. The student is also subject to a numerical limitation on H–1B visas. *See* § 6–8. The student may use this change to H–1B status as an intermediary step for obtaining permanent residence in future.

An F–1 nonimmigrant student may directly qualify to adjust status to that of permanent resident either through her/his family or employer. If the student is the spouse, child, or parent of a U.S. citizen, the student may acquire permanent residence through that relative without regard to the availability of visas subject to numerical limitations. In an attempt to deter immigration-related marriage fraud, the Immigration Marriage Fraud Amendments of 1986 impose a two-year conditional residency requirement on alien spouses and children before they may obtain permanent resident status on the basis of a "qualifying marriage" to a U.S. citizen or permanent resident alien. Permanent resident status is subject to verification that the marriage continued as a valid marriage for two years from the date of initial petition for permanent residence. INA § 216. For more information on visas for immediate relatives of U.S. citizens see § 5–2.1, *supra*. Other relationships to United States citizens and to permanent residents may qualify the student for a family-sponsored or employment-related preference visa, subject to numerical limitations. *See* § 5–3.1, *supra*. Availability of numerically limited visas may be subject to waiting periods for students from some countries.

A student seeking permanent resident status through an employer would most likely wish to apply for the second or third employment-related preference for professionals with advanced degrees or aliens of exceptional ability in science, art, or business. The third employment-related category is for professionals with baccalaureate degrees, skilled workers, and other workers. Both of these preference categories require the employer to obtain labor certification, showing that there is no U.S. citizen or resident available who can fill the position. Even if a labor certification is obtained, both preferences may be subject to waiting periods imposed by the numerical limitations on preference visas.

§ 7–9   VIOLATION OF STUDENT STATUS: CONSEQUENCES AND RISKS

§ 7–9.1   Reinstatement to Student Status

If the student has overstayed her/his authorized period of stay or has otherwise violated the conditions of her/his F–1 visa, the INS may consider reinstating the student to F–1 status. Reinstatement is difficult to obtain. The reinstatement will be considered only if the student:

(1) makes a written request for reinstatement, accompanied by a properly completed I–20 A–B from the school the student is attending or intends to attend;

(2) can establish that the violation of status resulted from circumstances beyond the student's control or that failure to reinstate the student would result in extreme hardship to the student;

(3) is currently pursuing or intends to pursue a full course of study;

(4) has not engaged in unauthorized off-campus employment;

(5) provides documentary proof of funding to continue in school and maintain full-time status; and

(6) is not deportable on any ground (other than her/his violation of student status). 8 C.F.R. § 214.2(f)(16).

The INS district director's decision to disallow reinstatement is not subject to review, except pursuant to a declaratory judgment action in a U.S. district court.

§ 7–9.2   Re-entry Upon Violation of the Student Status

F–1 students should carefully protect their status. According to implemented changes in IIRIRA, a violation of the terms of a student's F–1 visa can negatively affect her/his plans to travel or visit the U.S. in future.

If the F–1 student has violated the conditions of her/his status and cannot obtain reinstatement as discussed above, her/his entry visa is subject to automatic cancellation. Even if the visa is for duration of status or the expiration date on the visa stamp in the passport has not arrived, the student will need to obtain a new visa for re-entry into the U.S. The student must leave the United States to obtain a new entry visa ordinarily in her/his country of nationality. INA § 222(g)(2)(A).

Furthermore, since April 1997, a student who remains in the U.S. out of status for 180 days or more, after an immigration judge or district director determines that his/her duration of status has concluded, is barred from re-entering the U.S. for a period of three years. INA § 212(a)(9)(B)(i)(I). Students found to be remaining unlawfully in the U.S. for one year or more will not be allowed to re-enter the U.S. for 10 years. INA § 212(a)(9)(B)(i)(II). The three-year and ten-year bars on inadmissibility will usually prevent the alien from receiving a new visa, when s/he subsequently applies at a U.S. consulate abroad. *Cf.* 9–1.4, *infra.*

§ 7–9.3 Adjustment to Permanent Resident Status

In the past, when a student's request for reinstatement to F–1 status was denied, the student could leave the United States, reapply for a nonimmigrant F–1 visa, and return to the United States without adversely affecting her/his eligibility for adjustment to permanent resident status.

Current regulations, however, make ineligible for adjustment to permanent resident status any alien (other than an immediate relative as defined in INA § 201(b) or a special immigrant described in INA § 101(a)(27)(H)) who has failed (other than through no fault of her/his own for technical reasons) continuously to maintain a legal status since entry into the United States. 8 C.F.R. § 245.1(b). The student's departure and subsequent re-entry will not eliminate this bar to adjustment of status. 8 C.F.R. § 245.1(c).

This provision does not prevent any individual from leaving the United States and returning on an immigrant visa. Obtaining a numerically limited visa, however, may be a very lengthy process, depending on the current availability of the desired family-sponsored or employment-related preference category. Even when available, the application process may require many months of consular procedures before the visa interview is granted.

§ 7–9.4 Inadmissibility (Formerly "Exclusion")

Included in the Immigration Marriage Fraud Amendments of 1986 was an amendment to INA § 212(a)(19) which increased the sanctions applicable to a student who fraudulently or willfully violates the terms of her/his student status. This amendment provided that any alien who fraudulently or willfully misrepresents a material fact in order to procure any benefit conferred by the Immigration and Nationality Act is ineligible to receive a visa and will be denied admission into the United States. Before the 1986 amendment, the language of this provision denied admission to individuals who obtained a visa or other documentation or sought to enter the United States through the use of fraud or willful misrepresentation. The prior provision did not include as a ground for exclusion (now "inadmissibility") or denial of a visa the use of fraud to obtain "other benefit[s] provided under this Chapter." This broad inadmissibility provision could prevent a student from re-entering the United States, either as an immigrant or as a nonimmigrant, if that student misrepresented a material fact in order to qualify for immigration benefits such as permission to be employed or permission to take less than a full course of study.

CHAPTER 8

REMOVAL

§ 8–1 INTRODUCTION

Removal is the expulsion of an alien who has already been admitted to the United States. Under the Illegal Immigration Reform and Immigrant Responsibility Act of 1996 (IIRIRA), grounds for removal apply only after an alien has been inspected and admitted. Aliens who have entered but have not been admitted-aliens who entered without inspection-are now considered inadmissible rather than removable. IIRIRA abolished the separate proceedings for excludable and deportable aliens by replacing them with a single form of removal proceedings. Inadmissible and otherwise removable aliens, however, are still subject to different procedural rules with regard to burden of proof and discretionary relief.

The Immigration and Nationality Act lists six major categories of aliens subject to removal. Due to the large number of subcategories within each category, however, there are many more grounds for removal. For example, the first category alone establishes seven classes of aliens inadmissible at the time of entry, in adjustment of status, or in violation of status. The 1990 Act reduced the number of grounds for removal (formerly "deportation") in an attempt to make the list comprehensible and more current. The Technical Amendments Act of 1991, however, expanded the grounds for removal by adding the attempt or conspiracy to commit a crime. The Antiterrorism and Effective Death Penalty Act of 1996 (AEDPA) and IIRIRA facilitated the removal of aliens with criminal records, and further expanded crime-related grounds for removal.

In theory at least, removal is not a criminal punishment, but is a civil proceeding designed primarily to rid the United States of statutorily defined undesirables. The courts have long recognized the plenary power of Congress to expel and remove (formerly "deport") aliens. That Congress allows aliens to enter the United States "is a matter of permission and tolerance. The government's power to terminate hospitality has been asserted by this court since the question first arose." *Harisiades v. Shaughnessy* (Sup.Ct.1952).

Even though the courts do not recognize removal as criminal punishment, they recognize that removal penalizes the alien. The alien has voluntarily chosen to come to the United States and removal forces her/him to leave her/his home, job, friends, and in some cases, family. Indeed, removal may result "in loss of both property and life; or all that makes life worth living." *Ng Fung Ho v. White* (Sup.Ct.1922). Further, a removed alien is barred for five years from entering the United States unless s/he obtains special permission from the Immigration Service to re-enter. INA § 212. Because the consequences of removal are drastic, the student of immigration law should become familiar with the many and varied aspects of removal. This chapter examines first, the grounds for removal and second, the procedures incident to both the prehearing process and the removal hearing.

§ 8–2 GROUNDS FOR REMOVAL OF AN ALIEN

§ 8–2.1 General Considerations

The Immigration and Nationality Act—as amended by IIRIRA—presently contains six major broad categories of aliens subject to removal. INA § 237(a). The six categories cover aliens (1) who were inadmissible at time of entry or adjustment of status or have violated status, (2) have committed criminal offenses, (3) have failed to register or falsified documents, (4) were subject to security and related grounds, (5) have become a public charge, and (6) unlawfully voted. The various grounds for removal can be divided into two general classes—aliens removable for acts that rendered them inadmissible at the time of entry or adjustment of status and aliens removable for committing certain prohibited acts since their entry. Before examining these categories in any detail, some general aspects of removal will be examined.

Removal applies only to aliens, since only aliens may be removed. According to the INA, an alien is "any person not a citizen or national of the United States." INA § 101(a)(3). Hence, no matter how one obtained citizenship in the United States, s/he is not subject to removal and need only prove her/his citizenship to avoid removal. Removal proceedings may only be commenced against a naturalized citizen after the successful completion of denaturalization proceedings to remove the individual's U.S. citizenship. Aliens who have been admitted into the U.S., and who remain, even with permanent resident status, are subject to removal. There are several specific classes of aliens exempt from the removal statutes. Removal laws do not apply to ambassadors, public ministers, accredited career diplomats, consular officers, and the members of their families. Employees of international organizations such as the United Nations are also exempt from removal statutes. INA § 102.

Removing an alien often may result in the "de facto" removal of the alien's U.S. citizen children. The Third Circuit rejected the claim that removal (formerly "deportation") of an alien denies her/his child the right, as a U.S. citizen, to continue to reside in the United States. Removal of the child's parents will merely postpone, but not bar, the child's residence in the United States, if s/he should later choose to live in this country. The court reasoned that Congress did not intend to give such a child the ability to confer immigration benefits on her/his parents. *Acosta v. Gaffney* (3d Cir.1977).

Unlike most statutes regulating conduct, the INA frequently applies retroactively. The INS may remove an alien for conduct which was not a ground for removal at the time the alien committed the act. For example, a Nazi who legally entered the United States in 1965 may be removed under the provisions of a 1978 amendment to the act, even though s/he has resided in the United States for a number of years. Hence, removal (formerly "deportation") for acts which were not grounds for removal when committed does not violate the constitutional prohibition against *ex post facto* laws. *Mahler v. Eby* (Sup.Ct.1924). The INA also does not contain a general statute of limitations, although there are particular statutes of limitation contained within the classes of aliens subject to removal. For example, an alien who becomes a charge of the state is removable only if s/he becomes a public charge within five years of her/his entry into the United States. INA § 237(a)(5). Accordingly, the Immigration Service may remove a Greek who becomes a public charge four years after entry, but not an Italian who becomes a public charge five and a half years after entry. Because there is no general statute of limitations, however, the Immigration Service can remove the Greek who became a public charge within five years of entry *at any time*—even though s/he may no longer fit this description.

Like the public charge provision, many of the INA's provisions depend on when the alien entered the United States. IIRIRA, however, has diminished the significance of the concept of "entry" by replacing it with that of "admission." The critical distinction between "admission" and "entry" is the requirement that an immigration officer inspect and admit an alien whereas an "entry" may be achieved either after inspection or by successfully evading inspection. The practical effect of this shift is to deprive an alien who has achieved an "entry" without inspection by an immigration officer of substantive and procedural rights. Under the pre-IIRIRA process, an alien entering without inspection was entitled to greater rights in deportation hearings than aliens who were applying for admission and were subject to exclusion hearings. Generally speaking, it is easier for the United States government to refuse to admit an alien than it is to remove her/him after s/he has been admitted. Now, it is admission that determines whether an alien will be subject to the more stringent inadmissibility grounds or the slightly less demanding removal grounds. Entry, however, is still a concept in immigration law, and focuses on the physical act of crossing into the geographical jurisdiction of the United States. Some of the inadmissibility grounds still use the word entry. *See* INA §§ 212(a)(3)(C)(I), 212(a)(5)(A)(I). Some of the removal grounds similarly use the term.

See INA § 237(a)(1)(A) (inadmissibility at entry) and
§ 237 (a)(1)(A) (smuggling aliens within five years of
entry). The criminal provisions of the INA also continue
to make entry an essential element of various offenses.
Entry can occasionally make a difference when it comes
to procedure for removal. *See* § 9–2.1, *infra*. Further,
entry remains important because Congress's definition
of admission refers to entry. The terms "admission and
admitted mean, with respect to an alien, the lawful
entry of the alien into the U.S. after inspection and
authorization by an immigration officer." INA
§ 101(a)(13).

§ 8–2.2 Aliens Subject to Removal for Entry While Inadmissible and Related Conduct

The Immigration and Nationality Act provides for the
first category of aliens who are subject to removal for
acts that rendered them inadmissible at the time of entry
or adjustment of status or who violate their status following their admission. INA § 237(a)(1)(A). Section
237(a)(1)(A) allows the INS to "look back" at conditions
existing at the time of an alien's entry and remove aliens
who should not have been allowed admission into the
United States. This concept has profound implications.
An alien who may not have committed a removable
offense, discussed below, may still be subject to removal
if s/he can be shown to have committed acts which would
have amounted to inadmissible conduct before entry. *See*
§ 9–1, *infra*, for a detailed discussion of the inadmissibility provisions.

An alien who is present in the U.S. in violation of the
INA or any other law of the U.S. is removable. INA
§ 237(a)(1)(B). An alien who violates or fails to comply

with any of the terms of entry is subject to removal, as is any alien who fails to maintain the nonimmigrant or immigrant status that permitted her/his entry. INA § 237(a)(1)(C). Such violations include overstaying the time limit of a nonimmigrant visa or accepting employment without the requisite authorization. An alien accorded permanent resident status on a conditional basis under INA § 216 or § 216A must have her/his status converted from conditional to unconditional or s/he is removable. INA § 237(a)(1)(D). An alien who knowingly encourages, aids, or abets another alien to enter the United States illegally may be removed; the Attorney General, however, may waive this provision if the waiver would serve humanitarian purposes, assure family unity, or would be in the public interest. INA § 237(a)(1)(E).

Another category of aliens subject to removal for violating entry requirements are those aliens involved in marriage fraud. Aliens who marry United States citizens solely to obtain admission into the United States may be removed under the provisions of INA § 237(a)(1)(G). This statute covers annulled marriages and marriages otherwise terminated within two years, unless the alien demonstrates to the satisfaction of the Immigration Service that the marriage was not for the purpose of gaining admission into the United States. The INS also has authority to determine whether any previous alien-citizen marriage was fraudulent and if so, to remove the alien.

§ 8–2.3 Aliens Removable for Conduct After Entry

The INS also may remove aliens for engaging in certain prohibited activities after their entry into the United States. Since there is no statute of limitations in the

INA, the alien may be removed any time after the prohibited act is committed. Before the 1990 Act, a complex and often controversial set of provisions prescribed removal for membership in the Communist party or affiliation with a subversive organization. The 1990 Act amended and modernized those provisions, replacing them with a statute that reflected current national security and safety concerns. The subsequent IIRIRA amendments reflected the U.S. society's fear of terrorism by including terrorism as a ground of inadmissibility and removal. INA § 237(a)(4)(B). Prior to 1990, the statute classified the following as subversives:

1. Anarchists;

2. Aliens advocating or teaching opposition to all organized government;

3. Aliens who are members of or affiliated with the Communist Party or any other totalitarian organization;

4. Aliens, not already covered by the preceding classes, advocating the economic, international, and governmental doctrines of world communism;

5. Aliens advocating the overthrow, by force and violence, of the United States government, or any of its officers;

6. Aliens who write, publish, or distribute materials which are subversive;

7. Aliens who affiliate with persons who write, publish, or distribute subversive literature;

8. Aliens whom the Attorney General believes entered the United States principally or incidentally to

engage in activities endangering the welfare, safety, or national security of the United States.

The current law permits removal for any alien who violates U.S. espionage law, engages in criminal activity that endangers public safety or national security, or engages in any activity whose purpose is to overthrow the U.S. government by force or unlawful means. INA § 237(a)(4)(A). An alien who has engaged, is engaged, or at any time after admission engages in terrorist activity also is subject to removal. INA § 237(a)(4)(B). The Secretary of State has the discretion to recommend for removal an alien whose presence s/he believes will have serious adverse consequences for U.S. foreign policy. INA § 237(a)(4)(C).

In addition, a 1978 amendment to the INA updated in the 1990 Act, permits the INS to remove aliens who participated in Nazi activities. According to the act, any alien, who in association with the Nazi party, "ordered, incited, assisted, or otherwise participated in the persecution of any person because of race, religion, national origin, or political opinion" may be removed. INA §§ 237(a)(4)(D), 212(a)(3)(E). This provision has been unsuccessfully challenged as an unconstitutional bill of attainder and *ex post facto* law. The Second Circuit in *Linnas v. INS* (2d Cir.1986) held that the provision is not a bill of attainder because removal (formerly "deportation") is not punishment. Linnas, who was found to be chief of a Nazi concentration camp, was ordered removed to the Soviet Union, even though he was convicted *in absentia* in the Soviet Union and sentenced to death there for his war crimes. Linnas' argument that his removal would be unlawful extradition was likewise unsuccessful.

A second broad category of aliens removable for conduct which occurs after entry are those aliens convicted of various criminal offenses. INA § 237(a)(2). Because of the serious consequences of these removal grounds to immigrants and nonimmigrants, and their considerable expansion between 1986 and 1996, virtually any criminal activity other than the most petty offenses and misdemeanors can have serious adverse consequences to an alien and family members.

The first class of general crimes under this provision covers crimes of moral turpitude. An alien would be subject to removal if s/he is "convicted of a crime involving moral turpitude committed within five years after admission and convicted of a crime for which a sentence of one year or longer may be imposed, or who at any time after admission is convicted of two crimes involving moral turpitude.... " INA § 237(a)(2)(A). The alien must be convicted of the crime—a mere admission of the crime by the alien is not sufficient for removal.

In *Matter of Ozkok* (BIA 1988), the court stated that there must be three elements present to find a conviction for immigration purposes: (1) a judge or jury has found the alien guilty or s/he has entered a plea of guilty or nolo contendre or has admitted sufficient facts to warrant a finding of guilty; (2) the judge has ordered some form of punishment, penalty, or restraint on the person's liberty to be imposed; and (3) a judgment or adjudication of guilt may be entered if the person violates the terms of his probation or fails to comply with the requirements of the court's order, without availability of further proceedings regarding the person's guilt or innocence of the original charge. IIRIRA's amendments to the INA have narrowed *Ozkok* by codifying only the first two prongs of the *Ozkok* test. The INA thus currently defines conviction as "a formal judgment of guilt of the alien entered by a court or, if adjudication of guilt has been withheld, where (i) a judge or jury has found the alien guilty or the alien has entered a plea of guilty or nolo contendre or has admitted sufficient facts to warrant a finding of guilt, and (ii) the judge has ordered some form of punishment, penalty, or restraint on the alien's liberty to be imposed." INA § 101(a)(48)(A).

A difficult aspect of removing aliens for crimes of moral turpitude is defining which crimes involve "moral turpitude." The courts generally agree that crimes of moral turpitude include crimes of violence and crimes "commonly thought of as involving baseness, vileness or depravity." *Jordan v. De George* (Sup.Ct.1951). This definition, however, is nearly as vague and open-ended as "moral turpitude." The Supreme Court in *Jordan* held that the use of the term "moral turpitude" did not render the INA unconstitutionally vague because "the language conveys sufficiently definite warning as to the proscribed conduct when measured by common understanding and practices."

If the crime was not subject to a possible sentence of one year or more, the INS or reviewing court must decide whether the criminal law violated by the alien inherently involves moral turpitude; that is, whether violation of the law under any circumstance would involve moral turpitude. *Matter of R.__* (BIA 1954). In practice, the courts have held that the following crimes involve moral turpitude: assault with intent to kill or with a deadly weapon, bigamy, bribery, child beating, conspiracy, counterfeiting, narcotics offenses, forgery, fraud, most types of homicide, larceny, most sexual offenses, and certain misdemeanors, such as larceny. In order to determine if the alien's crime involved moral turpitude, the court can consider only the crime of which the alien was convicted or to which the alien pled guilty—not what the alien actually did or the particular nature of the alien's act.

INA § 237(a)(2)(iii) authorizes the removal of any alien who has been convicted of an aggravated felony at any time after entry. The term "aggravated felony" includes murder; rape or sexual abuse of a minor; drug trafficking; firearm trafficking; money laundering; crimes of violence for which the term of imprisonment, even if suspended, is at least one year or more; or any attempt or conspiracy to commit such acts, theft or burglary, gambling, tax fraud, transportation for prostitution purposes, commercial bribery, counterfeiting, forgery, stolen vehicle trafficking, obstruction of justice, perjury, bribery of a witness, and failure to appear to answer for a criminal offense. INA § 101(a)(43). This list, which reflects the Antiterrorism and Effective Death Penalty Act's (AEDPA) and IIRIRA's expansion of the aggravated felony definition, codifies *Application of Barrett* (BIA 1990) which interpreted the aggravated felony definition to apply to state as well as federal offenses. IIRIRA further expanded aggravated felony by reducing the previously required sentence for some crimes from five years to one year and by reducing the amount of loss required for some crimes from $200,000 to $10,000. An alien convicted of an aggravated felony is "presumed to be removable from the United States." INA § 242A(c). *See* § 10–2, *infra.*

Because of the serious, sometimes unanticipated consequences of criminal conduct on aliens and their families, lawyers representing aliens accused of a crime, prosecutors, and judges have several special considerations to keep in mind. First, if the alien is accused of a crime of moral turpitude, or an "aggravated felony," the lawyer may want to consider pleading the alien to a lesser offense not involving moral turpitude, with a mandatory sentence of less than one year, and/or not classified as an aggravated felony. Many of the provisions of the INA, as amended between 1986 and 1996, impose grave consequences upon aliens convicted of offenses, such as removal without waiver, incarceration, and ineligibility to acquire later immigration status after removal. Some prosecutors and judges are not aware of these consequences to aliens who may be the sole support of U.S. citizen or permanent resident family members. In many cases, the rehabilitative and punitive purposes of prosecuting and sentencing may actually be achieved through imposing a stronger sentence for a lesser level crime without causing collateral unwanted immigration consequences.

Second, the INA also specifies that the moral turpitude or aggravated felony provisions should not apply in the case of any alien who has after such conviction been granted a full and unconditional pardon by the President or the governor of the state of conviction. INA § 237(a)(2)(A)(v). Hence, as a last resort, the lawyer may attempt to obtain a full pardon for the alien. The statute does not provide, however, for offenses involving controlled substances or firearms, nor for an automatic stay of removal while the alien applies for a pardon and, therefore, for a stay of removal. The provisions of INA § 237(a)(2)(A) apply only to crimes involving moral turpitude or to which a sentence of one year or more may be imposed and do not apply to other crimes for which the alien may be removed, for example, drug offenses.

Other sections of the INA allow removal for conviction of specific crimes. INA § 237(a)(2)(A)(iv) provides for the removal of any alien convicted of a crime related to high speed flight from an immigration checkpoint. The INS may remove an alien convicted of violating any law or regulation relating to a controlled substance, such as narcotic drugs and marihuana. INA § 237(a)(2)(B). *Cf.* § 1–5, *supra.* Moreover, any alien who at any time after admission abuses or becomes addicted to drugs is subject to removal. INA § 237(a)(2)(B)(ii). Unlike the general moral turpitude category, an alien need not be sentenced in order to be removed for narcotics offenses. Likewise, an alien convicted of possessing or carrying any automatic weapon, semi-automatic, or sawed-off shotgun may be removed. INA § 237(a)(2)(C). Aliens convicted of violating the Selective Service Act, espionage statutes, or certain other statutes dealing with the national defense are subject to removal if the Immigration Service designates the alien as an undesirable. INA § 237(a)(2)(D).

The INA also provides for the removal of certain other statutorily defined undesirables. IIRIRA added a new ground for removal of aliens convicted of a crime of domestic violence, stalking, child abuse, child neglect, child abandonment, or of a violation of a protective order relating to domestic violence. INA § 237(a)(2)(E). The INS may also remove an alien who knowingly or recklessly prepares, files, or assists another in preparing or filing a false application or document for immigration benefits. INA § 237(a)(3)(C)(i). A waiver is available for a first violation by a permanent resident who committed a document fraud offense solely to assist or support a spouse or child. INA § 237(a)(3)(C)(ii). IIRIRA also added new grounds for removal and criminal penalties for aliens who falsely claim citizenship. INA § 237(a)(3)(D). Aliens, who in the opinion of the Immigration Service have become public charges within five years of their entry, from causes not affirmatively shown to have arisen after entry, may be removed. INA § 237(a)(5). Further, IIRIRA amendments provide for removal of those aliens who have voted unlawfully. INA § 237(a)(6).

§ 8–3 PROCEDURES FOR REMOVAL

§ 8–3.1 Prehearing Procedure

The INS uses a variety of techniques to investigate the presence of removable aliens both in and coming to the United States. The methods used by the INS include inspecting all vehicles, persons, and belongings before departure and at the border as well as at certain fixed check-points both inside the border and in other countries (referred to as "preinspection"); using roving patrols to stop and question persons in certain vehicles; conducting audits of I–9 forms (Employment eligibility verification) held by employers; searching businesses which are alleged to employ removable aliens; and acting on information obtained through informants. This section examines the scope of the INS' power in conducting prehearing investigations.

a. Immigration Service Powers Prior to Arrest

The INA provides that any officer of the Immigration Service may, without a warrant:

(1) Interrogate any alien or person believed to be an alien as to her/his right to be or remain in the United States;

(2) Arrest any alien who in the officer's presence or view is entering or attempting to enter the United States in violation of any law or if the officer has reason to believe the alien is in the United States in violation of any law and is likely to escape if not arrested;

(3) Board and search any vehicle to look for illegal aliens within a reasonable distance from the border. INA § 287(a).

The Code of Federal Regulations defines a reasonable distance from the border to be "100 air miles from any external boundary of the United States." 8 C.F.R. § 287.1(a)(2). The statute appears to confer broad investigatory powers on the INS. The Supreme Court has held that the Immigration and Naturalization Service may use evidence in a removal (formerly "deportation") proceeding which had been obtained in violation of the Fourth Amendment. Using a balancing test, the Court decided that the likely costs of excluding unlawfully obtained evidence outweigh the likely social benefits. Excluding such evidence would hinder the deliberately simple removal hearing system, would possibly suppress large amounts of information that had been obtained lawfully, and would "compel the courts to release from custody persons who would then immediately resume their commission of a crime through their continuing, unlawful presence in this country." In the Court's view, the social benefits from excluding such evidence would be minor because exclusion would have little deterrent effect on future Fourth Amendment violations by INS officials. *INS v. Lopez–Mendoza* (Sup.Ct.1984).

(1) OUTSIDE THE TERRITORIAL BOUNDS OF THE UNITED STATES

Ordinarily, the United States has power only over persons and property contained within its territorial bounds, including its territorial waters. One exception is the pre-boarding inspection offices established in foreign countries to inspect aliens before their departure to the United States. Congress has authorized the Attorney General, with the consent of the Secretary of State to detail immigration officers for duty in foreign countries. INA § 103(a). Pre-inspection occurs only when the vessel proceeds directly to this country and eliminates the need for inspection at the border.

In 1981 the President of the United States proclaimed that the entry of undocumented aliens from the high seas would be prevented by the interdiction of certain vessels carrying such aliens. Through Executive Order 12324 of September 29, 1981, the President gave the INS the authority to stop and board vessels which either came from the United States or from foreign nations having agreements with the United States (only Haiti), which allowed such stops. Once on board, the INS was authorized by the President to make inquiries of those on board and examine documents to determine the destination and purpose of the vessel. If the Service found or had reason to believe that an offense was being committed in violation of United States immigration laws, the Executive Order directed the INS to return the vessel and its passengers to the country from which the vessel comes.

The Executive Order apparently extended the INS' authority to the high seas. The D.C. Circuit in *Haitian Refugee Center v. Gracey* (D.C.Cir.1987) upheld the statu-

tory and constitutional authority of U.S. officials to inter-
dict on the high seas aliens who lack visas. The Haitian
Refugee Center challenged the 1981 agreement between
the United States and Haiti permitting U.S. authorities
to board Haitian vessels on the high seas to inspect,
among other things, the status of the people on board.
The court rejected the Center's allegations that the
agreement denied the aliens Due Process, on the ground
that aliens have no constitutional right to enter the
United States. This right of interdiction was upheld in
Haitian Refugee Center v. Baker (11th Cir.1992) which
denied judicial review of INS decisions under these circumstances on the ground that the aliens never presented themselves at the U.S. border. *See* § 9–2.4. Haiti has
since withdrawn its agreement to stopping its boats on
the high seas.

(2) AT THE BORDER

The INS has the authority to stop all vehicles and
persons at the border or its functional equivalent. Because Congress has the unquestioned power to admit or
exclude aliens, it can authorize inspection of all persons
as they cross the border. *See* INA § 235. Incident to this
inspection power at the border, the Immigration Service
may board and search any vehicle, including boats and
aircraft, which they believe contains aliens. These
searches may be legally conducted without a search warrant and can occur at the border or in the territorial
waters of the United States. INA §§ 235, 287.

When an alien arrives at the border, the INS is authorized to inspect her/him to determine whether the alien
may be admitted into the United States or whether s/he
is inadmissible. INA § 235(a). After the inspection, the
examining officer may elect to admit the alien. A visa is

usually essential for admission but it does not guarantee admission. The immigration officer reexamines the alien to determine whether s/he is subject to any inadmissibility grounds and should not be admitted. If the examining immigration officer determines that an alien seeking admission is not clearly and beyond doubt entitled to be admitted, the alien is detained for removal proceedings. INA § 235(b)(1)(A).

If the alien appears inadmissible, the officer may temporarily detain the alien for further inquiry. This procedure is customarily referred to as secondary inspection. The inquiry provides the INS with additional information about the alien's right to admission. Although a detained alien is interrogated by the Service, the Fifth Circuit held in *United States v. Henry* (5th Cir.1979) that no *Miranda*-type warning is necessary unless the questioning becomes custodial in nature. The Attorney General may at any time permit an alien applying for admission to withdraw his application and depart immediately from the U.S. INA § 235(a)(4).

The immigration officer also may elect to release the alien on parole pending further investigation. Under INA § 212(d)(5), the INS is authorized to parole, temporarily and under such conditions as the Service prescribes, any alien physically entering the United States subject to some constraints in case of aliens who are inadmissible on criminal and national security grounds. The Service grants parole chiefly as a matter of practicality. Often, time constraints prevent the Service from making a thorough investigation at the border and parole allows the Service additional time to determine the alien's right to be admitted to the United States. The alien who enters on parole has not been admitted, and may be removed without the formal removal proceedings which would be given to a person who had been admitted. Such aliens do have a statutory right to an abbreviated removal hearing (discussed *infra* chapter 9). The Board of Immigration Appeals held in *Matter of Castellon* (BIA 1981) that parole is purely discretionary and no administrative review of the decision is possible, although judicial review may lie in a district court for a declaratory judgment or habeas corpus action.

Alternatively, the immigration officer may choose to refer the alien to other immigration personnel. First, if the officer believes the alien can overcome a finding of inadmissibility, s/he may refer the alien to the district director for a waiver of inadmissability. 8 C.F.R. § 235.2(b). Second, after inspecting the alien, the officer may conclude s/he is inadmissible. The officer must then refer the alien to an immigration judge for a final determination. INA § 235(b). After the officer decides to refer the alien, the Code of Federal Regulations requires the officer to give notice to the alien of the hearing and to advise the alien of her/his right to counsel at no expense to the government. 8 C.F.R. § 235.6(a). Strictly speaking, there is no right to legal counsel in inspection proceedings, although the INS may permit an alien to have an attorney (or other advisor) present to provide advice during the inspection.

As a result of changes enacted by IIRIRA, immigration officers are authorized to remove certain arriving aliens through a special process known as expedited removal. If an immigration officer determines that an alien is inadmissible, the officer should order the alien removed without further hearing or review unless the alien indicates a fear of persecution or an intention to apply for asylum.

INA § 235(b)(1)(A). If an alien raises her/his unwilling-ness or fear of returning to her/his country of origin, the inspecting officer must give the alien a more detailed written explanation of the credible fear interview pro-cess. Pending the credible fear interview, the INS places the alien in detention. The INS expects to give the alien 48 hours after arrival at the detention facility to contact family members, friends, attorneys, or representatives. An asylum officer then interviews the alien; if the asylum officer finds that the alien has no credible fear of perse-cution on account of race, religion, political opinion or membership in a particular social group, the officer should inform the alien that s/he has a right to request review by an immigration judge. That review must take place within seven days after the asylum officer's deci-sion, and the alien is detained pending review by the immigration judge. If an asylum officer determines that an alien has a credible fear of persecution, the alien continues to be detained for further consideration of the application for asylum in the context of a normal removal proceeding under INA § 240. INA 235(b)(1)(B)(ii). Pend-ing these various procedures the INS ordinarily detains the alien, but may release her/him on parole, if required by a medical emergency or law enforcement objectives. 8 C.F.R. § 235.3. If the alien claims to be a permanent resident, to have been previously admitted as a refugee, or to have been granted asylum, the INS will attempt to verify this claim. If the claim cannot be verified, the alien may make a written declaration under penalty of perjury; then the immigration officer should issue an expedited order of removal and refer the case for review by an immigration judge. The expedited removal procedures may be applied to any arriving alien. The Attorney General has discretion to extend these expedited procedures to aliens who are present in the U.S., have not been admitted, and are unable to prove continuous physical presence in the U.S. for the immediately preceding two years. INA 235(b)(1)(A)(iii).

If an immigration officer or an immigration judge suspects that an arriving alien may be inadmissible under any of the security or foreign policy grounds (INA 212(a)(3)(A)(i or iii), (B), or (C)), the officer or judge shall order the alien removed. INA 235(c)(1). This provision covers aliens who seek to enter the U.S. to engage in acts involving sabotage, espionage, and violent overthrow of the government as well as aliens who are involved in terrorist activities and whose admission would adversely affect U.S. foreign policy. The Attorney General automatically reviews these removal orders. If the Attorney General concludes that the alien is inadmissible on one of the specified grounds, s/he may order the alien removed without further hearing. Otherwise, s/he decides what further inquiry is to be conducted. INA 235(c)(2). The alien may submit a written statement and additional information for the Attorney General to consider. INA 235(c)(3). IIRIRA also established a special removal procedure for terrorists which applies to both inadmissible and removable aliens. INA § 354.

(3) 100 MILES INSIDE THE BORDER

(a) Investigatory Stops for Identification. The Supreme Court applies a different standard to investigatory stops made by roving patrols and at fixed check-points. The Court in *United States v. Brignoni–Ponce* (Sup.Ct.1975) held that roving patrols may stop vehicles at points away from the border only if they are aware of specific articulable facts that reasonably warrant suspicion that the vehicle contains aliens illegally in the United States.

Even though the intrusion resulting from a brief stop is modest, the Court concluded that it is not reasonable under the Fourth Amendment to make random stops. Factors relevant to the existence of a reasonable suspicion include proximity to the border, traffic patterns, previous experience with alien traffic in the area, the driver's behavior, the appearance of the vehicle, and the officer's experience in recognizing the characteristic appearance of foreign nationals. Foreign appearance alone, however, is insufficient to support an inference of illegal presence. The Court applied this standard in *United States v. Cortez* (Sup.Ct.1981), where the Court held that the roving patrol did have a reasonable suspicion. While the Court disapproved of random stops in both *Cortez* and *Brignoni–Ponce,* the Court has indicated in *Delaware v. Prouse* (Sup.Ct.1979) that using patrols to stop every car, or perhaps some other systematic number of cars, may be consistent with the Fourth Amendment.

In addition, the INS can make routine investigatory stops at reasonably located fixed check-points even in the absence of any suspicion that the vehicle contains illegal aliens. The Court in *United States v. Martinez–Fuerte* (Sup.Ct.1976) reasoned that the Service's need to make such stops in order to control the entry of illegal aliens is great and the consequent intrusion on Fourth Amendment rights is limited since motorists are given advance warning of the stop which involves only the briefest detention—usually less than a minute. On balance, the Court supported the INS' right to make investigatory stops at fixed check-points.

(b) Searches. The INS also utilizes vehicle searches as another way of detecting illegal aliens. At areas removed from the border, Congress has empowered the INS to

board and search any vehicle to check for illegal aliens without a warrant. See INA § 287(a)(3). The courts, however, have limited this power when the officers act without a search warrant. In *Almeida–Sanchez v. United States* (Sup.Ct.1973), the Supreme Court held that a warrantless search of an automobile made by a roving patrol without probable cause or consent violated the alien's right to be free from unreasonable searches and seizures. The Court extended this holding to searches made at fixed check-points in *United States v. Ortiz* (Sup.Ct.1975). In *Ortiz*, the Court concluded that a vehicle search involves a substantial invasion of privacy; and to protect motorists from arbitrary searches, the INS must have probable cause to believe that the vehicle contains illegal aliens before a search is possible. When conducting the search, immigration officers may inspect only those areas of the car where an alien could reasonably hide. In other words, the officer may not, as the Supreme Court observed in *United States v. Ross* (Sup. Ct.1982), open and search small pieces of luggage or other small containers and compartments to look for aliens.

(c) Temporary Detention for Questioning. One step between an investigatory stop for identification and an actual arrest is a forcible detention of a suspected alien for interrogation. While the alien questioned during an investigatory stop is free to leave, an alien forcibly detained is not, even though s/he is not technically under arrest *Yam Sang Kwai v. INS* (D.C.Cir.1969). Immigration officers may forcibly detain persons temporarily when the circumstances warrant a reasonable suspicion that the alien is illegally in the United States. The First Circuit rationalized in *Navia–Duran v. INS* (1st Cir. 1977) that, since a forcible detention falls short of an

actual arrest, no *Miranda*-type warning is necessary before questioning the alien. Other circuits endorse this view. Courts will consider, however, the voluntariness of any statement given by the alien in the absence of a *Miranda*-type warning. If the INS coerced the alien, her/his right to Due Process, as guaranteed by the Fifth Amendment, may be violated. The court, as in *Navia–Duran*, may suppress any evidence obtained through coercion during the removal hearing.

(4) INTERIOR OF THE UNITED STATES

With the exception of areas within 100 miles of the external boundaries of the United States, the INS may not make investigatory stops using roving patrols or fixed check-points. INA § 283(a). The Service may, however, briefly detain aliens for interrogation. Like detentions made near the border, the INS must have a reasonable belief that the alien is illegally present in this country before detaining her/him for interrogation. Special circumstances, however, may permit greater INS authority. The D.C. Circuit Court of Appeals upheld the Attorney General's authority, during the Iranian hostage crisis, to order nonimmigrant Iranian students to report to INS district offices and to demonstrate their lawful status. *Narenji v. Civiletti* (D.D.C.1979).

The INS may also search vehicles inside the United States if there is probable cause. The INS may search not only vehicles, but business establishments as well, if they obtain an appropriate search warrant. While immigration officers have substantial authority to search if they have a warrant, the court in *Blackie's House of Beef, Inc. v. Castillo* (D.D.C.1978) held that the authority is limited. First, the warrant must have been properly issued. Second, the search warrant must be issued for persons, not property. As the court said in *Blackie's,* neither the Fourth Amendment nor any statute authorizes immigration officers to use a warrant commanding a search for property as permission to enter a private business establishment to search for illegal aliens employed there. Due to the large number of undocumented aliens in the United States and the difficulties in enforcing the immigration laws, however, the Supreme Court has increasingly applied a relaxed standard of review to alleged Fourth Amendment violations by immigration officers. *See, e.g., INS v. Delgado* (Sup.Ct.1984). If the INS makes the search in retaliation for the alien's union activities, however, a district court has held in *United States v. Turner* (N.D.Cal.1982) that the employer who requests such a search violates the National Labor Relations Act.

(a) Arrests Without a Warrant. The INA empowers immigration officers to arrest, without a warrant, "any alien in the United States, if he has reason to believe that the alien so arrested is in the United States in violation of any such law or regulation and is likely to escape before a warrant can be obtained for his arrest.... " INA § 287(a)(2). The Tenth Circuit in *Roa–Rodriguez v. United States* (10th Cir.1969) has limited this authority by holding that a belief that the alien intends to violate her/his entry conditions is insufficient for an arrest. The arresting officer must base her/his belief on something more than mere suspicion. After an arrest made without a warrant, specific administrative procedures for the INS must be followed. Once arrested, the alien is taken before a different immigration officer for questioning unless no other officer is readily available. 8 C.F.R. § 287.3. If the examining officer determines that a prima facie case exists for removing the alien, s/he refers the case to an immigration judge, orders

the alien's expedited removal, or takes other applicable action. 8 C.F.R. § 287.3.

Even though removal is a severe penalty, courts have concluded that removal is civil and not criminal in nature and hence, uniformly agree that a *Miranda* warning at the time of the arrest for removal is not required. After the INS makes the decision to proceed with removal (except in the case of the alien subject to expedited removal provision), however, section 287.3 of the Code of Federal Regulations requires the arresting officer to advise the alien of (1) the reason for the arrest; (2) the alien's right to counsel at no expense to the government and the availability of free legal service programs; and (3) the alien's right to remain silent. While not technically a *Miranda* warning, in essence, the arresting officer is required to advise the alien of her/his rights as defined by the Court in *Miranda v. Arizona* (Sup.Ct.1966). Although the statute requires the officer to give the warning only after s/he decides to proceed with removal, the court may scrutinize any statements given by the alien before the warning from the INS to determine whether the statements were made voluntarily. In addition, the alien must be informed within 24 hours whether s/he will be detained further or released on bond or recognizance and whether a Notice to Appear and warrant of arrest will be issued.

(b) Arrests With a Warrant. If the INS issues a warrant for arrest, it simultaneously issues a Notice to Appear before the immigration court to contest the removal. (*See* § 8–3.2, *infra* for a discussion of the Notice to Appear.) INS district directors, deputy district directors, and assistant directors; officers in charge; chief, deputy, and assistant patrol agents; the Assistant Com-

missioner, Investigations; Institutional Hearing Program
Directors; and port directors may issue an arrest warrant, but only if it is necessary to hold the alien in
custody. 8 C.F.R. § 287.5. Once issued, the INS must
serve the warrant within a reasonable period of time. *See
United States v. Weaver* (4th Cir.1967). Should the INS
determine the alien is not subject to removal, any officer
authorized to issue an arrest warrant may cancel it.

The Code of Federal Regulations also requires the
arresting officer to inform the alien at the time of her/his
arrest of the reason for the arrest and to advise the alien
of her/his rights. 8 C.F.R. § 242.2(b). The officer advises
the alien of: (1) the right to counsel at no expense to the
government; (2) that any statements made may be used
against her/him in subsequent proceedings; and (3)
whether or not s/he will remain in custody. Arrested
aliens are often advised of their rights through Form I–
214 which is served on the alien with the arrest warrant.
The form lists the *Miranda*-type warning in English;
hence, an alien who does not understand English may
sign the form without realizing its significance. If the
alien is not advised of these rights or fails to understand
them, s/he may move to suppress evidence obtained
because of the lack of warning. *Navia–Duran v. INS* (1st
Cir.1977).

(c) Release on Bond or Personal Recognizance. If an
alien is taken into custody, the INS has discretion either
to release the alien or continue the custody. According to
the INA, pending a final determination of whether the
alien is to be removed from the U.S., the Attorney
General may (1) continue to detain the arrested alien; (2)
release the alien upon bond in the amount of not less
than $1500 with security approved by the Attorney Gen-

eral, containing such conditions as the Attorney General may prescribe; or (3) release the alien on conditional parole. INA § 236(a). The INA also authorizes the INS to revoke the bond or parole at any time and rearrest the alien under the original warrant. INA § 236(b). A lawfully admitted alien convicted of an aggravated felony must demonstrate that s/he does not pose a danger to the community and that s/he will appear at any scheduled hearings to be eligible for release from custody. INA § 236(a)(2).

In practice, as the Board observed in *Matter of Patel* (BIA 1976), the alien is usually granted release on personal recognizance unless s/he poses a risk to national security or is a bail risk. The INS has discretion to determine whether the alien threatens national security and, as the Fifth Circuit concluded in *Barbour v. District Director* (Sup.Ct.1974), may base its decision on undisclosed security information. The factors considered relevant by the Board in *Patel* to determine whether the alien is a bail risk include prior arrests in this country, convictions in the alien's native country, illegal entry into the United States, participation in subversive activities, employment status, and the presence of relatives in the United States. The bail or parole decision is not subject to judicial review. INA § 236(e).

The INA gives the Attorney General the authority to provide for special expedited removal proceedings for aggravated felons. INA § 238(a)(1). These special proceedings are to take place at the federal, state, or local correctional facility where the felon is incarcerated. INA § 238(a)(1). The initiation and completion of removal proceedings, as well as subsequent administrative appeals should be completed "to the extent possible" before the aggravated felon's release from prison. INA § 238(a)(3).

The intention of allowing special expedited proceedings for aggravated felons is to have the entire removal process occur while the alien is serving her/his sentence. In that way the alien can be removed immediately upon release from incarceration with no intervening detention. In keeping with this goal of expediency, IIRIRA reduced the period during which an aggravated felon can seek judicial review to 14 days. INA § 238(b)(3).

Because Congress recognized the difficulty for an incarcerated felon to secure adequate counsel, witnesses, and other aspects of presenting her/his case, INA § 238(a)(2) provides that the "Attorney General shall make reasonable efforts to ensure that the alien's access to counsel" is not impaired. INA § 238(a)(2).

§ 8–3.2   Removal Hearing

a.   Notice to Appear

The removal process is officially commenced by the filing of the Notice to Appear (formerly "Order to Show Cause"). 8 C.F.R. § 239.1. Only those officials with power to issue warrants have the authority to issue a Notice to Appear and then, as the Supreme Court observed in *Abel v. United States* (Sup.Ct.1960), only on the basis of a prima facie showing of removability (formerly "deportability"). If an alien has been duly notified about the removal proceedings and s/he fails to attend, "[the alien] shall be removed in absentia if the INS establishes by clear, unequivocal, and convincing evidence that the written notice was so provided and that the alien is removable." INA § 240(b)(5). If the alien fails to appear for a removal hearing absent exceptional circumstances, s/he shall not be eligible for discretionary relief for ten years. INA § 240(b)(7). Sections 239 and 240 outline the basic requirements for the proceedings: (1) the alien must be given proper notice; (2) the alien may choose to be represented by counsel; (3) the alien shall have the opportunity to offer evidence in her/his behalf and examine evidence against her/him; (4) a decision of deportability [*sic*, "removal"] must be based upon "reasonable, substantial, and probative evidence." INA §§ 239(a), 240(b)(4)(A), 240 (b)(4)(B), 240(c)(3).

The INA lists the specific requirements for a Notice to Appear. It must contain a statement of the nature of the proceeding, the legal authority under which the proceeding is conducted, a concise statement of the factual allegations informing the alien of the act or conduct alleged to be in violation of the law, and a designation of the charges against the alien and of the statutory provisions alleged to have been violated. INA § 239(a)(1). In addition, the Notice to Appear lists the time and place when the alien will be required to appear before the immigration judge and notifies the alien of the need to keep the government apprised of her/his address and the consequences of failing to do so. INA § 239(a)(1).

The INA also provides for service of the notice. The INS may either deliver the notice by personal service or "routine service" which usually means registered mail. In either case, when the notice is served, the INS must inform the alien of the notice's contents, of her/his right to counsel at her/his own expense, that any statements may be used against her/him, and must provide a list of any free legal services programs available in the locale. INA §§ 239(a)(1), 239(b)(2). The Court of Appeals in

Attoh v. INS (D.C.Cir.1979) held that a failure to give the alien notice of these rights may result in a new hearing.

b. Participants in the Removal Hearing

Of course, the most obvious party to the proceedings is the alien. (The alien's rights will be discussed in a following subsection.) In addition to the alien, however, the removal hearing also involves an immigration judge, the service counsel, the alien's counsel, if necessary, an interpreter, and often witnesses.

(1) IMMIGRATION JUDGE

The immigration judge was previously identified as a special inquiry officer throughout the INA and regulations. The functions of an inquiry officer involved a blend of investigator, prosecutor, and judge. Modern structure has substantially increased the independence of the immigration judge. In 1982, the Attorney General gave final approval to a plan to reorganize the Board of Immigration Appeals and the immigration judges into the Executive Office for Immigration Review that became a part of the Department of Justice, separate from the INS, effective January 1, 1983. Immigration judges are selected by the Attorney General. The judges may conduct specified classes of proceedings, including removal hearings. INA § 101(b)(4). The INA authorizes the immigration judge to "conduct proceedings for deciding the inadmissibility or deportability [*sic*, "removability"] of the alien, and shall administer oaths, receive evidence, interrogate, examine, and cross-examine the alien and any witnesses, and ... shall decide whether an alien is removable from the United States." INA § 240. The INA allows the immigration judge to serve as both prosecutor and judge, although in practice the judge acts as a prosecutor rarely and only when the alien concedes removability. The Ninth Circuit in *LeTourneur v. INS* (9th Cir.1976) has, however, held that the dual role of the immigration judge is consistent with Due Process.

In addition, the Code of Federal Regulations provides the immigration judge with the authority to consider claims for discretionary relief and to determine the country of removal. 8 C.F.R. §§ 240.11, 240.10(f). As a presiding officer in a removal hearing, the immigration judge has the authority to hear motions for postponements, rules on the admissibility of evidence, orders the taking of depositions if a witness is not readily available and her/his testimony is essential, and issues subpoenas. 8 C.F.R. §§ 240.6, 240.7, 3.35(a), 3.35(b). The immigration judge may not, however, exercise authority in matters exclusively under the control of the district director, including, but not limited to, waivers of inadmissibility, Notices to Appear, and extensions of temporary stay. It was only recently that Immigration Judges were given subpoena and contempt authority. Finally, if the immigration judge considers her/himself unqualified to conduct the hearing, s/he may withdraw pursuant to the provisions of 8 C.F.R. § 240.1(b). According to the Fifth Circuit in *Marcello v. Ahrens* (5th Cir.1954), one such circumstance calling for withdrawal occurs when the immigration judge performed an investigatory function in the case. The alien must request the judge to withdraw if s/he is unqualified or biased and if the judge refuses, the ruling may be questioned on appeal.

(2) SERVICE COUNSEL

The district director assigns a service counsel to the case. 8 C.F.R. § 240.2(b). Pursuant to the INA the service counsel "shall have authority to present evidence, and to interrogate, examine and cross-examine the alien or other witness in the proceedings." 8 C.F.R. § 240.2(a). In effect, the service counsel acts as the prosecutor for the government. The service counsel need not be a lawyer. The Board of Immigration Appeals in *Matter of Reyes–Gomez* (BIA 1973) concluded that using a layperson as service counsel does not violate Due Process. The service counsel may appeal a decision of the immigration judge and may move for reconsideration. 8 C.F.R. § 240.2(a).

(3) ALIEN'S COUNSEL

The INA provides that the "alien shall have the privilege of being represented (at no expense to the Government) by counsel of the alien's choosing who is authorized to practice in such proceedings." INA § 240(b)(4). The alien is informed of this right several times during the removal process, including at the time of arrest, when served with the Notice to Appear, and at the outset of the removal hearing. As a matter of course, the immigration judge routinely grants one postponement during the hearing to allow the alien to obtain counsel. INA § 239(b)(1). In certain very rare circumstances, courts have found that Due Process requires that an indigent alien be appointed counsel in a removal proceeding. The indigent alien has a right to appointed counsel if, in the particular case, the assistance of counsel is necessary to provide "fundamental fairness." *Aguilera–Enriquez v. INS* (6th Cir.1975). The alien must be provided with a list of persons who have indicated their availability to represent the alien pro bono in the removal proceedings. INA § 230(b)(2). The Code of Federal Regulations allows the following persons to represent an alien in removal proceedings: (1) attorneys who are members in good standing of the highest court of any state, (2) under certain conditions, law students and law graduates not yet admitted to the bar, (3) reputable individuals of good moral character, (4) representatives of accredited organizations recognized by the Board of Immigration Appeals, and (5) accredited officials of the government to which the alien owes allegiance. 8 C.F.R. §§ 1.1(f), 292.1(1)-(5).

(4) INTERPRETER

If the alien does not understand English, an interpreter may form an integral part of the removal hearing. Although there is no statutorily defined right to have an interpreter present during the hearing, the alien may request an interpreter if s/he does not understand English. According to the Seventh Circuit in *Niarchos v. INS* (7th Cir.1968), a removal hearing conducted in a language the alien does not understand and without an interpreter present may result in a denial of Due Process. An interpreter in a removal case is sworn to interpret and translate accurately. 8 C.F.R. § 240.5. If the interpreter appears to be incompetent, the alien may raise the issue on appeal, but the Second Circuit in *United States ex rel. Catalano v. Shaughnessy* (2d Cir. 1952) held that the alien has the burden of proving the incompetence. Another difficulty is that the interpreter usually interprets only direct questions or statements to the alien and the alien's responses; accordingly, the alien may not understand additional testimony, arguments of counsel, and other matters arising in the hearing.

c. The Alien's Rights During the Removal Hearing

In 1903, the Supreme Court considered the Due Process rights of aliens during removal (formerly "deportation") proceedings in the *Japanese Immigrant Case* (Sup. Ct.1903). Included among those rights are the right to adequate "notice of the nature of the charges against him and of the time and place at which the proceedings will be held." INA § 239(a)(1).

The INA also provides that the "alien shall have a reasonable opportunity to examine the evidence against him, to present evidence in his own behalf, and to cross-examine witnesses presented by the Government." INA § 240(b)(4)(B). The alien may present any evidence that is material and relevant either to the issue of removability or discretionary relief. The alien also may present either oral testimony or written depositions. If an essential witness is unavailable to testify, the alien may request the immigration judge to order a deposition. The alien may also apply for a subpoena to compel the presence of a witness at the hearing. Before the immigration judge may issue a subpoena, the alien must state what s/he expects to prove by the testimony, and must affirmatively show that a diligent effort was made to produce the witness without the subpoena. 8 C.F.R. § 287.4(a)(2). The alien's right to cross-examine includes the right to examine government witnesses whose testimony was submitted via an affidavit, but, as the Sixth Circuit concluded in *Weinbrand v. Prentis* (6th Cir.1925), the alien must make the request at the time the witnesses' testimony is introduced.

The alien has the right to be present at and participate in the removal hearing. According to the INA, however, "any alien who, after written notice has been provided to him, does not attend a proceeding under this section, shall be removed in absentia if the Service establishes by clear, unequivocal, and convincing evidence that the written notice was so provided and that the alien is removable." INA § 240(b)(5). The Board of Immigration Appeals endorsed the fairness of this procedure in *In re S____* (BIA 1957), subject only to the conditions that the alien was served with the Notice to Appear (formerly "Order to Show Cause") and refused to appear without reasonable cause. If the alien is present at the hearing, s/he may choose either to testify or remain silent. The Supreme Court in *Hyun v. Landon* (Sup.Ct.1956), however, affirmed the right of the immigration judge to draw unfavorable inferences from the alien's silence. *See Cabral–Avila v. INS* (9th Cir.1978) (same holding). If necessary, the immigration judge can compel the alien to testify. According to the Seventh Circuit in *Laqui v. INS* (7th Cir.1970), the alien may claim the Fifth Amendment privilege against self-incrimination only if her/his alleged actions constitute a crime.

d. The Hearing

(1) CONDUCT OF THE HEARING

Removal hearings are open to the public unless the immigration judge closes the hearing entirely in order to protect witnesses, the alien, or the public interest. 8 C.F.R. § 3.27. At the outset of the hearing, the immigration judge must advise the alien of her/his rights during the hearing and inquire as to whether s/he waives any of those rights, place the alien under oath, read and explain the allegations of the Notice to Appear, enter the notice as an exhibit in the official record, and ask the alien to plead to the allegations in the Notice to Appear. 8 C.F.R. § 240.10(a). In a procedure analogous to pleading in the criminal context, the alien must either admit or deny the allegations of the Notice to Appear. If the alien admits the allegations and concedes removability, as usually occurs, the immigration judge accepts the plea and the hearing moves forward to determine issues of discretionary relief. 8 C.F.R. § 240.10(c). Alternatively, if the alien denies the allegations, the immigration judge requests the INS to assign a service counsel and continues with both sides presenting evidence. 8 C.F.R. § 240.10(d).

(2) EVIDENCE

Both the service counsel and the alien are allowed to present evidence to the removal hearing. The rules of evidence applicable to criminal proceedings, however, do not apply to removal hearings. The Supreme Court in *Bilokumsky v. Tod* (S.Ct.1923), noted that a failure to abide by judicial rules of evidence does not render a removal (formerly "deportation") hearing unfair. Evidence during a removal hearing is controlled by the Code of Federal Regulations; any type of evidence is admissible so long as it is material and relevant to the issues before the hearing. 8 C.F.R. § 240.7(a). The regulation allows hearsay evidence if it meets the test of relevance. In *Cunanan v. INS* (9th Cir.1988), however, the court refused to admit into evidence an affidavit from the alien's spouse indicating that her marriage was fraudulent. The court stated that admission of the affidavit would violate Due Process because the INS did not introduce the alien's spouse as a witness and did not inform the alien about her statement until the hearing date. Evidence may take the form of depositions and affidavits. If authenticated, tangible evidence is admissible. Either party may call witnesses to testify, but such testimony only will be taken under oath or affirmation administered by the immigration judge.

(3) ANCILLARY MATTERS

(a) Additional Charges. In most cases, the alien's removability is determined by the charges that appear in the Notice to Appear. The Ninth Circuit concluded in *Madrona Banez v. Boyd* (9th Cir.1956), that incorrect statements or errors in the Notice to Appear (formerly "Order to Show Cause") do not, however, render it invalid, if the service counsel establishes the correct information at the hearing. During the hearing, the service counsel may lodge additional charges for removal against the alien. 8 C.F.R. § 240.10(e). The additional charges must be submitted in writing. When submitted, the immigration judge reads and explains the additional charges to the alien. Again, the judge must inform the alien of her/his right to counsel and must recess the hearing to allow the alien additional time to meet the charges. 8 C.F.R. § 240.10(e). The Second Circuit in *United States ex rel. Catalano v. Shaughnessy* (2d Cir. 1952) upheld the procedure of lodging additional charges as consistent with Due Process.

(b) Designation of Country and Application for Discretionary Relief. During the hearing, the immigration judge must provide the alien with an opportunity to designate a country to which s/he would like to be sent in the event removal is ordered. INA § 241(b)(2). This designation does not constitute an admission of removability. After the alien has been given an opportunity to designate a country, the immigration judge may disregard her/his designation and name as an alternative country of removal any country of which the alien is a subject or national in the event that the alien's choice does not accept her/him. INA § 241(b)(2). The same section of the Immigration and Nationality Act sets up a system for

determining still another country of removal should the previous choices fail to accept the alien. Moreover, the Attorney General may disallow a country if s/he determines that removal would be prejudicial to the interests of the United States.

If the alien believes s/he is eligible for some form of discretionary relief, s/he must apply for it during the hearing. 8 C.F.R. § 240.11. (The types of discretionary relief available to the alien will be more fully discussed in "Relief From Removal" § 8–4, *infra*.) Again, an application for discretionary relief is not construed as an admission of removability. The alien may apply for cancellation of removal, adjustment of status, registry, or other appropriate relief. 8 C.F.R. § 240.11. The immigration judge must inform the alien of her/his apparent eligibility to apply for discretionary relief, and must allow the alien an opportunity to apply. The judge is not required to inform the alien about other types of available relief.

(c) The Decision

(1) Burden of Proof. The removal decision must be based on reasonable, substantial, and probative evidence in order to be valid. INA § 240(c)(3)(a). The INA provides that the INS has the burden of establishing by clear and convincing evidence that, in the case of an alien who has been admitted to the U.S., the alien is removable. INA § 240(c)(3)(a). The Supreme Court established this standard of proof in *Woodby v. INS* (Sup.Ct.1966). The Second Circuit held in *United States ex rel. Bishop v. Watkins* (2d Cir.1947) that initially, the government has the burden of proving, with clear and unequivocal evidence, that the alien is, indeed, an alien. The burden then shifts to the alien to prove the time, place, and manner of her/his entry into the United States. INA

§ 291. According to the Sixth Circuit in *Brader v. Zurbrick* (6th Cir.1930), the government must then meet and overcome positive evidence of the alien's legal right to be in the United States. If the government fails to meet its burden of proof, the immigration judge must decide for the alien.

(2) Rendering the Decision. The decision of the immigration judge may be either written or oral and must include a finding as to inadmissibility (formerly "excludability") or removability (formerly "deportability"). A formal enumeration of findings is not required. 8 C.F.R. § 240.12(a). The decision must either direct the alien's removal, the termination of the proceedings, or the granting of discretionary relief. The decision may be in the alternative. 8 C.F.R. § 240.12(c). If the decision is written, a copy must be served on the alien and the service counsel. Oral decisions, however, must be made with both parties present. 8 C.F.R. § 240.13. The decision is final unless there is an appeal. 8 C.F.R. § 240.14. The alien may appeal any decision to the board of immigration appeals (except there shall be no appeal from an order of removal entered in absentia), but must do so within thirty days of the decision. 8 C.F.R. § 240.15.

§ 8–4 RELIEF FROM REMOVAL

If the immigration judge finds the alien removable, the alien may seek relief from removal before the INS actually executes the order of removal. This section examines two major types of remedy available to the alien under a removal order—appeals, both administrative and judicial; and discretionary relief.

With IIRIRA's introduction of a single removal order, the judicial review scheme is correspondingly consolidat-

ed. AEDPA and IIRIRA enacted a number of outright
bars to judicial review. Furthermore, the still existing
standards of review are quite deferential to the administrative findings. *See* INA § 242(b)(4). The current statute consolidates several forms of pre-IIRIRA "relief from
deportation" into cancellation of removal. The new cancellation provisions are almost analogous to the pre-
IIRIRA forms of relief, but AEDPA and IIRIRA made it
more difficult for an alien to establish eligibility.

§ 8–4.1 Appeals and Relief

a. Motion to Reopen or Reconsider

An alien may move to reopen or to reconsider the
decision of the immigration judge by submitting Form I–
328 or the judge may do so on her/his own motion. 8
C.F.R. § 3.23(b)(ii). An alien may file one motion to
reopen proceedings within 90 days of a final administrative order of removal and one motion to reconsider the
decision within 30 days of the date of entry of a final
administrative order of removal. INA § 240(c)(5). The
INA does not impose a time limit on the filing of a
motion to reopen if the basis of the motion is to apply for
asylum and is based on changed country conditions. INA
§ 240(c)(6)(C)(ii). The immigration judge hears the motion unless the alien has already appealed the decision to
the Board of Immigration Appeals. The immigration
judge may grant the motion only if s/he is satisfied that
the evidence sought to be offered is material and was
unavailable at the time of the hearing. 8 C.F.R.
§ 3.23(b)(v)(3). The central characteristic of a motion to
reopen is the existence of new and additional facts which
were not and could not have reasonably been known in
the initial proceeding that would have a bearing on the

outcome. The motion to reopen should state with specificity the new facts and be supported by affidavits or other evidentiary material. INA § 240(c)(6)(B). The motion to reconsider should specify the errors of law or fact in the previous order and should be supported by pertinent authority. INA § 240(c)(5)(C). Motions to reconsider focus on errors of law or fact arising in the earlier proceedings and do not involve allegations of new facts. Hence, if the alien is seeking to have the judge reconsider the same evidence with no persuasive claim of legal error, the judge will deny the motion. The judge also may deny the motion because the alien has not established a prima facie case for the underlying substantive relief sought. *INS v. Abudu* (Sup.Ct.1988).

A motion to reopen for the purpose of providing the alien an opportunity to apply for discretionary relief that was available during the hearing will be denied unless the alien's right to make the application was not fully explained at the time of the hearing. 8 C.F.R. § 3.23. Likewise, in regard to a belated application for asylum, the judge may hold that the alien has not reasonably explained her/his failure to apply for asylum prior to completion of the initial removal proceedings, as required by 8 C.F.R. § 208.4. *Abudu*. Furthermore, in cases requesting discretionary relief (asylum, cancellation of removal, and adjustment of status, but not withholding of removal), the judge may ignore the above concerns and simply decide that even if the application were properly asserted, the alien is not entitled to the discretionary relief. *Id.* The appropriate standard of review of such denials on any of these grounds is abuse of discretion. The Court in *Abudu* stressed that motions to reopen are disfavored in removal proceedings because "[g]ranting such motions too freely will permit endless delay of deportation [now "removal"] by aliens creative and fertile enough to continuously produce new and material facts sufficient to establish a prima facie case." *Id.* After IIRIRA, a filing of a motion to reopen the hearing will no longer stay the execution of a pending removal order. The alien, therefore, must couple the motion to reopen with the request for a stay of removal.

b. Administrative Appeals

An appeal taken from a removal hearing is heard by the Board of Immigration Appeals (BIA). 8 C.F.R. § 3.1(b)(2). The BIA is supervised by the Department of Justice and is comprised of a Chairperson and fourteen additional members, all appointed by the Attorney General. 8 C.F.R. § 3.1(a)(1). The BIA has jurisdiction over the following appeals: decisions of the immigration judge in removal proceedings, decisions concerning discretionary relief, decisions involving administrative fines, decisions concerning petitions for immigrant status, decisions relating to bond or parole or detention of an alien, decisions of the immigration judge involving rescission of an adjustment of status, decisions of the immigration judge in asylum proceedings, and decisions of the immigration judge relating to Temporary Protected Status. 8 C.F.R. § 3.1(b).

In deciding the cases that come before it, the Board can exercise the discretion and authority conferred on it by the Attorney General. 8 C.F.R. § 3.1(d). Those powers include the right to dismiss summarily any appeal from removal proceedings if the party fails to substantiate the basis for the appeal. The Board may also dispose of a case by remanding it to the immigration judge, or in rare cases, by referring the case to the Attorney General for a decision. 8 C.F.R. § 3.1(d) & (h). Any decision made by the Board is administratively final although the alien may seek judicial review. 8 C.F.R. § 3.1(d)(2). The Board bases its decisions on the record of the removal hearing, briefs submitted by counsel, and oral argument. 8 C.F.R. §§ 3.1(e), 3.3(c), 3.5. Oral arguments are heard only if the petitioner requests an opportunity for an argument. 8 C.F.R. § 3.1(e). IIRIRA eliminated the automatic stay of a removal order upon service of a petition for review, unless the court orders otherwise. INA § 242(b)(3)(B).

c. Judicial Review of Orders of Removal

The INA authorizes the courts to take jurisdiction over certain decisions appealed from the BIA. *See* INA § 242. IIRIRA, however, has severely restricted judicial review of removal orders. The alien has thirty days from the administratively final order of removal to file a judicial appeal and such appeal no longer automatically stays removal unless the court affirmatively declares otherwise. INA §§ 242(b)(1), 242(b)(3)(B). In removal cases, the sole method for judicial review is by petition for review in the Court of Appeals. On a petition for review, the court may review not only a finding of removability, but also denials of motions to reopen. INA § 242(b)(6). The reviewing court decides the case on the basis of the administrative record, not by taking new evidence of its own. INA § 242(b)(4)(A).

The Eighth Circuit in *Daneshvar v. Chauvin* (8th Cir.1981) held that review of final orders of removal (formerly "deportation") lies exclusively in the Court of Appeals when removability (formerly "deportability") is in question and habeas corpus review is available only with respect to the denial of discretionary relief where removability itself is not an issue. Whenever the alien is being held in custody, habeas corpus is available to review the legality of the custody. (former INA § 106(a)(10)). The Fifth Circuit Court of Appeals in *United States ex rel. Marcello v. District Director* (5th Cir.1981) held that in enacting INA § 106(a)(10), Congress intended the phrase "held in custody" to mean actual physical custody in the place of detention. Until there is actual physical custody, the alien is required to seek review by direct appeal.

(1) REMOVAL APPEALS

The Supreme Court in *Foti v. INS* (Sup.Ct.1963) noted that the fundamental purpose behind the petition for review is to reduce the likelihood that the process of judicial review will be used by persons subject to removal to forestall departure by dilatory practices in the courts. The INA sets forth specific requirements for granting a petition for review. First, the appeal must be taken from a final order of removal. INA § 242(a)(1). According to the Supreme Court in *Cheng Fan Kwok v. INS* (Sup.Ct. 1968), Congress restricted review of removal orders to those orders entered during proceedings under INA § 240 (former INA § 242(b)).

IIRIRA eliminated judicial review over: (1) the summary removal provisions found in amended Section 235(b)(1) (except for habeas corpus petitions by aliens asserting lawful permanent resident status), (2) denials of discretionary relief from removal, and (3) orders of removal against criminal aliens. INA § 242. These limitations have caused considerable controversy as an unconstitutional limit on the right to petition for redress of grievance, a violation of Due Process, an impermissible suspension of habeas corpus, etc. *See* § 8–4.1.d(1), *infra*.

The Seventh Circuit Court of Appeals held that the district director's denial of a nonimmigrant student's applications for a school transfer and extension of stay was not reviewable in the Court of Appeals because the applications were not submitted pursuant to a proceeding under INA § 240 (former INA § 242(b)) or a motion to reopen such a proceeding. *Kavasji v. INS* (7th Cir. 1982). This rule was not altered by the Supreme Court when it held that the Ninth Circuit Court of Appeals had jurisdiction to review a constitutional challenge of the House of Representatives' authority to veto an immigration judge's suspension of deportation (now "a form of cancellation of removal"). *INS v. Chadha* (Sup.Ct.1983). Congress argued that the One–House veto authorized by the INA was not a proceeding under § 240 (former INA § 242(b)), and that the Court of Appeals therefore lacked jurisdiction under INA § 242 (former INA § 106) to review its constitutionality. The Court interpreted the term "final order" in § 242 to encompass all matters "on which the validity of the final order is contingent, rather than only those determinations actually made at the hearing." Because Chadha's deportation was contingent upon the validity of the challenged veto and because Chadha was directly attacking the deportation order, the Court of Appeals had jurisdiction under § 242.

In *Mohammadi–Motlagh v. INS* (9th Cir.1984), the Ninth Circuit confirmed that the *Chadha* decision did not signify a retreat from the narrow construction of § 242 (former INA § 106) adopted in *Cheng Fan Kwok*. The Court of Appeals in *Mohammadi–Motlagh* found no jurisdiction to review the denial of the alien's request for a school transfer because, in contrast to the purely legal question presented in *Chadha*, the alien's challenge of the district director's decision raised factual questions as to whether discretion was properly exercised.

Second, the INA authorizes judicial review only after the alien has exhausted administrative remedies available to her/him as of right. INA § 242(d)(1). Hence, if the alien has not appealed the decision of the immigration judge to the BIA, s/he may not seek review in the Court of Appeals. The Third Circuit in *Bak v. INS* (3d Cir. 1982) concluded that failure to exhaust administrative remedies deprives the Court of Appeals of jurisdiction to consider the case, but referred to a judge-made exception to the exhaustion requirement. Exhaustion is unnecessary if administrative appeal would be "futile." Administrative appeal would be futile if the BIA is absolutely bound by INS regulations and could not help but render the same decision.

Another potential exception to the exhaustion requirement is an allegation of "a wholesale, carefully orchestrated program of constitutional violations." *Haitian Refugee Center v. Smith* (5th Cir.1982). In *Haitian Refugee Center,* 4,000 Haitians claimed they had been denied Due Process and Equal Protection by accelerated INS removal (formerly "deportation") procedures instituted to achieve the mass removal of Haitian nationals seeking political asylum in the United States. The Haitians did not seek reversal of the district director's denial of their claims for asylum. Hence, the Fifth Circuit focused on the distinction between a constitutional challenge and a substantive claim of entitlement. The court held that the exhaustion requirement did not bar the district court from asserting jurisdiction. The Fifth Circuit decided that a pattern or scheme by immigration officials to violate the constitutional rights of aliens is independently reviewable in the district court under its federal question jurisdiction. The court, however, stressed the uniqueness of the case in warning that its holding was not to be construed as permitting a constitutional challenge in the district court based on a procedural ruling in a removal case with which an alien is dissatisfied.

Third, a federal court may review a final administrative order of removal only if another federal court has not decided the validity of the administrative order. The INA provides an exception for the cases when the reviewing court finds that the petition for review presents grounds that could not have been presented in the earlier proceeding, or that the remedy provided in that proceeding was inadequate or ineffective to test the validity of the administrative order. INA § 242(d)(2).

In addition, former INA § 106(c) precluded judicial review in cases where the alien has departed from the United States after entry of the removal order. The Ninth Circuit in *Mendez v. INS* (9th Cir.1977), however, held that if the government had illegally forced the alien to leave the United States, the court could grant a petition for review. The new judicial review provision in INA § 242(c) eliminated the requirement that the alien remain in the United States.

Finally, the scope of the review power of the Court of Appeals in removal cases is limited. The court is restricted to questioning whether the manner in which the proceeding was conducted was arbitrary, capricious, or illegal and whether the proceeding comported with the requirements of Due Process. *Biggin v. INS* (3d Cir. 1973). The appeals court may review only those issues which were raised during the removal hearing and which are part of the administrative record. INA § 242(b)(4).

The Tenth Circuit in *Pilapil v. INS* (10th Cir.1970), however, concluded that the Court of Appeals could consider constitutional issues raised by the alien on appeal even though they were not raised during the hearing, so long as the facts necessary to decide the issue are part of the administrative record.

d. Discretionary Relief

(1) GENERAL CONSIDERATIONS

The alien in a removal proceeding may apply for one or more of the available types of discretionary relief. If granted, discretionary relief eliminates or postpones the execution of the order of removal. The alien must generally apply for discretionary relief during the removal hearing. *See* 8 C.F.R. § 240.11. (The alien may apply for various types of discretionary relief, discussed below, prior to the removal hearing, *i.e.*, a request for asylum or registry. This section, however, examines discretionary relief only as it applies to the alien during removal proceedings.) In some circumstances, the alien may apply for discretionary relief after the removal hearing by moving to reopen the hearing. (*See* the previous section.) The immigration judge will grant a motion to reopen to apply for discretionary relief only if the circumstances which form the basis of the relief arose after the removal hearing. 8 C.F.R. § 3.23(b)(v)(3). Hence, if the alien believes s/he is eligible for any type of discretionary relief, s/he must apply during the removal hearing or risk being denied the opportunity to apply.

In determining whether to grant the requested relief, the judge undertakes a two-step process. First, the judge determines whether the alien is eligible for the particular form of relief. The alien has the burden of proving that s/he meets the statutory requirements. 8 C.F.R. § 240.8(d). Even though the alien may meet the requirements, however, the judge does not necessarily grant the relief. The immigration judge has the discretion to make the final determination as to whether the relief will be granted. Even though the alien may establish her/his eligibility, the Ninth Circuit in *Patel v. INS* (9th Cir. 1980), concluded that the judge may deny the requested relief.

IIRIRA specifically bars judicial review of any decision by the Attorney General with respect to discretionary relief. INA § 242(a)(2)(B)(i). This limitation on judicial review has caused considerable controversy. During the transitional period after the enactment of IIRIRA, various aliens in removal proceedings challenged the application of the 1996 amendments to their cases claiming it was unconstitutionally retroactive; in violation of their Due Process rights to a hearing prior to deportation/removal, and in violation of the Equal Protection principles as interpreted in the Fifth Amendment. In *Manuel Jurado–Gutierrez v. INS* (D.Colo.1997), the court stated that the application of IIRIRA to the petitioner's case was not unconstitutionally retroactive and that the petitioner had no Due Process right to a discretionary relief prior to deportation. The court, however, found that petitioner's Equal Protection claim of disparate treatment (i.e., between permanent residents who temporarily leave the country and those who do not) asserted a "substantial" constitutional violation for which habeas corpus review remains. During the next several years courts will need to consider many analogous challenges to the severe limitations on judicial review in IIRIRA.

(2) Types of Discretionary Relief

(a) *Voluntary Departure.* The Attorney General may permit an alien under removal proceedings to depart voluntarily from the United States at her/his own expense in lieu of removal proceedings or prior to the completion of such proceedings, if such alien is not removable as a result of her/his conviction of an aggravated felony at any time after admission or because s/he has engaged, is engaged, or at any time after admission engages in any terrorist activity. INA § 240B(a)(1). The Attorney General may also permit an alien voluntarily to depart at the alien's own expense after the conclusion of removal proceedings. INA § 240B(b). Relief under this section may be granted by district directors, assistant district directors for investigations, assistant district directors for examinations, officers in charge, chief patrol agents, service center directors, and assistant center directors for examinations. 8 C.F.R. § 240.25(a). Certain aliens are prohibited from applying for voluntary departure, including those found removable under aggravated felony or terrorism grounds, and those who were previously permitted voluntary departure after being found inadmissible for being present without admission or parole. INA §§ 240B(a)(1), 240B(b)(1)(C), 240B(c). Both versions of the voluntary departure, *i.e.* voluntary departure in lieu of or prior to the completion of removal proceedings (INA § 240B(a)), and at the conclusion of removal proceedings (INA § 240B(b)), are strictly limited in time. An alien who is granted permission to depart voluntarily in lieu of being subject to removal proceedings or prior to the completion of such proceedings must depart within 120 days (INA § 240B(a)(4)) and may be asked to post a bond. INA § 240B(a)(3). An alien who is granted voluntary departure at the conclusion of removal proceedings must depart within sixty days (INA § 240B(b)(2)) and *must* post a bond. INA § 240B(b)(3). Failure to depart, under either form of voluntary departure, results in a civil penalty, future inadmissibility for ten years, and ineligibility for several other forms of discretionary relief.

Voluntary departure is one of the most sought-after types of relief, especially when the alien concedes removability. Voluntary departure avoids the stigma of removal, enables the alien to select her/his own destination, and most importantly, facilitates the possibility of immediate return to the United States. An alien granted voluntary departure is not considered removed by the INS and, consequently, is not subject to any formal bar on return applicable to removed aliens. (Those aliens removed may not generally re-enter for at least ten years-twenty years if convicted for a second offense-and forever if convicted of an aggravated felony.)

In order to be eligible for voluntary departure, the alien must prove that s/he meets the statutory requirements. *Hibbert v. INS* (2d Cir.1977). First, an alien granted voluntary departure under INA § 240B must show that s/he has the ability to pay her/his own expenses of departing. According to the Ninth Circuit, in *Diric v. INS* (9th Cir.1968), failure to prove an ability to pay the expenses makes the alien ineligible for voluntary departure. (If, however, an alien granted voluntary departure under INA § 240B(a) is financially unable to depart at her/his own expense, the government may pay the departure expenses if the Attorney General deems the alien's removal to be in the best interest of the United States. INA § 240B(a).) Second, the INA provides that no individual shall be entitled to voluntary departure in lieu of removal proceedings or before the completion of removal proceedings if the alien is removable under (1) aggravated felony; or (2) terrorism grounds. INA § 240B(a)(1). The eligibility requirements for voluntary departure at the conclusion of removal proceedings are more extensive. To be entitled to voluntary departure at the conclusion of removal proceedings the alien (1) must have been physically present in the U.S. for at least one year immediately before the date the notice to appear was served; (2) must have been a person of good moral character for the previous five-year period; (3) must not have been removable under aggravated felony or national security (including terrorism) grounds; and (4) must show by clear and convincing evidence that s/he has the means to depart and intends to do so. INA § 240B(b)(1).

If the alien meets the statutory requirements, s/he is eligible for voluntary departure. The final decision, however, lies with the immigration judge and is discretionary. IIRIRA practically eliminated judicial review of voluntary departure decisions. INA §§ 240B(f), 242(a)(2)(B)(I). Further, the Attorney General may issue regulations that further limit eligibility for voluntary departure, and no court may review any such regulation. INA § 240B(e).

Another form of voluntary departure is "extended voluntary departure." Extended voluntary departure allows aliens from countries with dangerous public order situations to remain in the United States. Extended voluntary departure has been granted during certain periods to aliens from countries such as Afghanistan, Chile, Cuba, Ethiopia, Iran, Lebanon, Nicaragua, Poland, Uganda, and Vietnam. This policy has been increasingly criticized and challenged on the ground that extended voluntary departure is often granted or denied for improper political reasons. *See, e.g., Hotel & Restaurant Employees Union, Local 25 v. Smith* (D.D.C.1984). At the same time, others have advocated the extension of extended voluntary departure to individuals fleeing the strife in Central America. The practice of extended voluntary departure has been codified and largely replaced, at least for groups of aliens, by Temporary Protected Status under INA § 244. *See* §§ 10–2.4, 10–2.5. Extended voluntary departure may still be granted to individual aliens for humanitarian reasons.

(b) Cancellation of Removal. IIRIRA consolidates several forms of relief from removal into one single relief from removal: cancellation of removal. INA § 240. The first prong of relief for cancellation of removal is a remedy available only to certain lawfully admitted permanent residents and roughly corresponds to pre-IIRIRA "212(c) relief". INA § 240A(a). According to this section of the INA, "[t]he Attorney General may cancel removal in the case of an alien who is inadmissible or deportable [*sic*, "removable"] from the United States if the alien (1) has been lawfully admitted for permanent residence for not less than 5 years, (2) has resided in the U.S. continuously for seven years after having been admitted in any status, and (3) has not been convicted of any aggravated felony". INA § 240A(a). IIRIRA deleted the many previous disqualifications for this type of cancellation of removal. IIRIRA, however, also significantly expanded the definition of "aggravated felony" which now disqualifies a broader range of aliens. *See* INA § 101(a)(43). Further, even if the alien meets the statutory requirements, the BIA concluded in *In re Marin* (BIA 1978) that the granting of the relief is still discretionary.

The second prong of the cancellation of removal corresponds with the pre-IIRIRA "suspension of deportation." The INA § 240A(b) refers to cancellation of removal for "certain nonpermanent residents," but lawful permanent residents who do not meet the requirements of § 240A(a) are eligible for cancellation of removal under this section. The remedy under section § 240A(b) is available to both inadmissible and other removable aliens. In certain cases, the alien may be eligible for cancellation of removal and adjustment of status to that of an alien lawfully admitted for permanent residence. According to the Ninth Circuit in Fong v. INS (9th Cir.1962), the sole purpose of cancellation of removal (formerly "suspension of deportation") is to ameliorate the harsh consequences of removal for those aliens who have been present in the United States for long periods of time. The INA provides that the Attorney General or her/his designated representative may adjust to the status of an alien lawfully admitted for permanent residence any alien whom the Attorney General determines to meet the requirements of cancellation of removal. INA § 240A(b)(3). To be eligible, the alien must (1) have been physically present in the United States for a continuous period of not less than 10 years, (2) have been a person of good moral character, (3) have not been convicted of any of the crimes or document offenses that would make her/him inadmissible or removable, (4) not be subject to any of the security grounds of inadmissibility or removability, and (5) her/his removal would result in exceptional and extremely unusual hardship to her/his citizen or lawful permanent resident spouse, parent, or child. § 240A(b)(1).

Inadmissible or other removable battered spouses or children of U.S. citizens and permanent residents must meet less rigid eligibility requirements, although it is still difficult to qualify for cancellation of removal. The Attorney General may cancel removal if the alien (1) has been battered or subjected to extreme cruelty in the U.S. by a U.S. citizen or lawful permanent resident spouse or parent, (2) has a continuous physical presence in the U.S. for at least three years, (3) is a person of good moral character, (4) is not inadmissible or otherwise removable on criminal, document offense or security grounds, and (5) the removal would result in extreme hardship to the alien, the alien's child, or to the alien's parent.

The INA sets forth general eligibility rules that apply to both prongs of cancellation. INA § 240A(c). Aliens are ineligible for cancellation of removal if they are inadmissible or otherwise removable on national security grounds, fail to depart under a grant of voluntary departure, or are ordered removed after failing to appear at a removal proceedings. *See* INA § 240A(c)(1)-(6). Again, aliens applying for cancellation of removal bear the burden of proving statutory eligibility. 8 C.F.R. § 240.8(d). In determining whether the alien has been continuously present, the BIA in *Matter of Bufalino* (BIA 1965) concluded that the immigration judge must calculate the alien's residence from her/his last act which is subject to removal, and not from the time of admission into the United States.

In *INS v. Phinpathya* (Sup.Ct.1984) the Supreme Court construed the continuous physical presence requirement of INA § 240A strictly to forbid cancellation of removal (formerly "suspension of deportation") for an alien who had traveled three months outside the United States. The Court noted that Congress had changed the statute from "continuous residence" to limit the scope of discretionary relief from removal. Following the strict holding of *Phinpathya,* the 5th Circuit denied suspension of deportation to two otherwise eligible aliens who had been continuously physically present in the United States for twelve years except for a one night stay in Mexico. *Sanchez–Dominguez v. INS* (5th Cir.1986). The hardships resulting from *Phinpathya* led Congress to overturn the Court's holding by amending the statute to allow for "brief, casual, and innocent" absences from the United States which "did not meaningfully interrupt the continuous physical presence." Further, according to the most recent statutory amendments in IIRIRA, the statutory definition of continuous physical presence specifies the duration of any absences. INA § 240A(d)(2). An absence of more than 90 days or aggregate absence of more than 180 days interrupt continuous presence. INA § 240A(d)(2). The qualifying period for continuous residence or continuous physical presence ends with the service of a Notice to Appear for a removal proceeding, or when the alien commits certain offenses that would make him inadmissible or removable, whichever is earlier. INA § 240A(d)(1).

In addition to establishing continuous presence, the alien must also establish that s/he has been a person of good moral character for the same amount of time. Good moral character is determined by the provisions of INA § 101(f). The alien must not have been convicted of any of the crimes or document offenses that would make her/him inadmissible or otherwise subject to removal and not be subject to any of the security grounds of inadmissibility or removability. INA § 240A(b)(1)(C). Further, the alien must show that removal would result in "exceptional and extremely unusual hardship to the alien's citizen or permanent resident spouse, parent, or child."

INA § 240A(b)(1)(D). This statutory provision no longer refers to hardship to the alien. Battered spouses and children are subject to a less stringent "extreme hardship standard" including the hardship to the alien. INA § 240A(b)(2)(E).

The Supreme Court has held that the plain meaning of this statute controls. Hence, consideration of hardship does not extend to other relatives, even if the alien's relationship to that relative is the "functional equivalent" of a parent-child relationship. *INS v. Hector* (Sup. Ct.1986). The BIA has used several factors in determining the existence of unusual hardship, including age of the alien, family ties in the U.S. and abroad, length of residence in the U.S., condition of health, economic and political conditions in the alien's country, financial status, the possibility of adjustment of status, the alien's special assistance to the U.S., immigration history, and position in the community. *Matter of Anderson* (BIA 1978). The Ninth Circuit in *Villena v. INS* (9th Cir.1980) held that factors which support a finding of extreme hardship include (1) the alien's contribution to her/his community, (2) the effect of the alien's separation from family, including extreme hardship caused to the alien's citizen child by the alien's removal, and (3) economic hardship to the alien. In addition to the above factors, the BIA in *In re S__* (BIA 1953), considered the length of residence in the United States and the possibility of obtaining a visa abroad as factors relevant in determining whether the alien would suffer exceptional and extremely unusual hardship.

In *Matter of O–J–O-*, the BIA held that the removal of a twenty-four-year-old Nicaraguan who lived in the U.S. since the age of thirteen, would constitute extreme hardship since he lived in the U.S. during critical formative years and had become assimilated to life in the U.S. *See In re O–J–O–* (BIA 1996). Congress feared that this BIA decision would have a weakening impact on the extreme hardship standard. Accordingly, IIRIRA increased the required showing of hardship to "exceptional and extremely unusual hardship." This change was to emphasize that the alien must provide evidence of harm to his U.S. citizen or permanent resident spouse, parent, or child substantially beyond the harm that one would ordinarily expect to result solely from the removal.

A claim of the "extreme hardship" (for battered spouses or children) or "exceptional and extremely unusual hardship" (for others) must be supported by affidavit or other evidentiary material. The Attorney General and the INS have considerable discretion in determining what constitutes extreme hardship. *INS v. Jong Ha Wang* (Sup.Ct.1981). Furthermore, even if an alien's motion to reopen removal hearings is based on intervening circumstances demonstrating the required period of residence and extreme hardship, constituting a prima facie case of eligibility for cancellation of removal (formerly "suspension of deportation"), the Attorney General has the discretion to deny the motion to reopen. *INS v. Rios–Pineda* (Sup.Ct.1985); *INS v. Abudu* (Sup.Ct.1988). In *Rios–Pineda,* for example, the Court reasoned that the Attorney General can, in exercising his discretion, "legitimately avoid creating a further incentive for stalling by refusing to reopen [cancellation of removal] proceedings for those who became eligible for such [cancellation] only because of the passage of time while their meritless appeals dragged on." After IIRIRA, the discretionary authority of the Attorney General is no longer subject to any type of judicial review. INA § 242(a)(2)(B).

Until the decision in *INS v. Chadha* (Sup.Ct.1983), congressional approval was required for a suspension of deportation (now "cancellation of removal") even if the Attorney General had granted it. The suspensions (now "cancellations") granted under the INA § 244(a)(1) were considered approved by Congress if neither the House nor Senate passed a resolution against the suspension within a certain period of time. INA § 244(c). Suspensions authorized under INA § 244(a)(2), however, received congressional approval only if both the House and the Senate passed resolutions favoring the suspension. But, the Supreme Court in *Chadha* concluded that congressional vetoes of suspensions violated the constitutional separation of powers.

When adjustment to permanent resident status based on the cancellation of removal is granted, the Attorney General records the alien's admission to the United States as a permanent resident as of the date of the cancellation of removal or adjustment of status. INA § 240A(b)(3). The number of adjustments to permanent resident status based on such cancellations is limited to 4,000 per year. *Id.* The annual limitation upon adjustments evoked considerable debate when in February 1997, seven months before the fiscal year, the INS had almost reached the 4,000 annual cap on adjustments. The Office of the Chief Immigration Judge instructed immigration judges to reserve decision in any case in which cancellation (formerly "suspension") applications might otherwise be granted until a resolution could be reached within the Department of Justice. In November 1997, the President signed the Nicaraguan Adjustment and Central American Relief Act (NACARA) which permits certain Cubans and Nicaraguans to apply for permanent residence and allows certain Salvadorans, Guatemalans, and Eastern Europeans to apply for cancellation of removal under the more lenient rules available before the enactment of IIRIRA. The Act also provides relief for individuals affected by the annual cap by stating that the cap should only apply to cases decided after April 1, 1997, for the 1997 fiscal year. In addition, any unused numbers from fiscal year 1997 may carry over to the following fiscal year, and cases from protected class members and battered spouse cases will not count against the cap. The INS will regard the decisions reserved from fiscal year 1997 as decided in the fiscal year of the grant of adjustment. Accordingly, the INS will treat any case reserved in 1997 as adjusted during 1998 and as coming from an 8,000 allotment available for 1998, rather than a 4,000 allotment available for 1997. P.L. 105–100 (Nov. 19, 1997).

(c) *Adjustment of Status.* Still another type of discretionary relief for which the alien may apply during the removal proceedings is adjustment of status. Adjustment relieves certain aliens, whose status would otherwise entitle them to remain in the United States, from the hardship and expense of going abroad for long waits while an immigrant visa is processed. According to the INA, "[t]he status of an alien who was inspected and admitted or paroled into the United States may be adjusted by the Attorney General, in his discretion and under such regulations as he may prescribe, to that of an alien lawfully admitted for permanent residence if (1) the alien makes an application for such adjustment, (2) the alien is eligible to receive an immigrant visa and is admissible to the United States for permanent residence, and (3) an immigrant visa is immediately available to him at the time his application is filed." INA § 245(a).

Aliens who accept unauthorized employment prior to filing an application for adjustment of status are, in general, statutorily ineligible to adjust their status. INA § 245(c). The Immigration Reform and Control Act of 1986 (IRCA) amended INA § 245 to add to those aliens ineligible for adjustment of status any alien (other than an immediate relative of a U.S. citizen) who "is not in legal immigration status on the date of filing the application for adjustment of status or who has failed (other than through no fault of his own for technical reasons) to maintain continuously a legal status since entry into the United States." INA § 245(c). The Immigration Marriage Fraud Amendments of 1986 (IMFA) amended § 245(e) to make ineligible for adjustment of status any alien seeking to receive an immigrant visa on the basis of a marriage entered into during removal proceedings. The 1990 Act, however, softened this restriction by permitting an adjustment of status based on a marriage during deportation or exclusion proceedings (now "unified removal proceedings"), if the alien can show the marriage was entered in good faith. INA § 245(e). The IMFA also prohibited approval of a petition to grant an alien immediate relative or preference status by reason of a marriage entered into during removal proceedings until the alien has resided outside the United States for a two-year period beginning after the date of the marriage. INA § 204(g). These amendments substantially limit the availability of adjustment of status as a means to avoid removal.

In order to be eligible for adjustment of status the alien must show that s/he meets the statutory requirements. First, the alien must show that s/he has been inspected and admitted into the United States. Hence, according to the BIA in *In re Woo* (BIA 1966), aliens who enter illegally or on the basis of a willfully false claim of United States citizenship may not adjust their status. Second, the alien must show that s/he is eligible for a permanent resident visa. Since the alien applying for adjustment of status is considered to be "standing on the border," s/he must not be inadmissible under any of the categories of INA § 212(a). Aliens inadmissible for any reason are not eligible for adjustment of status. Third, and most importantly, the alien must show that there is an immigrant visa immediately available to her/him. The BIA concluded in *In re Wang* (BIA 1979) that the alien satisfied the requirement of immediate availability by showing that the visa was available when the application was filed—either with the district director before the Notice to Appear was issued or with the immigration judge after the removal proceedings commence. After IIRIRA, adjustment of status is one of the remedies unavailable for ten years to those aliens who fail to comply with the terms of their voluntary departure orders. INA §§ 240(b)(7), 240B(D). Aliens who have stayed in the U.S. after the expiration of the time authorized by the INS ("overstays") and aliens who entered without being admitted (formerly "entrants without inspection" (EWIs)) were, upon the payment of $1,000, able to apply for the adjustment of status to that of a lawful permanent resident, if an immigrant visa was available and no other bar applied. INA § 245(i). Section 245(i), which allowed overstays and entrants without inspection to avoid inadmissibility bars, expired on November 14, 1997. Congress, however, allowed aliens who filed visa petitions or labor certification applications by January 14, 1998, to continue to file 245(i) applications. P.L. 105–119 (Nov. 26, 1997). *See* § 9–1.4, *infra.*

(d) Asylum. Unlike the types of discretionary relief discussed above, the granting of asylum to an alien does not guarantee the alien permanent residence in the United States. (*See* chapter 10.) Asylum is the granting of temporary residence and the right to work in the United States for the period of time that the alien is entitled to refugee status. According to the INA, "an alien physically present in the United States or who arrives in the United States, irrespective of such alien's status, may be granted asylum in the discretion of the Attorney General if the Attorney General determines that such alien is a refugee.... " INA § 208(a). Hence, an alien may apply for asylum as a form of discretionary relief during a removal hearing, so long as s/he meets the requirements of refugee status. The INA defines "refugee" to mean "(A) any person who is outside any country of such person's nationality ... and who is unable or unwilling to return to, and is unable or unwilling to avail himself or herself of the protection of, that country because of persecution or a well-founded fear of persecution on account of race, religion, nationality, membership in a particular social group, or political opinion," or (B) "in such circumstances as the President may specify, any person who is within the country of such person's nationality and who is persecuted or who has a well-founded fear of persecution." INA § 101(a)(42).

An alien requesting asylum in removal proceedings may either apply for asylum during or after the removal hearing. 8 C.F.R. § 208.4. If the alien applies after the hearing, however, s/he must reasonably explain the failure to apply during the hearing. 8 C.F.R. § 208.4. The alien and the INS present evidence relating to the alien's request for asylum. If the immigration judge grants the requested asylum, the alien is admitted for one year.

After one year, any alien admitted under the provisions of the Refugee Act of 1980 (1) whose admission has not been terminated in the discretion of the Attorney General, (2) who has been physically present in the United States for at least one year, and (3) who has not acquired permanent resident status must report to the INS for inspection. INA § 209(a). After this inspection or after a hearing in front of an immigration judge, the INS will admit the alien as a lawful permanent resident if the alien is otherwise admissible as an immigrant. *Id.* The Attorney General may terminate the alien's asylum if s/he determines that the alien is no longer a "refugee" under the provisions of the INA. INA § 208(c)(2).

(e) Restriction on Removal (formerly Withholding of Deportation). Closely related to asylum is the relief identified by INA § 241(b)(3)(A) as "restriction on removal." This relief was previously known as "withholding of deportation" and the INS and immigration lawyers continue to use the phrase "withholding of removal" for this relief. The Nutshell uses these phrases interchangeably. The INA provides that "[t]he Attorney General may not remove an alien to a country if the Attorney General decides that the alien's life or freedom would be threatened in that country because of the alien's race, religion, nationality, membership in a particular social group, or political opinion." INA § 241(b)(3)(A). Certain aliens are not eligible for the relief of "restriction on removal": (1) who assisted in Nazi persecution or engaged in genocide; (2) who assisted in the persecution of an individual because of the individual's race, religion, nationality, membership in a particular social group, or political opinion; (3) who, having been convicted by a final judgment of a particularly serious crime, are a danger to the community of the U.S.; (4) who committed a serious

nonpolitical crime before entering the U.S., or (5) who otherwise represent a threat to the national security. INA § 241(b)(3)(B). Although similar in nature to asylum, restriction on removal differs in that the alien may request restriction on removal only as part of a removal hearing, while s/he may request asylum at any time.

The BIA had previously held that an alien under exclusion proceedings could not apply for withholding of deportation because s/he was not "within the United States" as required by the previous wording of the Act. *In re Cenatice* (BIA 1977). INA § 241(b)(3) now allows aliens to apply for "restriction on removal" as a relief from removal for inadmissibility (formerly "exclusion") as well as for other grounds (formerly "deportation").

The Supreme Court held in *INS v. Stevic* (Sup.Ct. 1984) that an alien seeking to avoid deportation (now "removal") pursuant to this section of the INA must establish a clear probability of persecution. According to the BIA in *Matter of McCullen* (BIA 1980), if the immigration judge determines that the alien meets the statutory requirements, the decision to grant withholding of deportation (now "restriction on removal") is mandatory. Asylum leads within one year to permanent residence; restriction on removal, however, only grants the alien temporary residence in the United States and only for so long as the alien's life or freedom is threatened.

(f) Stay of Removal. The alien may apply for a stay of removal by submitting Form I–246. The application is made to the district director of the INS. Such a stay is temporary and is granted at the discretion of the district director. Since the mere filing of a motion to reopen no longer automatically stays removal, the new regulations authorize the alien to couple a motion to reopen with a request for a stay to permit a decision on the motion. 8

C.F.R. § 3.8. Although a stay of removal is commonly used in connection with a motion to reopen or reconsider, the alien under a removal order may also move for a stay pending an application for permanent residence and in other exceptional circumstances. A pending application for immigration status, however, does not entitle an alien to a stay of removal; instead, the stay remains a discretionary matter. *Armstrong v. INS* (9th Cir.1971). If granted, the district director may impose such conditions as s/he decides are appropriate and s/he sets a specific time limit for the stay. An application for a stay does not relieve the alien from strict compliance with an outstanding order of removal. *Id.* The district director's decision on the application is not appealable, although the alien may renew the application before the BIA. *Id.*

(g) Other Discretionary Relief. In addition to the above types of discretionary relief, there are two other forms of relief that will not be as extensively discussed. The first, registry, is available to aliens who entered the United States prior to January 1, 1972. Registry is the creation of a record of lawful admission for permanent residence when the record is not otherwise available. INA § 249. In addition to proving that s/he entered prior to the specified date, the alien must also show that s/he has been a continuous resident of the United States, is a person of good moral character, and is otherwise eligible for citizenship. *Id.* The sole and limited purpose of registry is to ameliorate the harsh consequences of removal for those persons who have been long term residents of the United States. AEDPA amended Section 249(d) to make an alien "who has engaged, is engaged, or at any time after admission engages in any terrorist activity" ineligible for registry. INA § 249(d). Further, according to IIRIRA, aliens who have failed to appear at their removal hear-

ings or to comply with their voluntary departure orders are ineligible for registry for ten years. INA §§ 240(b)(7), 240(B)(D).

A second type of discretionary relief available to aliens is "deferred action status" or "non-priority status." The deferred action program is not created by statute but is an intra-agency administrative guideline contained within the Operations Instructions of the INS. District directors may place aliens under deferred action status, an act that gives some cases lower priority. "The deferred action category recognizes that the INS has limited enforcement resources and that every attempt should be made administratively to utilize these resources in a manner which will achieve the greatest impact under the immigration laws." O.I. 242.1a(22)(1993). Once placed under this status, the alien is informed that the INS will take no action to disturb her/his immigration status or that the alien's departure from the United States has been deferred indefinitely. *Id.*

In *Nicholas v. INS* (9th Cir.1979), the Ninth Circuit Court of Appeals found that, although the Operations Instructions create no substantive rights, they clearly and directly affect substantive rights—the ability of an individual to continue residence in the United States. The discretion allowed by the instructions should therefore be subject to review. The court held that the decision of an INS district director upon an application for non-priority status will stand unless it "so departs from an established pattern of treatment of others similarly situated without reason, as to be arbitrary and capricious, and an abuse of discretion."

After *Nicholas* the INS amended its Operations Instructions to indicate that deferred action does not create an entitlement and to specify the factors to be used in making deferred action determinations, including the likelihood of ultimately removing the alien and the presence of sympathetic factors. O.I. 242.1a(22)(1993).

(h) Estoppel. Occasionally, the conduct of the United States government is a substantial cause of an alien's removability, such as when an alien relies on false information given by a government employee. In these cases the courts have been quite reluctant to estop the government from removing the alien. Despite opportunities to do so, however, the Supreme Court has not completely ruled out the doctrine of estoppel in removal cases. In holding that an 18–month delay on the part of the INS in processing the alien's adjustment of status application falls short of affirmative misconduct in *INS v. Miranda* (Sup.Ct.1982), the Court was not required to reach the question of whether affirmative misconduct in a particular case would estop the government from enforcing the immigration laws.

Similarly, in most cases where the estoppel issue has been addressed by a lower court the decision has turned on whether affirmative misconduct occurred. The courts usually have held that there was no affirmative misconduct and therefore no estoppel was appropriate. A few lower courts, however, have held the government was estopped from removing the alien as a result of the government's affirmative misconduct. In *McLeod v. Peterson* (3d Cir.1960), the alien would have complied with the continuous presence requirement for cancellation of removal (formerly "suspension of deportation") had the INS not erroneously informed him that he was ineligible for nonquota status and advised him that his voluntary departure from the United States would aid his wife in making the necessary application for his legal re-entry. The Third Circuit Court of Appeals ignored the alien's departure and held that he had complied with the requirement of five years presence. In *Corniel–Rodriguez v. INS* (2d Cir.1976), U.S. consular officers in the Dominican Republic violated 22 C.F.R. § 42.122(d), by failing to warn an alien who was issued a visa as an unmarried minor child of a special immigrant that she would forfeit her exemption from the labor certification requirement for entry if she married before admission to the United States. This violation of a regulation by the consular officers precluded removal of the alien despite the alien's marriage three days before her departure from the Dominican Republic.

The estoppel doctrine also has been addressed in immigration cases outside the removal context. *See, e.g., Montana v. Kennedy* (Sup.Ct.1961) (refusal of a U.S. consular officer to issue a passport to a pregnant U.S. citizen to enable her to re-enter the U.S., at a time when the U.S. did not require passports for citizens to return to the U.S., was not misconduct such that the government was estopped from denying the child's U.S. citizenship when born abroad); *INS v. Hibi* (Sup.Ct.1973) (the government's failure after World War II to publicize fully the statutory right of Filipino servicemen to apply for naturalization and to provide a naturalization representative in the Philippines at all times during the period of eligibility did not rise to the level of affirmative misconduct); *INS v. Pangilinan* (Sup.Ct.1988) (Supreme Court rejected applicability of estoppel doctrine to claims about the same situation in the Philippines as in *Hibi*); *Podea v. Acheson* (2d Cir.1950) (alien did not lose his U.S. citizenship by serving in a foreign army and swearing allegiance to a foreign sovereign after an erroneous State Department ruling that the alien had already lost his U.S. citizenship because of certain prior acts).

CHAPTER 9

INADMISSIBILITY

Immigration law requires a higher standard of personal conduct for individuals who wish to be admitted to the United States than for aliens who have already been properly admitted and may have committed some offense for which they may be subject to removal. Individuals who have been admitted and lived in the United States ordinarily have jobs, family, friends, and other significant ties to this country; they should not be deprived of the right to remedies without a showing of very unacceptable conduct. IIRIRA for the first time in 1996 required that an alien have been admitted to the U.S. by an immigration officer in order to benefit from the application of the slightly less severe removal criteria. Previously, even aliens who entered the U.S. without inspection, often by unlawfully avoiding border officials, were allowed the benefits of the more favorable rules and criteria of deportation. As a result of these changes, aliens who had entered without inspection and have been present in the U.S. for many years will be subject to the same inadmissibility grounds as aliens arriving at a port of entry.

Accordingly, grounds for inadmissibility (formerly "grounds for exclusion") now apply to any alien who has not been properly admitted into the United States. IIRIRA replaced the term "inadmissible" for the previous concept of "excludable" aliens and redrew the line between aliens who are inadmissible and aliens who are otherwise removable (formerly "deportable"). Grounds for removal (formerly "grounds for deportation") only apply after an alien has been inspected and admitted. IIRIRA also consolidated the separate "exclusion" and "deportation" proceedings of the past into a single form of removal proceeding, but aliens who have been admitted have more procedural rights than those persons who have not been officially accepted. *See* chapter 8.

Ordinarily, the consular official who must determine the alien's eligibility for a visa considers whether any of the grounds for inadmissibility apply. Even if s/he determines that none do, however, an Immigration and Naturalization Service official can still make a contrary determination at the border when the alien actually attempts to be admitted to the United States.

§ 9–1 GROUNDS FOR INADMISSIBILITY

An alien seeking to be admitted into the U.S. must avoid any of the grounds for inadmissibility as detailed in INA § 212(a). Aliens fitting one or more of the classes listed in this section, are "ineligible to receive visas and ineligible to be admitted to the United States." INA § 212(a).

Before the 1990 Act, the INA listed 34 classes of inadmissibility (formerly "exclusion"). The 1990 Act updated what was previously considered an unnecessarily complex classification scheme. Until the 1990 changes, even the most archaic classes remained intact; *e.g.,* inadmissibility of "paupers, professional beggars, or vagrants" as one class and homosexuals as another. The 1990 Act eliminated both classes. In 1996, IIRIRA added a number of new grounds of inadmissibility. Section 212(a) as it now stands divides the classes into ten categories: health-related grounds; criminal and related grounds; security and related grounds; public charge proscription; labor certification requirements and qualifications for certain immigrants; illegal entrants and immigration violators proscription; documentation requirements; ineligibility for citizenship; aliens unlawfully present; and miscellaneous. After 1996 among aliens newly barred from being admitted are persons who have been unlawfully present in the U.S., former citizens who renounced citizenship to avoid taxation, certain "student visa abusers," individuals who falsely claim citizenship or voted unlawfully, uncertified foreign health-care workers, and immigrants who cannot document that they have been vaccinated against vaccine-preventable diseases. IIRIRA also made more stringent the existing grounds for document fraud, terrorist activities, and for persons previously ordered removed.

§ 9–1.1 Health–related Grounds

Section 212(a) begins with grounds for inadmissibility based on the alien's physical or mental health. Aliens who have a "communicable disease of public health significance" are inadmissible as are those persons with a "physical or mental disorder and behavior associated with the disorder that may pose ... a threat to the property, safety, or welfare of the alien or others." INA § 212(a)(1)(A). Moreover, a drug addict or abuser is inadmissible under this section. INA § 212(a)(1)(A)(iv). IIRIRA amended this section to render inadmissible an alien who seeks admission as an immigrant, or who seeks to adjust to the status of lawful permanent resident, and who failed to document that s/he has been vaccinated against   vaccine-preventable   diseases.   INA § 212(a)(1)(A)(ii).

The Congress and the Executive branch have for some time debated whether to declare inadmissible people who have tested positive for the Human Immunodeficiency Virus (HIV), the virus believed to cause Acquired Immune Deficiency Syndrome (AIDS). Congress declared inadmissible people testing HIV-positive originally under an appropriations bill rider in 1987. The 1990 Act then incorporated the reference to "communicable diseases of public health significance." In response, the Department of Health and Human Services (HHS) promulgated proposed regulations that restricted this class to diseases whose public health significance resulted from their contagious nature. Because AIDS/HIV cannot be spread through casual contact, it was removed from the list of grounds for inadmissibility, leaving the provision on health-related grounds limited to carriers of tuberculosis and similar communicable diseases.

The HHS proposal generated considerable criticism, particularly from conservatives in Congress and the Bush administration. In May 1991 the INS implemented the 1990 Act by defining "communicable diseases of public significance" to make inadmissible to the United States persons who have tested positive for HIV, as well as tuberculosis, syphilis in its infectious stage, gonorrhea, leprosy, and several other diseases. The INA, as it currently reads, makes inadmissible any alien "who is determined to have a communicable disease of public health significance, which shall include infection with the etiologic agent for acquired immune deficiency syndrome." INA § 212(a)(1)(I). Under INA § 212(g), however, the Attorney General may waive inadmissibility for an alien who has communicable disease of public health significance, including HIV, and who is the spouse, unmarried son or daughter, or the minor unmarried lawfully adopted child of a U.S. citizen or permanent resident. In addition, INA § 212(d) authorizes a waiver for nonimmigrants, which would allow persons who have tested positive for HIV to attend conferences in the U.S. and visit this country.

§ 9–1.2   Criminal and Related Grounds

Section 212(a)(2) renders inadmissible any alien who has committed a "crime involving moral turpitude" but provides exceptions for minor offenses and crimes committed by juveniles. *See* Grounds for Removal, § 8–2, *supra* for a discussion of how courts have defined "moral turpitude." The INA makes inadmissible aliens violating laws relating to controlled substances, or aliens reasonably believed by a consular or immigration official to be engaged in drug trafficking. INA § 212(a)(2)(C). An alien participating in prostitution or otherwise benefitting from prostitution or commercialized vice is inadmissible. INA § 212(a)(2)(D). In addition, aliens who departed from the U.S. after receiving immunity for a serious criminal offense in the U.S. are inadmissible unless they subsequently submitted to the jurisdiction of a U.S. court with respect to that offense. INA § 212(a)(2)(E).

§ 9–1.3   Security and Related Grounds

Prior to the 1990 Act, the national security grounds of inadmissibility were extremely detailed—excluding anarchists, Communists, subversives, and individuals who advocated overthrow of the government through violent means. The Supreme Court upheld this provision against a First Amendment challenge in *Kleindienst v. Mandel*

(Sup.Ct.1972). The Court reasoned that aliens have no constitutional right to be admitted into the United States, and U.S. citizens have no right to insist that aliens be admitted to the country so that ideas may be exchanged. Essentially, Congress' plenary power to control immigration supersedes a citizen's right to receive information under the First Amendment.

Section 212(a)(3), as modified by the 1990 Act, rendered inadmissible aliens believed to seek entry "solely, principally, or incidentally" to engage in activities which violate espionage laws or whose purpose it is to overthrow the U.S. government by unlawful means. INA § 212(a)(3)(A). Any alien who has engaged in terrorist activity, is engaged in, or is believed likely to do so in the future is inadmissible. INA § 212(a)(3)(B). The INA specifically states that a member of the Palestine Liberation Organization will be considered engaged in terrorist activity for the purposes of inadmissibility. INA § 212(a)(3)(B)(i)(II). *See United States v. P.L.O.* (S.D.N.Y.1988). AEDPA expanded the terrorist ground by rendering inadmissible an alien who is a representative or member of a foreign terrorist organization. INA § 212(a)(3)(B)(i)(III), (IV). Further, according to IIRIRA, an alien who has, under circumstances indicating an intention to cause death or serious bodily harm, incited terrorist activity, is inadmissible. INA § 212(a)(3)(B)(i)(III).

The D.C. Circuit held in *Abourezk v. Reagan* (D.C.Cir. 1986) that the government's decision that an anarchist or a Communist party member is inadmissible (formerly "excludable") must be based on projected engagement in activities prejudicial to the public interest, and such perception must be independent of the fact of membership alone in an organization.

Any alien who the Secretary of State believes will have adverse foreign policy consequences is inadmissible. INA § 212(a)(3)(C)(i). The INA, however, provides less stringent standards of inadmissibility for foreign government officials or candidates for election to a foreign government position. INA § 212(a)(3)(C)(ii). An immigrant who is or has been a member or affiliated with the Communist or other totalitarian party is inadmissible. INA § 212(a)(3)(D)(i). (This ground of inadmissibility is not applicable to nonimmigrants.) Inadmissibility for membership in the Communist or other totalitarian party is waived if the alien was an involuntary member; terminated her/his membership at least two years before the date of application for admission into the U.S., and s/he is not a threat to the security of the U.S.; or when waiver will serve a humanitarian purpose, assure family unity, or when it is otherwise in the public interest. INA § 212(a)(3)(D)(ii),(iii),(iv). Furthermore, any alien who participated in or was affiliated with the Nazi government is inadmissible. INA § 212(a)(3)(E).

§ 9–1.4   Grounds for Inadmissibility for Previously Removed and Unlawfully Present Aliens

Any alien is inadmissible if s/he has been ordered summarily removed within five years, ordered removed within ten years, departed the U.S. while an order of removal was outstanding within ten years, ordered removed in the case of a second or subsequent removal within twenty years, or removed for an aggravated felony within twenty years. INA § 212(a)(9)(A). IIRIRA amended this section to add new grounds for inadmissibility for aliens who have been "unlawfully present" in the United States and then seek admission. According to the INA, "an alien is deemed to be unlawfully present in the United States if the alien is present in the United States after the expiration of the period of stay authorized by the Attorney General or is present in the United States without being admitted or paroled." INA § 212(a)(9)(B)(ii). *(cf.* 7–9.2, *supra).* An alien who has been unlawfully present for a period of more than 180 days but less than one year and voluntarily departs is barred from admission into the U.S. for three years. INA § 212(a)(9)(B)(i)(I) . An alien who has been unlawfully present for one year or more is barred from admission into the U.S. for ten years. INA § 212 (a)(9)(B)(i)(II). The three year and ten year bars apply to both (1) aliens who have stayed in the U.S. after the expiration of the time authorized by the INS ("overstays") and (2) aliens who entered without being admitted (formerly "entrants without inspection" (EWIs)). Persons who have engaged in unauthorized employment in the U.S., overstays who became eligible to become immigrants within one of the preference classifications, and all entrants without inspection were, upon the payment of $1,000, eligible to apply for adjustment of status to that of a lawful permanent resident, if an immigrant visa was available and no other bar applied. INA § 245(i). Section 245(i), which allowed overstays and entrants without inspection to avoid inadmissibility bars, expired on November 14, 1997. Congress, however, allowed aliens who have filed visa petitions or labor certification applications to continue to file 245(i) applications until January 14, 1998. P.L. 105–119 (Nov. 26, 1997).

The three-and ten-year bars do not apply to permanent residents, minors, asylees, persons protected by family unity, and certain battered women and children. INA § 212(a)(9)(B)(iii). (Family unity protects aliens who are the parent, spouse, son, daughter, brother, or sister of a U.S. citizen or lawful permanent resident, and whose removal would result in hardship to the U.S. citizen or lawful permanent resident relative.) Inadmissibility may also be waived for an immigrant, who is a spouse, son or daughter of a U.S. citizen or permanent resident provided that extreme hardship to the citizen or permanent resident spouse or parent is established. INA § 212 (a)(9)(B)(v). An alien who has not been admitted and has been unlawfully present for an aggregate period of more than one year or has been ordered removed and then enters or attempts to enter without being admitted may be permanently barred from returning to the U.S. INA § 212(a)(9)(C)(i). This permanent bar applies to aliens who entered without being admitted and not to aliens who overstayed their visas ("overstays"). The Attorney General may waive inadmissibility under this bar for an alien seeking admission more than ten years after the date of the alien's last departure from the U.S. INA § 212(a)(9)(C)(ii).

§ 9–1.5 Other Grounds for Inadmissibility

a. Public Charge

Any alien who is believed likely to become a public charge is inadmissible at the time of application. INA § 212(a)(4)(A). The amended INA lists the alien's age, health, family status, assets, resources, financial status, and affidavit of support as factors to be considered in determining whether the alien is likely to become a public charge. INA § 212 (a)(4)(B).

Immediate relatives of U.S. citizens and immigrants under family-based preferences are inadmissible without an affidavit of support. INA § 212 (a)(4)(D). A sponsor must agree in the affidavit to provide support for the alien at an annual income that is not less than 125% of the federal poverty line during the period in which the affidavit is enforceable. INA § 213A(a)(1)(A). The affidavit is enforceable with respect to benefits provided for an alien before her/his naturalization, or before the alien has worked 40 qualifying quarters, that is, ten years. INA § 213A(a)(2). The sponsored alien, the federal government, any state, or any other entity that provides any means-tested public benefit may enforce the affidavit against the sponsor. INA § 213A(A)(1)(B). The entity that provided the sponsored alien with means-tested public benefits shall request reimbursement by the sponsor, and may bring legal action in federal or state court if the sponsor fails to repay. INA § 213A(b)(A),(B).

b. Alien Employment Certification

The INA lists the criteria for labor certification, without which an alien immigrating under § 203(b) would be inadmissible. INA § 212(a)(5). This ground of inadmissibility has resulted in a process, administered by the U.S. Department of Labor and the State Employment Services, known as labor certification. In the labor certification process an employer or prospective employer must demonstrate to the satisfaction of the Department of Labor that there are not sufficient qualified, willing U.S. workers to serve in jobs for which the aliens are qualified and willing to perform. In filing a labor certification application, the employer or prospective employer must demonstrate a need for foreign workers by explaining that the procedure used to recruit U.S. workers had not revealed any qualified and available employees. *See* 5–5.1, *supra.*

c. Illegal Entrants and Immigration Violators

IIRIRA in 1996 amended the grounds for inadmissibility to render inadmissible any alien who is present in the U.S. "without being admitted or paroled, or who arrives in the United States at any time or place other than as designated by the Attorney General." INA § 212(a)(6)(A)(i). Aliens who entered without being admitted are considered as applicants for admission.

An alien who entered without being admitted and who has not been physically present in the U.S. for two years may be subjected to expedited removal. INA § 235(b)(1)(A)(iii)(II). Such an alien may also be ordered removed pursuant to the ordinary removal procedures under INA § 240 in which s/he has the burden of proving admissibility beyond doubt or lawful presence by clear and convincing evidence. (*See* § 8–3.2, *supra* for further discussion of removal proceedings under § 240.) An alien who without reasonable cause fails or refuses to attend or remain in attendance at a removal proceeding is inadmissible for five years. INA § 212(a)(6)(B). Aliens who entered without being admitted are also subject to three and ten year bars to admissibility for aliens unlawfully present. *See* § 9–1.4, *supra*; INA § 212 (a)(9)(B)(ii). In addition, those aliens are subject to civil penalties for illegal entry of $50 to $250 for each entry or attempted entry. The fine doubles for an alien who has previously been subjected to a civil penalty under this section. INA §§ 212(a)(6)(F), 275(b). Any alien who has made a material misrepresentation of fact in the application process, who falsely claims or has claimed U.S. citizenship, or who was admitted as a nonimmigrant and who has obtained benefits for which s/he was not eligible, is inadmissible. INA § 212(a)(6)(C). Further, any alien who is a stowaway, who has encouraged, induced, assisted, abetted, or aided the illegal entry of other aliens, or who violated the terms of her/his F–1 visa status is inadmissible. The violators of F–1 visa status are inadmissible until they have been outside the U.S. for a continuous period of 5 years after the date of violation. INA § 212(a)(6)(D),(E),(G). The INA, however, does provide an exception to inadmissibility for certain battered women and children. INA § 212(a)(6)(A)(ii).

d. *Documentation Requirements*

Section 212(a)(7) spells out the documentation requirements for an alien seeking admission. An unexcused failure to possess the travel documents renders an alien inadmissible. The alien at the time of application must have a valid immigrant visa, re-entry permit, border crossing identification card, other valid entry document, and a valid unexpired passport, other suitable travel document, or document of identity and nationality. INA § 212(a)(7).

e. *Aliens Ineligible for Citizenship and "Miscellaneous"*

Immigrants permanently ineligible for citizenship are inadmissible, as are those persons who departed from the United States solely to evade military conscription. INA § 212(a)(8). Further, any alien is inadmissible if s/he is entering the U.S. to be a polygamist, an international child abductor, an unlawful voter, or a former U.S. citizen but renounced her/his citizenship to avoid taxation. INA § 212(a)(10).

§ 9–2 PROCEDURAL PROCESS

IIRIRA replaced the separate "exclusion" and "deportation" proceedings with a single "removal proceeding." The removal proceeding is used to compel the departure of both an alien who has already been admitted into the United States and an alien who is seeking admission or who had entered the U.S. without inspection. Inadmissible and otherwise removable (formerly "deportable") aliens are still subject to different procedural rules as to burden of proof and discretionary relief. *See* § 9–2.3, *infra*.

§ 9–2.1 Admission, Entry, and Re–entry

Before IIRIRA, aliens who were outside the U.S. and were seeking to enter (now "to be admitted") were subject to various inadmissibility (formerly "exclusion") grounds. The aliens who had already entered, either legally or illegally, could not have been removed unless they fell within a separate list of deportation grounds. Entry determined the grounds and procedures which would govern. An alien who successfully "entered" the U.S.—either by being inspected and admitted or by avoiding inspection and becoming free from official restraint in the U.S.—was entitled to the greater rights at a deportation hearing rather than an exclusion proceeding. These previous distinctions between aliens who "entered" and those who had not were difficult to apply and achieved rather perverse results. It was not always easy to determine whether an alien had successfully evaded inspection and become free of restraint. Also, such a distinction actually encouraged aliens to evade inspection, so that they would obtain the greater rights under deportation.

IIRIRA instead focused on admission rather than entry. According to the amended INA, "[the] terms admission and admitted mean, with respect to an alien, the lawful entry of the alien into the United States after inspection and authorization by an immigration officer." INA § 101(a)(13)(A). An admission thus involves physical presence, inspection, and entry. Any alien present in the U.S. who has not been admitted is regarded as an applicant for admission. INA § 235(a)(1). Even though IIRIRA replaced the definition of "entry" with the new definition for "admission," various provisions of the INA still refer to entry. Entry thus remains a concept in the immigration law, but its impact on the legal rights of aliens is much less pivotal.

The pre-IIRIRA "re-entry doctrine" held that the word "entry" in the INA refers to any coming into the U.S., not simply the *first* entry of the alien. Hence, a permanent resident alien may have been subject to the grounds of inadmissibility at the border when s/he leaves and returns to the United States.

In *United States ex rel. Volpe v. Smith* (Sup.Ct.1933) the Supreme Court upheld the removal of an alien who, after 24 years of residence in the U.S. following a lawful entry, was held to be inadmissible on his return from a brief visit to Cuba. The Court's restrictive view concluded that "entry" included any coming of an alien from a foreign country whether such coming was the alien's first entry or not. The Court in *Rosenberg v. Fleuti* (Sup.Ct. 1963) departed from this rigid application, recognizing that an alien does not make an "entry" upon his return to the United States where he had no intent to leave, or did not in fact leave the country voluntarily. Hence, an innocent, casual, and brief excursion outside the United

States was not intended as a departure disruptive of the resident alien's status, and the alien should not be subject to the conditions of an entry.

IIRIRA apparently did not change this basic analysis of the re-entry doctrine but gave it a somewhat clearer definition. When the returning permanent resident seeks admission under § 101(a)(13)(C), s/he becomes subject to inadmissibility grounds at the border. *See* INA § 212(a). A permanent resident alien is regarded as seeking an admission when s/he (1) has abandoned or relinquished her/his status, (2) has been absent from the United States for a continuous period in excess of 180 days, (3) has engaged in illegal activity after her/his departure from the U.S., (4) has departed from the U.S. while in removal proceedings, (5) has committed criminal and related offense identified in section 212(a)(2), or (6) is attempting to enter at a time or place other than that designated by the INS or has not been admitted to the U.S. after the inspection and authorization by the immigration officer. INA § 101(a)(13)(C). If the alien is nonetheless admitted, s/he may be later subject to removal for having been inadmissible at the time of entry. *See* INA § 237(a)(1)(A). When s/he is removed, the five year time ban against admission begins again to run. *See* INA § 237(a)(2)(A)(I).

§ 9–2.2 Parole

If an alien is seeking admission to the U.S., the inspecting immigration officer may elect to release the alien on parole pending further investigation. Parole allows an alien to travel away from the border and detention facilities while remaining subject to the same procedural rights in removal proceedings as a person who is just arriving at the frontier. The alien who is admitted on parole is not officially "admitted" and is not entitled to the greater procedural rights in a later removal proceeding of a person who has been inspected and accepted. The court in *Leng May Ma v. Barber* (Sup.Ct.1958) held that a parolee still has not satisfied the criteria for "admission," (formerly "entry," *i.e.,* freedom from official restraint).

IIRIRA discourages the INS from granting parole to large groups or classes of aliens and requires each parole decision to be rendered on a case-by-case basis for humanitarian reasons or reasons of a public interest. Parole can be used for a variety of reasons, such as preventing the separation of families. The concept of parole has been extended by the INS to include "advance parole" where an alien in the U.S., who wishes to leave, but who will not possess a status entitling her/him to admission may be issued advance parole before departing, thus ensuring a successful return to the U.S.

§ 9–2.3 The Removal Hearing for Inadmissible Aliens

In a removal hearing, an applicant for admission must prove that s/he is "clearly and beyond doubt" entitled to be admitted and is not inadmissible under Section 212. INA § 240(c)(2)(A). If the alien is not applying for admission, s/he must establish "by clear and convincing evidence that s/he is lawfully present in the United States pursuant to prior admission." INA § 240(c)(3)(A). The INS then has the burden to establish "by clear and convincing evidence that the alien who has been admitted into the United States is subject to removal." *See* INA § 240(c)(3)(A).

Removal proceedings commence when the INS serves on the alien a Notice to Appear at the immigration court. The notice contains the time and place of the hearing, the alleged facts and charged inadmissibility grounds, and the alien's procedural rights. INA § 239. During the hearing, the arriving alien is entitled to many attributes of procedural Due Process just as the alien who has been admitted into the United States. Unless the alien requests otherwise, the hearing may not start until ten days after service of the Notice to Appear to allow the alien an opportunity to secure counsel. INA § 239(b)(1). If the alien is unable to procure counsel within 10 days, the hearing may proceed. INA § 239(b)(3). *See also* § 8–3.2, *supra* on discussion of Notice to Appear.

An alien arriving in the United States may not, however, designate a place of removal, but is removed to the country where the alien boarded the carrier of arrival. INA § 240A(b). An alien who has previously been admitted may designate the country to which s/he will be sent after removal. Similarly, some forms of relief from removal are not available for the arriving alien but only to an alien who has been admitted. Indeed, several forms of relief are available only to persons who have been physically present in the United States for a continuous period of not less than ten years. *See* § 240A(b), chapter 8. The INA established separate provisions governing the detention of arriving aliens as well as detention and release on bond pending removal proceedings for aliens apprehended within the United States. INA §§ 235(b)(2), 236. The INA also sets out specific removal rules for aliens arriving at a port of entry who are ordered removed and general rules for the detention and release of aliens ordered removed. INA §§ 241(c), 241(a).

In *Landon v. Plasencia* (Sup.Ct.1982) the Supreme Court reaffirmed that a permanent resident, who had been outside the United States for a few days and was attempting to return, must be entitled to procedural Due Process in any removal (formerly "exclusion") hearing. The Court particularly questioned whether Due Process was accorded when (1) it was unclear whether the government or the alien had the burden of proof, (2) the alien received only 11 hours notice of the charges and the hearing, and (3) the alien was allowed to waive the right to counsel without being informed of the availability of free legal services. An alien seeking initial admission to the U.S. does not, however, have the constitutional right to Due Process beyond the procedures afforded by statutes and regulations.

Before IIRIRA, the usual procedure for obtaining judicial review of an administratively final removal order for inadmissible aliens was to petition for a writ of habeas corpus. The Supreme Court in *Brownell v. We Shung* (Sup.Ct.1956) upheld a habeas corpus petition as the proper method of review of removal orders for inadmissible aliens (formerly "exclusion orders"). After IIRIRA, judicial review of expedited removal under INA § 235(b)(1) is available only in habeas corpus proceedings. *See* 8–4.1.c(1), *supra*. In habeas proceedings, review is limited to determinations of whether the petitioner (1) is an alien; (2) was ordered removed under INA § 235(b)(1); (3) can prove by a preponderance of the evidence that s/he is a lawful permanent resident; and (4) is entitled to further inquiry by the INS as to her/his status as a refugee or asylee. INA § 242(e)(2).

This severe limitation on judicial review has proved to be one of the most controversial aspects of IIRIRA, which has been the subject of objection and challenge either as a suspension of habeas corpus or as a denial of constitutional rights. IIRIRA, by effectively baring judicial review of expedited removal, gave individual INS officers tremendous unreviewed discretion to remove an alien, and prevent her/him from reentering the United States for five years. The 1996 Act allows judicial review of expedited removal only in habeas corpus proceedings by aliens asserting that they are refugees or asylees with permanent residence in the United States. In addition, the 1996 Act states that no court has jurisdiction to review (1) a decision by the Attorney General to invoke the expedited removal provision; or (2) the application of expedited removal to individual aliens, including the determination regarding the alien's "credible fear of persecution" (see chapter 10, *infra*); or (3) procedures and policies adopted by the Attorney General to implement the expedited removal provisions. INA § 242(a)(2)(A).

§ 9–2.4   Interdiction

In the wake of political and economic upheavals in Haiti, large numbers of Haitians fled their country and sought admission into the United States. Pursuant to a 1981 agreement between Haiti and the U.S., the Coast Guard intercepted vessels carrying these Haitians, interviewed them briefly as to their reasons for wanting to enter the U.S., and forcibly repatriated almost all of them. The interdiction agreement provided that those aliens who apparently qualified for refugee status would not be returned to Haiti. It should be noted that Haiti was the only country with which the U.S. had an interdiction agreement. In *Haitian Refugee Center v. Gracey* (D.C.Cir.1987) the D.C. Circuit found that plaintiffs lacked standing to challenge the validity of the interdiction. See §§ 2–2.1, 8–3.1.

During fall-winter of 1991–92, more than 16,000 Haitians were intercepted on the high seas and were taken to the U.S. Naval Base at Guantanamo Bay in Eastern Cuba. They were questioned as to whether they had a prima facie claim to asylum status. Except for a very brief period the Haitians had no access to lawyers. They also had no right to appeal. Although some Members of Congress sought Temporary Protected Status (TPS) for the Haitians, the Bush administration refused to stop enforcement of the agreement. The interdiction and interview procedures were challenged in federal court; their claims were initially sustained in federal district court.

Nonetheless, the U.S. Court of Appeals for the Eleventh Circuit held in *Haitian Refugee Center v. Baker* (11th Cir.1992) that aliens who were detained on the high seas and, thus, had never presented themselves at a U.S. border, had no right to judicial review of INS decisions under the Administrative Procedure Act. Moreover, the court concluded that these aliens had no private right of action, unless they qualified for refugee status. Further, the court stated that the Refugee Center and their attorneys had no First Amendment claim for gaining access to the detained aliens. The Supreme Court denied certiorari over the objections of Justice Blackmun, who argued that this challenge to U.S. procedure for determining whether a group of aliens faces political persecution deserved a hearing by the Supreme Court.

While the courts provided no relief to the Haitians interdicted on the high seas and taken to Guantanamo, the litigation may have increased the number of Haitians found to have prima facie claims to refugee status. Over 35 percent of the Haitians were eventually found to have prima facie claims and were to be transported to the U.S. for adjudication of their asylum cases. Almost all of the others were transported back to Haiti.

In May 1992 the Bush administration ordered the Coast Guard to return any Haitians leaving their country in boats without an inquiry as to whether they qualified for asylum. The U.N. High Commissioner for Refugees and the Haitian Refugee Center challenged this measure as a violation of the U.S. government's obligations under the Protocol relating to the Status of Refugees.

In *Sale v. Haitian Centers Council, Inc.* (Sup.Ct.1993), the Court again upheld an executive order that authorized summary return of Haitians intercepted on the high seas without considering asylum claims. The court did not find any violation of Article 33 of the U.N. Protocol relating to the Status of Refugees or INA § 243(h)(now INA § 241(b)(3)) both of which prohibit a return of refugees to territories where their lives or freedom would be threatened. On April 4, 1994, Haitian President Aristide withdrew his government's agreement to stopping Haitian boats on the high seas and President Clinton ordered that Haitians would no longer be subject to interdiction without individualized inquiry as to whether they qualify for refugee or asylum status.

CHAPTER 10
REFUGEES AND ASYLUM

The United States has a long-standing commitment to the protection of victims or potential victims of serious human rights violations who have fled their country. An alien may be considered for refugee or asylum status in the United States if the alien has a well-founded fear of persecution in her/his home country. To be eligible for either refugee or asylum status, the applicant must qualify as a refugee, pursuant to the definition in INA § 101(a)(42). The asylum applicant is already present in the United States or at its borders, whereas refugee status may be sought from outside of the United States. Refugee or asylum status, along with occasional lotteries (see chapters 1 and 5), constitute the only significant avenues for immigrating to the United States for individuals without family ties or employment opportunities in the U.S. Refugee and asylum status differ in several other aspects, as discussed below.

§ 10–1 REFUGEES

The President has the power under INA § 207 to admit as refugees those aliens who are outside the United States and who qualify for refugee status. The President, after consultation with Congress and before the beginning of the fiscal year, is permitted to set a worldwide refugee admission ceiling for the year at such number as the President determines is "justified by humanitarian concerns or is otherwise in the national interest." INA § 207(a)(2). The President must also allocate this number among refugees from regions of the world which are of special humanitarian concern to the United States. In the event of an "unforeseen emergency refugee situation," the President may, after appropriate consultation with the relevant congressional committees, expand the admissible number of refugees if such action is justified by "grave humanitarian concerns or is otherwise in the national interest." INA § 207(b).

For example, President Clinton set the refugee admission ceiling for fiscal year 1996 at 90,000, which was a significant decrease from 111,000 refugee admissions authorized in 1995. This reduction results from a phaseout of admissions from East Asia and the former Soviet Union which historically constituted eighty percent of overall admissions. The President allocated the total number regionally as follows: Africa, 7,000; East Asia, 25,000; former Soviet Union/Eastern Europe 45,000; Latin America and the Caribbean, 6,000; Near East/South Asia, 4,000; undesignated, publicly funded, 3,000. The regional allocations do not reflect the distribution of refugees throughout the world, but instead, show U.S. foreign policy interests. Similarly, in the last few years, several hundred Cubans have been admitted through the undesignated allocation as a result of funding by the Cuban American National Foundation. Also, unused allocations may be transferred to regions where needed.

Like an asylum applicant, an applicant for refugee status must meet the definition of a refugee contained in INA § 101(a)(42), which includes the possession of a "well-founded fear of persecution on account of race, religion, nationality, membership in a particular social group, or political opinion." While the applicable standard is the same, the refugee applicant applies from abroad, whereas the asylum applicant applies while present in the United States or at its border. Applicants for refugee status are subject to numerical limitations, but no such limitations are imposed upon asylum. In addition, the beneficiaries of the Lautenberg amendment— Soviet Jews, Soviet Evangelical Christians, and most Indochinese—need only claim persecution and show a credible basis for concern about the possibility of such persecution. P.L. 101–167 (Nov. 21, 1989).

In addition to meeting the statutory definition of refugee, the alien must be generally admissible as an immigrant under INA § 212(a), must not be firmly resettled in any other country, and must be determined to be of special humanitarian concern to the United States. INA § 207(c). Several of the inadmissibility provisions of INA § 212(a) do not apply to refugees, including those provisions relating to labor certification, self-sufficiency, valid entry documents and visas, literacy, and foreign medical graduates. The Attorney General may, for humanitarian purposes, to assure family unity, or when it is otherwise in the public interest, waive other inadmissibility provisions. INA § 207(c)(3).

Each refugee, however, must be sponsored by a responsible person (usually a relative) and/or an organization which will assist the refugee in getting settled in the United States. See 8 C.F.R. § 207.2(d). Churches, community organizations, and other voluntary agencies often fill this role. The International Organization for Migration ordinarily provides transportation for the refugee from her/his place of abode to the place of resettlement in the United States, but the refugee is eventually expected to reimburse the cost of travel.

To apply for refugee status, the alien must complete Form I–590 (Registration for Classification as a Refugee). Applicants 14 years of age or older also must submit Form G–325C (Biographic Information) and Form FD–258 (Applicant Card). 8 C.F.R. § 207.2. The alien must file these completed forms, along with supplementary statements and documentary evidence, at an INS office outside the United States. The alien then will be interviewed by an immigration officer to determine eligibility, and a medical examination will be performed. 8 C.F.R. § 207.2(b) and (c).

Waiting lists are maintained for each designated refugee group of special humanitarian concern. The date on which the alien's approvable application was filed determines the alien's position on the waiting list. The Attorney General may, however, adopt appropriate criteria for selecting refugees and assigning priorities for each designated group based on considerations of family reunification, close association with the United States, compelling humanitarian concerns, and public interest factors. 8 C.F.R. § 207.5.

If the alien's application is approved, the alien must enter the United States within four months. 8 C.F.R. § 207.4. Spouses and children (unmarried and under the age of 21) accompanying or following to join a refugee may be admitted if not otherwise entitled to admission, and if they have not participated in the persecution of others. Spouses and children are charged against the numerical limitation under which the refugee's entry was charged. 8 C.F.R. § 207.1(e).

After one year in the United States, the refugee is eligible to apply for adjustment of status to lawful permanent residence. INA §§ 209(a)(1)(B). Whereas asylum status may be terminated during this period if conditions improve in the alien's home country, making asylum unnecessary, refugee status is not conditional in this respect. INA §§ 207(c)(4), 208(c)(2). The alien who seeks adjustment must return to the INS for an inspection and examination in order to determine admissibility. INA § 209(a)(1). Although INA § 209(a) provides for the adjustment of status of those aliens *admitted* to the United States under § 207, a refugee may be removed from the United States through removal proceedings for inadmissible aliens (formerly "exclusion proceedings") rather than removal proceedings for aliens already present in the U.S. (formerly "deportation proceedings") if it is subsequently determined that the alien was not in fact a refugee within the meaning of § 101(a)(42) at the time of the alien's "admission." INA §§ 207(c)(4), 209(a). If the alien is found to be admissible, permanent resident status will be granted and made effective as of the date the alien arrived in the United States. INA § 209(a)(2). While there is an annual numerical limitation of 10,000 on adjustment of status for asylees, there is no numerical limitation on adjustment of status for refugees. INA § 209(b). *See* O.I. 209.3K.

§ 10–2   ASYLUM

An alien who is present in the United States or arrives at its border may apply for asylum if the alien qualifies as a refugee. INA § 208. A refugee is defined in INA § 101(a)(42)(A) as "any person who is outside any country of such person's nationality or ... any country in which such person last habitually resided, and who is unable or unwilling to return to, and is unable or unwilling to avail himself or herself of the protection of that country because of persecution or a well-founded fear of persecution on account of race, religion, nationality, membership in a particular social group, or political opinion." IIRIRA amended the definition of refugee to count "forced abortion or involuntary sterilization, or persecution for failure or refusal to undergo such procedure or for other resistance to a coercive population control program" as persecution on account of political opinion. INA § 101(a)(42). Asylum can provide relief from removal of inadmissible aliens (formerly "exclusion"), as well as removal of aliens already present in the U.S. (formerly "deportation"), and a grant of asylum may lead to permanent residence. Moreover, there is no waiting period before one qualifies for asylum.

IIRIRA amendments significantly affect the asylum procedures. According to the new INA, an alien must file the asylum application within one year after her/his arrival in the U.S., may not receive work authorization until 180 days after filing an asylum application, and may be permanently ineligible for any immigration benefits if s/he knowingly files a frivolous application for asylum. Furthermore, any alien who is inadmissible or removable on terrorism grounds is ineligible for asylum. In addition, IIRIRA amendments provide that an aggravated felony is a particularly serious crime that renders an alien ineligible for asylum. The definition of "aggravated felony" has been considerably expanded. See § 8–2.3, supra.

In In re Q–T–M–T (BIA 1996), the Board dealt with a Vietnamese man sentenced to illegal sale of firearms prior to the date on which the IIRIRA amendments became effective, i.e., April 1, 1997. For this transitional period, the BIA stated that an alien convicted of an aggravated felony who has been sentenced to less than 5 years' imprisonment, is subject to a rebuttable presumption that s/he has been convicted of a particularly serious crime which bars her/his eligibility for withholding of deportation under INA § 243(h)(now "withholding of removal"; new INA § 241(b)(3)). The appropriate standard to evaluate whether the alien has overcome the presumption that s/he has committed a particularly serious crime is "whether there is any unusual aspect of the alien's criminal conduct that convincingly evidences that the crime cannot rationally be deemed 'particularly serious' in light of treaty obligation under the Protocol [relating to the Status of Refugees]." In the *Q-T-M-T* case, the nature and circumstances of the respondent's convictions for illicit trafficking in firearms fulfilled the definitions of both "aggravated felony" under INA § 101(a)(43)(C) and also "particularly serious crime" under the Protocol, such that the alien was disqualified from relief from removal.

§ 10–2.1   Burden and Standard of Proof in Asylum Cases

The burden of establishing eligibility as a refugee is on the applicant. 8 C.F.R. § 208.13. The applicant must show that s/he has a well-founded fear of persecution in the home country on account of race, religion, nationality, membership in a particular social group, or political opinion. The requirement of a "well-founded fear," however, has not been clearly defined. In *INS v. Stevic* (Sup.Ct.1984) and *INS v. Cardoza–Fonseca* (Sup.Ct.1987) the Supreme Court established the standard of proof which the INS must apply in considering asylum applications and examined the procedures available for review if such applications are denied. Stevic was a Yugoslav citizen who was ordered removed (formerly "deported") from the United States; while his motion to reopen his removal (formerly "deportation") was pending before an immigration judge, he applied for asylum. The immigration judge denied the reopening and his appeal to the Board of Immigration Appeals was dismissed. The Board noted that "[a] motion to reopen based on a . . . claim of persecution must contain prima facie evidence there is a clear probability of persecution to be directed at the individual [alien]." The Board concluded that Stevic had failed to prove that he would be singled out for persecution if he returned to Yugoslavia.

Stevic sought review by the U.S. Court of Appeals of the Board's denial of his motion to reopen the removal (formerly "deportation") proceedings on the asylum matter; this appeal was consolidated with his appeal from the denial of his habeas corpus petition in the federal district court concerning an earlier motion to seek withholding of deportation on the basis of INA § 243(h)(now "withholding of removal"; new INA § 241(b)(3)).

The Court of Appeals for the Second Circuit held that when the United States acceded to the United Nations Protocol relating to the Status of Refugees in 1968, and later adopted the Refugee Act of 1980, it intended to establish a more generous standard in evaluating asylum claims than the " 'clear probability' that an individual will be singled out for persecution" approach used by the Board of Immigration Appeals. The Court of Appeals indicated that the same burden of proof should apply to both the withholding procedure and to affirmative applications for asylum.

The Supreme Court granted certiorari and concluded from an analysis of legislative history and statutory language that the alien must show a clear probability of persecution in order to obtain withholding of deportation under INA § 243(h) (now "withholding of removal" under INA § 241(b)(3)). The Court defined the clear probability of persecution standard as inquiring whether it is more likely than not that the alien would be subject to persecution. The Supreme Court suggested that a different standard might be applicable to an affirmative asylum application.

In *INS v. Cardoza–Fonseca* (Sup.Ct.1987) the Supreme Court directly addressed the standard of proof applicable to applications for asylum under § 208(a). Cardoza–Fonseca was a Nicaraguan citizen who overstayed her nonimmigrant visa. When the INS commenced removal (formerly "deportation") proceedings, Cardoza–Fonseca requested withholding of deportation (now "withholding of removal") pursuant to INA § 243(h) and asylum pursuant to § 208(a). To support her asylum claim, she attempted to show a "well-founded fear of persecution" upon her return to Nicaragua with evidence that her brother had been tortured and imprisoned because of his political activities in Nicaragua. Cardoza–Fonseca claimed that she, too, would be tortured if forced to return, because the Sandinistas knew she had fled Nicaragua with her brother and would want to interrogate her about her brother's whereabouts. Because of the status of her brother, the Nicaraguan government would become aware of her own political opposition to the Sandinistas.

At the removal (formerly "deportation") hearing, the immigration judge applied the § 243(h) (now INA § 241(b)(3)) "more likely than not" standard of proof to Cardoza–Fonseca's § 208(a) asylum claim. The judge held that she was not entitled to asylum because she had failed to establish "a clear probability of persecution." The Board of Immigration Appeals (BIA) affirmed the decision. The Court of Appeals reversed, holding that the § 208(a) "well-founded fear" standard is more generous than the § 243(h) (now § 241(b)(3)) clear probability standard in that § 208(a) requires only a showing of past persecution or "good reason" to fear future persecution. The Court of Appeals remanded the case to the BIA, to be evaluated under this standard.

The Supreme Court affirmed the judgment of the Court of Appeals, holding that the § 243(h) (now § 241(b)(3)) clear probability standard does not govern asylum applications under § 208(a), and that "the reference to 'fear' in the § 208(a) standard obviously makes the eligibility determination turn to some extent on the subjective mental state of the alien." The Court, however, declined to give concrete meaning to the term "well-founded fear," leaving this task to the process of case-by-case adjudication.

If the asylum applicant has satisfied the § 243(h) (now § 241(b)(3)) clear probability standard as to withholding of deportation (now "withholding of removal"), the alien has *a fortiori* satisfied the more generous "well-founded fear" standard governing asylum claims. *Hernandez–Ortiz v. INS* (9th Cir.1985). In *Hernandez–Ortiz*, the alien's evidence of threats or acts of violence against members of her family in El Salvador showed a clear probability that her life would be threatened by return to El Salvador, and that the threat of persecution was related to the alien's political opinion. Having established a clear probability of persecution, the alien had *a fortiori* established a well-founded fear of persecution, thereby entitling her to asylum status.

Under the 1996 regulations, the applicant for asylum can sustain the burden of proving a well-founded fear of persecution if s/he establishes that a pattern or practice of persecution exists in her/his country on account of race, religion, nationality, or political opinion and s/he establishes her/his inclusion or identification with one such persecuted group. 8 C.F.R. § 208.13(b)(2).

The Ninth Circuit has determined that an applicant's petition for asylum must satisfy both a subjective and an objective component. Subjectively, the applicant must show that her/his fear is genuine. The objective component requires a showing by credible and specific evidence in the record of facts that would support a reasonable fear of persecution. *Arriaga–Barrientos v. INS* (9th Cir. 1991).

In a 1992 case, the Supreme Court held that a guerrilla organization's coercion to join its organization does not necessarily constitute persecution on account of political opinion for the purposes of INA §§ 101(a)(42) & 208. *INS v. Elias–Zacarias* (Sup.Ct.1992). In that case, Jairo Jonathan Elias–Zacarias testified during removal (formerly "deportation") proceedings that he was subject to persecution if he returned to his native Guatemala. He described how guerrillas had forced their way into his home and requested that Elias–Zacarias and his parents join their organization. They refused, and the guerrillas promised to return. Elias–Zacarias testified that he believed joining the organization would subject him to retaliation by the government.

In his opinion for the Court, Justice Scalia reviewed the applicable standards for granting asylum under § 208(a). First, he noted, the fear of persecution had to be such that a reasonable factfinder would conclude that it existed. He reasoned that, in this case, the political opinion in question was not that of the applicant, but rather, that of the guerrilla organization (the persecutor). In response, Elias–Zacarias had argued that failure to join the guerrillas was itself tantamount to expressing a political opinion, but the Court was not persuaded, holding instead that Elias–Zacarias had failed to show evidence which compelled a reversal of the BIA decision.

In a dissenting opinion, Justice Stevens stated that "A political opinion can be expressed negatively as well as affirmatively," and that in these circumstances, expression led to a reasonable fear of persecution. For a period after the decision in *Elias–Zacarias* it was unclear whether the "forcible recruitment" and imputed political opinion theory could still prevail with the proper evidence. Indeed, it now appears that the doctrine of imputed political opinion is still viable. *Shirazi-Parsa v. INS* (9th Cir. 1994). The Board granted asylum to a Sri Lankan national who was kidnapped by the Tamil Tigers and forced him to work in their camp. *In re S–P-* (BIA 1996). When the Tiger's camp was raided by the Sri Lankan Army, the soldiers accused the applicant of being a Tamil Tiger, imprisoned him, and ill-treated him during interrogations. The Board reasoned that in the context of general civil unrest, "it is not easy to evaluate whether the applicant's harm was inflicted because of imputed political views rather than a desire to obtain intelligence information." The difficulty of determining motive in such situations should not, however, "diminish the protections of asylum for persons who have been punished because of their actual or imputed political views, as opposed to their criminal or violent conduct."

In re Kasinga (BIA 1996) held that the practice of female genital mutilation ("FGM") can form the basis for a grant of asylum. Kasinga, a 19–year old native of Togo, feared that she would be subjected to FGM and a forced marriage upon her return to her country. The BIA stated the "applicant's testimony in *Kasinga* established that she had a well-founded fear of persecution on account of her membership in a 'particular social group,' *i.e.*, young women of the Tchamba–Kunsuntu Tribe who have not suffered FGM and who oppose the practice." *In re H-* (BIA 1996) granted asylum to a Somali national because of the persecution that he had suffered as a member of the Marehan subclan (to which the ousted Somali President also belonged). The Board held that the applicant was a member of a "particular social group." "The fact that almost all Somalis can claim clan membership and that interclan conflict is prevalent should not create undue concern that virtually all Somalis would qualify for refugee status, as an applicant must establish he is being persecuted on account of that membership."

If the applicant had suffered past persecution, it is presumed that her/his life or freedom would be threatened upon return. This presumption can be rebutted if the INS established by a preponderance of evidence that conditions in the country have changed to an extent that it is no longer more likely than not that the applicant would face persecution. 8 C.F.R. § 208.13(b)(1)(I). If the INS successfully rebuts the presumption of a well-founded fear of future persecution, an alien may still be granted asylum when s/he demonstrates compelling reasons for being unwilling to return to her/his country of nationality or last habitual residence due to the severity of the past persecution. 8 C.F.R. § 208.13(b)(1)(ii).

§ 10–2.2 Basic Asylum Application Procedures

Asylum is not a right; rather it is granted at the discretion of the asylum officer or immigration judge in the district where the alien resides or enters the U.S. 8 C.F.R. § 208.14. The Refugee Act of 1980 established the basic standard for granting asylum in a new INA § 208. In 1990, regulations were promulgated to respond to problems in adjudicating asylum cases. The 1995 regulations imposed restrictions upon asylum that were outside the language of the statute. For example, the 1995 regulations provided that an aggravated felon is *ipso facto* a danger to the community for withholding purposes and that an alien who committed a serious nonpolitical crime outside the U.S. prior to arrival is ineligible for asylum. The 1995 regulations also required an alien to submit fingerprints and photographs with the application. Asylum advocates argued that these regulations were *ultra vires* because they imposed restrictions outside the scope of the statute. IIRIRA, by codifying most of the 1995 regulations, eliminates the argument that the 1995 regulations were *ultra vires*. Furthermore, IIRIRA provides additional restrictive rules regarding timing, eligibility for judicial review, and procedures for filing an asylum claim.

a. Jurisdiction

The 1990 regulations took the determination of asylum applications out of the hands of the district director.

Currently, the asylum officers in the Office of International Affairs in the INS have initial jurisdiction over an asylum application filed by an alien physically present in the U.S. or seeking admission at a port of entry. 8 C.F.R. § 208.2. Asylum officers receive special training in international human rights law, non-adversarial interview techniques, and other relevant national and international refugee laws. The Director of International Affairs in cooperation with the Department of State compiles and disseminates to asylum officers information concerning the persecution of persons in other countries, as well as other information relevant to asylum determinations. 8 C.F.R. § 208.1(b).

Asylum officers have jurisdiction over all asylum applications except those filed by aliens in removal proceedings for inadmissible aliens (formerly "exclusion proceedings") or removal proceedings for aliens already present in the U.S. (formerly "deportation proceedings"), which are evaluated by immigration judges. If the asylum officer does not grant political asylum, and, instead, refers the application to an immigration judge, the judge will review the application *de novo*. The decision of the immigration judge is subject to both a BIA appeal and judicial review under the usual rules.

b. *The Application Process*

The alien must submit an application for asylum, Form I–589, along with biographic information, Form G–325A, an FD–258 fingerprint chart, and a photograph. INA § 208(d)(1), 8 C.F.R. § 208.3. The alien must also demonstrate that s/he is filing an application within one year after the date of arrival in U.S. INA § 208(a)(2)(B). If the INS has denied a previous application for asylum, the alien is ineligible to submit another application. INA

§ 208 (a)(2)(C). These conditions may be waived by the Attorney General if the alien proves "either the existence of changed circumstances which materially affect her/his eligibility for asylum or extraordinary circumstances relating to the delay in filing the application." INA § 208(a)(2)(D).

Provided the alien is not in removal proceedings for inadmissible aliens (formerly "exclusion proceedings") or removal proceedings for aliens already present in the U.S. (formerly "deportation proceedings"), s/he files the application materials with the district director who then forwards them to the asylum officer. The asylum officer may grant asylum in the exercise of discretion to an applicant who qualifies as a refugee under INA § 101(a)(42). If the alien appears to be removable under INA § 240, the asylum officer must either grant asylum or refer the application to an immigration judge for adjudication in removal proceedings for inadmissible or otherwise removable aliens. 8 C.F.R. § 208.14(b).

Since the adoption of IIRIRA in 1996, an alien who has a pending application for asylum is not eligible for employment authorization prior to 180 days after the date of filing of the application for asylum. INA § 208(d)(2). The applicant must file an initial application for employment authorization (I–765) not earlier than 150 days after the date on which s/he submitted a complete asylum application. The INS shall grant or deny the application for employment in 30 days from the date of filing of the form I–765. The authorization is good for one year, provided the application for asylum is not frivolous, and is renewable in one-year increments. The employment authorization remains valid until the end of the authorization period or sixty days after an asylum officer's denial of asylum, whichever is longer.

The asylum officer shall interview each applicant for asylum in a non-adversarial manner (except for expedited removal cases), and not in public, unless the applicant requests otherwise. 8 C.F.R. § 208.9. The applicant may have counsel and may submit affidavits of witnesses. In making a determination, the asylum officer may rely on information provided by the State Department and the Office of International Affairs, as well as other "credible" sources, such as international organizations. 8 C.F.R. § 208.12.

Prior to 1990 regulations, comments from the Bureau of Human Rights and Humanitarian Affairs (BHRHA) of the Department of State were required. Courts, however, were critical of the weight given to BHRHA opinions. The Second Circuit affirmed the admissibility of the State Department's opinions on the degree of persecution that exists in the country of prospective deportation. *Zamora v. INS* (2d Cir.1976). The advisory opinions are admissible provided the State Department reveals, so far as possible, the basis for its views and does not attempt to apply such knowledge to the particular case.

In *Arteaga v. INS* (9th Cir.1988), however, the Ninth Circuit overruled a BIA decision because the Board erred when it determined that guerrillas did not engage in forced recruitment. Under the current regulations, comment from the Department of State is optional. 8 C.F.R. § 208.12.

The decision by an asylum officer to grant or deny asylum, or to refer the asylum application to the immigration judge, shall be communicated in writing to the applicant. 8 C.F.R. § 208.17. After IIRIRA, an asylum officer rather than denying the cases refers most of them to the immigration judge. An asylum officer is allowed to deny only a few exceptional categories of cases such as cases of nonimmigrants in valid status. The rest of the cases that were not granted must be referred to the immigration judge for the initiation of removal proceedings. 8 C.F.R. § 208.14(b). The regulations do not require an asylum officer to state reasons for referrals which constitute the majority of decisions. There is no right to appeal a decision of an asylum officer; however, the application can be renewed *de novo* in removal proceedings.

An applicant who leaves the United States is presumed to have abandoned his application for asylum or restriction on removal (formerly "withholding of deportation"). 8 C.F.R. § 208.8. Moreover, an unexcused failure to appear for a scheduled interview may result in the dismissal of her/his application. 8 C.F.R. § 208.10.

Asylum will be denied as a matter of statutory eligibility if (1) the alien fails to qualify as a refugee; (2) the alien participated in the persecution of any other person on account of race, religion, nationality, membership in a particular group, or political opinion; (3) the alien, having been convicted by a final judgment of a particularly serious crime, constitutes a danger to the community of the United States; (4) there are serious reasons for considering that the alien has committed a serious nonpolitical crime outside the United States prior to the arrival of the alien in the United States; (5) there are reasonable grounds for regarding the alien as a danger to the security of the United States; (6) the alien is inadmissible or removable on terrorist activity grounds; or (7) the alien has been firmly resettled in another country.

INA § 208(b). The 1996 Act provides that "an alien who has been convicted of an aggravated felony shall be considered to have been convicted of a particularly serious crime" that disqualifies her/him from asylum. INA §§ 208(b)(2)(A)(ii), 208(b)(2)(B)(i).

In addition to statutory ineligibility, asylum may be denied as a matter of discretion by either the asylum officer or the immigration judge with jurisdiction over the case. A common basis for discretionary denial of asylum, even though statutory eligibility has been proved, involves cases where the alien has fraudulently or grossly circumvented U.S. legal procedures to enter the U.S. and make an asylum claim. *See, e.g., Matter of Salim* (BIA 1982). In *Matter of Pula* (BIA 1987), however, the Board did not find the applicant's use of false documents to enter the U.S. such a disqualifying factor as to justify denial of asylum or the exercise of discretion. The negative factor of fraud had to be weighed against such positive factors as fear of persecution, lack of knowledge about procedures for seeking refugee status, family ties in the U.S., etc.

The Board of Immigration Appeals in *Matter of McMullen* (BIA 1984) concluded that the alien's effective membership in the Provisional Irish Republican Army, a "clandestine, terrorist organization" engaged in the persecution of individuals opposed to the organization and its terrorist activities, constituted persecution of others on account of political opinion, making the alien ineligible for asylum. The Board also found that the organization's random bombing of civilian targets during the period of the alien's active membership provided "serious reasons for considering that the alien has committed a serious non-political crime outside the United States."

The Board held that a crime is non-political if the crime is grossly out of proportion to the political objective or if it involves acts of an atrocious nature.

After IIRIRA, the Attorney General may in her/his discretion deny an asylum application if the alien may be removed to a third country which has offered resettlement and "in which the alien's life or freedom would not be threatened on account of race, religion, nationality, membership in a particular social group, or political opinion." INA § 208(a)(2). The Attorney General's determination with regard to such a safe third country is not subject to judicial review. *See* INA § 208(a)(3).

If asylum is denied, the alien will be placed under removal proceedings for inadmissible aliens (formerly "exclusion proceedings") if the application was made at the border of the U.S., unless the alien is allowed to withdraw her/his application. 8 C.F.R. § 235.4. After IIRIRA, if an applicant for asylum has not yet been admitted to the U.S., s/he may be subject to expedited removal procedure. An alien will be subject to expedited removal if an immigration officer determines that s/he is inadmissible for lack of documents or for presenting fraudulent documents. INA § 235(b)(1)(A). An alien will be removed without further hearing or review unless s/he requests asylum or otherwise indicates a fear of persecution. INA § 235(b)(1)(B). If the alien so indicates, s/he will be referred to an asylum officer who conducts an interview to determine if the alien has a credible fear of persecution. If the asylum officer finds a credible fear, the alien is detained for "further consideration of the application for asylum." INA § 235(b)(1)(B)(ii). If the officer finds that the alien does not have a credible fear of persecution, s/he orders the alien removed and writes a report summarizing the reasons for the finding. INA § 235(b)(1)(B)(iii)(I, II). The alien may request review by an immigration judge. The review must take place within 24 hours if practicable, and in no case later than seven days after the asylum officer's decision. INA § 235(b)(1)(B)(iii)(III). The alien will be detained pending the review. There is no other administrative review unless the alien testifies that s/he already has been admitted as a permanent resident, a refugee, or an asylee. INA § 235(b)(1)(C).

If asylum is denied for an alien already present in the U.S., regardless of whether the application was for an original grant of asylum or a renewal, the asylum officer shall either commence removal proceedings for aliens already present within the U.S. (formerly "deportation proceedings") or grant voluntary departure. 8 C.F.R. § 208.8(f)(4).

The courts have differed over whether inadmissible (formerly "excludable") and otherwise removable (formerly "deportable") aliens must be informed of their right to apply for asylum. The court in *Nunez v. Boldin* (S.D.Tex.1982) decided that the Due Process protection of aliens within the borders of the United States requires that citizens of El Salvador and Guatemala held at an INS detention facility be informed of their right to apply for asylum. The United States has "by treaty, statute, and regulations, manifested its intention of hearing the pleas of aliens who come to this country claiming a fear of being persecuted in their homelands." The court stated that although no regulation specifically requires the INS to inform detainees of their right to apply for asylum, failure to do so may effectively render these treaties and statutes virtually nonexistent for the majority of aliens who would otherwise claim their benefits.

The court in *Jean v. Nelson* (11th Cir.1984) took an opposing view. The court concluded that "too many asylum applications may only bury the truth by straining INS resources and preventing careful assessment of individual claims. If the volume of asylum claims rises significantly, the INS may feel compelled to rely more and more on group profiles and less on individual evidence and credibility." The court held that although aliens have a protected statutory and regulatory right to apply for asylum, the Constitution, the Refugee Act, and its regulations do not require the INS to inform aliens of this right.

The decision in *Orantes–Hernandez v. Thornburg* (9th Cir.1990) and the settlement in *American Baptist Churches v. Thornburg* (N.D.Cal.1991) imply that aliens must be notified of their right to apply for political asylum and the right to be represented by counsel at no cost to the government. In *Orantes–Hernandez,* the court held that the INS had to advise the Salvadorans seeking entry of their rights in English and Spanish. The INS must tell them orally that they are being detained by the INS, that they will be given written notice of their rights prior to their deciding whether to return voluntarily to El Salvador, and that they will have to acknowledge that they received the written notice of their rights (called an "*Orantes* advisal").

The written notice advises the alien that s/he has the privilege to be represented by counsel, the right to a removal hearing, the right to apply for political asylum, and the right to request a voluntary departure. In addition, each alien must be given a list of organizations that provide free legal services in the area. The *ABC* settlement, discussed in greater detail below, reiterates these requirements. Moreover, 8 C.F.R. § 240.11(c) requires the immigration judge presiding over a removal proceeding to advise the alien that s/he may apply for asylum in the U.S. if the alien expresses a fear of persecution upon returning to her/his country of origin.

An alien who has been found removable (formerly "deportable") and requests a reopening of removal proceedings (formerly "deportation proceedings") for aliens already present in the U.S. to enable her/him to apply for asylum may be denied that opportunity if s/he has not reasonably explained her/his failure to apply for asylum prior to completion of the initial removal proceedings. *INS v. Abudu* (Sup.Ct.1988). Abudu, a citizen of Ghana, had expressly declined to seek asylum during removal proceedings (formerly "deportation proceedings"). Upon motion to reopen, Abudu alleged that a surprise visit from a former acquaintance, who had become a high official in the government of Ghana, was aimed at enticing Abudu to return to Ghana in order to force him to disclose the whereabouts of his brother and other enemies of the government. All the other facts upon which Abudu based his claim were available at the time of the removal (formerly "deportation") hearing. The Supreme Court held that the Board of Immigration Appeals did not abuse its discretion in holding that the alien had not reasonably explained his failure to request asylum during the initial removal proceedings (formerly "deportation proceedings") as required by 8 C.F.R. § 3.2. If Abudu had made a timely application for asylum, supported by the same factual allegations and evidence set forth in his motion to reopen, the immigration judge would have been required to grant him an evidentiary hearing. But an "alien who has already been found deportable [now "removable"] has a much heavier burden when he first advances his request for asylum in a motion to reopen."

If the application for asylum is approved, asylum status is granted for an indefinite period. Employment authorization is automatically granted as well. In addition, a spouse or children may be granted asylum. 8 C.F.R. § 208.19(g). An immigration judge or the BIA may reopen proceedings to terminate a grant of asylum. The INS must establish by a preponderance of the evidence that conditions have changed in the alien's country of origin, that the alien was guilty of fraud in the application process, or that the alien had committed any act that would have been grounds for denial. In addition, an immigration judge may terminate asylum made under the jurisdiction of the INS at any time after the alien has been provided a notice of intent to terminate by the INS. The termination may occur in conjunction with a removal of inadmissible aliens (formerly "exclusion") or removal of aliens already present within the U.S. 8 C.F.R. § 208.22(e).

An alien who has been granted asylum and who remains in the U.S. for one year may apply for adjustment of status to that of a permanent resident alien. 8 C.F.R. § 209.1. The applicant for asylum must generally meet the normal admission requirements of any immigrant with the exceptions that an applicant for asylum does not require labor certification, proof of self-sufficiency, a valid visa, or proof of literacy. The acceptance of unauthorized employment by the asylee will not bar her/his adjustment of status as it would under INA § 245(c). The alien also must continue to be a refugee within the meaning of INA § 101(a)(42) and not have been firmly resettled in a foreign country. 8 C.F.R. § 209.2(a)(iii). Further, there must be a number available from the admission allowance for refugees in general, as provided by INA § 207(a), and there is an annual numerical limitation of 10,000 on the number of adjustments for asylees. 8 C.F.R. § 209.2(a); INA § 209(b). If that number is exceeded, a waiting list is established. Such a numerical limitation on the number of aliens whose status may be adjusted under section 209(b) shall not apply to an alien who: (a) was granted asylum before November 29, 1990; (b) is no longer a refugee due to a change in circumstances in a foreign state; and (c) meets other requirements for adjustment of status under this section.

The denial of an application for adjustment of status is without prejudice to the alien's right to renew the application in removal proceedings for inadmissible and otherwise removable aliens (formerly "exclusion" or "deportation" proceedings). 8 C.F.R. § 209.2(f). If the application is granted, the date of admission as a permanent resident alien is recorded as one year prior to the actual date of approval. INA § 209(b). The date on which the alien becomes a permanent resident will determine when the alien may apply for citizenship. The existence of a waiting list for asylee adjustment of status is significant since the alien must frequently wait several years before actually qualifying for permanent residence.

§ 10–2.3 Asylum and Withholding of Removal (Formerly "Withholding of Deportation")

The provisions of INA § 241(b)(3)(A) governing "restriction on removal" are closely connected to those of

INA § 208(a) governing asylum. This relief was previously known as "withholding of deportation" and the INS and immigration lawyers continue to use the phrase "withholding of removal" for this relief. The Nutshell uses these phrases interchangeably. See § 8–4.1.d(2)(e), supra. Section 241(b)(3) (old INA § 243(h)) provides that the Attorney General shall not deport an alien, with certain exceptions, if the alien's "life or freedom would be threatened ... on account of race, religion, nationality, membership in a particular social group, or political opinion." An alien most often will apply for asylum as relief in removal proceedings along with a request for withholding of removal under § 241(b)(3) (formerly "withholding of deportation" under old INA § 243(h)). If an undocumented alien, residing in the United States and not under removal proceedings, applies for asylum, the INS will become aware of that alien's undocumented status and will force the alien to return to the country of alleged persecution if her/his asylum application is denied and a request for a de novo review before an immigration judge is unsuccessful. In light of the small percentage of aliens actually granted asylum, many aliens do not risk exposure to the INS, but bring the asylum claim along with a request for a withholding of removal if subjected to removal proceedings.

An asylum officer or district director may, following the interview, terminate withholding of removal (formerly "withholding of deportation") due to changed country conditions, fraud, or commission of an act which is grounds for denial under § 241(b)(3)(B). 8 C.F.R. § 208.22. Asylum is a discretionary matter, however, § 241(b)(3) relief (old 243(h) relief) is mandatory if the Attorney General determines that the alien is qualified. An alien, therefore, having established the requisite likelihood of persecution, must be granted a withholding of removal (formerly "withholding of deportation") to the country of persecution, but may be denied asylum at the discretion of the INS asylum officer or immigration judge. The alien in *Matter of Salim* (BIA 1982), for example, established the requisite probability of persecution in Afghanistan, but was denied asylum as a matter of discretion because of his arrival in the United States with a fraudulently obtained passport. The court ordered the alien's removal (formerly "deportation") to Pakistan. The standard for reviewing withholding of deportation or asylum is slightly stricter than the clear error standard. The appellate court will reverse only "if we conclude that the Board's evaluation is not supported by substantial evidence. This standard requires only that the Board's conclusion based on the evidence presented is substantially reasonable." *Arriaga–Barrientos v. INS* (9th Cir. 1991).

§ 10–2.4 Extended Voluntary Departure

Rather than grant asylum which can mature into permanent residence, the executive branch devised a temporary relief from removal (formerly "deportation") known as "extended voluntary departure." Extended voluntary departure was granted to aliens who could not return to their country of origin because of a civil war or a similar crisis. It reflected the volatile nature of the political or armed conflict situation which can change with unpredictable world events. Extended Voluntary Departure (EVD) was an ad hoc process in which the Attorney General and the INS granted blanket temporary relief to nationals of designated countries. Beneficiaries received unrestricted employment authorization. Under EVD, there were no standards for adjustment to lawful permanent status, nor any guidelines as to what federal programs a beneficiary could have been entitled.

EVD status was extended to Ugandans who suffered under Idi Amin, and to Nicaraguans and Iranians who faced the consequences of revolution in their respective countries. Afghans (1980), Ethiopians (1977), and Poles (1981) have also received EVD. In 1989, when the Chinese government suppressed dissident activity in the wake of the Tiananmen Square massacre, the State Department halted forceful removals (formerly "deportations") but did not grant EVD. Later, Chinese nationals in the United States were given a "deferred departure" status, ensuring their ability to remain in the U.S. through 1994. Extended Voluntary Departure was also considered as a form of relief from removal.

§ 10–2.5 Temporary Protected Status

Extended Voluntary Departure was devised by the executive branch to respond to changing world events; it was not, however, codified in the INA or other statute. The 1990 Act amended the INA by including a program that is quite similar to EVD and designed to replace it: Temporary Protected Status (TPS). INA § 244. Under TPS, the Attorney General may designate a country or region as too unstable for aliens to return. One of the three conditions must be met before the Attorney General can grant TPS: (1) ongoing war or armed conflict would pose a serious threat to an alien who sought to return to that country; (2) earthquake, flood, drought, or other environmental disaster has caused the country to seek TPS designation because it temporarily cannot handle the return of its nationals; (3) the safe return of aliens is prevented by "extraordinary and temporary conditions" and the national interest is not compromised by allowing their temporary stay. INA § 244(b)(1). TPS may be granted for up to eighteen months, and the Attorney General's decision to do so is not subject to review. INA §§ 244(b)(2), 244(b)(5)(A).

A national of a designated country should apply to the INS district director, even if removal proceedings for inadmissible or otherwise removable aliens (formerly "exclusion" or "deportation" proceedings) were underway before the country was so designated. 8 C.F.R. § 240.7(a) & (d). If, however, facts proved in those prior proceedings are sufficient to deny the alien eligibility under TPS, the immigration judge or the BIA must make a final determination. 8 C.F.R. § 240.7(d).

The 1990 Act provided eligibility for Salvadorans who were in this country as of September 19, 1990, and applied for TPS between January 1 and June 30, 1991. Salvadorans meeting § 303 of the 1990 Act requirements received protected status for 18 months. Soon after the 1990 Act, Kuwait, Liberia, and Lebanon received TPS designations as well. 56 Fed.Reg. 12745–47. Bosnia–Herzegovina, Burundi, Rwanda, Sierra Leone, Somalia, and Sudan have also received TPS designation. The 1997 extension of the TPS designation to Montserrat is the first example of granting this status to the victims of natural disaster. In the future, TPS status may be given to other groups in need of temporary protection.

The benefit of TPS is freedom from removal (formerly "deportation") during the period of protection and an authorization for employment. The alien is restricted, however, in her/his ability to travel abroad and in her/his ability to receive welfare. As soon as the alien's TPS terminates, removal proceedings (formerly "deportation proceedings") may begin. The *ABC* settlement discussed below, however, required that each Salvadoran be given the opportunity for a new asylum interview and adjudication.

a. The ABC Settlement

In *American Baptist Church v. Thornburg* (N.D.Cal. 1991) the INS and ABC reached a settlement in a class action suit against the Service for discriminatory handling of asylum cases involving Guatemalans and Salvadorans. In this landmark settlement, all Salvadorans in the U.S. as of September 19, 1990, and all Guatemalans in the U.S. as of October 1, 1990, who had previously been denied asylum can have their cases reopened and reheard before an asylum officer. This benefit also extends to all class members who had not previously filed for asylum. Only aggravated felons are excluded from the settlement.

Removal proceedings (formerly "deportation proceedings") for aliens already present in the U.S. are stayed during the pendency of their *de novo* asylum adjudications; removal proceedings for inadmissible aliens (formerly "exclusion proceedings") and removal proceedings for aliens already present in the U.S. (formerly "deportation proceedings") are closed until the new adjudications have been made. If, however, removal is based on criminal conduct or the proceedings were commenced after November 30, 1990, the applicant must make an affirmative request for closure of removal proceedings for inadmissible aliens and removal proceedings for aliens already present in the U.S. All members of the class are entitled to employment authorization in the meantime and the "non-frivolous" standard does not apply.

A significant aspect of the settlement is that the government is barred from considering the following factors in making asylum determinations: (1) U.S. foreign policy as regards the applicant's country of origin; (2) border enforcement considerations; (3) the U.S. support of the applicant's country of origin; and (4) the applicant's political or ideological beliefs. All Salvadorans and Guatemalans in detention were to be released, advised of their "*ABC* rights," and given the appropriate forms for complying with formal procedures.

b.   Procedures

Under TPS, the Salvadoran must have been continuously physically present in the United States since September 19, 1990; any departure precludes eligibility. The alien must be admissible as an immigrant, not have committed a felony or two misdemeanors, not have engaged in activities prejudicial to the interests of the U.S., and not have been involved in the persecution of any group of people.

To register for TPS, the alien must complete an I–104 registration form, an I–765 work authorization form, an I–263W Record of Sworn Statement with Addendum Questionnaire, and a fingerprint card. An interview is scheduled and a work authorization issued. If the applicant fails to appear for the interview, s/he will be presumed to have abandoned her/his application. Also, an alien subject to removal proceedings (formerly "deportation proceedings") may raise eligibility for TPS as a defense.

When TPS for Salvadorans expired in 1992, the INS created for them deferred enforced departure status which included a blanket authorization to work. Salvadorans had to file by January 31, 1996, any asylum application they planned. A blanket work authorization expired on April 30, 1996, and all Salvadorans who did not a have a pending asylum case became ineligible to work.

CHAPTER 11

INTERNATIONAL LAW ISSUES RELATED TO IMMIGRATION

§ 11–1 FREEDOM OF MOVEMENT

§ 11–1.1 Freedom of Exit

The right of an individual to leave a nation first was mentioned in the Magna Carta of 1215, which stated that everyone had the right to leave England, subject to feudal obligations. In the following centuries, a common law writ of *Ne Exeat Regno* developed in England, conferring on the King the right to refuse exit to specific persons without special authorization. Everyone else enjoyed freedom of exit and even this royal prerogative gradually lost its importance. Blackstone stated that there was an absolute right to leave England, subject to an injunction to remain, but he also advocated the common law doctrine of perpetual allegiance, or citizenship.

In Medieval Germany, free departure was recognized as release from the feudal structure. Peasants and townspeople, who were "freemen," normally had the right to leave, but they had to pay a tribute for the privilege. Serfs, however, could not claim this right until they had bought themselves free from their bondage. In 1555 the Edict of Augsburg conferred the right to leave Germany for religious reasons. The Peace of Westphalia of 1648 also contained the right of departure. During the subsequent period, however, emigration from Germany was permitted only in exceptional situations.

The right to leave a nation was further recognized near the end of the Eighteenth Century. The U.S. Declaration of Independence and the Bill of Rights, and the French Declaration des Droits de l'Homme et du Citoyen of 1789 did not mention the right of exit, but were, of course, important foundations of human rights. The French Constitution of 1791 specifically proclaimed the right to leave a nation. By the middle of the Nineteenth Century, most European nations in practice allowed individuals to leave freely, though no generally accepted right to emigrate existed.

The right to leave a nation became more generally recognized after World War II, with the adoption of several international instruments. The Charter of the United Nations, which came into force on December 24, 1945, is the most prominent international document dealing with human rights. The Charter announces a duty of states to promote and respect human rights; it does not specifically mention the right to leave. The Universal Declaration of Human Rights, adopted by the General Assembly on December 10, 1948, provides an authoritative interpretation of the human rights proclaimed by the Charter and states that "everyone has the right to leave any country, including his own.... " Article 12(2) of the International Covenant on Civil and Political Rights contains almost identical language that is binding on the more than 140 nations which have ratified the Covenant. The Fourth Protocol, Article 2(2), of the European Convention on Human Rights also contains nearly identical wording. Further, the right to leave is recognized in Article 22(2) of the American Convention on Human Rights and in Article 12(2) of the African Charter on Human and Peoples' Rights. These documents mention only the right to leave a nation, but one may infer that this right also includes the right to renounce one's citizenship.

§ 11–1.2 Right to Return

An individual may leave her/his home state, only to find that the home state will not allow her/his return. This problem may occur especially when an unpopular individual temporarily leaves the country to travel abroad. Article 13(2) of the Universal Declaration of Human Rights, Article 12(4) of the International Covenant on Civil and Political Rights, the Fourth Protocol to the European Convention on Human Rights, Article 22(5) of the American Convention on Human Rights, and Article 12(2) of the African Charter recognize the right of an individual to return to her/his home state. The United Nations Sub–Commission on Prevention of Discrimination and Protection of Minorities has considered but not adopted a draft declaration on freedom and non-discrimination in respect to the right of everyone to leave any country, including her/his own, and to return to her/his country.

§ 11–1.3 Right to Enter

There is no corresponding right to enter any nation of which the individual is not a citizen. Based on the theory of sovereignty, both Blackstone and Vattel recognized the right of every nation to exclude aliens, or to place upon their entrance whatever restrictions the nation may want. Most nations place the greatest restrictions on immigration. Nations regularly admit aliens for limited period if there is a treaty of commerce, establishment, and navigation between the alien's home state and the admitting state. Parties to these treaties usually retain the right to exclude individuals who are deemed physically, medically, morally, or socially undesirable. The international human rights treaties do not grant individuals the right to enter any nation other than their own, but the Convention and Protocol relating to the Status of Refugees protect a refugee from being expelled or returned to a country where her/his life or freedom will be threatened. *See* § 11–3.1; ch. 10.

§ 11–1.4 Right to Travel

No general international right to travel between nations exists. While an individual has a right to leave any nation, the individual does not have a right to enter another nation. Special travel rights are, however, given to stateless persons and to refugees. These groups will be considered in the sections below. Nations do, however, admit aliens more readily for temporary travel than for immigration, especially if the nation is a party to a treaty of commerce, establishment, and navigation. The Helsinki Accord, which is a European/North American regional agreement adopted in 1975 at the European Conference on Security and Cooperation in Europe (CSCE), provides for freer movement of individuals between the signatories. In particular, the agreement provides for freer movement on the basis of family ties, family reunification, proposed marriages, and personal or professional travel. In addition, further agreements in the CSCE context, changes in Eastern Europe and the Confederation of Independent States (former Soviet Union), as well as European unification indicate a trend away from obstacles to free travel. In 1994, the CSCE changed its name to the Organization for Security and Cooperation in Europe (OSCE). The new name reflects the development of an administrative structure and increased activity.

In *Haig v. Agee* (Sup.Ct.1981), the Supreme Court upheld a regulation granting the Secretary of State broad discretion to revoke or withhold passports for reasons of national security or foreign policy. In so doing, the Court expressly limited the right to travel abroad, first announced by the Court in *Kent v. Dulles* (Sup.Ct.1958). Chief Justice Burger reasoned in *Agee* that Congress had implicitly authorized passport denials and revocations in the Passport Act of 1926 by remaining inactive in the years during which that act has been construed. Under *Agee,* the Secretary of State can deny or revoke a passport only if s/he finds that "serious damage" has been done to U.S. foreign policy or national security.

The Universal Declaration of Human Rights (Art. 13(1)), the International Covenant on Civil and Political Rights (Art. 12(1)), the Fourth Protocol to the European Convention on Human Rights (Art. 2(1)), the American Convention on Human Rights (Art. 22(1)), and the African Charter (Art. 12(1)) do not provide for travel between nations, but they do provide for freedom of movement within a state. The Convention and Protocol relating to the Status of Refugees as well as the Convention relating to the Status of Stateless Persons also provide for freer movement within a state for these groups. These last three instruments subject the right of free movement to any regulations generally applicable to aliens in the same circumstances.

§ 11–2   THE RIGHTS OF STATELESS PERSONS

Traditionally, states had full authority to determine who could be citizens. This authority led to dual nationalities for some, and statelessness for others. Statelessness also can occur through denationalization, voluntary renunciation of citizenship, or territorial transfer. In addition, citizenship can be lost because of a conflict of nationality laws. For example, statelessness can arise at birth when the state in which the child is born only recognizes the child as receiving the nationality of the parents, while the parent's home state recognizes only the nationality of the state where the child is born.

Stateless persons had no right under traditional principles of international law, because they had no home state to protect them. Stateless persons were therefore totally at the mercy of the nation in which they lived.

The traditional law regarding stateless persons began to change after World War I. Little effort was made to address the issue before World War I because the problem of statelessness had not occurred on a large scale. Most of the progress, however, was made after World War II in connection with two types of international instruments.

The first type of agreement gives rights to stateless persons. The leading document is the Convention relating to the Status of Stateless Persons. This treaty grants three types of rights. First, stateless persons are given rights at least as favorable as aliens in the particular nation where they live, for activities such as the acquisition of property. Second, stateless persons have the same rights as citizens in regard to government services such as elementary public education and public relief. Third, stateless persons are given special rights with respect to identity papers and travel documents for the purpose of traveling outside the host state.

The second type of instrument tries to prevent statelessness. Article 15 of the Universal Declaration of Human Rights says "1. Everyone has a right to a nationality. 2. No one shall be arbitrarily deprived of his nationality nor denied the right to change his nationality." Article 32 of the Convention relating to the Status of Stateless Persons provides that "the Contracting States shall as far as possible facilitate the assimilation and naturalization of stateless persons." The Convention on the Nationality of Married Women provides that a woman's nationality is not dependent on her husband's nationality. The Convention on the Reduction of Statelessness similarly deals with the problem of statelessness at birth. A state may not deprive a person of her/his nationality under this Convention if the deprivation would render the person stateless. Finally, this Convention provides that no person shall become stateless as a result of a transfer of territory. None of these instruments does much to gain citizenship for people who are already stateless. Granting these people the citizenship of the nation where they live may be the only adequate way to solve this problem. Most nations, however, have not gone that far yet.

In 1997 the International Law Commission adopted a draft Declaration on Nationality in Relation to the Succession of States, which *inter alia* attempts to prevent statelessness and assist in the determination of nationality for persons who live in countries that previously were part of such nations as the former Czechoslovakia, the Soviet Union, and Yugoslavia. The draft declaration deals with general principles of nationality in relation to the succession of states and also specific categories of succession as to which model legislation is provided.

§ 11–3 THE RIGHTS OF REFUGEES

Refugees have problems concerning travel, social and political rights, as well as resettlement. In 1922 the High Commissioner for Russian Refugees, in conjunction with the League of Nations, created the Nansen passport. This document, which was a certificate of identity in the form of a passport, was intended to permit the bearer to travel abroad during the period of its validity, and, if specifically stated, to permit the bearer to return to the issuing country. The state where the refugee was located issued the passport, not the League of Nations.

The 1951 Convention relating to the Status of Refugees and the 1967 Protocol relating to the Status of Refugees define a refugee as:

"Any person who owing to well-founded fear of being persecuted for reasons of race, religion, nationality, membership of a particular social group or political opinion, is outside the country of his nationality and is unable or, owing to such fear, is unwilling to avail himself of the protection of that country; or who, not having a nationality and being outside the country, of his former habitual residence is unable or, owing to such fear, is unwilling to return to it."

The Convention applies to persons affected by events in Europe occurring prior to January 1, 1951. The Protocol extends the protections of the Convention without the geographic and date limitations. For the 131 nations (including the U.S.) that are parties to either the Convention or the Protocol, those treaties establish the basic norm of *non-refoulement* that prohibits states from expelling or returning refugees to frontiers or territories where they would be threatened on account of race, religion, nationality, membership of a particular social group, or political opinion. These instruments also prohibit a state from expelling a refugee lawfully in its territory without due process of law.

Article 13 of the Covenant on Civil and Political Rights similarly provides that unless national security requires otherwise, the expulsion of an alien who is lawfully present is to be carried out in accordance with domestic law, and the alien is to be allowed to have her/his reasons for expulsion reviewed by a competent authority. A General Comment of the Human Rights Committee in 1986 concerning Article 13 says that the rights of Article 13 also apply if the legality of an alien's presence is in dispute. If a refugee is found to be inadmissible, s/he should be given an opportunity to find another country that will grant refuge. In views adopted by the Human Rights Committee in 1981 concerning *Maroufidou v. Sweden*, the Committee found that Sweden's expulsion of Anna Maroufidou had followed the requirements of Article 13. In views adopted in 1986 concerning Hammel v. Madagascar, however, the Human Rights Committee found that Eric Hammel was expelled from Madagascar in violation of Article 13 because he did not have an opportunity to submit reasons against his expulsion or to have his case reviewed by a competent authority.

The United States' obligations under the Protocol to protect refugees are apparently neglected by the Illegal Immigration Reform and Immigrant Responsibility Act of 1996 (IIRIRA). The expedited removal process (IIRIRA § 302) is not consistent with the international standards identified in Executive Committee Conclusions of the United Nations High Commissioner for Refugees (UNHCR). Executive Committee Conclusions are attained by consensus of the member states. In 1983, the UNHCR Executive Committee concluded that unless an asylum seeker's claims are "manifestly unfounded or abusive," full review of a negative decision should be available to unsuccessful applicants. Under IIRIRA § 302, however, asylum seekers are required to establish a "credible fear" before being allowed to present claims for asylum to an immigration judge. INA § 235(b)(1)(B)(iii). IIRIRA's reduces opportunities for review.

Other examples of differences between IIRIRA and decisions of the UNHCR Executive Committee concern the detention of asylum seekers and the filing deadlines for asylum applications. In 1986, the UNHCR Executive Committee concluded that detention should be avoided. Under IIRIRA § 302, however, detention is mandatory even when an alien has established a "credible fear." INA § 235(b)(1)(B)(ii). In 1977, the UNHCR Executive Committee concluded that the failure of asylum seekers to apply for asylum within a certain time period should not prevent the consideration of late applications. Under IIRIRA § 604, an asylum seeker must apply for asylum within a year of arrival unless the asylum seeker can show changed country conditions or extraordinary circumstances relating to the delay. IIRIRA's filing deadline removes the option of asylum for at least some of those persons whom the Protocol seeks to protect.

In a 1994 speech, the United Nations High Commissioner for Refugees, Sadako Ogata, linked the norm of *non-refoulement* with the rights to life and freedom from cruel, inhuman, or degrading treatment. Her statement echoes earlier statements by the Executive Committee of UNHCR that the refusing of admission to stowaway asylum-seekers could be cruel or degrading treatment and that treaty provisions are increasingly interpreted to protect against the expulsion of a person to a country where that person is at risk of being tortured or subjected to inhuman or cruel treatment or punishment.

The Refugee Convention of 1951 and the Protocol of 1967 give refugees certain travel rights. Article 26 of the Convention affords refugees the same right as aliens, in the same circumstances, to travel within a state. Article 27 provides that states "shall issue identity papers to any refugee in the territory who does not possess a valid travel document." Furthermore, Article 28 provides that states shall issue travel documents to refugees lawfully staying in their territory for the purpose of traveling outside their territory.

The Refugee Convention of 1951 and 1967 Protocol also give rights to refugees almost identical to the rights given stateless persons in the Convention relating to the Status of Stateless Persons. Under the 1951 Convention, refugees have rights at least as great as other aliens in the same state in regard to such subjects as the acquisition of property. The Universal Declaration of Human Rights and the two International Covenants on Human Rights provide civil, political, economic, social, and cultural rights to all people, including refugees. The rights of people displaced by armed conflicts are also protected by the Fourth Geneva Convention of 1949, as extended by the two Additional Protocols of 1977.

The Organization of African Unity Convention Governing the Specific Aspects of Refugee Problems in Africa of 1969 broadens the definition and thus the protection of refugees to include as refugees:

" . . . every person who, owing to external aggression, occupation, foreign domination or events seriously disturbing public order in either part or the whole of his country of origin or nationality, is compelled to leave his place of habitual residence in order to seek refuge in another place outside his country of origin or nationality."

A similarly broad definition of refugee was also accepted by the Colloquium on the International Protection of Refugees in Central America, Mexico and Panama in its Cartegena Declaration of 1984 to include persons who have fled their country because their lives, safety, or freedom have been threatened by generalized violence, foreign aggression, internal conflicts, massive violations of human rights, or other circumstances that have seriously disturbed public order.

There are several international organizations that protect and provide assistance to refugees. The UNHCR provides "for the protection of refugees falling under the competence of his [her] office." The UNHCR also helps to house, feed, resettle, repatriate, and integrate refugees. The International Organization for Migration and many voluntary agencies assist the UNHCR in these tasks. The International Committee of the Red Cross and the Red Cross/Red Crescent Societies around the world assist victims of armed conflicts.

In 1996 there were 26.1 million persons who were of concern to the UNHCR. This number included 15.4 million refugees; 4.7 million internally displaced; 3.3 million returnees; and 2.7 million others of concern (that is, who were in a refugee-like situation but have not been formally recognized as refugees). The UNHCR has been requested by the Secretary–General or other U.N. organs to assist some, but not all internally displaced persons. In part because of the relationship between external and internal displacement, the UNHCR has been involved with internally displaced in Central America, Africa, countries of the former Soviet Union and former Yugoslavia, and elsewhere. In 1994, UNHCR Executive Committee Conclusions emphasized the need for the international community to respond to the problem of internally displaced persons.

At the request of the U.N. Commission on Human Rights, a Special Representative of the Secretary–General on internally displaced persons has been appointed. The U.N. Special Representative on internally displaced persons estimated that there were more than 16 million internally displaced in the world during 1994. The Special Representative has raised consciousness about the treatment of the internally displaced and has made efforts to develop guiding principles that address the needs of the internally displaced. In recent years, the UNHCR increased its involvement with internally displaced, returnees, and persons threatened with displacement by armed conflict.

§ 11–3.1 Right Not to Be Returned, and Suffer Torture or Ill-treatment

The Convention against Torture, which has 104 parties (including the U.S.), states that "No State Party shall expel, return ('refouler') or extradite a person to another State where there are substantial grounds for believing that he would be in danger of being subjected to torture." The presence of "a consistent pattern of gross, flagrant or mass violations of human rights" is to be considered in determining if substantial grounds are present. The United Nations Committee against Torture has applied Article 3 of the Convention Against Torture to find an obligation not to expel a person to a country when that individual is personally at risk of being expelled or returned to a country to be tortured. The norm of *non-refoulement* under the Convention against Torture does not require that the torture that an individual faces be for reasons of race, religion, nationality, membership of a particular social group or political opinion. The Committee against Torture, in a 1994 communication concerning *Khan v. Canada*, found a violation of Article 3 because of substantial grounds for believing that Tahir Hussain Khan would be subjected to torture if returned to Pakistan.

The Covenant on Civil and Political Rights has been interpreted even more broadly than the Convention against Torture to prohibit the sending back of a person to her/his country of origin where that person would be at risk of either torture or ill-treatment. Article 7 of the Covenant on Civil and Political Rights prohibits the subjection of anyone to "cruel, inhuman or degrading treatment or punishment." As with the Convention against Torture, the interpretation of the Covenant on Civil and Political Rights in the context of returning a person to her/his country of origin applies Article 7 even to persons who have committed serious offenses.

Cruel and inhuman treatment within the meaning of Article 7 of the Covenant can include capital punishment if the punishment is not carried out with a minimum of suffering. The Human Rights Committee in 1993 considered a communication concerning *Ng v. Canada* and determined that the possibility that Charles Ng would be executed by gas asphyxiation if he were returned to California would make complying with a request for his extradition a violation of the Covenant. The same year, the Committee rejected a communication concerning *Kindler v. Canada*, holding that capital punishment is not always a violation of the Covenant and found that the potential execution of Joseph Kindler by lethal injection would not violate the Covenant. Similarly in *Cox v. Canada*, the Human Rights Committee in 1994 adopted the view that the confinement of Keith Cox on death row would not violate the Covenant, at least in part because of the possibility of appeal or pardon.

Article 3 of the European Convention for the Protection of Human Rights and Fundamental Freedoms states that a person shall not be "subjected to torture or to inhuman or degrading treatment or punishment." In 1989, the European Court of Human Rights, in *Soering v. United Kingdom*, found that the extradition of Jens Soering to the U.S. would violate Article 3. In making this finding, the European Court held that it would inflict inhuman and degrading treatment on Soering if he were subjected to a prolonged detention on death row in Virginia. (Eventually, he was extradited to stand trial for murder under an assurance that he would not be sentenced to death.) In 1991, the European Court of Human Rights in *Vilvarahah v. United Kingdom* stated that the possibility of ill-treatment of Nadarajah Vilvarahah and others when they were returned to Sri Lanka did not violate Article 3 because there were not substantial grounds for believing that the applicants would be subject to a real risk. In 1996, the European Court, in *Chahal v. United Kingdom*, held that there was a real risk of Mr. Chahal being subjected to treatment contrary to Article 3 if he were to returned to India. Chahal was a leading Sikh militant supporting the cause of separatism and was likely to be targeted by Punjab police and/or the security forces, irrespective of which part of India to which he returned. The Court gave little credence to assurances of the Indian government that Chahal would not be subjected to ill-treatment, because the government had been unable to curb human rights violations by the Punjab police and other security forces.

Article 8 of the European Convention for the Protection of Human Rights and Fundamental Freedoms states that "everyone has the right to respect for his private and family life, his home and his correspondence and there shall be no interference by a public authority with the exercise of this right except such as is in accordance with the law and is necessary in a democratic society, in the interests of national security, public safety or the economic well-being of the country, for the prevention of disorder or crime, for the protection of health or morals, or for the protection of the rights and freedoms of others." In 1997, the European Court of Human Rights, in *Boujlifa v. France*, held that the deportation of a Moroccan national did not constitute a violation of Article 8. Mr. Boujlifa claimed that deportation would interfere with his private and family life. He had lived in France since he was five years old and received his education there; his parents and eight brothers and sisters live in France; and he is currently living with a French woman. The Court noted that the offences of armed robbery and robbery, for which Mr. Boujlifa's deportation was sought, constituted a particularly serious violation of the security and of public order. Under the circumstances of this case, the requirements of public order outweighed the interference with Boujlifa's personal and family life. Hence, the Court found that deportation cannot be regarded as disproportionate to the legitimate aims pursued.

§ 11–4 ASYLUM

§ 11–4.1 The Right to Grant Asylum

A nation may grant either asylum within its territory ("territorial asylum") or within its embassies, consular offices, military ships, or other such locations. The idea of asylum developed before the Middle Ages when churches granted a refuge in holy places where persons fleeing from danger could be free from seizure. As the power of governments grew, asylum in churches became less prevalent.

European governments began granting territorial asylum as the Reformation divided the continent. An increase in the granting of territorial asylum occurred in the Eighteenth Century. Legal writers in the Eighteenth Century began invoking asylum for those persons guilty of political crimes and for victims of religious persecution. Grotius went so far as to view asylum as both a state's right and duty. Most other writers, however, did not go as far as saying that states had a duty to grant political asylum. During and after the French Revolution, this notion was transformed into a juridical principle. The Revolution considered it a duty of countries to help the oppressed. The French Constitution of 1793 provided asylum for foreigners who were exiled from their home state in the cause of human rights and liberty.

The right to grant asylum is reflected in several international instruments. Article 14 of the Universal Declaration of Human Rights provides the right to "seek and enjoy" asylum. This right, however, "may not be invoked in the case of prosecutions genuinely arising from non-political crimes or from acts contrary to the purposes and principles of the United Nations." The U.N. General Assembly Resolution 2312 (XXII) on Territorial Asylum of 1967 reaffirmed the right to grant asylum contained in Article 14 of the Universal Declaration of Human Rights.

§ 11–4.2   The Right to Receive Asylum

While it is generally agreed that nations have the right to grant asylum, there is no similar agreement on the right of an individual to demand asylum. Article 14 of the Universal Declaration of Human Rights provides a "right to seek and to enjoy in other countries asylum from persecution." There is no right, however, to be granted asylum. An earlier draft provided for a right to "seek and be granted" asylum. This language was amended to make clear that states were not willing to accept an obligation to open their borders in advance to an unascertainable and possibly large number of refugees.

Although an individual may not have a right to asylum, the Convention and Protocol relating to the Status of Refugees forbid a nation from forcibly returning a refugee who is fleeing from a neighboring state. The admitting nation is then free to force the individual to go to another nation. This right is reflected in U.N. General Assembly Resolution 2312 (XXII) on Territorial Asylum of 1967. Article 3, paragraph 1 states that "no person referred to in Article 1, paragraph 1, shall be subjected to measures such as rejection at the frontier or, if he has already entered the territory in which he seeks asylum, expulsion or compulsory return to any state where he may be subjected to persecution." Paragraph 2 provides an exception in the case of national security, public safety, or massive influx of persons.

The UNHCR attempted in 1977 to establish a treaty on territorial asylum along the same lines as the Declaration on Territorial Asylum by convening a Conference of Plenipotentiaries in Geneva. The participating states, however, were unable to agree; the UNHCR adjourned the conference indefinitely because of the concern that the states would diminish the international protections for those persons who seek asylum.

The Executive Committee of the UNHCR in 1981 adopted non-binding recommendations regarding the protection of asylum seekers particularly in the context of massive movements of population. The Executive Committee recommended that asylum seekers be admitted to the state where they first seek entry, so that they may be afforded protection and assistance, even for a temporary period. The recommendations also state that asylum seekers should not be punished for illegal entry, should enjoy the rights established in the Universal Declaration of Human Rights, should be granted all the necessary facilities to enable them to obtain a satisfactory durable solution, etc.

There seems to be a growing recognition that the Convention on Refugees, the related Protocol, and national asylum procedures do not establish a satisfactory legal framework for dealing with the recent large influxes of asylum seekers. The Convention, the Protocol, and the national procedures, which they inspired, are premised upon the need for an individual determination of eligibility for asylum. Massive population movements in which many claim asylum do not permit such individual determinations. Also, intended immigrants claim asylum in many countries knowing that the procedures for individual adjudication are so overloaded that they effectively will be able to remain indefinitely. Governments have begun to respond by detaining large numbers of asylum seekers and by developing expedited asylum procedures.

While there is a need for a new legal structure, there is concern that such a structure may be less protective of the rights of asylum seekers than the present approach. Rather than seek a new legal structure, the UNHCR has used ad hoc approaches in which, for example, a prima facie determination of eligibility for asylum is made for whole groups at a time. Governments have began to provide temporary protected status and similarly restricted entry rather than refugee status as a way of dealing with major influxes. Nonetheless, there is little doubt that the problem of mass exodus and asylum represents a continuing challenge for both domestic and international legal systems.

§ 11–5 THE RIGHTS OF MIGRANT WORKERS

The International Labour Organization (ILO) in 1949 promulgated Convention No. 97 concerning Migration for Employment and the related Recommendation No. 86 concerning Migration for Employment. These two instruments provide:

1. Safeguards against misleading information relating to emigration and immigration;

2. assurance of medical services for migrants;

3. a prohibition against discrimination in regard to conditions of employment, trade union membership, social security, and taxes;

4. a prohibition against returning a migrant to her/his country of origin after s/he was admitted on a

permanent basis, but is no longer able to work by reason of illness; and

5. similar protections for migrants.

The Migrant Workers (Supplementary Provisions) Convention of 1975 (No. 143) and the Migrant Workers Recommendations of 1975 (No. 151) supplement these legal protections by providing that governments should not only repeal discriminatory legislation, but enact promotional legislation to guarantee equality of opportunity and treatment in respect of employment, occupation, social security, trade union and cultural rights, as well as individual and collective freedoms of migrant workers. The ILO also has adopted a convention supporting the rights of migrant workers to social security.

Forty countries have ratified Convention No. 97, including Belgium, France, the Federal Republic of Germany, Italy, Netherlands, Portugal, Spain, and the United Kingdom. The United States is conspicuously absent from this list. Only 17 countries have, so far, ratified the supplementary Convention No. 143; of the countries just mentioned, only Italy and Portugal have ratified this instrument.

There is also a European Convention on the Legal Status of Migrant Workers. This convention came into force on 1 May 1983. It has been ratified by France, Italy, Netherlands, Norway, Portugal, Spain, Sweden, and Turkey.

After eleven years of drafting, the U.N. General Assembly on December 18, 1990, adopted the International Convention on the Protection of the Rights of All Migrant Workers and Members of Their Families. The Convention provides further protection for the rights of all migrant workers and their families, including frontier workers, seasonal workers, itinerant workers, and project-tied workers. The Convention does not apply to investors, students, trainees, refugees, and stateless persons. Furthermore, Article 35 of the Convention provides that none of its provisions shall be interpreted to imply the regularization of undocumented migrant workers. Only Colombia, Egypt, Malawi, Morocco, Philippines, Seychelles, Sri Lanka, and Uganda are parties to this 1990 convention. A total of twenty parties (twelve more) are required for the treaty to come into force.

With regard to certain rights the U.N. Convention is broader and more specific than the existing ILO instruments. Articles 43 and 45 of the U.N. Convention provide for equality of treatment for migrant workers and their families in access to educational institutions, vocational training, social and health services, and to cultural life. Furthermore, the migrant worker is guaranteed equality of treatment in access to co-operatives and self-management enterprises without change in migration status, and to housing. Further rights provided in the Convention include: the right to equality of treatment with nationals of the state concerned before courts and tribunals (Article 18); the prohibition of collective expulsion (Article 22); equal treatment with nationals as regards remuneration (Article 25); trade union rights and freedom of association (Articles 26 and 40); the facilitation of reunification of migrant workers with their families (Article 44); and the right to transfer earnings, particularly for the support of their families, to the country of origin (Article 47).

Further, once it comes into force, the Convention establishes a Committee on the Protection of the Rights of All Migrant Workers and Members of Their Families to examine government reports to be submitted every five years on their laws and practices with regard to the rights recognized in the Convention. This Committee will also consider complaints made by one state party concerning the laws and practices of another state party and will consider individual complaints if that individual's government declares that it is willing to authorize the Committee to receive such complaints. Because there has been a delay in the coming into force of the Convention on Migrant Workers, the U.N. Commission on Human Rights in 1997 established a Working Group on Migrants and Human Rights which reports annually to the Commission.

§ 11–6 RIGHTS OF NON–CITIZENS

In 1985, the U.N. General Assembly adopted by consensus a declaration on the human rights of individuals who are not citizens of the country in which they live. The declaration covers all individuals who are not nationals of the state in which they are present. The declaration provides for the respect of fundamental human rights of aliens (Article 5—right to life; right to privacy; equality before the courts and tribunals; freedom of opinion and religion; and retention of language, culture, and tradition). Subject to certain national restrictions, aliens shall also be guaranteed the right to leave the country, to freedom of expression, to peaceful assembly, and to own property alone or collectively.

Articles 7 and 8 provide rights for aliens lawfully in the country. Article 7 prohibits individual or collective expulsion on discriminatory grounds. Article 8 provides for trade union rights as well as the right to safe and healthy working conditions and the right to medical care, social security, and education.

The rights of aliens are also set forth in the General Comment of the Human Rights Committee issued in 1986 to interpret the relevant provisions of the International Covenant on Civil and Political Rights.

§ 11–7 POPULATION TRANSFER

In 1992 the U.N. Sub–Commission on Prevention of Discrimination and Protection of Minorities initiated a study on the human rights dimensions of population transfer, including the implantation of settlers and settlements. The Sub–Commission considered the final report in 1997, which found that international law prohibits the transfer of persons, including the implantation of settlers unless they give their consent. The study noted that consent may be assessed in the light of the use of force, coercive measures, and inducements to flee. In the context of development programs, population transfers are lawful if they are non-discriminatory, are based upon the will of the people, and do not deprive a "people" of their means of subsistence. The general consent of the population sought to be transferred must be obtained by means of dialogue and negotiation with elected representatives of the population on terms of equality, fairness, and transparency; equivalent land, housing, occupation, employment, and adequate monetary compensation must be provided; and the transfer must be justified by the public interest. Population transfers during armed conflicts may be justified by military necessity, which must be strictly construed to protect the people involved. The Sub–Commission also reviewed, but did not adopt a draft

Declaration on Population Transfer and the Implantation of Settlers.

CHAPTER 12

CITIZENSHIP

§ 12-1 CONCEPTS OF CITIZENSHIP

§ 12-1.1 Citizenship and Alienage

Citizenship connotes membership in a political society to which a duty of permanent allegiance is implied. The United States Supreme Court in *United States v. Cruikshank* (1875), stated:

Citizens are the members of the political community to which they belong. They are the people who compose the community, and who, in their associated capacity, have established or submitted themselves to the dominion of a government for the promotion of their general welfare and the protection of their individual as well as collective rights.

Alienage has the opposite meaning and signifies a condition of not belonging to the nation. The allegiance required of aliens is temporary and consists of willingness to comply with the nation's laws while residing in its territory.

The status of citizens in the United States carries with it all the rights and privileges embodied in the Constitution. Although aliens also enjoy certain constitutional protections, some provisions protect only "citizens," such as the Privileges and Immunities Clause of Article IV and the Fourteenth Amendment. Moreover, only citizens have the right to vote and to hold office (see § 13-4.1); a citizen cannot be barred or expelled from the United States.

With the additional rights of citizenship come added responsibilities, such as the obligation to perform military service, required of able-bodied adults. 50 U.S.C.A. §§ 453, 454. Aliens have served in the armed forces (which is one means by which an alien may expedite the acquisition of citizenship), but they have traditionally been exempt from military conscription—at least until they become permanent residents. Citizenship also imposes the obligation to accept jury duty when called. 28 U.S.C.A. § 1861. In contrast, aliens are disqualified from serving on a jury, and an alien's presence on the jury in a felony trial has served as grounds to vacate a conviction.

The degree of connections one must have with the nation to be a citizen varies with the manner by which citizenship is acquired. Almost all persons born in the United States, for example, acquire citizenship automatically and cannot lose it involuntarily, even if they leave the United States immediately after birth and never return. Aliens seeking citizenship by naturalization, however, generally must reside in the United States for five years after having been granted permanent residence and demonstrate their good moral character, attachment to the United States, as well as their understanding of United States history and principles of government. INA § 316(a).

When the United States acquired outlying territorial possessions near the turn of the century, native populations were not considered citizens, though their allegiance to the United States was expected. The Supreme Court held in the "Insular Cases" that these territories were not "incorporated" into the United States, and hence, local populations were to be accorded a reduced level of constitutional protection. *See Balzac v. Pörto Rico* (S.Ct.1922). The continued vitality of the incorporation doctrine is unclear. *See, e.g., Torres v. Puerto Rico* (S.Ct.1978).

This chapter examines the two major methods by which citizenship may be acquired—birth and naturalization. It describes the substantive requirements of naturalization and the procedures involved in seeking citizenship under the naturalization laws. The final section focuses on loss of nationality through either denaturalization or expatriation. As a preliminary matter, however, the discussion first considers the two rules for determining citizenship—the principles of *jus soli* and *jus sanguinis*.

§ 12–1.2   The Principles of Jus Soli and Jus Sanguinis

Citizenship at birth in the United States is conferred automatically—the person's volition plays no part. Such automatic acquisition of citizenship assures that each person will have a nationality in the United States. In light of experience such a result appears reasonable, as people have traditionally remained loyal and committed to the citizenship they acquire at birth. There exists no universal nationality rule, however. While some nations adhere to the principle of *jus soli*—citizenship by the place of one's birth, others embrace the principle of *jus sanguinis*—citizenship by descent, or literally, blood relationship. Moreover, a number of nations, including the United States and Great Britain, have adopted a combination of the two principles.

The principle of *jus soli* was a tenet of the common law of England. Although it has its roots in feudalism, it still serves well as a basic rule of citizenship in many parts of the world. *Jus sanguinis* was the rule of civil law countries in Europe which determined an individual's citizenship at birth by the citizenship of her/his parents. The concept of nationality based upon blood took hold in Europe during the French Revolution, which had created a spirit of patriotism and fraternity for the French as a distinct people, and this sort of nationalistic fervor eventually spread to other peoples of Europe.

Jus soli continued to establish the citizenship of people born in England even after feudalism no longer existed. The rule's primary advantage as the criterion for citizenship lay in the certainty it provided each person's political status. In Great Britain the principle of *jus soli* remains the basis of nationality law. Nonetheless, the development of the British Empire, resulting foreign trade, and travel led to statutory provisions which followed the approach of *jus sanguinis*—granting citizenship to children born abroad of British parents.

Similarly, in the United States the principle of *jus soli* generally was accepted as part and parcel of the common law inherited from England. *See United States v. Wong Kim Ark* (Sup.Ct.1898). Hence, citizenship was conferred ordinarily upon the native born, although large groups of native born persons—American Indians, blacks, and Asians—did not enjoy citizenship status for many years after the formation of the republic. *See Elk v. Wilkins* (Sup.Ct.1884). The principle of *jus soli* was codified in the Fourteenth Amendment of 1868. The principle of *jus sanguinis* in United States nationality law was first established by the Act of 1790, which provided that children born abroad of United States citizens who had resided in the United States "shall be considered as natural-born citizens." 1 Stat. 103. Every subsequent statute has precluded acquisition of United States citizenship by a child born abroad unless the citizen parent or parents have resided in the United States. *See* INA § 301.

§ 12–1.3   Dual Nationality

The problem of dual nationality principally results from the existence of two different rules for conferring citizenship. For example, an individual born of alien parents in the United States ordinarily obtains U.S. citizenship at birth yet s/he also may be vested with the citizenship of her/his parents by the *jus sanguinis* laws of the foreign state. *See, e.g., Mandoli v. Acheson* (Sup.Ct. 1952). Such dual nationality is generally regarded as undesirable, as it inevitably leads to conflicts of loyalty which are inconsistent with the unitary allegiance normally required for citizenship.

These conflicts become particularly serious in times of war, as the case of *Kawakita v. United States* (Sup.Ct. 1952) demonstrated. Tomoya Kawakita was born in the United States of Japanese parents and obtained dual citizenship by virtue of the nationality laws of each country. He lived in the United States until 1939, when at age seventeen he went to Japan and undertook studies at the Meiji University. After December 7, 1941, the United States and Japan were engaged in war but Kawakita remained in Japan to continue his studies. In March 1943, he registered in the Koseki, a family census register, after being told by the Japanese police that he must make a choice of citizenship. He never served in the armed forces of Japan. Rather, he obtained employment as an interpreter with the Oeyama Nickel Industry Co., Ltd., where he worked until Japan's surrender. He was hired to interpret communications between the Japanese and the prisoners of war who were assigned to work at the mine and in the factory of the company. During his employment he allegedly committed acts of brutality against United States prisoners.

In December 1945, Kawakita went to the United States consul at Yokohama and applied for registration as a U.S. citizen, stating under oath that he was a citizen of the United States and had not done any acts amounting to expatriation. He obtained a passport and returned to the United States in 1946. Shortly thereafter he was recognized by one of the former prisoners of war; Kawakita was arrested, charged, and tried for treason.

At his trial Kawakita argued that he had terminated his United States citizenship in 1943 before the alleged acts of brutality, and thus could not be guilty of treason. The trial court submitted the issue as to whether he had expatriated himself to the jury, and charged that upon finding Kawakita had lost his citizenship prior to the time specified in the indictment, they must acquit him, since his duty of allegiance would have ceased with the termination of his United States citizenship. The jury found that Kawakita had not expatriated himself under any of the methods prescribed by Congress, and he was found guilty of treason and sentenced to death. The Court of Appeals for the Ninth Circuit affirmed in 1951.

On writ of certiorari the United States Supreme Court (by a 4–3 majority) affirmed the conviction and death sentence, upholding the jury's findings of fact. The Court further stated: "He cannot turn (his United States citizenship) into a fair-weather citizenship, retaining it for possible contingent benefits but meanwhile playing the part of the traitor. An American citizen owes allegiance to the United States wherever he may reside." President Eisenhower later commuted Kawakita's death sentence to life imprisonment. In 1963 he obtained his release and returned to Japan.

Partly in response to the problems *Kawakita* and similar cases present, many nations have attempted to eliminate dual nationality by statute. A typical solution is to require the individual, who has acquired two citizenships while a minor, to choose a single nationality upon reaching the age of majority. Section 349(a)(1) of the INA provides that a U.S. citizen will lose her/his nationality by voluntarily obtaining naturalization in a foreign state upon her/his own application, or upon an application filed by a duly authorized agent, after having obtained the age of eighteen years. INA § 349(a)(1). *See* § 12–3.3, *infra.* Nonetheless, the statute does not address the issue of the individual obtaining dual nationality at birth or before the age of eighteen. So long as different national rules for conferring citizenship exist, dual nationality and its attendant problems will remain an issue for the law of citizenship.

§ 12–2   METHODS OF OBTAINING CITIZENSHIP

§ 12–2.1   Citizenship at Birth

a. Birth Within the United States

There are four ways to obtain citizenship: by birth in the United States or its territories, by birth outside the U.S. to a U.S. parent, by naturalization, or by naturalization of a parent while a child is under 18 years old.

All persons born in the United States and subject to its jurisdiction automatically acquire citizenship. INA § 301(a). This principle of common law was codified by the Fourteenth Amendment to the Constitution, adopted in 1868:

All persons born or naturalized in the United States, and subject to the jurisdiction thereof, are citizens of the United States and of the State wherein they reside.

The Citizenship Clause was intended to go further than the common law and included all African–Americans born in the United States. Before the amendment, African–Americans—whether slaves or free—had been denied the status of U.S. citizen. The Supreme Court in *Scott v. Sanford* (S.Ct.1857) had declared that Dred Scott was not a "citizen" but a "Negro" of African descent, whose ancestors were slaves. He was thus barred from filing suit in U.S. District Court to obtain recognition of the freedom he had gained by entering and residing in free territory. The resulting Civil War led to the abolition of slavery. Because of the *Dred Scott* decision, however, proponents of the Fourteenth Amendment argued that while the Emancipation Proclamation had freed African–Americans, they could not become citizens without a constitutional amendment. The Fourteenth Amendment was thus adopted.

The Fourteenth Amendment also eliminated any doubt that persons born in the United States of alien parents were citizens. Such a proposition was confirmed by the Court in *United States v. Wong Kim Ark* (S.Ct.1898). Wong Kim Ark was born in San Francisco in 1873. His parents were native-born Chinese merchants who lived in this country as resident aliens. They left the United States in 1890 and returned to China permanently. Wong

Kim Ark made a temporary visit to his parents in 1894, but upon return the following year to the United States, was not permitted to land at San Francisco. The government claimed Wong Kim Ark was not a U.S. citizen but a Chinese laborer, and was properly barred entrance under the Chinese Exclusion Act. 22 Stat. 58. He challenged his exclusion in federal court, claiming citizenship under the Fourteenth Amendment. Justice Gray, in delivering the opinion of the United States Supreme Court, rejected the government's contention that the rule of *jus sanguinis*— citizenship by blood relationship—determined nationality in the United States. To the contrary, both the Fourteenth Amendment and the Civil Rights Act of 1866 (14 Stat. 27) had explicitly reaffirmed "the fundamental principle of citizenship by birth within the dominion." *Wong Kim Ark*. Hence, children born in this country were citizens without regard to the nationality of their parents. Wong Kim Ark won readmission to the United States.

The words "subject to the jurisdiction thereof" suggest exceptions to the general rule of *jus soli* or citizenship by birth within the dominion. For example, where a child was born in the United States to parents in the diplomatic service of the French government, the child was subject to the jurisdiction of the French Republic, not that of the United States. The physical fact of birth in this country did not alone confer citizenship. *In re Thenault* (D.D.C.1942).

A second exception concerned Native Americans, illustrated by the case of *Elk v. Wilkins* (Sup.Ct.1884). John Elk was born a member of a Native American tribe. He severed his tribal relations and moved to Omaha, Nebraska. He asked to be registered and permitted to vote in local elections, but registrar Wilkins refused him, claiming Elk—as a Native American—was not a citizen of the United States and thus not qualified to vote. Elk claimed citizenship under the Fourteenth Amendment in his suit against the registrar. The Supreme Court held that the Fourteenth Amendment failed to confer citizenship upon Elk, who was born subject to the jurisdiction of his tribe rather than that of the United States. His subsequent renunciation of his tribal allegiance was irrelevant. He only would become a U.S. citizen by being "naturalized in the United States."

The Citizenship Act of 1924, however, established the citizenship status of Native Americans born after its enactment in the United States. 43 Stat. 253. The Nationality Act of 1940 reconfirmed the citizenship of all Native Americans born in the U.S. 54 Stat. 1137. INA § 289 also recognized the right of many "American Indians born in Canada" to pass the border of the United States. INA § 301(b) provides:

The following shall be nationals and citizens of the United States at birth:

(b) A person born in the United States to a member of an Indian, Eskimo, Aleutian, or other aboriginal tribe: *provided,* that the granting of citizenship under this subsection shall not in any manner impair or otherwise affect the right of such person to tribal or other property.

By its proviso expressly excepting tribal property rights, Congress emphasized its intention to impose all other obligations of citizenship, or so found the Second Circuit in *Ex parte Green* (2d Cir.1941). Accordingly, appellant Green, a member of the Onondaga Tribe, was a citizen within the meaning of § 3(a) of the Selective Service Act of 1940, and subject to military service.

Two additional exceptions to the general rule of *jus soli* merit mention. Children born on foreign public ships while such vessels sit in the territorial waters of the United States, are not subject to U.S. jurisdiction and thus do not receive U.S. citizenship. *United States v. Wong Kim Ark* (Sup.Ct.1898). Persons born in private vessels within the territorial sovereignty of the United States, however, would acquire United States citizenship. Finally, children born to alien enemies in hostile occupation of United States territory would not be subject to United States jurisdiction and would not gain citizenship upon their birth.

b. Birth in the Territories of the United States

Near the end of the nineteenth century the United States began to acquire territories and possessions beyond its mainland. The issue of how and whether to grant the peoples of these territories United States citizenship generated much debate. Congress has passed several statutes granting nationality to the residents of some but not all territories and possessions of the United States.

(1) *Hawaii*—The Hawaiian Islands became part of the United States on July 7, 1898, and persons born in Hawaii after that date are United States citizens. 30 Stat. 750. A person who was a citizen of the Republic of Hawaii on August 12, 1898, obtained United States citizenship as of April 30, 1900, the date Congress enacted a statute incorporating Hawaii into the Union as a territory. 31 Stat. 141. Hawaii became a state on August 21, 1959. 73 Stat. 4.

(2) *Alaska*—Russia owned Alaska until 1867 when it sold the territory to the United States. 15 Stat. 539. All persons born in Alaska after March 30, 1867, except noncitizen Native Americans acquired United States citizenship. A Native American living or born in Alaska as of June 2, 1924, is a citizen of the United States. 43 Stat. 253. Alaska gained statehood on January 3, 1959. 72 Stat. 339.

(3) *Puerto Rico*—In 1899, the island of Puerto Rico was ceded to the United States by Spain in the treaty concluding the Spanish–American War. 30 Stat. 1154. Persons born in Puerto Rico from the date of cession to January 13, 1941, did not acquire citizenship at birth. With the Nationality Act of 1940, persons born there after January 13, 1941, and subject to the jurisdiction of the United States became U.S. citizens. 54 Stat. 1137. Persons born between April 11, 1899, and January 12, 1941, gained U.S. citizenship as of January 13, 1941, if they were residing in territory over which the United States exercised sovereignty.

(4) *Canal Zone and Panama*—The United States acquired the Canal Zone by treaty with Panama in 1904, to lease it in perpetuity. 33 Stat. 1234. By legislation first enacted in 1937 (50 Stat. 558), children born in the Canal Zone after February 25, 1904, became U.S. citizens if either the father or mother was a U.S. citizen. INA § 303(a). A child born in the Republic of Panama also received U.S. citizenship if either parent was a citizen employed by the United States, by the Panama Railroad Company, or by its successor in title. INA § 303(b).

In 1977, a treaty was negotiated returning sovereignty over the Canal Zone to Panama which Congress ratified in 1979. 93 Stat. 452. Citizenship acquired under the statute prior to the transfer is unaffected; but since the Canal Zone no longer constitutes U.S. territory, children born in the region of United States citizens are subject to the general rules applicable to children born outside the United States.

(5) *Virgin Islands*—The United States purchased the Virgin Islands from Denmark pursuant to an Act of January 25, 1917. 39 Stat. 1706. The Act of 1952 (66 Stat. 237) grants citizenship to all persons born in the Virgin Islands after January 17, 1917, and to any former Danish citizens who (1) did not declare an intent to preserve their Danish citizenship as provided under the treaty of purchase or (2) had subsequently renounced the declaration. INA § 306(a)(1). Several other categories of Virgin Island residents also became U.S. citizens after 1917.

(6) *Guam*—The Island of Guam was acquired from Spain in settlement of the Spanish–American War. Persons living in Guam on April 11, 1899, and their children born on or after that date were declared citizens of the United States as of August 1, 1950, if on this date they were residing in Guam or in other territory over which the United States exercises sovereignty and had taken no steps to retain or acquire a different nationality. All persons born in Guam on or after April 11, 1899, are citizens of the United States as of the date of their birth, provided that if the person was born before August 1, 1950, s/he has taken no steps to retain or acquire a different nationality. INA § 307.

(7) *The Philippines*—The United States acquired the Philippines as a result of the Spanish–American War. Filipinos never collectively obtained the status of U.S. citizens, instead being designated "noncitizen nationals."

INA § 308. They owed allegiance to the United States, but received none of the privileges of citizenship. In 1946, the Philippines obtained independence (61 Stat. 1174); Filipinos thus acquired a new nationality and the status of aliens in regard to the United States.

c. Birth Outside the United States

Individuals born abroad of United States citizen parents can acquire United States citizenship. This acquired form of citizenship is controlled by statute, rather than by the Constitution or the Fourteenth Amendment. Each statute dating from the original 1790 Act has required the citizen parent or parents to have lived in the United States prior to the child's birth. 1 Stat. 103. The statutes conferring citizenship by *jus sanguinis* (blood relationship) underwent substantive changes in 1934, 1940, and 1952. Hence, in order to determine whether an individual obtained citizenship at birth outside the United States, it must be determined which statutory period is applicable. *See* 66 Interp.Rel. 444 (1989) (containing a reprinted chart illustrating the rules that apply to legitimate and illegitimate children born at various time periods).

(1) PERSONS BORN ABROAD BEFORE MAY 24, 1934

The first Congress exercised its constitutionally granted power to "establish an Uniform Rule of Naturalization" by enacting the Act of March 26, 1790, which provided: "And the children of citizens of the United States, that may be born beyond sea, or out of the limits of the United States, shall be considered as natural born citizens: *Provided*, That the right of citizenship shall not descend to persons whose fathers have never been resident in the United States." 1 Stat. 103. This provision, with minor phrasing changes and with the same emphasis on paternal residence, was retained by three subsequently enacted naturalization statutes. 1 Stat. 415, 2 Stat. 155, 10 Stat. 604.

(2) BIRTH ABROAD BETWEEN MAY 24, 1934, AND JANUARY 12, 1941

The Act of May 24, 1934, extended acquired citizenship to persons whose *mothers* were citizens and past residents of the United States. 48 Stat. 797. Consequently, in cases where one parent is an alien and the other a citizen, a foreign-born child could acquire citizenship through the citizen parent, whether it be a father or mother. To have retained citizenship, however, the child must have resided continuously in the United States during the period immediately prior to the child's eighteenth birthday. Persons born abroad between May 24, 1934, and January 12, 1941, were governed by the 1934 statute. Congress later passed retroactive legislation which abolished the retention requirement for any person under age 26 as of October 10, 1978.

(3) BIRTH ABROAD BETWEEN JANUARY 13, 1941, AND DECEMBER 23, 1952

The Nationality Act of 1940 conferred citizenship at birth to children of parents who were both United States citizens, or of which one was a citizen and the other a national, as long as a citizen parent had previously resided in the United States or its outlying possessions. 54 Stat. 1138. If only one parent was a citizen and the other an alien, the citizen parent was required to have resided previously in the United States or its outlying possessions for ten years, at least five of which were after attaining the age of sixteen. Moreover, a child lost her/his acquired citizenship by failure to take up residence in the United States for a period or periods totaling five years between the ages of thirteen and twenty-one. This residency requirement did not apply to a child born abroad whose U.S. citizen parent was, at the time of the child's birth, residing abroad solely or principally in the employment of the United States government, certain U.S. organizations having their principal place of business in the United States, or an international agency in which the United States participates. Persons born between January 13, 1941, and December 23, 1952, are covered by the provisions of the 1940 Act.

(4) PERSONS BORN ABROAD AFTER DECEMBER 23, 1952

Under the Immigration and Nationality Act of 1952 (66 Stat. 163), where both parents of a foreign-born child are United States citizens, the child inherits citizenship in the same manner as provided by the 1940 Act. If one parent is a citizen and the other a U.S. "national" (*see, e.g.,* § 12–2.1.b(7)), the citizen parent must have been physically present in the United States or its outlying possessions for one year prior to the child's birth. INA § 301(d). If one parent is a citizen and the other an alien, the 1952 statute provided that the citizen parent must have been physically present in the United States or its outlying possessions for a period of ten years, at least five of which were after attaining the age of fourteen. INA § 301(g). In 1986 this physical presence requirement was reduced to five years, at least two of which were after attaining the age of fourteen.

(5) AMENDMENTS TO THE 1952 ACT

(i) *Exemption for Foreign Service.* In 1966 Congress passed an amendment to section 301(g) of the 1952 Act (80 Stat. 1322) attaching a proviso which allowed periods of overseas service in the armed forces, in the employment of the United States government, or in the employment of an international organization to which the United States is a member, as counting towards satisfaction of the ten year physical presence requirement. INA § 301(g). Congress retained this provision when it reduced the physical residence requirement to five years in 1986. In addition, any period during which the citizen parent was physically present abroad as an unmarried dependent of a person in such service counts towards satisfying the requirement.

The amendment specifically was designed to alleviate the hardship of the children of parents in foreign civilian service who, if they were to marry a foreign national, were precluded by law from transmitting their United States citizenship to their foreign-born children, because they lacked the requisite years of physical presence in the United States. As the State Department wrote in its letter to then Vice–President Humphrey, requesting the legislation:

> It is not uncommon for the children of a foreign service officer to spend most of their youthful years abroad accompanying the parents from one assignment to another. The proposed amendment, in effect, would treat the time spent abroad in such cases as constructive physical presence in the United States for the purpose of transmitting U.S. citizenship.

(ii) *Elimination of Retention Requirement for Children Born Abroad.* Until 1972, INA § 301(b) required that the citizen child born abroad of parents, one of whom was a citizen and the other an alien, had to reside in the United States for five consecutive years after attaining the age of fourteen but before reaching age twenty-four.

Congress decided in 1972 that the intent of the law could be met by a lesser period of residence, "thereby alleviating the hardship that is often caused by the separation of children or young adults from their families and the attendant financial burden imposed by such separation." Therefore, Congress reduced the residence requirement to two years of physical presence in the United States for a continuous period between the ages of fourteen and twenty-eight, further providing that absence of less than sixty days in the aggregate would not break the continuity of such physical presence. Finally, the legislation provided that these residence requirements would not apply in the case of a child whose alien parent was naturalized while the child was under age eighteen.

Despite the liberalized residence requirement of the 1972 amendment, 693 citizens lost their citizenship for failure to comply between 1972 and 1977. This unhappy result prompted Congress in 1978 to eliminate altogether the residence requirement for children born of one citizen parent and one alien parent. In its report accompanying the bill the House Judiciary Committee stated: "The Committee believes that section 301(b) of the Immigration and Nationality Act currently creates an inconsistency in our citizenship laws, in that this is the only class of United States citizens who are subject to any residence requirement in order to retain their citizenship."

The Judiciary Committee felt that repeal of section 301(b) would best redress the inequity. While some members of Congress expressed concern that repeal of section 301(b) would create the possibility of "generations of citizens residing with little or no connection with the United States," such fears were groundless. Until 1986, section 301(g) continued to provide that in order for a United States citizen to transmit citizenship to her/his child born abroad of the citizen parent and an alien parent, the citizen parent must have resided in the United States for ten years at least five of which were after attaining the age of fourteen. In 1986, this residency requirement was reduced to five years, at least two of which were after attaining the age of fourteen.

§ 12–2.2 Citizenship by Naturalization

a. Historical Development

Naturalization is the principal process by which persons not acquiring citizenship at birth may obtain citizen status. The power to confer citizenship in this manner derives from Article I, section 8 of the Constitution which authorized Congress "to establish a uniform Rule of Naturalization." Since the initial naturalization statute of 1790 (1 Stat. 103), Congress has exclusively exercised the power to establish the conditions upon which aliens might be naturalized. *See Collet v. Collet* (C.C.D.Pa.1792).

In the original statute of 1790 Congress prescribed that a "free white alien" who had resided in the United States for two years might be naturalized in a court proceeding, provided s/he was of good moral character and took an oath to support the Constitution. 1 Stat. 103. The Act of 1795 lengthened the residency requirement to five years and enacted additional conditions that the applicant for naturalization declare formal intent to seek citizenship three years before actual admission; that the applicant renounce any former allegiance and swear allegiance to the United States; that the applicant satisfy the court s/he "has behaved as a man [sic] of good moral character, attached to the principles of the Constitution of the United States, and [be] well disposed to the good order and happiness of the same." 1 Stat. 414.

An unfortunate period (1798–1802) of hysteria against foreigners produced the Alien and Sedition Acts and much more restrictive naturalization requirements (residence requirement increased to fourteen years, declaration of intent period increased to five years). 1 Stat. 566. The hysteria soon dissipated, however, and Congress enacted the more lenient provisions of the 1795 Act in the Act of April 14, 1802. 2 Stat. 153. The substantive provisions of 1795 closely resemble the general requirements of the present law, notwithstanding several refinements discussed *infra*.

Congress established substantive requirements for naturalization in the first years of the republic, but failed to provide uniform procedures and administration until passage of the Naturalization Act of 1906. 34 Stat. 596. The statute vested responsibility for administrative supervision of naturalization in the Bureau of Immigration and Naturalization within the U.S. Department of Commerce and Labor; it prescribed uniform naturalization forms; required that each petitioner for naturalization obtain an official certificate of lawful admission and attach it to the petition for naturalization; required uniform naturalization fees; established time limitations for the courts to hear and grant petitions (minimum of 90 days after filing, no hearings permitted within 30 days of a general election); and finally, required that each petition be supported by two citizen witnesses who would testify to the petitioner's qualifications for citizenship.

Subsequent procedural revisions included permitting heretofore excluded "alien enemies" to petition for naturalization and the establishment of court-appointed naturalization examiners who would hear the evidence in naturalization cases and recommend dispositions to the federal courts. 44 Stat. 709. Congress added several substantive revisions in the Nationality Act of 1940. 54 Stat. 1137. Most significantly, the act eased racial restrictions on naturalization. Persons from races indigenous to the Western Hemisphere became eligible for naturalization. Up until that time only white persons and persons of African nativity or descent had been eligible. 1 Stat. 414; 16 Stat. 254. In 1943 Congress added Chinese immigrants as a fourth class of eligible persons, (57 Stat. 600) while at the same time repealing the Chinese Exclusion Act (22 Stat. 58) which had specifically prohibited naturalization of Chinese persons.

The Immigration and Nationality Act of 1952 provided comprehensive codification of the law governing citizenship. 66 Stat. 163. Among the most significant changes enacted by the 1952 law was elimination of all racial and gender qualifications for naturalization. The statute finally ended the blatantly racist formulations of previous naturalization provisions. INA § 311. The statute did, however, preclude naturalization (1) of persons belonging to certain subversive groups (INA § 313), (2) of persons who had sought relief from United States military services on the ground of their alienage (INA § 315), or who had deserted from the armed forces during wartime (INA § 314), and (3) of aliens against whom a deportation proceeding or order was outstanding. INA § 318. Congress also enacted provisions to facilitate naturalization of aliens who had actively served in the armed forces during World War I, World War II, the Korean hostilities, the Vietnam Conflict, or later conflicts. INA § 329.

The 1990 Act and the 1991 Act made the INS the sole decisionmaker in naturalization cases, but the court should administer the oath of allegiance within 45 days or the district director will give the oath.

During the last few years the INS has been placing increasing emphasis on its efforts to naturalize as many permanent residents as possible. For example, during 1960 the INS assisted 119,442 permanent residents in receiving U.S. citizenship by naturalization. In 1970 the number of naturalizations declined to 110,399. But by the most recent year for which there is data, that is 1994, more than 406,223 people received U.S. citizenship through naturalization. In addition to the INS efforts to promote naturalization, many permanent residents have been encouraged to apply for citizenship because of concern that they would be denied education, health benefits, and participation in other governmental programs by such measures as Proposition 187 in California and the Illegal Immigration and Reform and Immigrant Responsibility Act of 1996. *See* chapter 1, *supra*.

b.　*Requirements of Naturalization*

(1) RESIDENCE AND PHYSICAL PRESENCE

Section 316(a) of the Immigration and Nationality Act requires that, except as otherwise provided, no person shall become a U.S. citizen by being naturalized unless (1) s/he has resided continuously in the United States for five years as a lawfully admitted permanent resident, (2) during the five years immediately prior to filing the petition for naturalization s/he has been physically present in the United States for at least half of the time, and (3) s/he has resided within the district in which s/he filed the petition for at least three months. The applicant must reside continuously within the United States from the date of the petition up to the time of admission to citizenship. INA § 316. The purpose of the residency requirements is to create a reasonable period of "probation" that will enable candidates to discard their foreign attachments, to learn the principles of the U.S. system of government, and to develop an identification with the national community.

To comply with the statute a legal residence is necessary; a valid statutory residence prior to naturalization cannot be founded on an illegal entry into the country. Congress has defined "residence" under the 1952 Act to mean "the place of general abode ... [a person's] principal, actual dwelling place in fact, without regard to intent." INA § 101(a)(33). The question of residence thus turns on a determination of where an applicant has held the status of lawful permanent resident alien, not on declarations of where s/he intends to live.

An applicant for citizenship need not show that s/he stayed at the claimed residence each day of the five year statutory period. Temporary absences from the place of abode—even from the United States—do not alone break the continuity of an applicant's residence. Absence from the United States for less than six months during the statutory period do not affect continuous residence, while an absence of more than six months but less than one year presumptively breaks the continuity. INA § 316(b). The applicant can overcome the presumption by "establish[ing] to the satisfaction of the Attorney General that he did not in fact abandon his residence in the United States during such period." An absence from the United States for one year or more will as a matter of law break the continuity of residence; the applicant will be required to complete a new period of residence after s/he returns to the United States.

As an exception to the physical residency requirement, persons who expect to be away from the United States for a year or more in service of the United States government, a recognized U.S. institution of research, a U.S. corporation engaged in foreign trade and commerce, a public international organization of which the United States is a member by treaty or statute, or a religious organization, may apply for permission to be absent without breaking their residence for purposes of naturalization. Before seeking such exception with Form N–470, an applicant must continuously reside in the United States—following lawful admission—for one year or more. INA §§ 316(b), 317. The applicant must establish to the satisfaction of the Immigration and Naturalization Service that her/his absence from the United States for such period is in service of the government, for the purpose of conducting scientific research, for the purpose of developing trade or commerce necessary to protect property rights in a foreign country, or as a member of a public international organization. INA § 316(b)(1). A 1981 amendment provides that dependent unmarried sons and daughters of a person who qualifies for benefits under this provision are also entitled to such benefits during the period for which they were residing abroad as dependent members of the person's household. INA § 316(b).

Recognizing the peculiar difficulties individuals employed on seagoing vessels face in meeting the normal residency requirements, Congress has traditionally relaxed those requirements for persons serving on certain United States vessels. 40 Stat. 542; 54 Stat. 1137. Under current law the benefit of "constructive residence" is granted to aliens lawfully admitted for permanent residence who thereafter serve with good conduct, in any capacity other than as a member of the armed forces, on board (a) a vessel owned and operated by the United States government, or (b) a vessel whose "home port" is in the United States. INA § 330. Such service is deemed residence *and* physical presence for the purpose of satisfying the residency requirements of section 316(a). Similarly, INA § 317 preserves both the residence and physical presence of ordained persons who are sent outside the U.S. by a recognized U.S. religious institution.

The exemption to the one year absence limitation concerning continuity of residence, which is provided for certain applicants (INA § 316(b)(1)), does not relieve such persons from the requirement of physical presence within the United States for one-half of the statutory five year period. INA § 316(c). Persons employed by the United States government, however, are exempted completely from the physical presence requirements of section 316(a). INA § 316(c).

Where an alien's absence from the United States is involuntary, courts have excused the absence for the purpose of residence and physical presence requirements. In the case of *In re Yarina* (N.D.Ohio 1947), a Czech immigrant, who had spent his entire childhood in the United States, was employed by a U.S. company at Wake Island, a United States territory in the South Pacific. In December 1941, the Japanese captured the island and took petitioner Yarina and many others prisoner. He remained a captive in a Japanese prisoner of war camp until September 1945. He filed his petition for naturalization in the year following his liberation and return to the United States. The court held that the provision depriving an alien of the right to naturalization, in case of absence from the United States for a year or more during the statutory period preceding the application, contemplated a voluntary departure from this country. Since the forces of the enemy transported Yarina from Wake Island to the prison camp, petitioner "never left his residence in the United States within the purview of the statute." He was thus granted his naturalization petition.

Nonetheless, if a petitioner departs the United States voluntarily but is prevented from returning by events beyond her/his control, the absence is unexcused. Mary Holzer, an Israeli national, was a lawfully admitted permanent resident alien who left the United States to visit Israel in October 1952. She cited financial reasons for her inability to return to the United States within the one year period. The court found that her extended absence barred the petition for naturalization, stating "the rule applies even where the absence from the United States beyond the statutory period was involuntary." *Petition of Holzer* (S.D.N.Y.1956). The court applied the same reasoning in the case of *In Re Petition For Naturalization of Vafaei–Makhsoos* (D.Minn.1984). Petitioner, a lawful permanent resident in the United States, while visiting Iran during the hostage crisis of 1979–81, was prevented by the U.S. government's travel restrictions from returning to the U.S. for more than a year. The involuntary character of the petitioner's absence did not provide an exception to the one year absence rule which broke the continuity of residence for the purposes of naturalization.

(2) Age

To apply for naturalization an applicant must generally have attained the age of eighteen years. INA § 334(b)(1). A parent or adoptive parent, however, can file an application on behalf of a child under age eighteen, if the parent is a citizen—either by birth or naturalization—at the time the petition is filed. The child must be residing with the citizen parent in the United States as a lawful permanent resident. INA § 322. Most children acquire citizenship at the time their parents are naturalized; they are not subject to the five year waiting period. Their naturalization is by operation of law; hence, no application or proceeding is necessary. This method of obtaining citizenship is called derivative naturalization.

(3) Literacy and Educational Requirements

Unless s/he is physically unable to do so through blindness or deafness, an applicant for naturalization must be able to speak and understand simple English, as well as read and write it. INA § 312(1). Before 1978, the Act provided an exemption to the literacy requirement for persons who, on the effective date of this chapter (1952), were over fifty years of age and had been living in the United States for periods totaling at least twenty years. In 1978 Congress amended the provision to exempt any person who was over the age of fifty years *at the time of filing their petition,* and who had been lawfully admitted for permanent residence for periods totaling twenty years. 92 Stat. 2474. The legislative history to this amendment pointed to the original exemption's lack of flexibility in addressing the language problems of persons who were slightly under fifty years of age as of

December 24, 1952. In addition, the 1990 Act provided an exemption from the literacy requirement for any person who had been a permanent resident for 15 years and who is over 55 years of age as of the date of application for naturalization.

The statute further requires "a knowledge and understanding of the fundamentals of the history, and of the principles and form of government, of the United States." INA § 312(2). Each person applying for naturalization, including the older persons mentioned above, must pass an examination demonstrating the requisite knowledge of the United States. An interpreter or sign language may be used to test the applicant's knowledge of United States history, principles, and form of government, if s/he is exempt from the literacy requirement. 8 C.F.R. § 332.11(b). The Immigration Service generally applies the educational requirements in a lenient manner with due consideration given to such factors as the extent of the applicant's education, background, age, and length of residence in the United States. 8 C.F.R. § 312.2. Moreover, the regulations provide for second and third opportunities to pass the examinations. 8 C.F.R. § 312.3.

The power of Congress to establish these literacy requirements has withstood constitutional challenge. In *Trujillo–Hernandez v. Farrell* (5th Cir.1974), petitioner brought a class action, attacking the statute on equal protection grounds. The Court of Appeals for the Fifth Circuit held that a direct attack on Congress' exercise of its naturalization power was foreclosed and nonjusticiable, as such power was part of the foreign relations responsibilities committed to Congress.

(4) GOOD MORAL CHARACTER

An applicant for naturalization must show that, during the five year statutory period before filing and up until the final hearing of the naturalization petition, s/he "has been and still is a person of good moral character. ..." INA § 316(a). The burden of establishing good moral character falls upon the petitioner, as an applicant must prove her/his eligibility for citizenship in every respect. *Berenyi v. INS* (Sup.Ct.1967).

Courts have struggled with the issue of what constitutes good moral character. Judge Learned Hand stated that it is a "test, incapable of exact definition; the best we can do is to improvise the response that the 'ordinary' man or woman would make, if the question were put whether the conduct was consistent with a 'good moral character'." *Posusta v. United States* (2d Cir.1961). Prior to 1952, no attempt had been made to define good moral character by statute. Then, in the 1952 Act, Congress chose to define by enumerated exclusions what would *preclude* a finding of good moral character. 66 Stat. 166. A person could not be considered of good moral character if s/he was at any time during the five year period:

(1) a habitual drunkard;

(2) one who during this period has committed adultery;

(3) a polygamist or a person illegally connected with prostitution, narcotics, or the unlawful entry of other aliens;

(4) one whose income is principally from illegal gambling activities;

(5) a person who had been convicted of two or more gambling offenses committed during this period;

(6) one who has given false testimony for the purpose of obtaining any benefits under the Act;

(7) a person who had been convicted and jailed for 180 days or more, regardless of whether the offense was committed within this period;

(8) one who *at any time* has been convicted of the crime of murder. INA § 101(f) (emphasis added). (The 1990 Act changed the words "the crime of murder" to "an aggravated felony.")

The fact that a person is not within the classes enumerated does not preclude a finding for other reasons that s/he lacks the requisite good moral character.

Congress hoped by this provision to establish some nationally uniform standards for determining good moral character. This objective was not fully realized, however, at least with respect to one of the most controversial bars to citizenship—adultery. For example, the Immigration and Naturalization Service took the position that what constituted adultery was to be determined under the law of the state where the act was committed. Laws concerning adultery varied considerably from state to state, raising the obvious question: what about the goal of uniformity? The Board of Immigration Appeals, which reviews the administrative decisions, sought to rationalize the Service's interpretation in *In re Pitzoff* (BIA 1962):

Congress' desire that there be uniformity related not to the methods to be used in determining whether adultery had been committed but related rather to the desire that *all* who had committed adultery should be barred from the prizes of the law. (emphasis added).

The Service's position was followed by some but not all courts. In *Moon Ho Kim v. INS* (D.C.Cir.1975), the U.S. Court of Appeals for the District of Columbia Circuit held that the definition of "adultery," as the term is used in the act, is not that definition which applies in the state where the extramarital act took place; rather, the appropriate approach is the application of a uniform federal definition, namely, "extramarital intercourse which tends to destroy an existing, viable marriage, and which would represent a threat to public morality."

If a person committed "technical adultery" but acted in good faith, as where petitioner obtained a Mexican divorce from his first wife and remarried, unaware of the invalidity of the divorce, he did not fall within the sanction of the act concerning adultery. *Dickhoff v. Shaughnessy* (S.D.N.Y.1956). In addition, the existence of extenuating circumstances were generally deemed relevant in determining whether an alien had established good moral character despite the commission of adultery. Hence, in *Wadman v. Immigration & Naturalization Service* (9th Cir.1964), petitioner's isolated acts of sexual intercourse with another, after his wife had willfully and permanently abandoned him, did not preclude him from establishing good moral character. But some courts insisted upon a stricter application of the statutory provision, such as the U.S. District Court for the Southern District of New York in *Petition for Naturalization of O_____ N_____* (S.D.N.Y.1964), which refused to consider as extenuating circumstances that the cohabiting petitioners were recent immigrants who wanted to marry but were unfamiliar with American divorce procedure. Referring to the legislative history, the court stated, "[T]he two Senate reports ... support the view that Section 1101(f)(2) [INA § 101(f)(2)] was an attempt to tighten the law and exclude the relevance of extenuating circumstances.... "

Ultimately, in 1981, Congress acknowledged the problems that the adultery classification had created for the courts in evaluating moral character on the individual facts of each case. It therefore repealed the adultery provision. 95 Stat. 1611. A person can still be found to lack good moral character under the discretionary provision that permits a finding of a lack of good moral character "for other reasons." INA § 101(f). Adultery, however, is no longer a mandatory bar to citizenship. Congress stated its rationale for repeal in the report accompanying the legislation:

> With respect to adultery, the Committee believes that the Immigration Service should not be required to inquire into the sex lives of applicants for naturalization. Such questions clearly represent an invasion of privacy. Furthermore, in testimony before the 96th Congress witnesses concurred in the view that the adultery bar was merely "window dressing" in the law; INS estimated that "7 out of 10 persons today who would admit to that conduct would fall within one or more of the judicial interpretations which excuse that conduct for purposes of naturalization."

INA § 316(e) provides that, in determining whether the applying alien is of good moral character, "the Attorney General shall not be limited to the applicant's conduct during the five years preceding the filing of the application, but may take into consideration ... the applicant's conduct and acts at any time prior to that period." The U.S. Court of Appeals for the Second Circuit in *Tieri v. INS* (2d Cir.1972) held that in evaluating petitioner's application for naturalization in 1966, the district court properly considered evidence of the petitioner's six arrests between 1922 and 1959, two of which resulted in convictions of robbery and bookmaking. The Second Circuit concluded that "petitioner persistently attempted to obscure any past conduct which he feared might prove suspicious or embarrassing to his cause, and that, accordingly, the district court was not mistaken in discerning a pattern of deception in the whole mosaic of petitioner's testimony."

The Third Circuit Court of Appeals held that INA § 101(f)(6), regarding the giving of false testimony for the purpose of obtaining benefits under the act, is mandatory in its terms and not subject to a distinction between material and immaterial matters. *In re Haniatakis* (3d Cir.1967). Haniatakis falsely stated on her naturalization application that she was unmarried for fear that her naturalization would be delayed for 5 more years if the INS knew of her marriage to another alien. The petitioner also misrepresented her prior places of residence.

The INS declared that her marriage to another alien would not have affected her application. The district court concluded that the false testimony did not affirmatively demonstrate the absence of good moral character because the misrepresentations were immaterial and the facts concealed would not have been a barrier to her naturalization. In reversing the judgment of the district court, the Third Circuit reasoned that naturalization is denied whenever false testimony is given for a practical reason; and in addition, that one who gives false testimony to deceive the government is unworthy of citizenship. A false answer which appears immaterial may nonetheless cut off a line of inquiry which might have revealed facts material to the applicant's eligibility for citizenship. The court distinguished *Chaunt v. United States* (Sup.Ct. 1960), in which the Supreme Court refused to denaturalize a citizen who had twenty years before failed to reveal on his naturalization application that he had previously been arrested. The provision of the act involved in *Chaunt,* INA § 340(a), specifically required that the fact concealed be "material." The government in *Chaunt* was attempting to deny the privileges of citizenship to one who had already been granted them.

(5) Attachment to Constitutional Principles

An applicant must show that s/he is "attached to the principles of the Constitution of the United States, and well disposed to the good order and happiness of the United States." INA § 316(a). The purpose behind this requirement is the admission to citizenship of only those persons who are in general accord with the basic principles of the community. *Petition of Sittler* (S.D.N.Y.1961). Courts have defined attachment to the Constitution as a belief in representative democracy, a commitment to the ideals embodied in the Bill of Rights, and a willingness to accept the basic social premise that political change only be effected in an orderly manner. Similarly, a favorable disposition to the good order and happiness of the United States has been characterized as a belief in the political processes of the United States, a general satisfaction with life in the United States, and a hope for future progress and prosperity. Neither requirement is thought to preclude a belief that change in the U.S. form of government within constitutional limits is desirable.

Whether an applicant for citizenship is attached to the principles of the Constitution depends on her/his state of mind, which must be determined on the basis of the applicant's conduct and expressions over a period of time. The INS cannot safely base its judgment on isolated statements of the applicant. Hence, the federal court in *In re Kullman* (W.D.Mo.1949) found that petitioner's isolated statement made before America's involvement in World War II expressing sympathy for the German people and praise for Adolf Hitler would not deny him citizenship, in light of his thirty-seven years of law-abiding residence in the United States and his aid to U.S. armed forces during World War I.

Although the general requirement of attachment to the Constitution allows discretion in evaluating a case on its own facts, several statutes enacted in 1952 specifically and automatically preclude naturalization of certain persons. Individuals belonging to the Communist Party or other totalitarian groups (INA § 101(a)(37)), and persons who—irrespective of membership in any organization— advocate the overthrow of the United States government by force or violence or other unconstitutional means may not obtain naturalization. INA § 313(a)(4). An applicant is not disqualified, however, if s/he can show that the membership in the prescribed organization is or was involuntary. INA § 313(d). Moreover, if the applicant can establish that such membership or affiliation occurred and terminated prior to the alien's attaining sixteen years of age, or such membership or affiliation was by operation of law or for purposes of obtaining employment, food, or other essentials, he or she may yet qualify for naturalization. In *Grzymala–Siedlecki v. United States* (5th Cir.1961), therefore, petitioner's enrollment in the Polish Naval Academy, which automatically conferred Communist Party membership, did not disqualify him from naturalization where the college education was necessary to the applicant's earning a livelihood in Poland.

A few courts have added another exception to the disqualification for Communist membership. Such membership or affiliation does not disqualify an applicant unless it is or was a "meaningful association." The Supreme Court had held, in the context of deportation proceedings, that a "meaningful association" signifies at minimum "[an] awareness of the Party's political aspect." *Rowoldt v. Perfetto* (Sup.Ct.1957). The federal district court of Puerto Rico applied the same analysis in *In re Pruna* (D.Puerto Rico 1968) holding that where petitioner's membership in an organization supporting Fidel Castro's revolution in Cuba in 1958 resulted from a belief that the organization's objective was to restore to the Cuban people a representative democracy, and where he was unaware that the organization was connected with the Communist Party, his participation did not constitute a "meaningful association" with a subversive group. His membership thus did not preclude him from naturalization.

An applicant may escape the preclusion statute if more than ten years have passed, between her/his membership in the subversive organization or the act of advocating overthrow of the government, and the filing of the petition for naturalization. INA § 313(c).

Section 314 of the INA permanently precludes the naturalization of anyone who, during the time that the U.S. "has been or shall be at war," deserts the U.S. armed forces or leaves the country with the intent of avoiding the military draft, and is convicted of that offense by a court-martial or a court of competent jurisdiction. INA § 314. The provision also specifically prohibits such people from ever holding an official position of the United States. Uncertainty remains whether the term "at war" includes hostilities lacking a formal declaration of war—such as the Korean, Vietnam, and Persian Gulf conflicts of recent years. The Immigration Service has stated that the Korean conflict constituted a "time of war" within the meaning of the 1940 version of this provision. To the date of this writing, no reported judicial determinations exist.

INA § 315(a) provides that an alien who seeks or obtains exemption from service in the armed forces on the ground that s/he is an alien becomes permanently ineligible for citizenship, unless the alien had served in the military of a country having a treaty with the U.S. INA § 315(a). Selective Service records are conclusive on the issue of whether an alien secured the exemption because of alienage. INA § 315(b).

(6) OATH OF ALLEGIANCE TO THE UNITED STATES

Related to the requirement that an applicant be attached to the Constitution of the United States, s/he also must take an oath of renunciation and allegiance in open court. Section 337(a) of the INA requires that the applicant pledge (1) to support and bear true faith and allegiance to the Constitution of the United States; (2) to renounce all allegiance to any foreign state or sovereign; (3) to support and defend the Constitution and laws of the United States against all enemies, foreign and domestic; and (4) to bear arms on behalf of the United States when required by law, or to perform noncombatant service in the armed forces, or to perform civilian work of national importance when required by law. INA § 337.

If an applicant can show by clear and convincing evidence, that s/he is opposed to the bearing of arms, the applicant may revise the pledge to perform only noncombatant services in the armed forces. Similarly, if the applicant can show by the same standard of proof that s/he opposes any type of service in the armed forces by reason of "religious training and belief," s/he may pledge merely to perform important civilian work. INA § 337(a).

The present statute was designed to codify judicial decisions relieving conscientious objectors of naturalization requirements to bear arms. The moral stand taken by conscientious objectors frequently resulted in the denial of their naturalization petitions between the world wars—a result the Supreme Court affirmed in *United States v. Schwimmer* (Sup.Ct.1929) and *United States v. MacIntosh* (Sup.Ct.1931). In the 1946 case of *Girouard v. United States* (Sup.Ct.1946), however, the Court overruled these prior cases and held that religious objection to bearing arms was not of itself incompatible with allegiance to the United States. Congress adopted the Supreme Court's holding by enacting the statute currently in effect.

Congress followed *United States v. Seeger* (Sup.Ct. 1965), a later Supreme Court decision on conscientious objection to military service, in defining the phrase "religious training and belief" as "an individual's belief in a relation to a Supreme Being involving duties superior to those arising from any human relation, but does not include essentially political, sociological, or philosophical views or a merely personal moral code. . . . " INA § 337(a). The Supreme Court has construed this language in *Seeger* to apply to persons who, while not believing in a personalized God, possess a sincere and meaningful belief which occupies in the life of the believer a place "parallel" to that filled by the God of persons who clearly qualify for the exemption. Hence, the applicant need not found a claim of conscientious objector status upon the precepts of an organized religion or a belief in a Supreme Being. *In re Weitzman* (8th Cir.1970).

GENERAL RULES OF NATURALIZATION

SECTION INA	STATE RESIDENCE Sec. 101(a)(33)	LPR* STATUS REQUIRED	LENGTH OF STATUS REQUIRED	PHYSICAL PRESENCE	GOOD MORAL CHARACTER	ENGLISH LITERACY (Sec. 312)	GOVERNMENT TEST (Sec. 312)	OATH OF ALLEGIANCE (Sec. 312)	OTHER REQUIREMENTS
316	3 Months in state or INS District where filed	YES	5 Years	30/60 Aggregate	5 yrs. +	YES, unless exempt **	YES	YES, unless exempt	None
319(a)	3 Months in state or INS District where filed	YES	3 Years	18/36 Aggregate	3 yrs. +	YES, unless exempt**	YES	YES, unless exempt	Married to same USC*** for 3 yrs. and living in marital union
319(b)	N.P.****	YES	N.P.****	N.P.****	N.P.****	YES, unless exempt**	YES	YES, unless exempt	Married to USC**** (N.P.****), & living in marital union & USC spouse to be employed abroad 1 yr. with US gov=t or corp., etc. appl. will join
328	N.P.****	YES	N.P.****	N.P.****	N.P.****	YES, unless exempt**	YES	YES, unless exempt	3 years honorable active military less than 6 mo. since discharged
329	N.P.****	YES - But not if enlisted or inducted in US	N.P.****	N.P.****	N.P.****	YES, unless exempt**	YES	YES, unless exempt	1 day honorable active service during certain periods of hostilities (WWI, WWII, Korea, Vietnam, Granada, Gulf War)
322	N.P.****	NO	N.P.****	N.P.****	If 14 yrs. or older	NO	NO	If 14 yrs. or older	Biological or adopted child under 18 yrs. old

* LPR = Lawful permanent resident
** Test Exemptions: 15/55, 20/50, 20/65, mental or physical disability, or 15/65 and disability
*** USC = United States Citizen
**** N.P. = No particular time period

In *Petition for Naturalization of Kassas* (M.D.Tenn. 1992), the petitioner, who was a native of Syria, expressed reservations based on his Islamic faith, about bearing arms on behalf of the U.S. against persons of the Islamic faith or a predominantly Islamic country. The court held that the petitioner is not eligible for an exemption from swearing to bear arms on behalf of the U.S. because he is opposed only to some but not all war.

c. Relaxed Requirements for Particular Persons

Although the naturalization requirements discussed in the preceding subsections apply to most applicants for citizenship, Congress has chosen for various policy reasons to relax the requirements with respect to particular persons. The most significant special classes are: persons serving in the armed forces, spouses of United States citizens, and minor children of U.S. citizens. The table on the preceding page summarizes some of the special rules applicable in naturalization of particular categories of persons.

(1) PERSONS SERVING IN THE ARMED FORCES

A lawful permanent resident alien who has served honorably in the armed forces of the United States for periods totaling three years may apply for naturalization without meeting the standard residence and physical presence requirements, provided such application is filed while the applicant is still in the service or within six months of discharge. INA § 328(a). If the applicant's service was continuous, a certificate of honorable service establishes compliance with the requirements of good moral character. INA § 328(e). Where the service was not continuous, the applicant must establish good moral character by the standards applicable to other naturalization applicants. INA § 328(c).

The statute further provides that an alien whose service in the armed forces terminated more than six months prior to filing of the application is not exempted from the standard residence and physical presence requirements. INA § 328(d). Nonetheless, the period of time served in the military, if within five years immediately preceding the date of filing, shall constitute residence and physical presence for the purpose of meeting the standard requirements.

Another statute provides even broader exemptions for aliens who have actively and honorably served in the armed forces for at least one day during periods of hostilities—from World War I to the Gulf conflict or during any periods which the President designates involving armed conflict with a hostile foreign force. INA § 329. Such persons may be naturalized without having been lawfully admitted to the United States if they were in the United States or specified territories at the time of induction. INA § 329(a). If an applicant was not within these territories when enlistment occurred, s/he must subsequently obtain lawful admission to qualify under the provision.

An applicant seeking naturalization through active duty service in the armed forces is exempt from the standard age requirement; the generally prescribed residence and physical presence requirements; and the provision precluding the naturalization of persons subject to an outstanding deportation order. INA § 329(b).

(2) Spouses of United States Citizens

Section 319 of the Immigration and Nationality Act relaxes the naturalization requirements for spouses of

United States citizens. The applicant spouse must have resided continuously in the United States for three years—instead of five—immediately before filing the petition for naturalization. INA § 319(a). The residence must follow lawful admission, and the applicant must live "in marital union" with the citizen spouse throughout this period. The phrase "living in marital union" is not interpreted so strictly as to require that one spouse refrain from seeking a temporary separation from the other in situations of domestic violence. Hence, in *Petition of Omar* (S.D.N.Y.1957) the court ordered a separation of petitioner from his citizen spouse for two weeks as a "cooling off" period, following the petitioner's arrest (at his wife's request) for allegedly striking her. The judicially enforced separation did not preclude compliance with the statute.

Although a short separation, such as the two weeks involved in *Omar*, will not operate to destroy the marital union for purposes of the statute, an extended estrangement produces a different result. The rationale behind section 319(a), said the federal court in *Petition of Kostas* (D.Del.1958), was "the congressional expectation that a non-citizen spouse who lived in close association with a citizen spouse for three years would more speedily absorb the basic concepts of citizenship than one not so situated." In *Kostas* the facts showed an "uneasy union marked by frequent separations of substantial duration," to the extent that it appeared the couple spent more time apart than together during the three year statutory period. On that record the court determined that petitioner fell far short of the "marital union" requirement.

The statute does not relieve the spouse applicant of the burden of establishing good moral character and attachment to the principles of the Constitution.

If the citizen spouse is an employee of the United States government, a U.S. firm engaged in foreign commerce, a recognized U.S. institution of research, a public international organization in which the United States participates by treaty or statute, or s/he performs qualified religious functions abroad, and is regularly stationed abroad in such activity, the applying spouse may be naturalized without any prior residence in the United States. The applying spouse, however, must declare to the Immigration Service in good faith an intention to take up residence in the United States immediately upon the termination of such employment abroad of the citizen spouse. INA § 319(b). The applicant also must comply with all other requirements for naturalization.

Further, the surviving spouse of a citizen, whose citizen spouse dies while serving honorably in the armed forces, may be naturalized without any prior residence or physical presence in the United States. INA § 319(d).

(3) CHILDREN OF CITIZENS

A minor child born outside of the United States may be naturalized upon the petition of a natural parent who, at the time of application is a citizen of the United States either by birth or naturalization. INA § 322(a). Residence and physical presence requirements do not apply under this provision. Good moral character and attachment to the principles of the Constitution will be presumed for a child of tender years.

A citizen parent may apply for the naturalization of her/his adopted minor child. The child must be lawfully admitted to the United States for permanent residence, but no specified period of residence is required. INA § 322(b)–(c). A prior statute prescribing a minimum of two years residence before an adopted child could be naturalized was repealed in 1978. Children adopted by two U.S. citizen parents can also derive citizenship under INA § 341(c).

d. Naturalization Procedures

(1) JURISDICTION TO NATURALIZE

Exclusive authority to naturalize is conferred upon the Attorney General. INA § 310(a). Prior to the 1990 Act, the court decided whether a petitioner had complied with statutory conditions for citizenship. An INS designated examiner recommended whether naturalization should be granted, but the court could decide regardless of the INS recommendation. The 1990 Act shifted both the decision on naturalization and the principal responsibility for administration of the oath of allegiance to the INS. The 1990 Act authorized the federal district court to review *de novo* denials of naturalization and determine the matter if the INS fails to decide within 120 days after hearing. INA §§ 210(d), 336(b). The 1991 Technical Amendments returned principal responsibility for administration of oaths to the federal district courts, but left the substantive determination with the INS. Title I of the Technical Amendments Act gives the courts 45 days to administer the oath of naturalization, after which an applicant can choose to have the oath administered by the INS. This compromise gives the courts an important role in naturalization, without creating backlogs due to crowded court dockets. INA § 310 *et seq.* State courts of record are also authorized, but not required, to aid in the administration of oaths of allegiance.

(2) APPLICATION

An applicant for naturalization first must file an application to enable the Immigration and Naturalization

Service to conduct an investigation of the applicant's qualifications. INA § 334(a). The application (Form N–400) consists of several pages wherein the applicant must provide background information regarding family history, periods of residence in the United States, and the names of witnesses who will support the petition for naturalization.

A 1981 amendment removed the two-witness requirement (95 Stat. 1619) because the rule had become too time consuming and unproductive. Moreover, the INS should be sufficiently thorough in its investigation to determine the applicant's fitness for citizenship. The INS can still seek witnesses as part of the investigation.

In *Price v. INS* (Sup.Ct.1992), the Court approved the Attorney General's broad authority to make inquiries as long as they are related in some way to the naturalization requirements. Hence, U.K. citizen Price was denied naturalization because he refused to list on his application all the organizations with which he had ever been affiliated. The Court found that the identity of the organizations with which a petitioner is associated might be relevant to one or more requirements of citizenship.

An applicant may also file a formal declaration of intention to naturalize, but such a declaration is no longer mandatory. INA § 334(g). Several documents and pieces of information must accompany the application, including three identical photographs of the applicant to be affixed to the naturalization certificates and application form (INA § 333(a)), a record of the applicant's fingerprints, alien registration number, biographical information, and the date of arrival in the United States.

(3) EXAMINATION

The applicant and witnesses who can testify to the applicant's qualifications for citizenship appear before a naturalization examiner. INA § 335(b). Each applicant and witness is interrogated separately, during which questioning the applicant's attorney or representative may be present (provided the attorney or representative has filed a notice of appearance) to observe without taking part. The proceeding may be videotaped or tape recorded; the hearing is not formal and rules of evidence do not apply. The record of the examination is admissible in any subsequent hearing under INA § 336(a).

If after completion of the questioning, the examiner determines that the application lacks any necessary qualifications, s/he advises the applicant of that determination. An applicant is not bound, however, by the examiner's findings, and may as a matter of right file a request for a hearing before an immigration officer and then may seek *de novo* review by the federal district court. INA §§ 310(c), 336.

(4) HEARING ON DENIAL OF APPLICATION

If the application is initially denied, a new hearing takes place before another immigration officer. INA § 336(a). The applicant's attorney may take an active part in this hearing, present evidence, subpoena witnesses, make objections, and conduct cross-examination of the government's witnesses. The hearing is scheduled within 180 days after a request is filed; it is tape-recorded or videotaped for purposes of judicial review. Upon consideration of the testimony and review of all documents properly submitted in support or opposition, the immigration officer decides whether the application for naturalization should be granted or denied. If the immigration officer fails to decide the matter within 120 days after the examination, the federal district court may determine the naturalization or remand the matter to the INS with instructions. INA § 336(b).

(5) ADMINISTRATION OF OATH AND JUDICIAL REVIEW

If the examiner approves the naturalization, the applicant will be granted citizenship at a hearing in open court after s/he takes the oath of allegiance to the United States. INA § 337. In the case of verified illness or disability of the applicant, the court may excuse her/his attendance at the final hearing. INA § 337(c). As provided under the technical amendments to the 1990 Act, if the court cannot administer the oath within 45 days, the applicant may choose to have the oath administered by the INS.

If the INS denies the application, the applicant can seek judicial review in federal district court. Upon request by the applicant, the court can consider all issues *de novo*. If the INS does not act upon the application within 120 days, the applicant can request a hearing in federal district court. These procedures have been designed and modified to expedite the naturalization process, which, given the benefits that naturalization confers, is significant to the applicant.

(6) CERTIFICATE OF NATURALIZATION

Upon granting the citizenship, the INS issues a certificate of naturalization. INA § 338. The certificate itself does not convey citizenship, but simply serves as evidence that the INS has granted citizenship. The statute prescribes the information that the naturalization certificate will contain, including the number of the petition and the certificate; date of naturalization; the name, signature, place of residence, signed photograph, and personal description of the naturalized person (including age, sex, marital status, and country of former nationality); and a statement that the INS has found the application in full compliance with the requirements of the naturalization laws and has ordered the applicant be admitted to citizenship. INA § 338.

Minor clerical errors do not affect the evidentiary value of the certificate nor do informalities in the certificate—such as the misspelling of names or the misnaming of the applicant. *Brassert v. Biddle* (2d Cir.1945).

The date on the certificate of naturalization is determined by the date of the oath. If the oath is waived for children under six, the date is the day on which the application is granted. If the court administers the oath, it may also grant a name change.

A naturalization order is subject to *direct* attack in independent denaturalization proceedings as prescribed by the Congress. INA § 340(a). Revocation of naturalization is discussed below.

§ 12–3 LOSS OF NATIONALITY

§ 12–3.1 Introduction

There are two ways by which a citizen may lose citizenship: denaturalization and expatriation. Denaturalization involves the judicial revocation of the naturalization order based on a finding that the naturalization was illegally or fraudulently procured. INA § 340(a). Obviously, denaturalization applies only to naturalized citizens. Expatriation, however, applies to both naturalized and all other citizens, and does not assume a defect in the original acquisition of citizenship. Rather, expatriation results from certain actions enumerated in the statute (INA § 349) by which the citizen voluntarily relinquished her/his citizenship.

§ 12–3.2   Denaturalization

a.   Congress' Power to Denaturalize

The authority of Congress to provide for cancellation of wrongfully procured naturalization certificates is derived from the constitutional power of Congress to establish a uniform rule of naturalization under Article I, section 8, and the "Necessary and Proper" clause.

The Supreme Court in *Costello v. United States* (Sup. Ct.1961) sustained the constitutionality of the 1952 version of the denaturalization statute with respect to Congress' powers to cancel certificates procured "by concealment of a material fact or by willful misrepresentation." But while the power of Congress to prescribe grounds for revoking naturalization has been repeatedly upheld, the Supreme Court has stricken those provisions it deemed arbitrary or discriminatory. Hence, in *Schneider v. Rusk* (Sup.Ct.1964) the Court invalidated the provision prescribing loss of nationality by a naturalized citizen who resided in a foreign state for three years or more. Native-born citizens faced no such punishment. Justice Douglas wrote:

This statute proceeds on the impermissible assumption that naturalized citizens as a class are less reliable and bear less allegiance to this country than do the native born. This is an assumption that is impossible for us to make. Moreover, while the Fifth Amendment contains no equal protection clause, it does forbid discrimination that is "so unjustifiable as to be violative of due process"....

The court thus held that the provision discriminated against naturalized citizens in violation of Due Process, creating a "second-class citizenship" without a rational justification.

The revocation statute empowers United States district attorneys, upon an affidavit showing good cause, to institute proceedings in equity to cancel the naturalization certificate. INA § 340(a). The original naturalization order has no res judicata effect against this independent attack by the United States, *Johannessen v. United States* (Sup.Ct.1912), in contrast to the immunity it enjoys from collateral attack. *Tutun v. United States* (Sup.Ct.1926).

b. *Grounds for Denaturalization*

(1) CONCEALMENT OF MATERIAL FACT
OR WILLFUL MISREPRESENTATION

Naturalization may be revoked if the certificate of naturalization was "procured by concealment of a material fact or by willful misrepresentation" or was "illegally procured." INA § 340(a). Fraud and illegal procurement as grounds for denaturalization date back to the original 1906 statute. 34 Stat. 596. The introduction of the term "concealment of a material fact by willful misrepresentation" was intended to assure that both "extrinsic fraud" (outside of the proceedings—like concealment of witnesses) and "intrinsic fraud" (perjured testimony) would serve as grounds for denaturalization. *Costello v. United States* (Sup.Ct.1961).

Clearly, facts suppressed or concealed in a naturalization proceeding are "material" if disclosure of those facts alone would justify denial of citizenship. But the scope of materiality also includes concealed facts which, if disclosed, would have led to the investigation and discovery of other facts bearing on the applicant's eligibility for naturalization. In *Chaunt v. United States* (S.Ct.1960), the Supreme Court considered the materiality of Chaunt's failure to disclose three prior arrests for petty offenses in his naturalization application. The government argued that the arrests were material because, if disclosed, the Immigration Service would have investigated and *might* have discovered that Chaunt was (as one witness testified) an active member of the Communist Party. The Court established a two-part test for materiality, by which it concluded on the facts before it that "the government failed to show by 'clear, unequivocal, and convincing' evidence *either* (1) that facts were suppressed which, if known, would have warranted denial of citizenship, or (2) that their disclosure *might* have been useful in an investigation *possibly* leading to the discovery of other facts *warranting* denial of citizenship." (emphasis added).

Confusion has ensued as to the second part of the *Chaunt* test—that "disclosure might have been useful in an investigation possibly leading to the discovery of other facts warranting denial of citizenship." The Ninth Circuit in *United States v. Rossi* (9th Cir.1962) held that a concealed or suppressed fact is material only "if disclosure of the true facts would have justified a refusal to issue a visa." The Sixth Circuit, however, took a different view in *Kassab v. Immigration and Naturalization Service* (6th Cir.1966), holding it sufficient if the suppressed fact, if revealed, "*might* have led to further action and the discovery of facts which would have justified the refusal of the visa" (emphasis in original).

More recently, the Southern District Court of Florida in *United States v. Fedorenko* (S.D.Fla.1978) ruled that the government must *prove the existence* of the facts which would have warranted denial of naturalization, although it need only show that an investigation leading to discovery of these facts *possibly* would have taken place. The court found the government had failed to establish that the defendant had voluntarily served as a guard and committed atrocities at a German death camp while a prisoner of war during World War II, which the government contended it might have discovered through investigation, had the defendant disclosed on his visa application that he had resided at the particular concentration camp. The Fifth Circuit reversed, stating that the government need only prove "that disclosure of the true facts would have [prompted] an inquiry that might have uncovered other factors warranting denial of citizenship." The government would not be burdened with the overwhelming task of conducting an investigation into the past, discovering ultimate facts warranting disqualification, and proving those facts in court by clear and convincing evidence.

The Supreme Court affirmed the Fifth Circuit, but on other grounds, not addressing the materiality question. The U.S. Court of Appeals for the Tenth Circuit, however, in *United States v. Sheshtawy* (10th Cir.1983), adopted Justice Blackmun's views expressed in his concurring opinion to the *Fedorenko* case. The court concluded that the *Chaunt* test "requires that the government demonstrate the existence of actual disqualifying facts—facts that themselves would have warranted denial of petitioner's citizenship." Since the government had not claimed to have established facts that would have warranted denial of citizenship, it had not met the rigorous *Chaunt* test, and revocation of naturalization under INA § 340(a) was not justified.

In *Kungys v. United States* (Sup.Ct.1988), the Supreme Court attempted to clarify the *Chaunt* holding. The Court held that the test of whether concealments or misrepresentations are "material" under INA § 340(a) is whether they can be shown by clear, unequivocal, and convincing evidence to have been predictably capable of affecting the decisions of the INS, *i.e.*, to have "had a natural tendency to influence the decisions of the INS." Of the seven other participating justices, four joined this part of Justice Scalia's opinion.

Kungys was admitted to the United States for permanent residence in 1948 and became a naturalized citizen in 1954. In 1982 the United States commenced denaturalization proceedings. The government alleged that Kungys had participated in executing over 2,000 Lithuanians, most of them Jewish, in Kedainiai, Lithuania, between July and August 1941. The government also demonstrated that, in his visa application and in his naturalization petition, Kungys misrepresented his date and place of birth, as well as his occupation and residence during World War II.

In determining whether Kungys' misrepresentations met the Court's new standard of materiality, the Court held that § 340(a) is limited to falsehoods or deceptions in the naturalization proceedings and not misrepresentations made in the visa process, because it is the former falsehoods which "procure" the naturalization. The Court concluded that Kungys' misrepresentations of the date and place of his birth in his naturalization petition were not material. There was no suggestion that the facts were themselves relevant to Kungys' qualifications for citizenship. Likewise, there was no showing that the true date and place of birth would have disclosed other facts relevant to his qualifications and would have resulted either in outright denial or an investigation resulting in denial of the naturalization application. Hence, the government failed to establish clearly, unequivocally, and convincingly that Kungys' misrepresentations had a natural tendency to influence the decision of the INS. Only two justices joined Justice Scalia in this part of the opinion.

As an alternative basis for upholding denaturalization, the government argued that Kungys' naturalization had been "illegally procured" because, at the time of his naturalization, he lacked the good moral character required under INA § 316(a). (Illegal procurement of naturalization is discussed further in the following section of this chapter.) In the government's view, Kungys' misrepresentations, whether material or not, constituted false testimony given for the purpose of obtaining benefits in both the visa and naturalization proceedings, which indicates a lack of good moral character under INA § 101(f)(6).

The Court decided in favor of the government on this issue, holding that § 101(f)(6) does not contain a materiality requirement for false testimony for the purposes of determining whether naturalization was "illegally procured" because of a lack of good moral character. In the Court's view, lack of good moral character is present to some degree whenever there is subjective intent to deceive, no matter how immaterial the deception. The Court pointed out, however, that "testimony" is limited to oral statements made under oath and that the false testimony provisions do not apply to "concealments."

Section 101(f)(6) applies to only those misrepresentations made with the subjective intent of obtaining immigration benefits, and this intent must be proven by clear, unequivocal, and convincing evidence. The Court concluded that it would be "relatively rare that the Government will be able to prove that a misrepresentation that does not have the natural tendency to influence the decision regarding immigration or naturalization benefits was nonetheless made with subjective intent of obtaining those benefits." A majority of the justices joined this part of the opinion.

Although a majority of the justices agreed that § 101(f)(6) contains no materiality requirement, only three of the justices concurred in Justice Scalia's opinion holding that denaturalization could not be affirmed under that provision. The question whether Kungys' misrepresentations constituted false testimony for the purpose of obtaining immigration or naturalization benefits cannot be answered without first resolving two issues: (1) whether Kungys' misrepresentations constituted "testimony" and (2) whether in making the misrepresentations, Kungys possessed the subjective intent to obtain immigration or naturalization benefits. The latter question is one of fact to be resolved by the trier of fact. Since the case had to be remanded in any event, the Court chose not to resolve the former question of law.

Five separate opinions were filed in the *Kungys* case and there was no clear majority holding on many of the issues presented in the majority opinion. Hence, *Kungys* did little to dispel the uncertainty about the *Chaunt* standard of materiality.

In addition to being material, the misrepresentation must be intentional. Hence, where the defendant in

Maisenberg v. United States (Sup.Ct.1958) had answered "no" to a question on her preliminary application for naturalization asking whether she belonged to or was associated with any organization which teaches or advocates anarchy or overthrow of the existing government, she did not conceal a material fact or commit willful misrepresentation. Although she was at the time a member of the Communist Party, the question was ambiguous and she could reasonably have interpreted it as relating solely to anarchy, and not as calling for disclosure of membership in nonanarchistic organizations advocating violent overthrow of the government. Moreover, an applicant does not "conceal" a material fact, within the meaning of the statute, if s/he merely fails to *volunteer* facts which might have a bearing on eligibility. In *Cufari v. United States* (1st Cir.1954) the First Circuit held that a naturalized citizen could not be denaturalized for failing to disclose his criminal record at the time of naturalization, unless the government could prove that he had been asked during the proceedings whether he had a criminal record and that he had answered in the negative.

Specific concealments and misrepresentations which courts have found sufficient to warrant denaturalization include: deliberate suppression of criminal records where there is a duty to disclose (*United States v. Oddo* (2d Cir.1963))—unlike the situation in *Cufari, supra;* knowingly false statements concerning marital or family status (*United States v. D'Agostino* (2d Cir.1964)); and deliberate misstatement concerning an applicant's fulfillment of the residence requirements. *Rosenberg v. United States* (3d Cir.1932).

(2) Illegal Procurement of Naturalization

Illegal procurement provides an independent ground for revoking naturalization. The term has been held to convey something wider in scope than fraud, not restricted to intentional deception. It has encompassed naturalizations procured when prescribed requirements—for example, attachment to the principles of the Constitution or lack of good moral character—had no existence in fact. *United States v. Ginsberg* (Sup.Ct.1917). In *Kungys v. United States* (Sup.Ct.1988), the Supreme Court held that false testimony given for the purpose of obtaining benefits in a naturalization proceeding indicates a lack of good moral character under INA § 101(f)(6) and may render the naturalization "illegally procured," even though the misrepresentations may not have been material. This case is discussed in more detail in the immediately preceding section. The term also connotes affirmative misconduct by the applicant to induce the court or governmental agents to act in a manner not authorized by law; it encompasses the granting of certificates upon an error of law, for example, as to jurisdiction or procedural irregularities such as denying the government the opportunity to question the applicant in open court or to introduce evidence.

To justify denaturalization, however, the error must be substantial. Hence, clerical mistakes in connection with the issuance of a naturalization certificate will not constitute grounds for revocation and errors of judgment in granting citizenship against the preponderance of the evidence are better corrected on appeal in the original naturalization proceeding than in an action to revoke naturalization.

(3) Residence in Foreign Country Within One Year After Naturalization

Section 340 provides that if a naturalized citizen takes up permanent residence in a foreign country within one year after naturalization, it shall be considered prima facie evidence of a lack of intention to establish permanent residence in the United States at the time of the application for citizenship. In the absence of countervailing evidence, this prima facie evidence shall be sufficient to justify revocation of naturalization, as having been obtained by concealment of a material fact or by willful misrepresentation. INA § 340(d). The naturalized person may rebut the presumption by testimony that s/he intended in good faith to establish permanent residence in the United States. The court, not wishing to cancel lightly the valuable right of citizenship, will grant the defendant every reasonable doubt, and show great receptiveness to consideration of extenuating circumstances. For example, in *United States v. Delmendo* (9th Cir. 1974), the Ninth Circuit held that a naturalized citizen's years of residence in the Philippines did not show intent to establish permanent residence in the Philippines or an intent not to reside permanently in the United States at the time he applied for naturalization, because the citizen was very ill, poor, and had been given erroneous legal advice by the State Department that his three-year residence abroad had automatically deprived him of citizenship.

(4) Other Grounds for Denaturalization

The denaturalization statute provides two additional grounds for revoking naturalization: (1) Refusal on the part of the naturalized citizen, within ten years following her/his naturalization, to testify as a witness before a congressional committee concerning her/his subversive activities, will be a ground for revocation of naturalization, if such refusal resulted in a conviction for contempt. INA § 340(a). The refusal to testify establishes as a matter of law that naturalization was procured by concealment of a material fact or by willful misrepresentation and the naturalized citizen is not granted an opportunity within this provision to present countervailing evidence. (2) If within five years of naturalization a naturalized citizen becomes a member of any of the proscribed subversive organizations, of which membership would have precluded naturalization in the first place, it shall constitute prima facie evidence that such person was not attached to the principles of the Constitution at the time of naturalization. INA § 340(c). In the absence of countervailing evidence it will be sufficient to revoke the person's citizenship as having been obtained by concealment of a material fact or by willful misrepresentation. Neither ground has been invoked in any naturalization proceeding to date and the constitutionality of these provisions may be in doubt because of the discrimination they impose on naturalized citizens. *Cf. Schneider v. Rusk* (Sup.Ct.1964).

§ 12–3.3 Expatriation

a. Introduction

Expatriation provides the second means for loss of nationality, to which both naturalized and all other citizens are subject. INA § 349(a). The term is defined as the *voluntary* act of abandoning one's country and becoming the citizen or subject of another. Under current Supreme Court jurisprudence, the specific intent of the alleged expatriate to renounce citizenship must accompany the expatriating act, in order to constitute relinquishment of citizenship. In 1986, Congress amended INA § 349(a) to conform to the rulings of the Supreme Court, by providing that a person will lose her/his U.S. citizenship only by "voluntarily performing any of the following acts with the intention of relinquishing United States nationality."

b. Development of the Law of Expatriation

The Constitution makes no mention of expatriation. Courts were reluctant in the early days of the United States to acknowledge expatriation of a citizen without express consent of the government. The right of a citizen to voluntary expatriation notwithstanding lack of the sovereign's consent was first recognized by Congress in 1868. 15 Stat. 223. The 1868 Act proclaimed that "the right of expatriation is a natural and inherent right of all people, indispensable to the enjoyment of the rights of life, liberty and the pursuit of happiness." Although intended to protect naturalized United States citizens from claims of allegiance by their former sovereigns, the Attorney General construed the statute to permit U.S. citizens to abandon their citizenship. 14 Ops. Att'y Gen. 295. Also in 1868 the United States initiated a series of treaties—named the Bancroft Treaties for George Bancroft, a United States diplomat who negotiated the first of these treaties with the North German Confederation (15 Stat. 615)—which provided that each country would regard as citizens of the other, those of its own subjects who became naturalized by the other.

Although the right of expatriation was thus established, Congress did not first define the manner by which a citizen may lose citizenship until the Expatriation Act of 1907. 34 Stat. 1228. The statute provided that a citizen was deemed expatriated if s/he was naturalized in any foreign state in conformity with its laws or took the oath of allegiance to any foreign state; a female citizen who married an alien assumed the nationality of her husband; and a naturalized citizen returning to the country of her/his origin and living there for two years was presumed to have effected expatriation. 34 Stat. 1228. Marriage to a foreigner ceased to be an expatriating act in 1922. 42 Stat. 1022.

The Nationality Act of 1940 expanded the grounds for expatriation, to include: service in the military or government of a foreign state, voting in a political election in a foreign state, formal renunciation of United States citizenship, court martial conviction and discharge from the armed services for desertion in wartime, conviction for treason against the United States, and failure for nationals born abroad to take up permanent residence in the United States before attaining 16 years of age. 54 Stat. 1137. In addition, naturalized citizens could be expatriated for three years continuous residence in the state of their birth, or for five years continuous residence in any other foreign state. Many of these provisions reflected the trying economic times and the security consciousness resulting from the onset of World War II. The Immigration and Nationality Act of 1952 essentially re-enacted the expatriation provisions of the 1940 statute, with some minor additions. INA § 349 (examined in section 12–3.3d, *infra*).

c. *The Power of Congress to Prescribe Grounds for Expatriation*

The 1907 statute prescribed specific methods of expatriation. 34 Stat. 1228. Certain provisions appeared to mandate loss of nationality without regard to intent, most notably, marriage of a female citizen to an alien. In *MacKenzie v. Hare* (Sup.Ct.1915), the petitioner challenged this provision, which withdrew her citizenship upon her marriage to a British national. She argued that expatriation required not merely the act of marrying a foreign national, but a subjective intent to "permanently reside elsewhere [and] to throw off the former allegiance, and become a citizen or subject of a foreign power." The Court determined that Mrs. MacKenzie had voluntarily relinquished her citizenship because her marriage was voluntary, and she had notice of the consequences.

The Court further held that Congress had authority to prescribe grounds for expatriation, based on powers "implied, necessary or incidental" to its expressed power over nationality and foreign relations. The Court viewed the law in controversy as a reasonable exercise of government power for the prevention of potential international controversies arising out of dual nationality.

Subsequent cases over the next forty years reinforced an "objective intent" standard for determining relinquishment of citizenship. In *Savorgnan v. United States* (Sup.Ct.1950), the petitioner was a native-born U.S. citizen who was engaged to an Italian government official. To obtain royal approval of her marriage, she was informed she would have to become naturalized as an Italian citizen, recite an oath of allegiance to Italy, and sign a document renouncing her United States citizenship. She believed her signing was only a technical requirement, and she asserted that she never intended to renounce her United States citizenship. The Court held that under the statute one who obtained citizenship in a foreign country loses United States citizenship, regardless of her/his subjective intent:

[T]he acts upon which the statutes expressly condition the consent of our Government to the expatriation of its citizens are stated objectively. There is no suggestion in the statutory language that the effect of the specified overt acts, when voluntarily done, is conditioned upon the undisclosed intent of the person doing them.

The Supreme Court's attitude, heretofore one of deference to Congress regarding laws of expatriation, began to change in 1958. In *Perez v. Brownell* (Sup.Ct.1958), the Court upheld the constitutionality of the provision prescribing loss of nationality for voting in a foreign political election. 54 Stat. 1137. Justice Frankfurter, speaking for the majority, ruled that a "rational nexus" existed between the congressional power to regulate foreign affairs and the withdrawal of citizenship for voting in a foreign election. The power of Congress to terminate citizenship did not depend on consent of the citizen but the voluntary performance of the expatriating act. The holding thus reaffirmed the power of Congress to prescribe acts which would constitute loss of nationality, but the Court was closely divided, five justices to four. Chief Justice Warren wrote a vigorous dissent, maintaining that Congress did not have the power to take away the "most basic right" of citizenship. Congress could only acquiesce in the wishes of the citizen to abandon her/his nationality.

On the same day, March 31, 1958, the Court for the first time held an expatriation provision unconstitutional; Chief Justice Warren wrote the plurality opinion in another five to four decision, *Trop v. Dulles* (Sup.Ct. 1958). The suit challenged section 401(g) of the Nationality Act of 1940, which provided for expatriation upon conviction by court martial and dishonorable discharge for desertion in time of war. 54 Stat. 1137. Private Trop, serving abroad in the United States army, escaped from a stockade where he had been confined for disciplinary reasons. He turned himself in several hours later, but for his offense he was court martialed and convicted of desertion, sentenced to three years of hard labor and dishonorably discharged. Chief Justice Warren concluded that section 401(g) was a penal statute, violative of the Eighth Amendment's prohibition against cruel and unusual punishment, as it stripped the individual of any nationality, leaving him stateless. (In 1978 Congress repealed the statute. 92 Stat. 1046.)

A second expatriation provision was invalidated in *Kennedy v. Mendoza–Martinez* (Sup.Ct.1963). The challenged statute provided loss of citizenship for those persons who had left the United States in time of war to evade military service. 58 Stat. 746. In 1942, Mendoza–Martinez (a native born U.S. citizen with dual Mexican nationality) went to Mexico solely, as he admitted, for the purpose of evading service in the armed forces. He further conceded that he remained there for that purpose until November 1946, when he voluntarily returned to the United States. In 1947, he pleaded guilty to and was convicted of, evasion of his service obligation, and sentenced to imprisonment of a year and one day. He served his sentence and upon his release lived undisturbed until 1953 when, after a lapse of five years, he was arrested and subjected to deportation proceedings. The government asserted that Mendoza–Martinez was deportable as he had expatriated himself by committing the act specified in the provision. Justice Goldberg wrote for the majority, holding that the statute's automatic deprivation of nationality for the offense of evading military service was an unconstitutional punishment, in violation of rights to Due Process and trial by jury.

In 1964, the Court again limited the power of Congress to expatriate in *Schneider v. Rusk* (Sup.Ct.1964). It decided that the statute expatriating a naturalized citizen for three years continuous residence in the state of their former nationality was an invalid discrimination against naturalized citizens.

In *Trop, Mendoza–Martinez,* and *Schneider,* the Court utilized an *ad hoc* approach for restricting congressional power to expatriate, by invalidating several provisions as violative of specific constitutional rights. The issue of the requisite intent for finding a voluntary relinquishment of citizenship had not been addressed since *Perez v. Brownell, supra.* In *Afroyim v. Rusk* (Sup.Ct.1967), the Supreme Court overruled its 1958 decision in *Perez,* holding that Congress had no general power, express or implied, to expatriate without the citizen's assent. Afroyim was a naturalized citizen who went to Israel and while in that country voted in an Israeli election. The State Department subsequently refused to renew his passport, asserting Afroyim's loss of citizenship under section 401(e) of the Nationality Act of 1940. 54 Stat. 1137. Afroyim contended that neither the Fourteenth Amendment nor any other provision of the Constitution allowed Congress to extinguish his citizenship without his voluntary renunciation. Writing for the majority, Justice Black agreed, and held that the Fourteenth Amendment "can most reasonably be read as defining a citizenship which a citizen keeps unless he voluntarily relinquishes it. Once acquired, this Fourteenth Amendment citizenship was not to be shifted, canceled, or diluted at the will of the

Federal Government, the States or any other governmental unit."

The expansive language of Justice Black's majority opinion caused speculation as to its meaning. Some reasoned that *Afroyim* had invalidated all expatriation statutes, leaving the decision as to one's nationality at all times with the individual. With the right of citizenship judicially defined as absolute, it was not necessary for the allegedly expatriated individual to do more than assert her/his claim to citizenship in order to recover it. Others believed that *Afroyim* had reinstated a subjective intent test, which required for expatriation a finding that not only did the citizen commit the expatriating act, but s/he did so with the specific intent of relinquishing citizenship.

The Court's next opportunity to consider the scope and vitality of the *Afroyim* holding occurred in *Rogers v. Bellei* (Sup.Ct.1971). Bellei acquired citizenship by birth outside the United States to a U.S. citizen mother and Italian father. He lived abroad, although he visited the United States several times on a United States passport. He was warned shortly before his twenty-third birthday that the statute conferring his citizenship required him to remain in the United States for five years in order to preserve his citizenship. Bellei left the United States one year later and was notified that he had lost his citizenship. He sought to enjoin the statute, claiming it was violative of Due Process, and constituted cruel and unusual punishment. The district court ruled the statute unconstitutional, citing *Afroyim* and *Schneider*. The Supreme Court reversed in another five to four decision, holding that Bellei's citizenship acquired upon birth abroad was not constitutionally conferred, nor was it protected under the Fourteenth Amendment, which referred in its first sentence to "persons born or naturalized *in the United States.*" (emphasis added). As a mere creation of statute his citizenship was subject to congressional restrictions, and it was perfectly reasonable for Congress to impose a "condition subsequent" to the grant of citizenship. In dissent, Justice Black saw no distinction between the various forms of citizenship which justified the second class treatment afforded citizens born abroad. "I cannot accept the Court's conclusion that the Fourteenth Amendment protects the citizenship of some Americans and not others." (Congress has since repealed the statute at issue in *Bellei*. 92 Stat. 1046.)

The Supreme Court's 1980 pronouncement on the issue of congressional power to expatriate, *Vance v. Terrazas* (Sup.Ct.1980), went in two directions. Terrazas was born in the United States of Mexican parents, thus acquiring dual nationality. He obtained a certificate of Mexican nationality while in Mexico in 1970, which included renunciation of all other nationalities. He claimed it was not his intent to relinquish U.S. citizenship. On the one hand, the Court unanimously reaffirmed the basic holding of *Afroyim*—that expatriation required a showing of specific intent to relinquish citizenship voluntarily, in addition to proof that the expatriating act itself was committed voluntarily. The specific intent could be expressed in words or fairly inferred from proven conduct. On the other hand, the Court upheld a statute providing that the government must prove merely by "a preponderance of the evidence" that citizenship was voluntarily relinquished. The Court of Appeals had declared the statute unconstitutional, believing a "clear and convincing" standard of proof was required. In reversing,

Justice White stated "[We do not] agree with the Court of Appeals that, because under *Afroyim* Congress is constitutionally devoid of power to impose expatriation on a citizen, it is also without power to prescribe the evidentiary standard to govern expatriation proceedings." The "preponderance of the evidence" standard was held to apply, for both the government's burden of proving voluntary relinquishment, and for the citizen's burden of rebutting the presumption that the expatriating act, which the government proved to have been committed, was voluntary.

The case of Rabbi Meir Kahane illustrates the difference between an intent-based and an allegiance-based approach to expatriation. Kahane was a U.S. citizen at birth. He moved to Israel where he became active in politics and was elected to the Israeli Parliament. Kahane, aware of the fact that accepting an office under a foreign government was an expatriating act listed in INA § 349 (a)(4) communicated on several occasions with the State Department that he did not intend to give up his U.S. citizenship. The State Department nonetheless claimed that Kahane committed the expatriating act by shifting his allegiance to Israel. The court rejected this argument because an actor who contemporaneously with the expatriating act declares his intent to stay a U.S. citizen automatically preserves his citizenship. *Kahane v. Shultz* (E.D.N.Y.1987).

One year later, the Israeli Parliament passed a law providing that its members could only be Israeli citizens. Kahane executed a formal oath of renunciation of his U.S. citizenship to remain eligible for a seat in the Parliament. After Kahane's party was barred, on different grounds, from running in the elections, Kahane tried to revoke his renunciation of U.S. citizenship claiming that the Israeli law compelled his act. The court ruled against Kahane who remained expatriated, although he was permitted to visit the United States and was eventually assassinated in New York City. *Kahane v. Secretary of State* (D.D.C.1988).

d. Methods of Expatriation

(1) OBTAINING NATURALIZATION IN A FOREIGN STATE

Subject to the constitutional and statutory requirement of voluntariness, INA § 349 provides that a person who is a citizen may lose her/his nationality by obtaining naturalization in a foreign state, either upon personal application or that of a parent or duly authorized agent, after having obtained the age of eighteen years.

(2) OATH OF ALLEGIANCE TO A FOREIGN STATE

If a citizen, having obtained the age of eighteen years, takes an oath or other formal declaration of allegiance to a foreign state, s/he is expatriated under the current statute. INA § 349(a)(2). Under *Vance v. Terrazas* (Sup. Ct.1980) the courts again will inquire if the person taking the oath actually intended to abandon United States citizenship. If the oath is taken in circumstances indicating lack of voluntariness, such as military conscription, the requisite intent to transfer allegiance may not be found. *Riccio v. Dulles* (D.D.C.1953).

(3) MILITARY SERVICE IN A FOREIGN STATE

If a citizen enters the armed forces of a foreign country, s/he is expatriated if such armed forces are engaged in hostilities against the United States or s/he served as a commissioned or noncommissioned officer. INA § 349(a)(3). Again, the requirement that the expatriating act be done with the intention of relinquishing United

States nationality applies to service in foreign armed forces. INA § 349(a).

(4) FOREIGN GOVERNMENT EMPLOYMENT

Employment in the government of a foreign state coupled with (as a condition of employment) acquisition of nationality in or declaration of allegiance to the foreign state will serve as grounds for expatriation. INA § 349(a)(4). This broad language has, however, been restricted by the courts. For example, in *Kenji Kamada v. Dulles* (N.D.Cal.1956) petitioner had taught public school in Japan during and after World War II, for which the United States government claimed she was expatriated. A federal district court disagreed, focusing not only on the voluntariness question but upon the nature of the government service. Teaching school, reasoned the district judge, was not the type of foreign government employment envisioned by the act; rather, the law was intended to encompass service to a foreign government the performance of which required absolute allegiance to the foreign government. Teaching, as such, did not come within this category.

(5) FORMAL RENUNCIATION OF NATIONALITY

Making a formal renunciation of nationality before a diplomatic or consular officer of the United States in a foreign country will lead to expatriation, if performed in a manner prescribed by the Secretary of State. INA § 349(a)(5). Informal renunciations of citizenship are ineffective, however, as are other methods not meeting the State Department regulations. *Vance v. Terrazas* (Sup.Ct.1980).

Davis v. District Director (D.D.C.1979) is, perhaps, the most dramatic case in which a citizen's renunciation was held to be effective. In 1948 Davis, a native born citizen, voluntarily signed an oath of renunciation before the U.S. Consul in Paris, on the form provided by the Consul. Davis indicated at the time that he wanted to become "a citizen of the world." He set up a "World Service Authority" and issued himself a passport. The Immigration Service refused to permit Davis to enter the U.S. in 1977 on the ground that he was not a U.S. citizen and lacked a visa to enter as an alien. Even though Davis failed to obtain another citizenship when he renounced his U.S. citizenship, the federal district court sustained the Immigration Service's decision to exclude Davis from this country.

If renunciation occurs in the United States, it must be in writing and during time of war to take effect. INA § 349(a)(6). The Attorney General is empowered to designate the officer to receive such renunciations and to promulgate procedures for accepting them. The current statute has not been invoked, although a prior version was used to expatriate several citizens of Japanese descent during World War II.

(6) Acts of Treason and Subversion

A citizen will lose nationality, if convicted of committing any act of treason against the United States, of attempting to overthrow the government of the United States, or of conspiring to incite insurrection against the government. INA § 349(a)(7). The constitutionality of this provision has not been tested in the courts.

(7) Repealed Expatriation Provisions; Burden of Proof; and Age of Maturity

Several expatriation provisions have been repealed as a result of Supreme Court decisions declaring them unconstitutional. Specifically, they are: (1) residence abroad by naturalized citizen in excess of three years (in the country of former nationality) or five years (in another foreign state), declared unconstitutional by *Schneider v. Rusk* (Sup.Ct.1964); (2) voting in a foreign political election, declared invalid by *Afroyim v. Rusk* (Sup.Ct.1967); (3) desertion from the United States armed forces in time of war, struck down in *Trop v. Dulles* (Sup.Ct.1958); and (4) departing from the United States to avoid military service, declared unconstitutional by *Kennedy v. Mendoza–Martinez* (Sup.Ct.1963).

Regarding the burden of proof, the statute places the initial burden on the proponent of expatriation, requiring proof by a "preponderance of the evidence" that the expatriating act occurred. INA § 349(c). The act shall be presumed to have been done voluntarily, but such presumption may be rebutted upon a showing by a preponderance of the evidence that the act was not committed voluntarily. The Supreme Court upheld the constitutionality of this provision in *Vance v. Terrazas* (Sup.Ct.1980).

A second general restriction applicable to most expatriating acts is the requirement that the citizen (at the time of the act) must have attained the age of legal maturity. The statute sets the age of maturity at eighteen years for performance of several expatriating acts—obtaining foreign naturalization, oath of foreign allegiance, military service in a foreign state, renunciation of nationality, and employment in a foreign government. INA § 351(b).

In 1990, the State Department issued new and more lenient evidentiary standards applicable to expatriation cases. The new evidentiary standards are based upon the presumption that United States citizens intend to retain U.S. citizenship when they (1) obtain naturalization in a foreign state; (2) subscribe to routine declarations of allegiance to a foreign state; or (3) accept non-policy level employment with a foreign government. Based on this presumption, a U.S. citizen who naturalizes in a foreign state, takes a routine oath of allegiance, or accepts foreign government employment, is not required to state her/his intent to retain the U.S. citizenship. The intent to retain United States citizenship is not presumed when a person: (1) renounces U.S. citizenship before a consular officer; (2) takes a policy level of employment in a foreign government; (3) is convicted of treason, or (4) performs a potentially expatriating act under the statute accompanied by conduct which is inconsistent with retention of United States citizenship to such an extent that it compels a conclusion that s/he intended to relinquish U.S. citizenship. These new standards are subject to change and reflect only evidential presumptions. A citizen who does a potentially expatriating act may still be well advised to record her/his intent to remain a U.S. citizen, if that is the case.

CHAPTER 13

THE RIGHTS OF ALIENS IN THE UNITED STATES

§ 13–1 INTRODUCTION

Generally, persons seeking to be admitted to this country have virtually no rights recognizable under United States law. The judiciary is very reluctant to interfere with Congress's authority over immigration matters. As a result, Congress and immigration officials lawfully exercise a great deal of discretion in establishing and applying immigration law; they control the hopeful immigrant's application for admission. Far from having any right to be admitted to this country, an individual's admission is granted exclusively by Congress under whatever terms it chooses. In determining who shall be admitted, Congress has the authority to discriminate with impunity; it has done so on the basis of national origin and race, and currently employs a system of priorities that excludes, among others, persons with undesirable political beliefs, moral character, and mental or physical disability. INA § 212(a). Special preference is granted to certain relatives of U.S. residents, and to persons possessing work skills needed in the U.S. economy. INA §§ 201 and 203. The Supreme Court has unwaveringly held that the decisions to exclude or expel certain aliens are within the exclusive province of Congress. *Chae Chan Ping v. United States* (Sup.Ct.1889); *Fiallo v. Bell* (Sup.Ct.1977).

Aliens who are admitted, however, can claim certain general protections under the Constitution. Almost all constitutional guarantees of individual freedom have no personal designation and are extended by terms to "persons." The right to hold federal elective office is reserved for citizens, as is the entitlement to the "privileges and immunities of citizens." Therefore, all aliens admitted to the U.S. appear to be guaranteed the rights secured by the Bill of Rights including the freedoms of speech, association, religion, and the press; the rights to be free from unreasonable searches and seizures as well as self-incrimination; and other criminal procedure protections. In removal proceedings, resident aliens are entitled to the safeguards of Due Process as guaranteed by the Fifth Amendment.

This chapter sets forth the rights enjoyed by aliens once they reside in or are admitted to the United States, the limitations imposed on those rights, and their theoretical rationale. The first section briefly reminds the student of immigration law about the often hostile social reality faced by immigrants to this country. The second section concentrates on official discrimination against aliens. Third, specific rights and liabilities are discussed with regard to use of the courts, welfare, education, military service, payment of taxes, property ownership, and other areas of concern to the alien living in the United States.

§ 13–2 THE EXPERIENCE OF BEING AN ALIEN IN THE UNITED STATES

Despite legal guarantees of equal treatment and the image of the Statue of Liberty welcoming distressed immigrants, resident aliens have experienced difficulties with adjustment and assimilation. Official hostility, expressed in immigration law and other restrictive legislation, has been especially flagrant in periods of war, racial animosity, and high unemployment. At various times, some academics theorized that certain racial and ethnic groups were unfit or unacceptable for "Americanization." Many U.S. citizens readily adopted such justifications for their own prejudice. Thousands of immigrants, historically poor, were faced with social stigma, language barriers, unfamiliar customs, and a complete lack of political representation.

Some improvement in official and popular thought has been won since the great waves of immigration occurred in the 19th and early 20th centuries. Immigrants to the United States today still, however, encounter discrimination sanctioned by state and federal governments as well as the racial and ethnic prejudice of many U.S. citizens. A recognition of the immigrant's difficult experience in adjusting to life in the United States is essential to an understanding of the full impact of U.S. law and policy.

§ 13–3 DISCRIMINATION ON THE BASIS OF ALIENAGE

§ 13–3.1 Introduction

For purposes of immigration and other laws affecting aliens, four broad classes of aliens can be identified: (1) persons seeking admission to the United States; (2) persons admitted as immigrants or permanent resident aliens; (3) persons admitted as nonimmigrants or temporary visitors; and (4) undocumented persons or "illegal" aliens who are present in the country without the official knowledge or permission of the federal government.

Most of the law involving discrimination on the basis of alienage has developed in cases concerning resident aliens. These individuals are most like citizens of the United States: this country is their permanent home; they pay taxes, are subject to military service, contribute to the economic and cultural life of their communities, and generally have a stake in the country that a nonimmigrant alien cannot ordinarily claim. Courts have provided less protection to individuals who are less like citizens.

The immigrant or permanent resident alien is entitled to protection under the Equal Protection guarantees of the Fifth and Fourteenth Amendments. The judicial review of discrimination on the basis of alienage, however, varies with the particular restriction and whether the state or federal government has imposed it. In *Plyler v. Doe* (Sup.Ct.1982) the United States Supreme Court decided that even undocumented aliens are entitled to Equal Protection—at least in so far as the children of undocumented aliens have the right to attend public schools.

This section will discuss the historical and modern treatment of discrimination against aliens. Because of the distinct governmental interests involved and because of markedly different judicial treatment, state and federal discrimination will be considered separately.

§ 13–3.2 State Discrimination

a. Historical Treatment: Pre–graham v. Richardson

In 1886 the Supreme Court declared in *Yick Wo v. Hopkins* (Sup.Ct.1886) that the guarantees of the Fourteenth Amendment extended universally to all persons within the territorial jurisdiction of the United States, without regard to race, color, or nationality. *Yick Wo* invalidated the discriminatory application of a San Francisco ordinance, effectively prohibiting Chinese residents from operating laundry facilities, while allowing white citizens under similar circumstances to own laundries. In *Yick Wo,* the Court definitively established that aliens must be treated on a basis equal to citizens and that the state had no authority to restrict arbitrarily an alien's "life, or the means of living, or any material right essential to the enjoyment of life. . . . "

In practice, however, the strictures of *Yick Wo* have not been followed. The Supreme Court for many years applied an extremely lax standard of review in alienage discrimination cases, upholding severe restrictions on resident aliens. Only in recent years has the alien enjoyed a degree of the protection guaranteed by the Equal Protection Clause of the Fourteenth Amendment so clearly enunciated in *Yick Wo.*

Throughout the late 19th and early 20th centuries, when massive immigration to the United States was occurring, states imposed a wide variety of restrictions on the activities of resident aliens. Most of these discriminatory measures easily withstood Equal Protection challenges. Several theories justified state discrimination:

(1) If a public resource or "special public interest" was involved, public monies could properly be reserved for citizens and withheld from aliens. On this ground, the Court in 1915 upheld New York's exclusion of aliens from employment on public works and other public employment. *Heim v. McCall* (Sup.Ct.1915).

(2) If the resource in question was viewed as "common property" of the citizens of the state, non-citizens could be prohibited from enjoying it. Therefore, Pennsylvania

could limit permission to hunt wildlife and carry firearms to citizens (*Patsone v. Pennsylvania* (Sup.Ct.1914)), and Virginia could reserve for its citizens the right to plant oysters in a stream bed within its boundaries. *McCready v. Virginia* (Sup.Ct.1876).

(3) If the limitation constituted a valid exercise of police power, the alien could be barred from activities routinely allowed citizens, including certain forms of private employment. Such reasoning perhaps was stretched the furthest in *Clarke v. Deckebach* (Sup.Ct. 1927), in which the Court upheld the requirement of citizenship for licensing of pool hall operators as a valid exercise of police power. The court's rationale was that pool halls often attracted criminals and other undesirable people and that non-citizens were less familiar with U.S. laws and customs than native-born or naturalized citizens. The court held that it was in the interest of the public welfare to limit pool hall operators to citizens.

(4) If the particular benefit was characterized as a "privilege" not a "right," it could be withheld from the alien who was not entitled to the privileges and immunities guaranteed to citizens by the Constitution. On this ground and because of the states' traditionally broad power over the regulation of property ownership, the Court approved prohibitions against the inheritance and ownership of land by aliens in the absence of a treaty to the contrary. *Hauenstein v. Lynham* (Sup.Ct.1879); *Terrace v. Thompson* (Sup.Ct.1923). It was not until 1948 that doubt was cast on the validity of such restrictions on property rights. *Oyama v. California* (Sup.Ct.1948).

In this tradition, the Court gave short shrift to most resident aliens' claims under the Equal Protection Clause. The standard of review was not very severe, indicating the Court's unwillingness to interfere with the judgments of local governments. The ordinance was affirmed where "the possibility of a rational basis for the legislative judgment" was not "preclud[ed]," and where the Court had "no such knowledge of local conditions . . . to say it is wrong." *Clarke v. Deckebach* (Sup.Ct.1927).

Despite this deference to state discriminatory actions, the Court in *Truax v. Raich* (Sup.Ct.1915) struck down an Arizona law which required private employers of more than five persons to employ at least 80% "qualified electors or native-born citizens." Noting that the discrimination in *Truax* was imposed on private enterprise, reaching broadly across all industries, the Court found no special public interest or public resource involved that could justify the restriction. The Court held that the discrimination was "an end in itself" and inimical to the Fourteenth Amendment's guarantee of personal freedom and opportunity. Significantly, the Court also found that the state's attempt to deny aliens the opportunity to work collided with the federal government's exclusive power to permit aliens to enter and reside in the United States. The Court reasoned that the privilege of living in the U.S., granted by Congress, would be destroyed if the state could severely restrict employment solely on the basis of alienage and that the privilege to reside here carried with it "the right to work for a living in the common occupations of the community." Arizona's attempt virtually to take away from resident aliens the opportunity to earn a livelihood impinged on the authority of Congress over immigration.

Truax v. Raich (Sup.Ct.1915) was a significant decision because it laid the foundation for the Court's later repudiation of the line of cases in which state discriminatory actions had been almost routinely upheld. It was not until 1948, however, that an alien was again successful in an Equal Protection challenge. In *Takahashi v. Fish and Game Commission* (Sup.Ct.1948), the Supreme Court considered a California statute which forbade the granting of commercial fishing licenses to persons "ineligible to citizenship." Federal law at that time provided that Japanese nationals were ineligible for United States citizenship. The Court quoted extensively from *Truax,* rejecting California's assertion that because the state owned the fish off the coast as trustee for its citizens, it had a "special public interest" in conserving fish for the benefit of its citizens. In holding that this ground was inadequate for discriminating against Japanese residents, the Court implicitly overruled its earlier line of cases. Justice Murphy's concurring opinion in *Takahashi* argued vigorously that California's action was racially motivated; he cited impressive historical evidence and claimed that the statute was invalid for that reason. The majority, however, did not address the race question. *Takahashi* represented a departure from traditional Equal Protection analysis in alien discrimination cases. In refusing to approve a state's citizenship requirement in a case that involved public interests as strong as many in earlier cases, the Court signaled that it would more carefully review such discrimination in the future.

b. Modern Treatment

Takahashi made clear that states would not be allowed to discriminate casually on the basis of alienage: "the power of a state to apply its laws exclusively to its alien inhabitants as a class is confined within narrow limits." Such language suggested that aliens should be protected more diligently than the traditional rational basis standard of review would demand. Finally in 1971, the Supreme Court explicitly held in *Graham v. Richardson* (Sup.Ct.1971) that aliens as a group constitute a "discrete and insular minority" deserving of heightened judicial protection, and that alienage is a "suspect classification" prompting strict scrutiny of state discrimination under the Equal Protection Clause.

Graham involved the denial of state welfare benefits to aliens. The state argued that the receipt of welfare benefits was a privilege, a share in the state's wealth, which could properly be reserved for members of the body politic. In rejecting this assertion, the Court laid to rest the special public interest doctrine and the right-privilege distinction that had justified many earlier restrictions on aliens. As it had in *Truax* and *Takahashi,* the Court also objected to the statute as an impermissible state interference with the exclusive federal power to regulate immigration. *See* § 2–2.2.

For several years following *Graham,* the Court analyzed cases of alienage discrimination by using the same Equal Protection mode that it had developed in racial discrimination and other cases: if a personal fundamental interest is at stake or if a suspect class is found, state laws invariably fall when submitted to strict judicial scrutiny. To sustain its burden, the state must show that its purpose or interest justifying the classification is "substantial" and that the classification is " 'necessary ... to the accomplishment' of its purpose or the safeguarding of its interest." *Application of Griffiths* (Sup.Ct. 1973). Many state restrictions on aliens were overturned by the lower courts.

Following this approach the Supreme Court in *Sugarman v. Dougall* (Sup.Ct.1973) struck down a New York statute that barred all aliens from competitive civil service employment. The state asserted that its interest in assuring the loyalty of its employees who implement government policy justified the bar. While recognizing a state's interest in limiting government participation to those persons who are within the "basic conception of a political community," and the state's authority to define that political community, the Court found that the statute swept far too broadly. Within New York's statutory framework, menial competitive civil service positions were subject to the citizenship requirement while other elective and high appointive offices were not. The Court declared that despite a valid state interest, the means employed were too imprecisely drawn to survive strict scrutiny.

Sugarman did recognize a state's prerogative to define a class of positions requiring citizenship in some situations: the power of the state to define the political community applied to persons holding state elective or important non-elective legislative and judicial positions, that is, for officers who participate directly in the formulation, execution, or review of broad public policy perform functions that go to the heart of representative government.

Decided the same day as *Sugarman,* the Court in *Application of Griffiths* invalidated a Connecticut law that limited to U.S. citizens licenses to practice law. The Court rejected the state's argument that because lawyers are officers of the Court, the state must be assured of undivided allegiance by requiring citizenship. Furthermore, in spite of their access to courts and their traditional leadership role in government, the Court found that a lawyer is not "so close to the core of the political process as to make him a formulator of government policy." In so ruling, the Court appeared to confine narrowly the reaches of the political function exception mentioned in *Sugarman.*

In similar fashion, the Court struck down a Puerto Rican statute that denied engineering licenses to nearly all aliens in *Examining Board v. Flores de Otero* (Sup.Ct. 1976), and a New York statute that denied higher education financial assistance to certain resident aliens in *Nyquist v. Mauclet* (Sup.Ct.1977). In *Mauclet* the Court held that a suspect class existed, even though non-citizens were eligible for assistance if they applied for citizenship or filed statements of intent to become citizens. New York's stated interest in encouraging naturalization was held, first, to be related insufficiently to preservation of the political community and, second, an interference with the federal government's power over immigration and naturalization, since only the national government was properly concerned with encouraging naturalization. Furthermore, the Court found that while the state has a legitimate interest in enhancing the educational level of the electorate, allowing aliens to participate in financial aid programs would not defeat that goal. By way of *dicta,* the Court explained that the political function exception to which the Court had alluded in *Sugarman* was very narrow, limited to the states' historical or constitutional powers to define such characteristics as the qualifications of voters or of government officers who directly participate in the formulation, execution, or review of broad public policy.

Despite the purported narrowness of the "political function" exception extracted from *Sugarman,* the Court has retreated from its suspect classification-strict scrutiny approach to alienage cases. In 1978 the Court read "political function" expansively in *Foley v. Connelie* (Sup.Ct.1978) to uphold a New York statute that allows only citizens to compete for the job of state trooper. In a clear withdrawal from the Court's previous position, Chief Justice Burger's majority opinion cited his own dissenting opinion in *Mauclet* to pronounce that every statutory restriction on aliens does not demand strict scrutiny. The Court theorized that as only citizens are entitled to participate in the political process, the right to govern thereby could be properly reserved to citizens; as states have the authority to delimit the political community, a state could permissibly exclude aliens from positions relating to "the right of the people to be governed by their citizen peers." If the position under review involves discretionary decision-making or execution of policy, "which substantially affects members of the political community," a lesser standard of review would be proper. The Court then held that police officers have considerable discretionary powers, exercise a high degree of judgment in executing state policy, and affect the public significantly. Therefore, the state may assume that citizens are "more familiar with and sympathetic to American traditions," which presumably the Court found important if citizens were to submit to such police powers as arrest, search, and seizure.

In *Ambach v. Norwick* (Sup.Ct.1979), the political function exception also was used as the basis for upholding New York's denial of permanent certification as public school teachers to any non-citizen unless that person declared an intention to become a citizen. The State Commissioner of Education was authorized to certify aliens provisionally only in certain narrowly prescribed situations. The Court first emphasized the im-

portance of education in preparing students for participation as citizens, in preserving societal values, and
instilling civic virtues. Second, the Court held that the
role of teachers was critical in developing students' attitudes toward government and the political process. In
order to place a teacher within the governmental function principle, the Court cited a teacher's discretion
over communication of course material and position as
a role model. The Court then held that (1) the state
has a valid interest in furthering its educational goals
and (2) in pursuit of that interest, it could rationally
conclude that non-citizens or permanent residents who
did not want to become citizens were inappropriate candidates for teachers. Strong dissenting opinions in both
Foley and *Norwick* protested the Court's opinions as
unjustified departures from Equal Protection precedents
and as an unwarranted expansion of the *Sugarman
dicta.*

Despite *Foley* and *Norwick* most lower courts have
continued to apply *Graham* after deciding that a political
function is not involved. For example, in striking down a
statute that required citizenship for appointment as a
notary public, the Florida Supreme Court determined
that notaries public do not perform political functions as
described in *Foley;* instead, they are more like public
employees performing routine ministerial duties. The
court applied strict scrutiny and ruled that the statute
violated the Equal Protection Clause. Applying *Graham*
outright, a district court struck down New Mexico State
University's attempt to deny admission to Iranian students until their government released U.S. hostages.
Tayyari v. New Mexico State University (D.N.M.1980).
The Supreme Court of Connecticut, however, held that a
criminal defendant was not entitled to a jury selected

from a panel which included resident aliens. Under *Foley* and *Norwick,* the court classified jury service as a political function from which aliens rationally could be excluded. *Connecticut v. Thigpen* (Conn.Sup.1978).

In 1982, the Supreme Court upheld a California statute that limits positions classified as "peace officers" to citizens. Plaintiffs were resident aliens seeking employment as deputy probation officers, positions within the statutory classification of "peace officers." The district court twice had held the statute unconstitutional both on its face and as applied, the latter decision rendered after consideration in light of *Foley.* In *Cabell v. Chavez–Salido* (Sup.Ct.1982), a 5–4 majority read *Sugarman, Foley,* and *Norwick* to require strict review of state restrictions on resident aliens only where an alien's *economic interests* were affected; here the restriction served a political function and a far less stringent standard of review was appropriate. The Court set out a two-step evaluation process to determine the character of the restriction. First, the specificity of the classification would be considered; substantial under-or over-inclusiveness would tend to negate the claim that the classification is intended to serve a political function. Second, even if "sufficiently tailored," the classification as applied must affect only persons who "perform functions that go to the heart of representative government." The Court would look at the extent of discretionary decision-making or policy implementation that affects members of the political community.

The statutory scheme in *Chavez–Salido* defined about 70 positions as peace officers, including toll service employees, cemetery sextons, and livestock identification inspectors. The Court found, however, that such over-inclusiveness is not fatal: "the classifications used need not be precise; there need only be a *substantial fit*" to support the state's claim that an important government function is involved. The Court held that nearly all peace officers shared a law enforcement function primarily because they had the power to arrest and must undergo training for arrests and the use of firearms. Such an exercise of the sovereign's "coercive police powers" could be limited to members of the political community under *Foley*.

In considering the statute as applied, the Court characterized the work of a probation officer as involving a great deal of discretion, because their decisions must be made in the first instance without supervision. Alluding to the "educational function" of probation officers, the Court also asserted that the position symbolized the state's sovereign power and the political community's control over the juvenile offender.

In a forceful dissent, Justice Blackmun reviewed the history of the challenged statute. No legislative rationale or common purpose behind the peace officer classification and citizenship requirement had been articulated. Justice Blackmun asserted that the majority distorted *Sugarman* by employing a weak standard of review and by approving a mere "substantial fit" between the classification and justifications asserted by the state. The dissenters would have found the statute to be fatally under-and over-inclusive as it limited to citizens some jobs which were not even rationally related to the political community, while in other areas failed to bar aliens from jobs which arguably encompassed a political function. In the view of the dissent, even *Foley* and *Norwick* required a substantial showing by the state. By abolishing a strict standard of review, Justice Blackmun stated, "*Sugarman*'s exception swallows *Sugarman*'s rule."

Justice Blackmun also took issue with the majority's "coercive power" characterization of the position of all peace officers, pointing out that probation officers are not allowed to carry guns, can arrest only probationers under their jurisdiction, and then only for the purpose of bringing them before a court to decide on detention or release. Further, their discretion is limited by judicial supervision and is extensively regulated by statute. After setting out compelling statutory inconsistencies that allow aliens to play integral roles in the criminal justice system and the considerable qualifications of the plaintiffs, the dissent concluded that the state discrimination "stems solely from state parochialism and hostility toward foreigners who have come to this country lawfully."

The Supreme Court, however, returned to its suspect classification—strict scrutiny approach to alienage cases in *Bernal v. Fainter* (S.Ct.1984). By a vote of 8–to–1, the Court struck down as a violation of the Equal Protection Clause a Texas statute requiring a notary public to be a U.S. citizen. Applying strict scrutiny, the Court found no legitimate political function to support a citizenship requirement. Because the functions of a notary public are primarily clerical and ministerial, the position is not one "such that the office holder would necessarily exercise broad discretionary power over the formulation or execution of public policies importantly affecting the citizen population, power of a sort that a self-governing community could properly entrust only to full-fledged members of that community." In contrast to the state troopers in *Foley,* notaries public do not routinely exercise the state's monopoly of "legitimate coercive force," nor do they "exercise the wide discretion typically enjoyed by public school teachers" as in *Norwick*.

Foley, Norwick, and *Chavez–Salido* indicate that the Court has increasingly been willing to find a political function that invokes only a minimal rationality standard of review. In contrast to *Sugarman* 's 8–1 majority, however, the Court in *Chavez–Salido* was sharply divided, with the dissent in vehement opposition to the majority's approach. Perhaps this sharp division, along with the Court's decision in *Bernal,* portends an eventual reexamination of the political function exception, or, at the least, signals that the outer limits of the exception have been reached. Certainly, the Court has changed directions without repudiating its holding in *Graham* that classifications on the basis of alienage are suspect. Commentators object that the Court has not set out a forthright or disciplined judicial analysis, although several alternative theories are available.

In cases involving a political function, the Court could have maintained its strict scrutiny review of alienage restrictions by finding a compelling state interest that justified the classification, if precisely drawn. The significance of citizenship in the political process cannot be dismissed: in certain situations the public or political character of the position in question may justify the requirement. In that way, the Court would have remained consistent with *Graham* and its progeny.

Alternatively, the Court could have straightforwardly re-evaluated the suspect classification rubric and concluded that aliens, indeed, do not require the judicial vigilance evident in racial classifications. Significantly, alienage is not an immutable characteristic, nor is it always evident. Certainly important state and federal interests are connected with citizenship that in some cases may warrant different treatment. But aliens comprise a class that is in many ways prototypic of a discrete and insular minority group which needs judicial protection against a political process which is often oblivious or hostile to its interests. Historically, aliens have been discriminated against, socially stigmatized, and ostracized, though arguably their experience has not been as severe as that of racial minorities. Deprived of political rights, aliens have no representative voice and thus need the protection of courts which must protect minority and under-represented interests. In any case, it undermines the integrity of the suspect classification approach to Equal Protection to hold that alienage is suspect for some purposes, but not for others.

Other commentators suggest that Equal Protection analysis is inappropriate in this area; that those cases that strike down state restrictions under the Equal Protection Clause are expounding an unarticulated preemption theory. In each case, the Court either specifically indicated or consistently could have indicated, that the state provision in question interfered with the federal government's exclusive authority over immigration and naturalization. *Truax* and *Takahashi* expressly held that a state's restriction on the alien's opportunity to earn a living conflicted with congressional power to set the terms and conditions of continued residence. Other cases involving employment could be similarly considered. Burdens on aliens other than those related to employment could also be overturned if they have an adverse effect on the conditions of residence as determined by Congress. Consistent with this preemption theory, those activities truly related to the political process could withstand challenge if not in conflict with federal policy.

Many lower courts have considered and decided the preemption issue, raised by plaintiffs as the alternative to an Equal Protection claim. For example, Louisiana's statute requiring citizenship for the granting of a license to practice dentistry was invalidated as a denial of Equal Protection under *Graham* 's strict scrutiny standard, but was held not to be an interference with the immigration and naturalization power of the federal government. *Szeto v. Louisiana State Board of Dentistry* (E.D.La. 1981). At least one state court apparently has adopted the preemption theory as the most logical approach to alienage discrimination cases. *Matter of Adoption of a Child by L.C.* (N.J.1981).

A clearly articulated approach to state restrictions on resident aliens is needed to assure minimally uniform treatment. The Supreme Court must re-examine its departures from Equal Protection analysis and provide more forthright guidance for lower courts and prospective litigants. Resident aliens at least are entitled to consistently reasoned judgments when challenging discrimination under a Constitution that promises equal treatment to all persons.

§ 13–3.3 Federal Discrimination

a. Introduction

In contrast to state discrimination, actions by the federal government that classify individuals on the basis of alienage touch upon policies and interests traditionally immune from searching judicial review. This section will examine the deferential judicial approach to alienage discrimination by the federal government and the special federal interests grounded in congressional power over immigration that are asserted in its defense.

b. Judicial Deference to the Political Branches: Special Federal Interests

The Court has long held that immigration and naturalization, like foreign policy generally, encompass an area over which Congress maintains almost plenary power and the judiciary has a very limited responsibility. *E.g., Fong Yue Ting v. United States* (Sup.Ct.1893). Immigration matters raise complex and sensitive questions of national policy, calling for informed political judgments. This country's treatment of prospective immigrants or temporary foreign visitors is intertwined with U.S. foreign policy. It may be a factor in treaty negotiations, contribute to this country's influence abroad, and influence how other governments treat U.S. citizens traveling abroad. Sometimes, national security matters may be implicated. The Supreme Court considers itself an inappropriate forum, and judges inexpert, for the weighing of policy choices presumably done by Congress in setting immigration and naturalization priorities.

In fact, in reviewing immigration legislation, the Court has stopped just short of applying the political question doctrine that is grounded in the separation of government powers and in effect would render nonjusticiable any challenges to congressional authority in this area. Historically, the Court has thus upheld discrimination on any basis Congress may choose in deciding what groups shall be admitted to this country and under what terms. Constitutional challenges to such admission and removal laws repeatedly have failed.

Although the Court has admitted to misgivings about the extent of congressional plenary power and its own virtual abdication of review, the strength of long-standing precedent has thus far prevented any effective reconsideration: As Justice Frankfurter explained,

> In light of the expansion of the concept of substantive Due Process as a limitation upon all powers of Congress, even the war power, ... much can be said for the view, were we writing on a clean slate, that the Due Process Clause qualifies the scope of political distinction heretofore recognized as belonging to Congress in regulating the entry and deportation of aliens.... But the slate is not clean. As to the extent of the power of Congress under review, there is not merely "a page of history," ... but a whole volume. Policies pertaining to the entry of aliens and their right to remain here are peculiarly concerned with the political conduct of government. In the enforcement of these policies, the Executive Branch of the Government must respect the procedural safeguards of Due Process.... But that the formulation of these policies is entrusted exclusively to Congress has become about as firmly embedded in the legislative and judicial tissues of our body politic as any aspect of our government. *Galvan v. Press* (Sup.Ct.1954).

Quoting the above passage, the Court declined again to expand the scope of judicial review in *Fiallo v. Bell* (Sup.Ct.1977), a case in which substantive constitutional rights of U.S. citizens and permanent resident aliens were compromised by provisions of the Immigration and Nationality Act. In *Fiallo,* the statutes in question granted special preference immigration status to aliens qualified as "children" or "parents" of U.S. citizens or permanent resident aliens. The INA's definition of "child" excluded illegitimate children whose claim to preferential status was based on their relationship with their natural fathers, while including those who claimed through their mothers. Further, a natural father was ineligible to claim a preference status for his illegitimate child, while a natural mother was eligible.

Plaintiffs were natural fathers and their illegitimate children who sought to be reunited under the special preference provisions, claiming, among other things, that the INA discriminated against them on the basis of gender, marital status, and illegitimacy. Despite the statute's clear detrimental impact on the rights of citizens and resident aliens, the Court refused to expand the scope of judicial review of immigration matters. In rather parrot-like fashion the Court reiterated that it had a limited role to play in such policy decisions, and applied an extremely lax minimum rationality standard of review to uphold the restrictions. (The Immigration Reform and Control Act of 1986 amended INA § 101(b)(1) to allow an illegitimate child to claim preferential status through its natural father "if the father has or had a bona fide parent-child relationship with" the child. INA § 101(b)(1)(D). The Supreme Court rejected a child's challenge to this provision, but hinted that a father's challenge might succeed. *Miller v. Albright* (Sup.Ct. 1998). *See* § 2–3.2, *supra*.)

The federal government regulates the lives of aliens in a myriad of ways, however, other than directly through its immigration and naturalization policies. Historically, federal, like state restrictions on the activities of resident aliens have been substantial and severe. Because congressional power is viewed as broadly encompassing "regula[tion] of the relationship between the United States and our alien visitors," *Mathews v. Diaz* (Sup.Ct.1976), those justifications for deferring to Congress and the Executive on matters of immigration, foreign policy, national security, etc. have apparently been extended to any federal actions that affect aliens. Consequently, the guarantee of Equal Protection of the law inferred from the Due Process Clause of the Fifth Amendment has had little meaning for resident aliens.

c. Protection Under the Fifth Amendment

The Court's treatment of federal discrimination on the basis of alienage departs sharply from Equal Protection jurisprudence in the areas of discrimination on the basis of race, national origin, and religion. Classification on these bases is immediately suspect, invokes strict judicial scrutiny, and virtually never survives an Equal Protection challenge. The federal government has been required to abide by similar standards under the Fifth Amendment as have the states under the Fourteenth Amendment.

Where the classification is on the basis of alienage, however, the Court has declared that the Equal Protection component of the Fifth Amendment is not co-extensive with that of the Fourteenth although the analysis is much the same:

> Not only does the language of the two Amendments differ, but more importantly, there may be overriding national interests which justify selective federal legislation that would be unacceptable for an individual State. *Hampton v. Mow Sun Wong* (Sup.Ct.1976) (fn. omitted).

Only where the federal government acts very much like a state, must it adhere to standards applicable to the states:

> [W]hen a federal rule is applicable to only a limited territory, such as the District of Columbia, or an

insular possession, and when there is no special national interest involved, the Due Process Clause has been construed as having the same significance as the Equal Protection Clause. *Hampton v. Mow Sun Wong* (fn. omitted).

Therefore, stepping outside its precedent in *Graham v. Richardson* (Sup.Ct.1971), the state discrimination case in which aliens' "discrete and insular minority" status prompted "heightened judicial solicitude," the Supreme Court has refused to scrutinize closely nationwide federal actions that burden aliens. Two leading cases (*Hampton* and *Diaz*), neither directly involving immigration or naturalization, firmly establish the Court's refusal to restrain the federal government in any area relating to aliens. Unfortunately, the Court's deference to Congress overshadows the significant deprivation of individual rights involved in those cases.

In *Hampton v. Mow Sun Wong* (Sup.Ct.1976), the Supreme Court considered a U.S. Civil Service Commission regulation that excluded non-citizens from employment in the competitive federal civil service. The resident alien plaintiffs argued that they had been deprived of Equal Protection of the laws. On that ground the Ninth Circuit Court of Appeals invalidated the regulation; the Supreme Court relied on rather narrow Due Process grounds to affirm the lower court.

In *Hampton* the Supreme Court first refused to use the same approach for federal as for state discrimination: "the paramount federal power over immigration and naturalization forecloses a simple extension of the holding in *Sugarman v. Dougall* (Sup.Ct.1973), in which New York's bar of non-citizen employment in state competitive civil service was held to be a violation of the Equal Protection Clause of the 14th Amendment." The Court did concede, however, that some judicial interference may be proper, noting that plenary federal power does not allow *any* agent of the federal government to discriminate between aliens and citizens. Writing for the Court, Justice Stevens recited the disabilities suffered by aliens due to lack of political rights and unfamiliarity with language and customs, holding that the inability to be employed by the federal civil service was a deprivation of a liberty interest which entitled the plaintiff aliens to Due Process of law. The Court set out the standard under which the deprivation was reviewable:

When the Federal Government asserts an overriding national interest as justification for a discriminatory rule which would violate the Equal Protection Clause if adopted by a State, Due Process requires that there be a legitimate basis for presuming that the rule was actually intended to serve that interest. If the agency which promulgates the rule has direct responsibility for fostering or protecting that interest, it may reasonably be presumed that the asserted interest was the actual predicate for the rule. That presumption would, of course, be fortified by an appropriate statement of reasons identifying the relevant interest. Alternatively, if the rule were expressly mandated by the Congress or the President, we might presume that any interest which might rationally be served by the rule did in fact give rise to its adoption.

Applying such presumptions, the Court found that the Civil Service Commission was not authorized or required by Congress or the President to promulgate the citizenship requirement. Although legitimate national interests could be asserted, only the interest in administrative convenience was within the concern of the Civil Service Commission. In the absence of specified reasons, the Court was unwilling to presume that the Commission was attempting to further national interests outside of its responsibility. Therefore, the regulation as promulgated deprived plaintiffs of Due Process. The Court strongly suggested, however, that had the President or Congress expressly adopted the rule or had the agency done so with justifications that were within its scope of concern, the rule would not have been invalid.

Indeed, within three months of the Court's decision in *Hampton,* President Ford issued an Executive Order that in effect restored the invalidated Commission rule barring aliens from competitive civil service. 5 C.F.R. § 7.4. He did not specify, as the Court had implied was important, the national interests to be furthered by this rule. The Ninth Circuit Court of Appeals later held the new Executive Order to be constitutional in *Mow Sun Wong v. Campbell* (9th Cir.1980); the Supreme Court denied certiorari. The Court of Appeals found the order to be within the President's constitutional and statutory authority. Under the standards set forth in *Hampton v. Mow Sun Wong* (Sup.Ct.1976), the national interest in creating an incentive for aliens to be naturalized was sufficient to justify the rule.

The Supreme Court did not hesitate to decide plaintiff's Equal Protection claim in *Mathews v. Diaz* (Sup.Ct. 1976), which was issued the same day as the Court's decision in *Hampton. Diaz* challenged the constitutionality of a statute limiting eligibility for certain Medicare benefits to citizens and resident aliens who have resided in the United States for at least five years. A unanimous Court held that such a classification was constitutional because it was not "wholly irrational." The Court invoked both the plenary power of Congress over immigration and naturalization as well as the political question doctrine to justify such an extremely lax standard of review:

> Any rule of constitutional law that would inhibit the flexibility of the political branches of government to respond to changing world conditions should be adopted only with the greatest caution. The reasons that preclude judicial review of political questions also dictate a narrow standard of review of decisions made by the Congress or the President in the area of immigration and naturalization.

Although the Court conceded that the five year residency requirement is longer than necessary to protect the fiscal integrity of the program and that unnecessary hardship is incurred by some persons, the Court found that the restriction reasonably insured that those qualified for the benefits have a greater affinity with the United States; accordingly, the classification was not "wholly irrational." The Court did not state why affinity with the United States is somehow significant in relation to Medicare; nor did it examine how well the classification furthered that end. The *Diaz* court distinguished *Graham v. Richardson* (Sup.Ct.1971), which had invalidated a similar restriction on state welfare benefits on the ground that a state's relationship with aliens differs substantially from that of the federal government.

The message from *Diaz* and *Hampton* appears clear: virtually no federal limitation on aliens would fail under the Fifth Amendment. Under the minimum rationality standard of *Diaz* no real evaluation of the asserted government interest nor the necessity of the means em-

RIGHTS OF ALIENS

ployed to further that interest would be undertaken. Although *Hampton* spoke in terms of an "overriding national interest," that case in effect requires only that an administrative agency, which is not officially concerned with national interests involving aliens, must spell out its reasons for imposing a restriction based on alienage. Where Congress or the President acts, or presumably the Immigration and Naturalization Service, virtually any national interest would sustain the restriction against an Equal Protection challenge.

Following *Diaz* and *Hampton,* Equal Protection challenges to federal legislation concerning resident aliens have failed in such diverse areas as employment in federal non-competitive civil service, eligibility for farm operating loans, licensure as commercial radio operators, and eligibility for certain Social Security benefits. In most cases plaintiffs were long time permanent resident aliens qualified in every way for the benefit in question except for their alienage. Courts usually applied minimum rational basis review, resulting in ready acceptance of the government interest asserted. One lower court has read *Hampton* as requiring an intermediate standard of review, at least where a liberty interest is involved and the statute in question is not directly related to the admission, exclusion, or expulsion of aliens. *Yuen v. IRS* (2d Cir.1981). In that case, however, the government nonetheless prevailed.

d. Implications of the Current Approach

Resident aliens can expect to be afforded more judicial protection when the state discriminates against them than when the federal government does so. This discrepancy may be entirely defensible in immigration or other areas that directly involve questions of foreign policy and where refined political judgments are crucial to maintaining consistency and strength as an international power. Unquestionably, the national government requires a degree of flexibility that a state does not in order to pursue the international affairs of the country.

Important national interests, however, should not obscure the impact of discrimination on the individual rights of aliens who have been lawfully admitted and have taken up permanent residence here. The Supreme Court has mechanically extended its deference to congressional plenary power and its restraint in the face of the political question implications of immigration to all other areas of federal control over aliens. This unfounded extrapolation subordinates constitutional rights to the interests of the national government regardless of the substantive area involved or the relative importance of the governmental interest asserted.

Rational basis review may be particularly misplaced in cases of alienage discrimination. Professor Rosberg in his article, *The Protection of Aliens From Discriminatory Treatment by the National Government,* argues that aliens are in as much need of protection from state-sponsored discrimination as are members of the more traditional suspect classifications. Like other groups given suspect classification status, aliens have suffered a history of discriminatory treatment. Although alienage is not an immutable characteristic, as is race, before an alien fulfills the five year residency requirement, her/his status is inescapable. Political powerlessness, however, is the alien's most obvious and significant debilitating condition. While other protected minorities may have seriously weakened political voices, an alien has no voice or vote. The suspect classification doctrine is at least partially based on the understanding that judicial vigilance is necessary because the political process does not adequately represent the interests of oppressed groups. In Rosberg's words:

> Where a group is systematically shut out of the political process, ... and is denied an opportunity to form alliances with any other group, it may well lose on every issue. At that point the proper functioning of the majoritarian political process is very much in question. In such case, the Court begins to fear that the injury to the members of the disadvantaged class, far from being an unintended by-product of the state's effort to serve a legitimate interest, was in fact the very purpose of the classification. And the likelihood increases that the classification was based on a stereotypical and erroneous view of the characteristics of the members of the group.

It would seem that the suspect classification rubric fits perfectly the particular needs of aliens for extra protection. In fact, the applicability of the political question doctrine is ironic: The Court's refusal to interfere with any congressional judgment regarding aliens assumes that debate and political reflection are essential. Yet the political powerlessness. of aliens guarantees a one-sided debate.

Of course, broad use of the suspect classification doctrine and strict scrutiny would make it very difficult for the federal government to carry out any legitimate immigration or foreign policy objectives with the use of alienage classifications. The Court's fear of imposing constitutional rigidity in an area in which flexibility is important would be justified. While adherence to strict scrutiny may hamstring the federal government, the current rational basis review virtually ignores the legitimate interests of resident aliens.

Unfortunately, the strict/rational dichotomy causes an all or nothing situation; the Court should explore alternative methods of analysis in which asserted government interests and the means employed to further them are balanced against the severity of the burden on resident aliens. At least three approaches provide for such balancing. First, within Equal Protection analysis, an intermediate standard of review could be applied. *See Reed v. Reed* (Sup.Ct.1971). Less severe than strict scrutiny, intermediate judicial review would nonetheless substitute more exacting justification than the weak rational basis standard.

Second, analysis under the Due Process Clause affords another alternative. The Court already has been innovative in this area. In *Hampton v. Mow Sun Wong* (Sup.Ct. 1976), the Court looked at the process of decision-making to declare invalid an administrative rule that discriminated against aliens. While in that case, the Court's intervention proved very short-lived, a more aggressive track could similarly examine the process of congressional decision-making.

To alleviate the concern that questions of national policy as to aliens must be left to Congress, the Court could first determine whether such issues are raised by the particular classification. If so, the Court could examine the statute and legislative history to assess whether Congress indeed considered the national interest that is to be served by the alienage classification. Such an approach would necessarily abandon any presumption that Congress made an informed policy judgment simply because the legislation relates to aliens. At the least, this approach would force the political branches to evaluate and justify discrimination against resident aliens. Depending on the vigor of the Court's review, it could succeed in weeding out arbitrary and very harmful discrimination that contributes little or nothing to U.S. immigration or foreign policies.

Third, focusing on fairness to the individual, cases of alienage discrimination by the federal government could be reviewed under the conclusive presumption doctrine. In essence, that doctrine requires that if an individual is disadvantaged by a classification which is premised on a congressional presumption, for a particular purpose, s/he must be given an opportunity to prove that the presumption is untrue. A restriction which *conclusively presumes* a characteristic or fact without allowing rebuttal would be a deprivation of Due Process. On the one hand, this approach to alienage discrimination cases would avoid the rigidity of an Equal Protection holding because even if struck down, a restriction could be re-instituted with a provision allowing for a rebuttable presumption. On the other hand, substantive review of congressional presumptions would assure greater protection of individual rights. Only some similar type of analysis that recognizes and investigates competing interests will result in fairness to both the individual alien and the federal government.

The real question that the federal government, including both the political and judicial branches, needs to answer is whether fairness is a goal in its treatment of aliens. The rationales advanced by the Court for its hands-off approach do not justify the poor treatment resident aliens sometimes suffer. Less laudable reasons probably explain it.

At the least, much legislation appears to be the effect of stereotypic thinking about foreigners, unwarranted assumptions about loyalty and the importance of "affinity" to the United States, and in some situations outright racial prejudice. The Court has ignored or avoided any significant curtailment of this abuse although such bases for law-making are repugnant.

Hundreds of lawful classifications are embodied in the immigration laws that set preferences for admittance and establish conditions under which an alien may remain in this country. In characterizing all legislation that burdens aliens after they have been admitted as part of an ongoing scheme with foreign policy overtones, the government may simply extend the prejudices expressed in the immigration laws. The U.S. government apparently prefers affluent immigrants who will not need Medicare; immigrants who will seek only private or state civil service employment, while refraining from federal employment; who will not request government farm loans, but who will nonetheless pay taxes, contribute to the community, and if necessary, serve in the military. A prospective immigrant could not know the true terms of entry without checking all federal legislation for restrictions as to citizenship.

In any case, unprincipled discrimination against resident aliens creates an image of the United States in the eyes of the world as being hypocritical and unfair. If, indeed, treatment of aliens is a crucial element in foreign relations, then the government has the opportunity to improve its international image by treating resident aliens fairly.

§ 13–3.4 Conclusion

Resident aliens can expect to suffer discrimination after immigration to this country. While technically the law guarantees treatment equal to that of citizens, such has never been the case. Historically, as waves of immigrants came to the United States to escape economic and political difficulties in their native countries, social stigma and official discrimination have been commonplace. While significant steps were taken during the early and middle 1970's to halt discrimination by states on the basis of alienage, the Supreme Court has since the late 1970's retreated from its briefly active role in that area.

Vis-a-vis the federal government, aliens have never been found to be deserving of significant protection and apparently can be disadvantaged with little or no justification.

§ 13–4 OTHER RIGHTS AND DUTIES OF ALIENS

§ 13–4.1 Right to Vote

The Constitution reserves for citizens only the right to vote, and no state presently allows aliens to vote in elections. Throughout much of the nineteenth and part of the twentieth century, however, aliens were able to vote in many states. Arkansas was the last state to end alien suffrage in 1928. The progressive disenfranchising of aliens in the early part of the twentieth century was due primarily to increased hostility to and distrust for foreigners. Anti-alien sentiment was fueled in part by the assassination of President McKinley, a large influx of immigrants who did not have Anglo–Saxon origins, and the outbreak of World War I.

When an opportunity arose for the Supreme Court to decide whether a state could deny aliens the right to vote, the Court declined to hear the case for failure to present a substantial federal question. *Skafte v. Rorex* (Sup.Ct.1977). (The Colorado Supreme Court had sustained a Colorado statute that denied aliens the right to vote in school elections.) While the Supreme Court has stated that citizenship is a permissible criterion for determining who may vote, the Court has not explained the basis for requiring voters to be citizens. *See, e.g., Sugarman v. Dougall* (Sup.Ct.1973). Many arguments have been suggested to preserve the citizenship requirement. Voting is seen by many as the quintessential right of citizenship. Others claim that aliens are unable to vote intelligently in elections because of unfamiliarity with U.S. institutions and values. Still others argue that aliens may be incapable of voting responsibly because they lack loyalty, due to strong ties with their native country.

Although aliens are a protected class in the eyes of the Supreme Court, it is unlikely that the Court would acknowledge a right to vote. But as a suspect class, aliens are provided some degree of protection in the courts without being held to the political responsibilities which accompany participation in the political processes.

§ 13–4.2   Capacity to Use the Courts

The Supreme Court held, in *Ex parte Kawato* (Sup.Ct. 1942), that lawful resident aliens have a full capacity to sue and be sued in state courts. This principle does not apply to nonresident aliens, who will usually be allowed to sue in state courts only where it is necessary to avoid injustice or to serve the interests of international comity.

Any alien may bring suit in federal court if the alien can claim federal question jurisdiction. This jurisdiction specifically covers cases where the alien's constitutional, treaty, or federal statutory rights have been violated. The Second Circuit in *Filartiga v. Peña–Irala* (2d Cir.1980), permitted the Paraguayan relatives of a Paraguayan youth who had been tortured to death in Paraguay by a police officer acting under the authority of the Paraguayan government to maintain an action in federal district court against the Paraguayan police officer, who was visiting the United States. Torture was held to violate the law of nations, which is part of the law of the land. 28 U.S.C.A. § 1350. The Court of Appeals did not, however, decide the difficult issues related to choice of laws to be applied and as to the doctrine of *forum non conveniens*. The trial court on remand applied Paraguayan law and awarded damages. *Filartiga v. Peña–Irala* (E.D.N.Y. 1984).

In *Forti v. Suarez–Mason* (N.D.Cal.1987)(*Forti I*), the court held that, as in *Filartiga*, the Alien Tort Claims Act provides the court with subject matter jurisdiction for violations "of the law of nations." 28 U.S.C.A. § 1350. In *Forti I*, the plaintiffs, including Alfredo Forti, sought damages from a general, Carlos Guillermo Suarez–Mason, who commanded an army in Argentina during the 1970s that was claimed to be responsible for official torture, prolonged arbitrary detention, and summary execution which the court found to be universally recognized torts. In *Forti v. Suarez–Mason* (N.D.Cal.1988)(*Forti II*), the court found that international consensus also existed on the recognition of the international tort of "causing disappearance." *Forti II* said that a plaintiff stating a claim under the Alien Tort Statute has the burden to establish general recognition, not unanimity, that a "specific practice is prohibited." The court, however, did not find that "cruel, inhuman or degrading treatment" was a specific practice.

The court in *In re Estate of Ferdinand E. Marcos Human Rights Litigation* (9th Cir.1992) allowed an alien mother to sue the former head of Philippine military intelligence for the torture and wrongful death of her son in the Philippines. The court found subject matter jurisdiction not only under the *Filartiga* interpretation of 28 U.S.C.A. § 1350, but also on the basis of the Torture Victim Protection Act. In *In re Estate of Ferdinand Marcos Human Rights Litigation* (9th Cir.1996) the court affirmed awards of 800 million dollars in compensatory damages plus 1.2 billion dollars in exemplary damages, but the plaintiffs have not yet been able to collect any of those funds.

The right of an alien to bring suit in federal court based on federal question jurisdiction was, however, limited in *Sanchez–Espinoza v. Reagan* (D.C.Cir.1985). Nicaraguan citizens sought damages from the President of the United States and other federal defendants for tortious injuries caused by the U.S.-backed Contra forces. The court found that no treaty made it unlawful for executive officials, in their private capacity, to support forces bearing arms against the government of Nicaragua, and absent a waiver of sovereign immunity, such officials were immune in their official capacity from actions for monetary damages. The court held that the Alien Tort Claims Act, 28 U.S.C.A. § 1350, is not a waiver of sovereign immunity, but "may conceivably have been meant to cover only private, nongovernmental acts that are contrary to treaty or the law of nations—the most prominent examples being piracy and assaults upon ambassadors." The Court also held that it would be an abuse of discretion to award discretionary, nonmonetary relief because the support for military operations was approved by the President, the Secretary of State, the Secretary of Defense, and the Director of the CIA, and involved the conduct of diplomatic relations with at least four foreign states. Furthermore, the court found that "[t]he danger of foreign citizens using the courts in situations such as this to obstruct the foreign policy of our government is sufficiently acute that we must leave to Congress the judgment whether a damage remedy should exist."

In 1990, the U.S. Drug Enforcement Administration (DEA) arranged for the kidnapping of Dr. Alvarez–Machain, a Mexican doctor, suspected of assisting in the murder of a DEA agent in Mexico. The kidnappers forcibly brought Alvarez–Machain to the United States to stand trial for murder. The Supreme Court rejected a claim that the U.S.-Mexico extradition treaty barred such kidnapping. *United States v. Alvarez–Machain* (Sup.Ct. 1992). Dr. Alvarez escaped prosecution when the district court dismissed his case for lack of sufficient evidence. He then filed a suit under 28 U.S.C.A. § 1350 against persons responsible for his kidnapping. His complaint alleged that the kidnappers' actions were "torts in violation of the law of nation, including ... torture; cruel, inhuman and degrading treatment or punishment; violations of the Fourth, Fifth and Eight Amendments ..." Amici argued that aliens have a Due Process right against physical abuse while in custody of United States agents, and that the Torture Victim Protection Act applies to this case. The Court of Appeals held that Dr. Alvarez could not bring Fifth Amendment claims, but found that the Torture Victim Protection Act was retroactive and that Dr. Alvarez could pursue his claims under the Act. *See Alvarez–Machain v. United States* (9th Cir.1996).

An alien may be able to claim jurisdiction in a suit against a foreign state under the Foreign Sovereign Immunities Act, 28 U.S.C.A. § 1330(a). In *Verlinden B.V. v. Central Bank of Nigeria* (Sup.Ct.1983), the Supreme Court held that a nonresident alien could sue a foreign state in a federal district court on any nonjury civil action under the Foreign Sovereign Immunities Act of 1976 (FSIA), 28 U.S.C.A. § 1330(a). In *Verlinden,* a Dutch corporation sued an instrumentality of Nigeria in a U.S. district court, alleging anticipatory breach of a letter of credit. The Court held that, under the FSIA, a foreign sovereign is immune to suits involving the foreign sovereign's public acts, but such immunity does not extend to cases arising out of its strictly commercial acts. If one of the exceptions to sovereign immunity specified under 28 U.S.C.A. §§ 1605–07 or under any applicable international agreement applies, a federal district court may exercise subject-matter jurisdiction under § 1330(a), and the FSIA contains no limitation based on the plaintiff's citizenship.

Any alien also may sue the U.S. in the Court of Claims if U.S. citizens are granted reciprocal rights by the alien's country and subject matter jurisdiction would otherwise exist. 28 U.S.C.A. § 2502.

Aliens may sue or be sued in federal court based on diversity of citizenship, but the Constitution limits such suits to those between U.S. citizens and subjects of a foreign state. U.S. Const. Art. III, § 2. Hence, an alien may not sue another alien based on diversity jurisdiction, even if a U.S. citizen is party to the suit. 28 U.S.C.A. § 1332. An alien may sue a citizen, however, even if the alien resides in the same state as the citizen. The alien thus has greater jurisdictional rights in this respect than a similarly situated citizen would have. *Breedlove v. Nicolet* (Sup.Ct.1833). Stateless aliens, though, can never meet diversity jurisdiction requirements, because they are not subjects of a foreign state.

Aliens, who are enemies during times of war, may also bring suit. Resident enemy aliens have full access to all courts. *Ex parte Kawato* (Sup.Ct.1942). Nonresident enemy aliens may also bring suit, but are subject to greater restrictions, especially if the judgment would hamper the war effort. The court may still deliver judgment, but the amount of the claim may be withheld pending termination of hostilities.

§ 13–4.3 Education

An alien's right to education depends both on the status of the alien in the U.S. and on the level of education sought. In general, an alien must apply for nonimmigrant visa status to study in the United States. The F visa for academic students, the J visa for exchange students, and the M visa for vocational students are discussed above in the Nonimmigrant Visa chapter 6. *See also* chapter 7 (academic student visas), *supra*. Nonetheless, the Supreme Court has rendered decisions delineating the limits of a state's power in relation to aliens and education.

The first of these decisions, *Plyler v. Doe* (Sup.Ct. 1982), considered the right of undocumented or illegal alien children to receive elementary education. The Court noted that undocumented aliens do not constitute a "suspect class," so that any statute on this subject would not be subject to "strict scrutiny." The Court then described the unique and lifelong effect that elementary education has on a person. The Court feared that denying these children an education might create a nearly permanent underclass of illegal aliens who probably would remain in the U.S. for the rest of their lives. Furthermore, any statute that discriminated against the illegal alien children would punish them for the acts of their parents, since the children had no choice in coming to the U.S. Accordingly, the Court held that any state statute which created special burdens for undocumented alien children to receive an elementary education would be voided unless it could be shown that the statute furthered some substantial state interest. No such interest was found in the *Plyler* case.

The second decision of the Supreme Court on aliens and education was *Toll v. Moreno* (S.Ct.1982). This case concerned the right of the children of aliens who are international organization employees (G–4 nonimmigrants) domiciled in a state to pay the lower in-state tuition rate at the state university. The Court noted that G–4 nonimmigrants were a special group of aliens to which Congress had granted the right of acquiring domicile in the U.S. If the state then required the children of a domiciled G–4 nonimmigrant to pay a higher out-of-state tuition, the state would be creating a burden on them not contemplated by Congress. The Court held that the imposition of such a burden would be impermissible, since it would frustrate the federal policy. Although the case only dealt with G–4 nonimmigrants, presumably other classes of nonimmigrants would also be covered by this decision if they, too, were not required to maintain their domicile outside the U.S. Hence, the reasoning of *Toll* might extend to the children of holders of a few other nonimmigrant visas, such as H and L visa holders.

In November 1994 California voters passed Proposition 187 to prohibit public schools in that state from admitting undocumented alien children to attend school. Each school was supposed to verify the immigration status of every student as well as their parents or guardians. The school was also to report to the INS the immigration status of any student, parent, or guardian suspected to be out of status. The court in *League of United Latin American Citizens v. Wilson* (C.D.Cal.1995) enjoined the enforcement of many Proposition 187 provisions. The court relied upon *Plyer v. Doe* to reject Proposition 187 in so far as it limited the right of undocumented alien children to attend public schools and relied upon federal preemption to forbid state and local employees from investigating and reporting the immigration status of students and their parents/guardians. The court, however, did not invalidate provisions preventing undocumented aliens from receiving public post-secondary education as well as certain welfare and medical benefits.

§ 13–4.4 Eligibility for Federal Benefit Programs

An alien's eligibility for federal benefit programs is largely determined by her/his status in the United States. Under the Personal Responsibility and Work Opportunity Reconciliation Act of 1996 (Welfare Act), this status will generally fall into one of three groups: (1) lawfully permanent residents who have worked at least 40 "qualifying quarters," (2) aliens who are "qualified," and (3) aliens who are "not qualified." Before 1996, permanent resident aliens and aliens "permanently residing in the U.S. under color of law" were generally eligible for benefits. The classification "permanently residing under color of law" was liberally construed to mean any alien permitted to remain in the U.S. indefinitely. *Holley v.*

Lavine (2d Cir.1977). The Welfare Act, however, removes eligibility for most legal immigrants, provides eligibility to lawfully permanent residents with 40 "qualifying quarters," allows eligibility for "qualified" aliens, and removes eligibility for aliens who are "not qualified." The restrictions in the Welfare Act and the related public discussion has encouraged many permanent residents to become U.S. citizens. *See* § 12–2.2, *supra*.

The Welfare Act § 402 allows two categories of non-citizens to be eligible for "federal public benefits," such as Food Stamps (7 C.F.R. § 273.4) and Supplemental Security Income (SSI)(20 C.F.R. § 416.202(b)). 8 U.S.C.A. §§ 1612(a) and 1641. Other federal public benefits with restricted eligibility include unemployment benefits, public or assisted housing, licenses, and grants or loans (including those for post-secondary education). 8 U.S.C.A. § 1611(c). Federal public benefits are unavailable to aliens who are "not qualified." 8 U.S.C.A. § 1611.

The first category of eligible non-citizens includes lawfully admitted permanent residents who have worked at least 40 "qualifying quarters." 8 U.S.C.A. § 1612. Approximately ten years of work would allow a permanent resident to qualify, although this period sometimes can be shorter because lawfully permanent residents can receive credit for the "qualifying quarters" of spouses and parents. 8 U.S.C.A. § 1645.

The second category of non-citizens who are eligible for "federal public benefits" includes "qualified" aliens who are refugees and aliens granted asylum or restriction on removal. The eligibility of such aliens is limited to five years. 8 U.S.C.A. § 1612(a). The second category also includes "qualified" aliens who are active duty service members, active duty veterans, the spouses and unmarried dependent children under 21 of such members and veterans, persons paroled into the U.S. for at least one year, and certain battered spouses and children. 8 U.S.C.A. § 1641. Some parolees and some lawfully admitted residents face a five-year bar from "any federal means-tested program." 8 U.S.C.A. § 1613.

Medicaid for emergency care, in-kind disaster relief, and certain immunizations are not included as "federal public benefits," and can still be available to aliens regardless of status. 8 U.S.C.A. § 1611. The Attorney General is also able to define "federal public benefit" to permit other programs, services, and assistance that are "necessary for the protection of life or safety." *Id*.

The Welfare Act § 421 also states that "federal means-tested programs" are to use the income and resources of the sponsor of the alien in addition to the income of the alien to determine eligibility for benefits. 8 U.S.C.A. § 1631. Unless the aliens are refugees or asylees, this sponsor-to-alien deeming rule may keep most aliens ineligible for federal benefits until they naturalize or have 40 "qualifying quarters." After IIRIRA, the federal government, a state government, or any other entity that provides means-tested public benefits may enforce an affidavit of support against the alien's sponsor. INA § 213A(A)(1)(B). *See* 9–1.5, *supra* discussing enforcement of affidavits of support.

States are allowed, but not required, under the Welfare Act to prevent legal aliens from being eligible for non-emergency Medicaid (42 C.F.R. § 435.406), Title XX social services block grants, and the Temporary Assistance for Needy Families program (formerly Aid to Families with Dependant Children) which are administered on the state level. 8 U.S.C.A. § 1612. The Welfare Act § 411, however, mandates that states and localities only provide state or locally funded programs to qualified aliens, parolees, and nonimmigrants unless the states enact laws specifically providing others with eligibility. 8 U.S.C.A. § 1621.

Under the Welfare Act § 412, states are also allowed to disqualify some aliens from state funded public benefits. 8 U.S.C.A. § 1622. Such disqualification by a state of lawful aliens for eligibility to state programs, however, could be challenged as a violation of Equal Protection under the Fourteenth Amendment. The U.S. Supreme Court has held, for example, that state legislation discriminating between citizens and permanent resident aliens violates the Equal Protection Clause. *Graham v. Richardson* (Sup.Ct.1971). *See* 13–3.2b. To the extent *Graham* is based on preemption theory, however, federal authorization to discriminate may sustain withdrawals of public benefits.

The largest category of federal benefits are authorized under the Social Security Act. Old Age, Survivors and Disability Insurance (OASDI) is available to holders of social security numbers for work purposes. In order to obtain a social security number for work purposes, a person must be a citizen, permanent resident alien, or an alien who, under authority of law, is permitted to work in the U.S. 20 C.F.R. § 422.104. Not all aliens who are permitted to work in the U.S. are "qualified aliens" and not all permanent resident aliens will have worked at least 40 "qualifying quarters." Where the alien already holds a social security number, the alien will be eligible to receive OASDI, assuming other qualifications are met.

Coverage with OASDI can be suspended, however, regardless of the alien's status, if the alien leaves the

U.S. for more than six months, 42 U.S.C.A. § 402(t). Coverage can also be suspended if the alien is removed for certain reasons. 42 U.S.C.A. § 402(n). This suspension is not a violation of Due Process. *Flemming v. Nestor* (Sup.Ct.1960). These conditions for OASDI also apply to hospital insurance benefits. 42 U.S.C.A. § 426. For the uninsured alien, Medicare is available, but this coverage is restricted to permanent resident aliens who have resided in the U.S. for five or more years. 42 C.F.R. § 405.205. The Supreme Court unanimously upheld this restriction as within the authority of Congress in *Mathews v. Diaz* (Sup.Ct.1976).

If the alien leaves the U.S. and then tries to re-enter, the INS may refuse to admit the alien as one likely to become a public charge, based on the alien's previous welfare history. There also may be an adverse effect if the alien applies for an adjustment of status to permanent resident. Further, in the extreme, an alien who becomes a public charge within five years after entry may be removed, unless the causes arise after entry. INA § 237(a)(5).

Temporary resident aliens who receive benefits for which they are not qualified, either through agency inadvertence or "grandfathering," will not necessarily be denied permanent residency. The INS applies two tests to determine whether an alien legalized under the 1986 Immigration Reform and Control Act (IRCA) is not admissible as "likely to become a public charge." 8 C.F.R. § 245a.3(g)(4). The first test examines the alien's current earnings, job history, skills, education, and past receipt of welfare. The second test, deemed the "special rule," considers only whether the alien has maintained a consistent job history without receiving public cash assistance. Formerly undocumented aliens who were legalized under IRCA are disqualified for a period of five years after the date of legalization from receiving "programs of financial assistance furnished under Federal law ... as such programs are identified by the Attorney General." INA § 245A(h)(1). This five year waiting period does not necessarily apply to Cuban and Haitian aliens, or aliens who are aged, blind, or disabled. INA § 245A(h)(2).

Refugee aliens, as defined by INA § 207(c)(2), may qualify for Refugee Assistance, a program through which the federal government makes grants to, and contracts with, public or private nonprofit agencies for initial re-settlement of refugees in the United States. INA § 412. The goals of the program are to (i) make available sufficient resources for employment training and place-ment in order to achieve economic self-sufficiency among refugees as quickly as possible, (ii) provide refugees with the opportunity to acquire sufficient English language training to enable them to be resettled effectively as quickly as possible, (iii) insure that cash assistance is made available to refugees in such a manner as not to discourage their economic self-sufficiency, and (iv) insure that women have the same opportunity as men to partici-pate in training and instruction. INA § 412(a)(1)(A). Through the Refugee Medical Assistance program, refu-gees who do not qualify for Medicaid may receive free health care.

Even aliens who are qualified may also find limitations in a number of lesser used programs. These programs include loans for farm purchases (7 C.F.R. § 1822), hous-ing financial assistance (42 U.S.C.A. § 1436a), student financial aid, or student eligibility for state resident tuition. *See Nyquist v. Mauclet* (Sup.Ct.1977). These programs are usually limited to permanent resident aliens, but other restrictions may exist, and they may change from time to time-particularly in regard to state welfare programs.

§ 13–4.5 Freedom of Speech

The Supreme Court decided in *Schneider v. New Jersey* (Sup.Ct.1939) that aliens present in the U.S. are entitled to the same right of freedom of speech as any citizen. Nonetheless, any alien may be removed if s/he has engaged at any time since entry in terrorism or in any activity a purpose of which is the overthrow of the U.S. government by force or other unconstitutional means. INA § 237(a)(4). An alien's statements could also be used to attack the alien's good moral character or attachment to the principles of the Constitution, which are both required for naturalization. INA § 313.

One federal district court declared portions of INA § 241 [currently INA § 237] unconstitutional on their face as being "substantially overbroad," but the U.S. Court of Appeals reversed for lack of standing and ripeness. *American–Arab Anti–Discrimination Committee v. Thornburgh* (9th Cir.1991). These provisions stated that nonresident aliens should be deported if they advocate the doctrines of world communism; advocate unlawful damage of property; write, publish, etc., material advocating world communism or the establishment of totalitarian dictatorship in the United States; and if they affiliate with any organization that writes, circulates, etc., material advocating world communism or establishment of a totalitarian dictatorship in the U.S. The district court reasoned that the provisions are applicable to both constitutionally permissible and impermissible activities. The statutes prohibit a range of conduct, including the teaching of organizational viewpoints, advocacy of imminent lawless violence, and even an alien's wearing of an organization's button. The district court noted that resident aliens have First Amendment rights generally and these rights cannot be infringed despite the plenary power of Congress over immigration matters. The 1990 Act modified INA § 241 [currently 237] considerably, restricting its application in this respect to an alien's activities after entry and removing the offending provisions.

This case continued when the INS instituted further deportation proceedings under the terrorist activity provision of the 1990 Act, because the seven Palestinians and one Kenyan were members of the Popular Front for the Liberation of Palestine. The aliens again filed suit claiming that the INS had singled them out for selective enforcement of the immigration laws in retaliation for their constitutionally protected associational activity. The district court enjoined deportation of those aliens with visas and the INS appealed. In *American–Arab Anti–Discrimination Committee v. Reno* (9th Cir. 1997), the court rejected the government's contentions that IIRIRA deprived federal courts of jurisdiction over the case. Even though the exclusive jurisdiction provision of IIRIRA applies retroactively, it incorporated a statutory exception for certain claims of injunctive relief. *See* § 2–2.1, *supra.*

An unadmitted nonresident alien has no right of free speech in the U.S. The Supreme Court stated in *Kleindienst v. Mandel* (Sup.Ct.1972), that aliens could be excluded for views held or opinions expressed because aliens have no constitutional right of entry to the U.S. Additionally, the Court held that U.S. citizens have no right to have aliens enter the country so that ideas may be exchanged. The plenary power of Congress to control admission of aliens overrides a citizen's right to receive information under the First Amendment.

§ 13-4.6   Right to Own Land

Land ownership laws in the United States originally developed from English land laws. England prohibited aliens from owning land because all land grants required an oath of loyalty to the King; that oath conflicted with the alien's allegiance to another sovereign. That prohibition, however, inhibited territorial expansion and was even a subject of complaint in the Declaration of Independence. Yet, after the U.S. gained independence, the common law restrictions against alien ownership remained intact; states relaxed them slowly over the next century as the needs of territorial growth and foreign investment dictated. By the end of the 1800's, however, when unlimited territorial expansion was no longer possible, both state and federal legislatures began re-establishing restrictions on alien landholding. Many federal enactments from this era are still in effect, although few of the state restrictions are.

Alien land ownership law is primarily a state concern, and there are only three principal areas of federal restriction. First, the federal government has been concerned in time of war when enemy aliens hold land; second, the federal government is concerned with safeguarding of natural resources for citizens or permanent residents; third, the federal government has an interest in seeing that foreigners are treated equitably and in a manner consistent with national policies regarding immigration and foreign affairs.

As to the *first* area of federal concern, the Trading with the Enemy Act, 50 U.S.C.A.App. § 1, empowers the government to control land transactions during times of *declared* war. The Foreign Assets Control Regulations limit land transactions for aliens of certain listed countries, such as Cuba and the Democratic People's Republic of Korea at present. The International Emergency Economic Powers Act, 50 U.S.C.A. § 1701, grants the President broad authority to control alien property during a time of declared national emergency. President Carter used this authority during the Iranian hostage crisis to freeze all Iranian assets, including land. Similarly, President Bush froze Iraqi and Kuwaiti assets in 1991 after Iraq invaded Kuwait.

Second, federal laws restrict alien exploitation of agricultural, grazing, mineral, or timber land. Foreigners are required to notify the Department of Agriculture if they own agricultural land. 7 U.S.C.A. § 3501. The Taylor Grazing Act, 43 U.S.C.A. § 315, restricts grazing rights on public lands to citizens or immigrants who have applied for citizenship. The Mining Law of 1882 and the Mineral Lands Leasing Act of 1920 (41 Stat. 437) create restrictions on alien ownership of mineral rights, including petroleum. 30 U.S.C.A. § 181. More recent laws restrict alien development of off-shore oil deposits and geothermal resources. In addition, the Forest Service places some restrictions on standing timber sales to aliens, using a national preference system.

The *third* area of federal concern is founded upon constitutional protections and treaty rights. The Equal Protection Clause of the Fourteenth Amendment invalidates state laws that forbid resident aliens from owning land. Furthermore, in *Zschernig v. Miller* (Sup.Ct.1968), the Supreme Court relied on the constitutional grant of the foreign affairs power to the federal government to invalidate state laws that restrict inheritance by nationals of totalitarian countries. The reasoning of this decision conceivably could be used to void any state restriction on alien investment as an infringement on the federal foreign affairs power. Also, if the federal government has granted another nation's citizens land ownership rights by treaty, the state cannot abridge these rights, since treaties are part of the "supreme law of the land."

In state law, there is a wide diversity of statutes that control alien land ownership. All states permit resident aliens who have applied for citizenship to purchase and inherit land, but the uniformity ends there. A few states prohibit nonresident alien ownership; a few others limit the duration of land ownership; and some place acreage limits on ownership in order to inhibit aliens from owning agricultural land. Some states have restricted ownership by "enemies" in times of war. Other states limit land ownership to those who are eligible for citizenship. Minor restrictions abound: For example, South Carolina restricts ownership to ½ million acres; other states will not sell state-owned property or mineral rights to aliens. States generally do not restrict inheritance of land by aliens, except that some states insist upon reciprocity by the foreign country, permitting inheritance by U.S. citizens and receipt of the land by the heir. A few states require that the land inherited by an alien be sold within a statutory period after inheritance. About a dozen states also place restrictions on alien corporate landholding.

In general, the practitioner must examine the laws of each state with regard to both the type of land transaction and the identity of the alien individual or corporation involved. These laws must also be examined for constitutionality, because alien land ownership or usage is still an unsettled area of law.

§ 13–4.7 Military Service

The United States currently has a Selective Service registration requirement, 50 U.S.C.A.App. § 453, even though there is no longer any military draft, 50 U.S.C.A.App. § 467. This registration requirement applies to all males between the ages of 18 and 26 who reside in the U.S. except for lawfully admitted nonimmigrant aliens (50 U.S.C.A.App. § 453), and aliens who have resided in the U.S. less than one year, 50 U.S.C.A.App. § 455(a)(1)(3). The U.S. also has treaties with a number of other countries granting exemption from military service on a reciprocal basis. A resident alien from one of these countries may apply for a classification of exemption from the Selective Service. 32 C.F.R. § 1630.42. If the alien is granted the exemption based on alienage, however, the alien is barred from becoming a citizen, unless the alien is covered by a treaty. INA § 315. Any alien permanently ineligible for citizenship is inadmissable. INA § 212(a)(8)(A). Therefore, a permanent resident alien who obtains an exemption from military service and then leaves the U.S. may be excluded from re-entering. An alien in this category may apply to the Attorney General for an authorization for admission, but such authorizations are discretionary. INA § 212(c). Aliens who have departed the U.S. in order to avoid military service are also inadmissible. INA § 212(a)(8)(B).

An alien who does enter military service will receive the benefit of reduced residency requirements when applying for naturalization. INA § 328(a). If the service is during a time of hostilities, additional benefits are granted, including waiver of any age and residency requirement. INA § 329(b). Aliens in the military are ineligible to become commissioned officers and if the alien deserts the service, s/he is permanently barred from naturalization. INA § 314.

§ 13–4.8 Taxation of Aliens

The liability of an alien in the United States to pay taxes will depend on the alien's status as a resident or a nonresident. This status for tax purposes is determined by the Internal Revenue Code (26 U.S.C.A. § 1 *et seq.*) and not by the Immigration and Naturalization Act. Under 26 U.S.C.A. § 7701(b)(1)(A), an alien is treated as a U.S. resident with respect to any calendar year if s/he is either a lawful permanent resident at any time during that year or s/he meets a "substantial presence" test. With certain exceptions, an alien meets the substantial presence test if s/he is present in the U.S. on at least 31 days during the current year, and on at least 183 days within the last three years, with each day present in the current year counting as a full day, each day in the first preceding year as one-third of a day, and each day in the second preceding year as one-sixth of a day. Qualified aliens may also make a special election to be taxed as U.S. residents. 26 U.S.C.A. § 7701(b)(1)(A).

A resident alien is generally taxed in the same way as a U.S. citizen. A resident is thus taxed on income derived from all sources, including sources outside the U.S., and this income is subject to the graduated tax rates that apply to U.S. citizens. An individual who was a resident alien for the entire tax year may also claim the same deductions allowed for U.S. citizens. 26 C.F.R. § 1.871–1. Certain tax laws, however, may have a greater impact on resident aliens than on citizens; examples include: (1) a taxpayer may claim as a dependent only a citizen, national, or resident of the United States, a resident of Canada or Mexico, or an alien child adopted by and living with the U.S. citizen or national taxpayer (26 U.S.C.A. § 152(b)(3), 26 C.F.R. § 1.152–2(a)(2)); (2) a qualified individual may elect to exclude from gross income up to $70,000 of income earned in a foreign country and a limited amount based on housing costs paid or incurred because of foreign employment (26 U.S.C.A. § 911); and (3) a tax credit or deduction may be taken for certain foreign tax paid (26 U.S.C.A. § 901, 26 C.F.R. §§ 1.901–1, 1.901–2).

The situation of a nonresident alien is considerably more complicated. Any income derived from U.S. sources is taxed at the same graduated rates as for a U.S. citizen, if the income is effectively connected with the alien's trade or business in the United States. 26 U.S.C.A. §§ 871, 872. Other income, not effectively connected with a trade or business in the United States, such as an annuity or the income from the sale of a capital asset, is taxed at either a flat 30% rate, or a lower rate if a separate treaty exists with the alien's country. 26 C.F.R. § 1.871–8.

Nonresident aliens engaged in a trade or business in the United States may be able to exclude certain U.S. income from their effectively connected gross income. Nonresident aliens whose U.S. business is performing personal services in the United States may exclude compensation from a foreign employer, if the nonresident was admitted to the U.S. under INA §§ 101(a)(15)(F), (J), or (M) (as a nonimmigrant student or exchange visitor), income from certain annuities, and income exempt by treaty.

In general, deductions for nonresident aliens are allowed only if they are effectively connected with a trade or business. The following deductions, however, are allowed whether or not the nonresident's income was effectively connected with a U.S. trade or business: (1) deductions for casualty and theft losses on property located within the U.S.; (2) deductions for charitable contributions; and (3) deductions for personal exemptions. 26 U.S.C.A. § 873. Nonresident aliens who receive income effectively connected with their U.S. trade or business may make certain itemized deductions, including state and local income taxes, charitable contributions to U.S. organizations, casualty and theft losses on property located in the U.S., moving expenses, and miscellaneous deductions.

Nonresident aliens may also claim credits against U.S. income tax liability for certain taxes paid, including certain foreign taxes paid. With limited exceptions, nonresident aliens engaged in a trade or business in the U.S. are allowed only one personal exemption. A fuller discussion, complete with examples, is available in Publication 519, U.S. Tax Guide for Aliens, from the local office of the Internal Revenue Service (IRS). This guide includes an updated list of tax treaties in effect.

In order to ensure that all taxes owed are paid, the departing alien is required to obtain a Certificate of Compliance from the IRS. Also known as a Sailing Permit or Exit Permit, this document shows that either the taxes have been paid or an adequate bond has been posted to cover taxes owed. Diplomats, certain employees of foreign governments and international organizations, aliens present in the U.S. for a short term with no taxable income, commuting residents of Canada or Mexico, and some students or trainees do not have to obtain a

Sailing Permit before departing. 26 C.F.R. § 1.6851–2(a)(2).

An alien who has obtained a social security number for work purposes also will pay social security taxes for work performed in the U.S. 26 U.S.C.A. § 3101. The United States has bilateral social security agreements with many foreign countries to coordinate social security coverage and generally to make sure that social security taxes are paid only to one country. Agreements are in effect with Austria, Belgium, Canada, France, Germany, Italy, Netherlands, Norway, Portugal, Spain, Sweden, Switzerland, and the United Kingdom. Under these agreements, aliens are generally subject to social security tax only in the country where they are working.

Resident aliens, like U.S. citizens, are subject to gift tax no matter where the gift property is situated and whether it is tangible or intangible property. 26 U.S.C.A. § 2501(a), 26 C.F.R. § 25.2501–1(a). Nonresident aliens are generally liable for gift tax only with respect to gifts of real property or tangible personal property situated in the U.S. when the alien made the gift. 26 U.S.C.A. §§ 2501(a), 2511(a). A marital deduction is not allowed for gifts made to a spouse who is not a U.S. citizen. 26 U.S.C.A. § 2523(i). The law, however, raises the tax exclusion to the first $100,000 of the value of the gift from the previous $10,000. Federal estate taxes are also applied to aliens and citizens on a similar basis, with a separate rate table for nonresidents. 26 U.S.C.A. § 2101. A marital deduction, however, is not allowed for bequests made to a surviving spouse who is not a U.S. citizen. 26 U.S.C.A. § 2056(d). In addition, aliens normally will be required to pay state taxes; states vary in their taxation of citizens and aliens, but ordinarily citizen and alien taxpayers are treated alike.

CHAPTER 14

CRIMINAL ASPECTS OF IMMIGRATION

§ 14–1 INTRODUCTION

In addition to the harsh penalties of removal and inadmissibility, aliens may incur actual criminal penalties for misconduct related to immigration. Criminal sanctions for aliens are found under both the Immigration and Nationality Act and portions of the U.S. Criminal Code. This chapter describes immigration-related conduct that may result in criminal penalties for aliens and citizens, including unlawful entry, bringing aliens into the U.S. without inspection, transporting or concealing an alien who entered unlawfully, encouraging an alien to enter unlawfully, misrepresentation or fraud in obtaining immigration status, failure to comply with removal regulations, and unlawful employment of aliens. The chapter also discusses the immigration consequences of an alien's criminal activity, including denial of asylum, inadmissibility, and removal.

§ 14–2 CRIMINAL PROVISIONS RELATED TO IMMIGRATION

§ 14–2.1 Unlawful Entry

a. *Entry of Alien at Improper Time or Place; Avoidance Of Examination or Inspection; Misrepresentation and Concealment of Facts*

Unlawful entry into the United States became a criminal offense in 1929. 45 Stat. 1551. Today, INA § 275 penalizes all aliens who enter or attempt to enter this country improperly—at any time or place other than as designated by immigration officials—by eluding examination or inspection or by being responsible for a willfully false or misleading representation or the willful concealment of a material fact. An alien who enters the country unlawfully can be fined under 18 U.S.C.A. (before 1991, INA § 275 set the amount of the fine at $2,000 or less) or imprisoned not more than six months, or both, for a first offense in violation of § 275. For a subsequent conviction the prison sentence increases to a maximum of two years. Note that in order for a felony sentence to be imposed under INA § 275, the alien must have previously been convicted of the offense. Title 18 U.S.C.A. directs courts to the sentencing guidelines established by the U.S. Sentencing Commission. Courts use the guidelines when someone is convicted of a federal offense in order to determine the amount of fines and length of sentences. The guidelines use categories of offense behavior and categories of offender characteristics in an attempt to achieve fairness and certainty in the setting of fines and sentences.

Mere proof that the alien entered the country unlawfully is insufficient. *United States v. Arambula–Alvarado* (9th Cir.1982). This fact is significant because prosecution under the misdemeanor provision of § 275 is not a high priority for prosecutors and is therefore fairly unusual. Prosecution is more often used as a threat by INS officers to get aliens to accept prompt removal. Criminal prosecution is more likely under a 1990 amendment to INA § 275 proscribing an individual from establishing a commercial enterprise for the purpose of evading immigration law. If convicted, such a person is subject to a fine according to 18 U.S.C.A. (before 1990, INA § 275 set the amount of the fine at $2,000), a prison term of not more than five years, or both.

The Illegal Immigration Reform and Immigrant Responsibility Act of 1996 (IIRIRA) adds civil penalties not exceeding $500 for aliens who are apprehended while entering or attempting to enter improperly. INA § 275(b). Before IIRIRA, INA § 275 did not reach attempted entries.

b. *Re-entry of Removed Alien*

Under INA § 276, an alien who has been removed and who re-enters or attempts to re-enter the United States without permission of the Attorney General is guilty of a felony. The penalty for this felony is imprisonment up to two years, a fine under title 18 U.S.C.A., or both. For example, in *United States v. Bernal–Gallegos* 726 F.2d 187 (5th Cir.1984) an alien was convicted under § 276 for an unlawful entry committed more than five years after removal.

Theoretically, when an alien re-enters the United States without permission after removal, s/he is subject to criminal penalties under both § 275 and § 276. In *United States v. Ortiz-Martinez* (9th Cir.1977), however, the Ninth Circuit Court of Appeals held that since one act of re-entering is involved, a person convicted of violating both statutes cannot be subjected to consecutive terms of imprisonment.

Specific intent to re-enter the country illegally is not required for a conviction under § 276. Hence, the government need not prove that the alien knew s/he was not entitled to re-enter the United States without permission of the Attorney General. *Pena-Cabanillas v. United States* (9th Cir.1968); *United States v. Hernandez* (10th Cir.1982). In *United States v. Anton* (7th Cir.1982), however, the Seventh Circuit Court of Appeals held that an alien's reasonable belief that he had the consent of the Attorney General to re-enter the country constitutes a viable mistake-of-law defense to a § 276 charge.

An alien prosecuted for unlawful entry after removal may be able to challenge collaterally the validity of the underlying removal order. In *United States v. Mendoza–Lopez* (Sup.Ct.1987), the Supreme Court held that although the language of § 276 does not require the removal (formerly deportation) to have been lawful and there is no evidence that Congress intended to permit a challenge to the validity of the prior removal order, "[i]f the statute envisions that a court may impose a criminal penalty for re-entry after *any* deportation, regardless of how violative of the rights of the alien the deportation proceedings may have been, such a statute does not comport with the constitutional requirement of due process." The Court further held that where the removal (formerly deportation) proceeding effectively eliminates the right of the alien to obtain judicial review, that review must be made available in any subsequent proceeding in which the result of the removal proceeding is used to establish an element of a criminal offense.

An alien may argue that he was compelled to incriminate himself, even if that argument was not made before the immigration judge. *Navia-Duran v. INS* (1st Cir. 1977). If INS agents arrest an alien without a warrant, they must comply with regulations requiring that the alien be advised of certain rights. *Id.* Moreover, an alien in INS custody must be advised of her/his rights under *Miranda v. Arizona* (Sup.Ct.1966). The 1990 Act provides that an officer or employee of the INS may arrest an alien without a warrant, if that officer or employee has reasonable grounds to believe the individual has committed or is committing a felony. Again, failure to give *Miranda* warnings may invalidate any confessions obtained during the custodial interrogations of the alien.

c. Removal Consequences of Unlawful Entry

Besides the criminal penalties imposed by INA §§ 275 and 276, an alien who enters or re-enters the United States unlawfully may also be subject to removal. The alien's guilty plea to a § 275 or § 276 charge will establish the alien's unlawful entry or re-entry for purposes of removal under § 237(a)(2). *See, e.g., Marroquin–Manriquez v. INS* (3d Cir.1983). The Fifth Circuit Court of Appeals in *Garcia-Trigo v. United States* (5th Cir.1982) held that the alien need not be informed of the collateral immigration consequences of her/his conviction under § 275.

Although removal, rather than criminal penalties, is more often enforced in cases of unlawful entry, an alien who may be removed under § 237(a)(1)(B) may still be subject to criminal prosecution. During the removal proceeding, once the INS has established that the respondent is an alien, the alien has the burden of proof to show the time, place, and manner of her/his entry into the United States. If this burden is not sustained, the alien will be presumed to be in the U.S. in violation of law and thereby subject to criminal prosecution. INA § 291. Generally, since a removal hearing is not a criminal proceeding, there is no presumption of innocence, and therefore, no abridgement of the alien's Fifth Amendment rights in requiring the alien to demonstrate the time, place, and manner of her/his entry into the United States. *Chavez–Raya v. INS* (7th Cir.1975); *Cabral–Avila v. INS* (9th Cir.1978).

Because of potential criminal liability for unlawful entry under § 275 or § 276, however, the right to remain silent is available in removal proceedings under § 237(a)(1)(B). In *Cabral–Avila*, the Ninth Circuit Court of Appeals held that the alien's decision to remain silent during removal (formerly deportation) proceedings is an appropriate exercise of the alien's Fifth Amendment privilege, but by doing so, the alien is not shielded from the inference that s/he is not legally in the country, and the alien's silence cannot be relied upon to carry forward her/his duty to rebut the government's prima facie case.

§ 14–2.2 Crimes Related to Facilitating an Alien's Unlawful Entry or Continued Unlawful Presence in the United States

a. Bringing in an Alien

The INA contains two sections that impose criminal penalties upon persons who unlawfully participate in bringing aliens into the U.S. The first, INA § 274(a)(1)(A), applies to any person who helps bring or attempt to bring an alien into the country without inspection, even if the alien had received prior official authorization to enter or reside in the United States. The penalties imposed for this violation include a fine under title 18, imprisonment up to five years, or both, for each alien in respect to whom the violation occurred. If the reason for the violation was commercial advantage or private financial gain, the imprisonment may be up to ten years. INA § 274(a)(1)(B).

The second section, INA § 274(a)(2), applies to any person who, knowing or in reckless disregard of the fact that an alien has not received prior official authorization to enter or reside in the United States, brings or attempts to bring that alien into the country, although not necessarily without inspection. The penalties under this section include a fine under title 18, imprisonment up to one year, or both, for each transaction constituting a violation of this section, regardless of the number of aliens involved. The penalty includes a fine and imprisonment up to ten years if the offense involves attempting to bring an alien unlawfully into the United States with the reasonable belief that the alien will commit an offense punishable by more than one year in prison. The penalty also includes a fine under title 18 and up to ten years imprisonment if the offense is committed for commercial advantage or private financial gain, or if the alien is not immediately presented to an appropriate immigration officer at a designated port of entry. If the offense is the third or more offense, imprisonment is not to exceed fifteen years or be less than five years.

Under § 274(a), penalties are to be imposed regardless of any further official action that may later be taken with respect to the alien. No consideration is given to the manner in which the offender brought or attempted to bring the alien into the United States. IIRIRA added § 274 (a)(1)(A)(v) that makes conspiring to do these acts a violation of the statute even if the alien is not actually brought within the territorial jurisdiction of the United States. (*See also* § 14–2.4, *infra.*)

It is interesting to note that the 1986 amendments to INA § 274(a)(1)(A) were expressly intended to correct "shortcomings and ambiguities" identified in *United States v. Anaya* (S.D.Fla.1980) and *United States v. Zayas–Morales* (11th Cir.1982). In those cases, the defendants had made no effort to land undocumented Cubans surreptitiously or evasively, but instead brought them directly into immigration officers in Key West, Florida, to apply for asylum. In House Report No. 99–682(1) to the Immigration Reform and Control Act of 1986, this perceived "gap" in the law was intentionally closed. Therefore, an individual may be charged and convicted under INA § 274(a)(1)(A) even if s/he is merely bringing an undocumented alien to the border for purposes of applying for asylum.

Problems may arise in a criminal prosecution under § 274(a)(1)(A) or (a)(2) if, before trial, the government removes the alien witnesses who allegedly were brought into the U.S. unlawfully. The defendant may claim that her/his Sixth Amendment right to compulsory process has been violated by the removal (formerly "deportation") of these witnesses. In *United States v. Valenzuela–Bernal* (Sup.Ct.1982), the Supreme Court held that to show a denial of Due Process through the removal of alien witnesses, the defendant must show that the testimony of the removed witnesses would have been material and favorable to her/his defense in ways not merely cumulative to the testimony of available witnesses.

b. *Transporting an Alien Within the United States*

INA § 274(a)(1)(A)(ii) imposes a criminal penalty on any person who "knowing or in reckless disregard of the fact that an alien has come to, entered, or remains in the United States in violation of law, transports, or moves or attempts to transport or move such alien within the United States by means of transportation or otherwise, in furtherance of such violation of law." To support a conviction for this offense, the government must prove that (1) the defendant transported or attempted to transport an alien within the United States; (2) the alien was in the United States in violation of the law; (3) the defendant knew the alien was in the United States in violation of the law or acted in reckless disregard of this fact; and (4) the defendant acted willfully in furtherance of the alien's violation of the law. The 1986 amendment to this section eliminated an earlier requirement that the defendant know or have reasonable grounds to believe that the alien's last entry into the United States occurred less than three years before. The penalties imposed under this section include a fine under title 18, imprisonment up to five years, or both, for each alien in respect to whom the violation occurred.

The mere transportation of a person known to be an alien unlawfully in the country is not a violation of this provision. The transportation must be "in furtherance of [the alien's] violation of law." The statute does not delineate the specific circumstances under which transportation of an alien will constitute transportation "in furtherance of such violation of law." In *United States v. Moreno* (9th Cir.1977), the Ninth Circuit Court of Appeals held that "there must be a direct or substantial relationship between [the] transportation and its furtherance of the alien's presence in the United States." If the act of transporting the alien is "only incidentally connected to the furtherance of the violation of law," it is "too attenuated to come within the boundaries of [INA

§ 274(a)(1)(A)(ii)]". *Moreno* involved the transportation of undocumented aliens by a foreman of a reforestation company who was required to transport employees from one job site to another. The court concluded that "his transportation of aliens was only incidentally connected with the furtherance of the violation of the law, if at all," and noted that the foreman's employer was not charged with any offense.

The Fifth Circuit Court of Appeals held, in *United States v. Merkt* (5th Cir.1985), that by definition, a person intending to help an alien in obtaining legal status, such as by transporting the alien to an INS office, is not acting in furtherance of the alien's illegal presence in the U.S. within the meaning the statutory provision now found at INA § 274(a)(1)(A). In *United States v. Shaddix* (5th Cir.1982), however, the Fifth Circuit held that an employer's offer of employment and voluntary transportation of the aliens to the place of employment had furthered the aliens' illegal presence in this country sufficiently to constitute a violation of the statute. Similarly, in *United States v. Pereira–Pineda* (5th Cir.1983) and in *United States v. Aguilar* (9th Cir.1989), the courts of appeal held that the possibility that aliens might apply for asylum, allowing them to remain at liberty while their rights were determined, did not mean that the aliens resided lawfully in the United States before applying for asylum. In *Aguilar* the court sustained the conviction of several individuals who had helped Arizona churches give sanctuary to Central Americans.

While a mistake of fact may constitute a valid defense to the crime of unlawfully transporting an alien, a mistake of law will not. In *Merkt,* the defendant's belief that the aliens' genuine qualifications for political asylum entitled them to legal status even though they had not yet filed an asylum claim was held to be based on a mistake of law and therefore did not constitute a defense.

c. Concealing, Harboring, or Shielding an Alien

Under INA § 274(a)(1)(A)(iii), criminal penalties are imposed upon any person who "knowing or in reckless disregard of the fact that an alien has come to, entered, or remains in the United States in violation of law, conceals, harbors, or shields from detection or attempts to conceal, harbor, or shield from detection, such alien in any place, including any buildings or any means of transportation." A violation will subject the defendant to a fine under title 18, imprisonment up to five years, or both, for each alien in respect to whom the violation occurred.

Because INA § 274 is aimed at preventing undocumented aliens from remaining in the United States, and preventing them from entering, the harboring need not be directly connected with the alien's illegal entry to be prohibited. The activity need only substantially facilitate the alien's continued unlawful presence in the United States. *United States v. Lopez* (2d Cir.1975); *United States v. Cantu* (5th Cir.1977).

Persons who warn aliens of the presence of immigration officers have been held to fall within this section. *United States v. Rubio–Gonzalez* (5th Cir.1982). INA § 274(a) previously contained a clause providing "[t]hat for the purposes of this section, employment (including the usual and normal practices incident to employment) shall not be deemed to constitute harboring." The 1986 amendment to INA § 274(a) eliminated this exception.

d. Inducing an Alien to Enter

Under INA § 274(a)(1)(A)(iv), it is a crime to "encourage or induce an alien to come to, enter, or reside in the United States, knowing or in reckless disregard of the fact that such coming to, entry or residence is or will be in violation of law." Persons convicted of this crime are punishable by a fine under title 18, imprisonment up to five years, or both, for each alien in respect to whom the violation occurred.

The defendant in *United States v. Hanna* (5th Cir. 1981) petitioned for a rehearing of his INA § 274(a)(1)(D) (currently § 274(a)(1)(A)(iv)) conviction, claiming that he did not violate the statute because his passengers were paroled into the United States. The Fifth Circuit Court of Appeals denied the rehearing, holding that parole "is simply a device through which needless confinement is avoided while administrative proceedings are conducted" and that parole "was never intended to affect an alien's status.... " The court concluded that "[i]t would be a misuse of the parole concept to conclude that one who physically transports into the United States persons not otherwise entitled to come in cannot be guilty under [INA § 274(a)(1)(A)] if the United States grants parole to those brought in while it determines whether they should be given asylum."

The act of inducement or encouragement need not have been committed in the United States. The Ninth Circuit Court of Appeals in *United States v. Castillo–Felix* (9th Cir.1976) reasoned that acts of inducement committed outside the United States may constitute crimes since such acts "have no purpose unless they are intended to facilitate the unlawful entry of an alien or his continued illegal presence in the United States." The effect of such crimes committed outside of the United States takes place in the United States and "in terms of the regulation of immigration, it is unimportant where acts constituting the crime occur."

e. *Aiding or Assisting a Subversive Alien to Enter the U.s.*

Any person who knowingly aids or assists any criminal or subversive alien inadmissible to enter the United States under INA § 212(a)(2) (because of an aggravated felony) or INA § 212(a)(3) (because of security or related grounds), or who connives or conspires with any person to permit any such alien to enter the United States, can be fined under title 18, or imprisoned not more than 10 years, or both. INA § 277.

f. *Importing an Alien for an Immoral Purpose*

Under INA § 278, it is a felony offense to import, directly or indirectly, any alien for prostitution or for any other immoral purpose. Attempts to import an alien for such purposes are also covered by the statute. Similarly, it is an offense "to hold any alien for any such purpose in pursuance of such illegal importation" or to "keep, maintain, control, support, employ, or harbor in any house or other place, for the purpose of prostitution or for any other immoral purpose, any alien, in pursuance of such illegal importation." Persons convicted of this offense may be punished by a fine under title 18, imprisonment up to ten years, or both.

g. *Related Civil Penalties*

In addition to the criminal penalties discussed above, several sections of the INA provide civil penalties for certain acts related to bringing in aliens. A fine of

$3,000, for example, may be imposed upon any person who improperly brings to the United States an alien (other than an alien crewman) who is inadmissible under INA § 212(a)(1). INA § 271(a).

INA § 271 imposes a duty upon "every person, including the owners, masters, officers, and agents of vessels, aircraft, transportation lines or international bridges or toll roads" (other than transportation lines that have entered into contracts with the Attorney General under INA § 238), bringing an alien to, or providing a means for an alien to come to the United States, to prevent the unauthorized landing of aliens. Violators are subject to a $3,000 fine. An owner or operator of a railroad line, international bridge, or toll road, however, may escape liability by establishing that it acted diligently and reasonably to prevent unauthorized landings, even though such a landing occurred. INA § 271(c)(1). Any owner or operator of a railroad line, international bridge, or toll road may request that the Attorney General inspect any facility or method used at a point of entry to the United States to comply with this provision. If the Attorney General has approved the facility or method, proof that the individual has diligently maintained the approved facility or used the approved method is prima facie evidence that the individual acted diligently and reasonably to fulfill the duty to prevent unauthorized landings. INA § 271(c).

The INA contains several other provisions that impose civil fines upon carriers. INA § 234 provides a $2,000 penalty for failure of an aircraft to land at a designated port of entry or for violating regulations related to such ports of entry. The failure or refusal of a transportation line to receive and remove an inadmissible alien or to pay removal expenses, as ordered by the Attorney General, will subject the carrier to a $2,000 penalty for each violation under INA § 243(c). The failure to remove an alien stowaway subjects a person to a $5,000 penalty. INA § 243(c)(B). A civil penalty also is imposed upon persons, including transportation lines and other vessel operators, who bring in aliens who do not have valid passports and unexpired visas, if a visa is required for such alien, or who fail to detain or remove a stowaway or removable crewmember. The penalty consists of a $3,000 fine per alien, and in the case of an alien without an unexpired visa who is not admitted or permitted to land temporarily, an additional amount equal to that amount paid by the alien for his transportation from the initial point of departure. This additional amount paid is then returned to the alien. Any amounts paid as a penalty for bringing in an alien without an unexpired visa may be refunded if the Attorney General is convinced that the violator did not know, and could not have discovered by the exercise of reasonable diligence, that the individual transported was an alien and that a visa was required. INA § 273.

§ 14–2.3   Failure to Comply With Registration Requirements

INA § 262 provides that every alien who remains in the United States for thirty days or more must be registered and fingerprinted. Any alien who "willfully fails or refuses" to register may be fined up to $1,000, imprisoned up to six months, or both. INA § 266(a). Similarly, this provision provides that every alien required to be registered must also give written notice of each change of address and provide other information as the Attorney General may require. Violators of this provision may be subject to a $200 fine, imprisonment up to thirty days, or both. After registering and being finger-printed, the alien is issued a certificate of alien registration or an alien registration receipt card. Aliens eighteen years old or older must "at all times carry with him and have in his personal possession" the certificate or card issued to her/him. INA § 264(e). Aliens who fail to comply with this requirement may be subject to a fine of $100, imprisonment up to thirty days, or both.

In actual practice, however, these registration requirements are not generally enforced. The INS has stopped reminding aliens that they ought to notify the INS of their address and effectively has ceased administering the address notification requirement. Although failure to give the written notice of address required by § 265 is a ground for removal under INA § 237(a)(3), Operating Instruction 265.1(a) provides that failure of an alien to comply with the § 265 requirements regarding notification of address "shall not normally serve as the sole basis for initiating prosecution" or removal proceedings. Therefore, an alien ordinarily will not be prosecuted under § 237(a)(3) unless the alien also is removable for another reason. Similarly, Operating Instruction 265.1(b) implies that an alien will not normally be prosecuted solely under § 264(e): "[a]ny alien not in possession of an alien registration card shall be advised of the requirements and sanctions of section 264 of the Act and shall be furnished an application for a replacement or duplicate card."

Any alien who files an application for registration containing statements known by her/him to be false or who registers or attempts to register through fraud is guilty of a misdemeanor. Upon conviction, such person may be fined up to $1,000, imprisoned up to six months, or both. Conviction will also render the alien removable under INA § 237(a)(3). INA § 266(c). Other statutes dealing with conspiracy to defraud the United States also may penalize fraud or falsification in registration. *See* § 14–2.4, *infra*. Counterfeiting a certificate of alien registration or an alien registration receipt card is an offense punishable by a fine of up to $5,000, imprisonment up to five years, or both. INA § 266(d). Persons who manufacture and sell counterfeit cards also are punishable under 18 U.S.C.A. § 1426.

§ 14–2.4 Misrepresentation, False Statements, Fraud, and Conspiracy

a. Perjury

Several statutes apply to perjury in immigration proceedings. These statutes overlap to some extent, and depending on the situation, a prosecution can be brought under any of them.

The perjury provision of the Immigration and Nationality Act is contained in INA § 287(b). This statute empowers INS officers and employees to administer oaths, and provides that:

[A]ny person to whom such oath has been administered (or who has executed an unsworn declaration, certificate, verification, or statement under penalty of perjury ...), ... who shall knowingly or willfully give false evidence or swear ... to any false statement concerning any matter referred to in this subsection shall be guilty of perjury and shall be punished as provided by section 1621 of Title 18.

18 U.S.C.A. § 1621 is the general perjury provision of the United States Code. § 1621 provides:

Whoever—(1) having taken an oath before a competent tribunal, officer, or person, in any case in which a law of the United States authorizes an oath to be administered, that he will testify, declare, depose, or certify truly, or that any written testimony, declaration, deposition, or certificate by him subscribed, is true, ... states or subscribes any material matter which he does not believe to be true; or (2) in any declaration, certificate, verification, or statement ... willfully subscribes as true any material matter which he does not believe to be true; is guilty of perjury, and shall, except as otherwise expressly provided by law, be fined under this title [see § 14–2.1; before 1994, § 1621 limited the amount of a fine to not more than $2,000] or imprisoned not more than five years, or both.

A third statute related to perjury in immigration proceedings is 22 U.S.C.A. § 4221. This statute authorizes certain embassy officials and consular officers to administer oaths, and directs that any person who "willfully and corruptly" commits perjury or "by any means procure[s] any person to commit perjury" before such officers may be prosecuted in any United States district court in the same manner as if the offense had been committed in the United States.

The fact that false statements made under oath may constitute perjury does not preclude prosecution under other applicable statutes. Because of the demanding requirements for proof of perjury, prosecutors often proceed under other statutes whose requirements are less stringent, such as laws dealing with false statements, fraud, misuse of documents, or conspiracy. *See* §§ 14–2.4c.–e.

b. *False Claim to Citizenship*

Under 18 U.S.C.A. § 911, any person who falsely and willfully represents her/himself to be a United States citizen may be fined (see § 14–2.1; before 1994, § 911 limited the amount of a fine to not more than $1,000) and imprisoned for not more than three years. The misrepresentation of citizenship must be willful, in addition to being false. The Ninth Circuit Court of Appeals in *Chow Bing Kew v. United States* (9th Cir.1957) held that "willfully" means only that the misrepresentation was made voluntarily and deliberately and, therefore, the prosecution need not show that the misrepresentation was made for a fraudulent purpose. In reaching this conclusion, the court pointed out that § 911 was an amendment to a prior statute (35 Stat. 1088, 1103) which, in contrast, specifically required a fraudulent purpose. *See also De Pratu v. United States* (9th Cir.1948); *United States v. Franklin* (7th Cir.1951).

The statute reaches misrepresentations of citizenship in many contexts, including statements made to private employers, to unions, in voting, in applying for a U.S. passport, in an immigration or naturalization proceeding, in a selective service questionnaire, in applying for a license, and in responding to questions of arresting police officers. Under some circumstances, the false representation of citizenship may constitute perjury. *See* § 14–2.4a. The false citizenship claim also may be punishable under 18 U.S.C.A. § 1001, which deals with false statements made to government officers, or under 18 U.S.C.A. § 1546, concerning fraud and misuse of visas and other documents. *See* §§ 14–2.4c. and d.

c. *False or Fraudulent Statements and Representations*

18 U.S.C.A. § 1001 establishes a broad foundation for criminal penalties against false statements and misrepresentations in general. The statute provides:

[W]hoever, in any matter within the jurisdiction of the executive, legislative, or judicial branch of the Government of the United States, knowingly and willfully— (1) falsifies, conceals, or covers up by any trick, scheme, or device a material fact; (2) makes any materially false, fictitious, or fraudulent statement or representation; or (3) makes or uses any false writing or document knowing the same to contain any materially false, fictitious, or fraudulent statement or entry; shall be fined under this title [see § 14–2.1; before 1994, § 1001 limited the amount of a fine to not more than $10,000] or imprisoned not more than 5 years, or both.

18 U.S.C.A. § 1001 imposes a penalty for false statements or misrepresentations made to any officer, department, or agency of the United States and thus covers false statements and misrepresentations made to immigration and consular officers in a broad variety of immigration contexts. False statements made in applying for or use of a passport are specifically punishable under 18 U.S.C.A. § 1542.

d. *Fraud and Misuse of Visas, Permits, and Other Documents*

18 U.S.C.A. § 1546 criminalizes a wide variety of acts involving misuse of a visa, permit, or other document required for entry into the United States or as evidence of authorized stay or employment in the United States. The following offenses are subject to criminal sanctions:

a. Knowingly forging, counterfeiting, altering, or falsely making any immigrant or nonimmigrant visa, permit, or other document required for entry into or as evidence of authorized stay in the United States, or using, possessing, obtaining, etc., such document knowing it to be fraudulently or unlawfully obtained;

b. Unauthorized possession of any blank permit; unauthorized creation, sale, transport, control, or possession of any plate in the likeness of a plate designed for printing permits; unauthorized making of any print, photograph, or impression in the likeness of any visa, permit, or other document required for entry into the United States; or unauthorized possession of the distinctive paper used for printing these documents; (Note: commonly used forms such as the I–94 (Arrival–Departure record) are routinely photocopied; because this proscription reaches all documents, however, photocopies should not be sent to the INS.)

c. Assuming a false identity when applying for a visa, permit, or other document required for entry into or admission to the United States;

d. Selling or offering to sell or dispose of a visa, permit, or other document to a person not authorized to receive such document; and

e. Knowingly making under oath or penalty of perjury any false statement with respect to a material fact in any application, affidavit, or other document required by the immigration laws or regulations; or knowingly presenting any such document containing a false statement.

f. Using an identification document, knowing or having reason to know that the document was not lawfully issued for the use of the possessor or that the document was false, or using a false attestation, for satisfying the requirements of the employment verification system under INA § 274A(b).

Persons who violate any of the first five offenses in § 1546 (a.-e., above) may be fined in accordance with title 18, imprisoned for up to five years, or both. Commission of the sixth offense (f.) subjects the violator to a fine, imprisonment up to two years, or both. Similarly, 18 U.S.C.A. §§ 1543 and 1544 provide for a fine (see § 14–2.1), imprisonment up to ten years, or both, for forgery or misuse of a passport. Before 1994, §§ 1543 and 1544 limited the amount of a fine to not more than $2,000.

Following IIRIRA in 1996, if an alien arrives with fraudulent or invalid documents under INA §§ 212(a)(6)(C) or 212(a)(7), s/he is inadmissible. INA § 235(b). Unless such alien expresses an intention to apply for asylum or a fear of persecution, s/he is to be removed "without further hearing or review." INA § 235(b)(1)(A)(i).

e. Conspiracy

The general conspiracy statute, 18 U.S.C.A. § 371, provides yet another means of penalizing false statements, misrepresentations, and other fraud in immigration matters. This statute provides:

If two or more persons conspire either to commit any offense against the United States, or to defraud the United States, or any agency thereof in any manner or for any purpose, and one or more of such persons do any act to effect the object of the conspiracy, each shall be fined not more than $10,000 or imprisoned not more than five years, or both.

If, however, the conspired offense is a misdemeanor only, the punishment for the conspiracy must not exceed the maximum punishment provided for the misdemeanor. 18 U.S.C.A. § 371.

An individual may be convicted under both 18 U.S.C.A. § 371 and the statute relating to the substantive offense.

Pereira v. United States (Sup.Ct.1954). Showing participation in a conspiracy is often easier than proving a substantive crime. IIRIRA added INA § 274 (a)(1)(A)(v) which imposes criminal penalties on persons who conspire to bring in or harbor certain aliens. This addition makes showing a violation for conspiracy possible under both the INA and 18 U.S.C.A. § 371.

f. Marriage Fraud

The Immigration Marriage Fraud Amendments of 1986 intended to deter aliens from seeking immigration benefits through a fraudulent marriage to a U.S. citizen or permanent resident alien. Those amendments, for example, impose a two-year conditional residency requirement on alien spouses before they may obtain permanent resident status on the basis of a "qualifying marriage" to a U.S. citizen or permanent resident alien. The Fraud Amendments also provide a criminal penalty for marriage fraud. INA § 275 states, "[a]ny individual who knowingly enters into a marriage for the purpose of evading any provision of the immigration laws shall be imprisoned for not more than five years, or fined not more than $250,000, or both." The statute applies to the U.S. citizen or permanent resident alien and also to the nonresident alien involved in the fraudulent marriage. *See* § 5–2.1 for a discussion of the Immigration Marriage Fraud Amendments of 1986.

§ 14–2.5 Failure to Comply With Removal Proceedings

a. Failure to Comply With Supervision Regulations

The Attorney General has a period of 90 days from the date of an alien's final removal order within which to effect the alien's departure from the United States. INA § 241(a)(1)(A). If the alien is not removed within this 90 day period, the alien is subject to supervision under regulations prescribed by the Attorney General. INA § 241(a)(3). These regulations include requirements of periodic reporting; submission, if necessary, to medical and psychiatric examination; testimony as to the alien's "nationality, circumstances, habits, associations, and activities" and other such information as the Attorney General deems proper; as well as conformity to other written restrictions. Any alien who willfully fails to comply with these requirements may be fined up to $1,000, imprisoned for up to one year, or both. INA § 243(b).

b. Failure to Depart

INA § 243(a) penalizes numerous categories of aliens who willfully fail to depart the United States within ninety days of the date of a final order of removal. The statute applies to any alien found to be subject to removal by reason of being a member of any of the classes described in INA §§ 237(a)(1)(E), (2), (3), and (4). Included in this list are subversive aliens, narcotic drug addicts, aliens associated with Nazi Germany, aliens who have violated registration requirements, aliens convicted of crimes involving moral turpitude or unlawful possession of certain weapons, aliens convicted of any listed offenses relating to national security, and aliens convicted of domestic abuse, stalking, or child abuse. In addition to willfully failing to depart, the statute penalizes aliens of the above-listed classes who do the following:

1. Willfully fail or refuse to make timely application in good faith for travel or other documents necessary for departure;

2. Connive, conspire, or take any other action with the purpose of preventing or hampering the alien's departure; or

3. Willfully fail or refuse to present himself or herself for removal at the time and place required by the Attorney General.

Before an alien can be convicted of a willful failure to depart, the country willing to receive the alien must be identified. *Heikkinen v. United States* (Sup.Ct.1958). In *Heikkinen,* an alien had been convicted for willful failure to depart. Because the government had not shown that any country would have admitted the alien, the Supreme Court reversed, holding the evidence insufficient to support conviction.

Violation of the statute constitutes a felony, punishable by imprisonment up to ten years. INA § 243(a)(1). The statute provides, however, that it is not illegal for an alien "to take any proper steps for the purpose of securing cancellation of or exemption from such order of removal or for the purpose of securing the alien's release from incarceration or custody." INA § 243(a)(2).

§ 14–2.6 Unlawful Employment of Aliens

The Immigration Reform and Control Act (IRCA) in 1986 was enacted as a response to growing concern that the United States had lost control over the influx of undocumented aliens to the country. IRCA attempted to control immigration by creating sanctions for the employment of unauthorized aliens.

IRCA makes it unlawful for any person or entity to hire, recruit, or refer for a fee for employment in the United States, an alien, knowing that the alien is unauthorized with respect to such employment, or any individual without complying with the employment verification system established under INA § 274A(b). INA § 274A(a)1. It is also unlawful for a person or entity to continue employing an alien, knowing that the alien is or has become unauthorized. INA § 274A(a)(2).

In addition to civil fines, which increase with multiple offenses, IRCA imposes criminal penalties upon persons and entities engaging in a "pattern or practice of violations." These penalties include a fine of up to $3,000 for each unauthorized alien, imprisonment up to six months for the entire pattern or practice, or both. INA § 274A(f)(1). The term "pattern or practice" means "regular, repeated and intentional activities, but does not include isolated, sporadic or accidental acts." *United States v. Mayton* (5th Cir.1964), *International Brotherhood of Teamsters v. United States* (Sup.Ct.1977), and *United States v. International Association of Iron Workers Local No. 1* (7th Cir.1971). These interpretations were incorporated expressly into the legislative history accompanying the Immigration Reform and Control Act of 1986 by House Report No. 99–682(I).

Although IRCA imposes no penalties upon unauthorized aliens merely for working illegally, an individual seeking employment in the United States must attest under penalty of perjury, that s/he is a citizen or national of the U.S.; a permanent resident alien; or an alien authorized to be hired, recruited, or referred for employment. INA § 274A(a)(1)(A). Similarly, the employer must attest under penalty of perjury that it has verified that the individual is not an unauthorized alien by examining documents that establish employment authorization and the identity of the individual.

The employer sanctions do not apply to individuals who were hired, recruited, or referred before November 6, 1986. An employer also may establish an affirmative defense to an allegation of unlawful employment by showing that it has complied in good faith with the requirements of the employment verification system. INA § 274A(a)(3). Although the employer sanctions do not apply to continuing employment of an alien who was hired before November 6, 1986, the felony provisions of INA § 274, which penalize the concealing, harboring, or shielding of undocumented aliens, may still apply. IRCA § 112(a) removed from INA § 274 an earlier clause providing that employment does not constitute harboring of an undocumented alien. The removal from INA § 274 of the so-called "Texas Proviso" was a considerable departure from prior law, which had excepted mere employment from conduct constituting a harboring offense.

§ 14–3   IMMIGRATION CONSEQUENCES OF CRIMINAL ACTIVITY

An alien convicted of a crime generally will suffer the penalties prescribed by statute. A criminal conviction, however, may have a direct effect on the alien's immigration status as well. The effect of the conviction may be felt almost immediately, as when conviction of the crime constitutes a ground for removal, or the impact of the conviction may not occur for several years, as when conviction of the crime precludes the showing of good moral character necessary for naturalization.

§ 14–3.1   Ineligibility for Admission

An alien seeking to enter the United States may be ineligible for admission because of prior criminal activity.

INA § 212 provides several categories of aliens who are ineligible to receive visas and are inadmissible to the United States because of criminal activity. These inadmissibility grounds apply equally to aliens who seek entry to the United States for the first time and to aliens who, after residing in the United States for a period of time, seek re-entry after a temporary departure.

Aliens convicted of a crime involving moral turpitude (other than a purely political offense), aliens who admit having committed such a crime, and aliens who admit committing acts which constitute the essential elements of a crime involving moral turpitude are inadmissible. INA § 212(a)(2)(A). A conviction occurs when a finding of guilt, a guilty or *nolo contendere* plea, or an admission of enough facts to warrant a finding of guilt is accompanied by a judicial order of punishment, penalty, or restraint on liberty. INA § 101(a)(48)(A); *Matter of Ozkok (BIA 1988)*, as limited by IIRIRA § 322(a)(1).

An exception to the normal consequence of inadmissibility is made under certain circumstances for aliens who have committed only one such crime while under the age of eighteen, provided the crime was committed and the alien has been released "from any confinement to a prison or correctional institution imposed for the crime" more than five years before the date of application for a visa and for admission to the United States. INA § 212(a)(2)(A)(ii)(I). An exception also is made for aliens who committed only one crime involving moral turpitude in which "the maximum penalty possible for the crime of which the alien was convicted (or which the alien admits having committed ...) did not exceed imprisonment for one year and, if the alien was convicted of such crime, the alien was not sentenced to a term of imprisonment in excess of 6 months (regardless of the extent to which the sentence was ultimately executed)." INA § 212(a)(2)(A)(ii)(II).

The courts generally agree that crimes of moral turpitude "include elements that necessarily demonstrate the baseness, vileness, and depravity of the perpetrator." *Tutrone v. Shaughnessy* (S.D.N.Y.1958). The following criminal offenses have been held to involve moral turpitude: offenses in which either an intent to defraud (*e.g.*, counterfeiting, forgery fraud) or an intent to steal is an element; offenses (usually felonies) in which great bodily harm is caused or threatened by an intentional or willful act (*e.g.*, homicide, aggravated assault, assault with a deadly weapon, assault with intent to kill) or by recklessness (*e.g.*, vehicular homicide, driving while intoxicated resulting in personal injury to another); offenses in which "malice" is an essential element; and sex offenses in which some "lewd" intent is required.

INA § 212(h) allows the Attorney General to waive the inadmissibility of an alien who has committed a crime involving moral turpitude if the alien is the spouse, parent, or child of a United States citizen or lawfully admitted permanent resident, provided the alien is inadmissible because of activities that occurred more than 15 years before the alien's application for an immigration benefit; the alien's admission would not be contrary to the national welfare, safety, or security; and the alien has been rehabilitated. IIRIRA limited the use of § 212(h) by adding that no waiver can be granted if the alien has been convicted of an "aggravated felony" or not resided continuously in the United states for at least seven years immediately before the beginning of proceedings to remove the alien. INA § 212(h)(2). The INA, with

IIRIRA's amendments and additions, defines aggravated felony to include murder, rape, sexual abuse of a minor, illicit trafficking, money laundering, firearms offenses, and offenses for which a term of imprisonment of at least one year may be imposed. INA § 101(43). A term of imprisonment includes the period of incarceration or confinement ordered by a court regardless of any suspension of the imposition or execution of that imprisonment or sentence in whole or in part. INA § 101(48)(B).

An alien is also inadmissible if s/he has been convicted of two or more offenses (other than purely political offenses) for which the aggregate sentences to confinement actually imposed were five years or more. INA § 212(a)(2)(B). This provision applies regardless of whether the conviction was in a single trial or whether the offenses arose from a single scheme of misconduct and regardless of whether the offenses involved moral turpitude. The Attorney General may issue a waiver of multiple criminal convictions under INA § 212(a)(2)(B) upon finding the same circumstances required for a waiver of a crime involving moral turpitude, *i.e.,* cases in which the alien is the spouse, parent, son, or daughter of a citizen of the United States or lawfully admitted permanent resident, s/he has not been convicted of an "aggravated felony," and s/he has resided continuously in the United States for at least seven years immediately before the beginning of removal proceedings. INA § 212(h).

INA § 212(a)(2)(A)(i)(II) makes inadmissible any alien convicted of a violation of, or a conspiracy to violate, any law or regulation of a state, the United States, or a foreign country relating to a controlled substance (as defined in 21 U.S.C.A. § 802). INA § 212(h) allows the

Attorney General to waive applicability of § 212(a)(2)(A)(i)(II) in so far as it relates to a single offense of simple possession of 30 grams or less of marijuana, provided the alien meets the same criteria for a waiver of crimes involving moral turpitude. Moreover, § 212(a)(2)(C) makes inadmissible "[a]ny alien who the consular or immigration officer knows or has reason to believe is or has been an illicit trafficker in any such controlled substances or is or has been a knowing assister, abettor, conspirator, or colluder with others in the illicit trafficking in any such controlled substance." No waiver is available for this ground of inadmissibility. INA § 212(a)(6)(E) also excludes any alien who at any time, knowingly and for gain, encouraged or assisted any other alien to enter the United States in violation of law. This section eliminates the "for gain" requirement under the previous law. INA § 212(d)(11) provides the Attorney General with the discretionary power to waive this ground of inadmissibility "for humanitarian purposes, to assure family unity, or when it is otherwise in the public interest." Other grounds of inadmissibility related to criminal activity include polygamy (INA § 212(a)(10)(A)), involvement in prostitution (INA § 212(a)(2)(D)), and aliens coming to the United States to engage in any other unlawful commercialized vice, whether or not related to prostitution (INA § 212(a)(2)(D)(iii)), terrorists (INA 212(a)(3)), and international child abductors (INA § 212(a)(10)(C)).

§ 14–3.2 Removal

Removal also may be a direct result of an alien's involvement in criminal activity. INA § 237 lists several grounds for removal related to criminal activity. For a discussion of these grounds, see § 8–2. An alien who has committed an "aggravated felony" is presumptively subject to special expedited removal proceedings. INA § 238. See §§ 8–2.3, 8–3.1. A full pardon by the President or the governor of the state of conviction would have the effect of removing convictions for offenses, not involving controlled substances or firearms, as the grounds for removal. INA § 237(a)(2)(A)(v); see also § 8–2.3. If an alien is convicted of an offense for which there is no pardoning authority under state or federal law, the conviction cannot be used to remove the alien. Under the Technical Amendments Act of 1991, an alien is not only removable for the commission of certain crimes, but for the attempt or conspiracy to commit these crimes as well.

Many jurisdictions have statutes permitting the expungement or sealing of criminal records, which also has the effect of eliminating some convictions as a ground for removal. Expungement of a conviction involving narcotics, however, cannot defeat removability. See Tsimbidy–Rochu v. INS (9th Cir.1969). Even if a conviction is expunged, the conduct that resulted in the conviction, may be a subject of inquiry if the alien applies for United States citizenship. See Petition of de la Cruz (S.D.N.Y. 1983). It may be possible for the alien to escape criminal charges by participating in various programs such as community service work or rehabilitation, thereby avoiding the immigration consequences of some convictions. If an alien pleads guilty to a crime for which s/he may be removed without being aware of the immigration consequences of that plea, it may be possible to vacate the guilty plea or to obtain a writ of error coram nobis. Many states now require defense attorneys to advise non-citizen defendants as to the immigration consequences of their pleas. See, e.g., People v. Soriano (Cal.1987). Some courts have allowed the withdrawal of a guilty plea upon a showing of ineffective assistance of counsel, for failure to research or explain the immigration consequences of the plea. *See, e.g., State v. Lopez* (Minn.App.1986) and *People v. Pozo* (Colo.1987).

§ 14–3.3 Failure to Establish Good Moral Character

Conviction of a crime may prevent an alien from establishing good moral character, which is a statutory prerequisite to a number of immigration benefits. These benefits include naturalization (INA § 316), voluntary departure (INA § 240B), cancellation of removal (INA § 240A), and registry (INA § 249). A petitioner for naturalization or voluntary departure must establish good moral character during the five years prior to application. An alien seeking cancellation of removal must show that s/he has been of good moral character during her/his continuous presence in the United States of at least ten years. INA § 240A(b)(1). If s/he is a battered spouse or child, a showing of good moral character during the three years before application is sufficient. INA § 240A(b)(2). An applicant for registry need only show that s/he is presently of good moral character. INA § 249(c). For a discussion of what constitutes "good moral character," see § 12–2.2b(4).

§ 14–3.4 Denial of Asylum

Another possible consequence of an alien's criminal activity is denial of the alien's application for asylum or termination of the alien's asylum status. An immigration judge or asylum officer must deny a request for asylum if it is determined that the alien has been convicted of an aggravated felony or "[h]aving been convicted by a final judgment of a particularly serious crime in the United

States, constitutes a danger to the community." 8 C.F.R. § 208.13(c)(2)(i). Further, even if the alien has not been convicted of a crime, asylum will be denied if s/he "[c]an reasonably be regarded as a danger to the security of the United States." 8 C.F.R. § 208.13(c)(2)(iii). Withholding of removal also must be denied for such reasons. INA § 241(b)(3)(B).

Similarly, once granted asylum, an alien's asylum status will be terminated if the alien poses a danger to the United States community because of conviction of a serious crime, as described in 8 C.F.R. § 208.16(c)(2). 8 C.F.R. § 208.24(b)(3). Asylum status also will be terminated if it appears that the alien was not, in fact, eligible for asylum at the time of application for the reasons specified in the previous paragraph. 8 C.F.R. 208.24. Once an alien's asylum status is terminated, the alien, unless eligible for other immigration benefits, will be subject to removal proceedings.

CHAPTER 15

ETHICAL DIMENSIONS OF IMMIGRATION PRACTICE

Immigration lawyers are confronted by ethical issues probably even more often than other practitioners. The alien clients of the immigration lawyer are often suspicious about the fairness of United States laws and administrative practices and are usually unfamiliar with them. Some aliens may try to suggest or pursue courses of conduct from their culture that might be inappropriate or, perhaps, unethical for a lawyer in the United States. Hence, the student of immigration law should be aware of the ethical dimensions of an immigration practice.

This chapter analyzes three typical ethical problems encountered by the immigration lawyer from the perspective of both the Model Rules of Professional Conduct and the Model Code of Professional Responsibility. The three problems deal with common situations faced by immigration lawyers:

(1) The alien is in violation of her/his immigration status, or has fraudulently married to gain permanent resident status. Must the lawyer report her/his client to the Immigration and Naturalization Service (INS)?

(2) An alien consults the lawyer about admission to the United States. The client is qualified for a nonimmigrant visa, but in discussing the alien's ultimate objectives, the lawyer learns that the client may want eventu-

ally to become an immigrant and a United States citizen. If the alien has a present intent to immigrate to the United States, s/he would be ineligible for the nonimmigrant visa. What should the lawyer tell the client?

(3) An immigration lawyer is paid by a company to obtain a visa for an employee or potential employee. In the course of the representation the lawyer learns facts such as the employee's career plans which may be adverse to the new employer's interest. What should the lawyer do? Can s/he tell the employer? Whom does the lawyer actually represent?

While each problem will be examined in some detail, this chapter does not attempt to provide definitive answers but merely raises the ethical issues. Several standards address these issues.

The Model Rules of Professional Conduct drafted by the American Bar Association (ABA) have now been adopted by more than two-thirds of the jurisdictions in the U.S., including Washington, D.C.,—either completely or with relatively minor changes. While the Model Rules constitute the predominant approach to legal ethics, there are other relevant standards. Immigration lawyers are subject to the ethical rules of practice before the Immigration and Naturalization Service. Also, there are still some states (*e.g.*, New York and Virginia) that still apply the Model Code of Professional Responsibility, which was the ABA-drafted predecessor of the Model Rules. Both the Model Rules and the Model Code have influenced the drafting of the American Law Institute's Restatement of the Law Governing Lawyers.

This chapter discusses three sources of ethical constraint on the immigration lawyer. The first source is the Model Rules adopted by the ABA in 1983. The Model

Rules include aspirational goals, rules of permissible conduct, and mandatory rules. In the Model Rules, the word "should" expresses an aspirational goal and the word "may" expresses other permissible conduct that lawyers are not necessarily required to follow. Almost all of the rules, however, mandate a minimum level of conduct for the lawyer. Should the attorney's conduct fall below this minimum level s/he may be subject to sanction. The Model Rules use the words "shall" and "shall not" to identify rules for which lawyers may be disciplined.

The second source derives from the regulations governing the conduct of lawyers who appear before the Immigration and Naturalization Service. In 1996, the Code of Federal Regulations listed fifteen nonexclusive reasons for suspending or disbarring the immigration lawyer, some of which overlap the Model Rules and some of which are unique to immigration practice. 8 C.F.R. § 292.3.

The third source is the Model Code adopted by the ABA in 1969. The Model Code identifies ethical considerations that the lawyer strives to achieve. Should the lawyer fail to abide by ethical considerations, however, there are theoretically no sanctions in most states. The Model Code also contains disciplinary rules that mandate a minimum level of conduct for the lawyer. Should the attorney's conduct fall below this minimum level s/he may be subject to disbarment, suspension, or other sanction.

§ 15–1 Must the Lawyer Report His/Her Client to the Immigration Service?

A situation which frequently confronts the immigration lawyer occurs when the attorney becomes aware—through discussions with the client, independent investigation, or other outside sources—that the client is not observing her/his visa conditions. For example, a student-client with an F–1 visa accepts employment outside the educational institution without the requisite permission. Under these circumstances, what is the lawyer's obligation to (a) report the client's violation of immigration status to the INS and/or (b) advise the client as to the possible consequences of accepting employment?

Similarly, an immigration attorney is frequently confronted with an alien who seeks permanent resident status after marrying a U.S. citizen. Preliminary results of an INS pilot study suggest fraud in as many as 30% of the spouse petitions that were intensively reviewed. What if the attorney becomes aware that her/his client is involved in a sham marriage solely to attain permanent resident status? Does the attorney have an obligation to report her/his client's fraudulent marriage to the INS? Would disclosure violate lawyer-client confidentiality requirements?

§ 15–1.1 Reporting the Client's Activities

Under the provisions of both the Model Rules and the Model Code, the lawyer appears to face competing mandates concerning whether to report the client. On the one hand, the Model Rules require the attorney not to reveal a confidence except in a limited number of circumstances. Model Rules of Professional Conduct Rule 1.6 (1983). The Model Code says that the lawyer has a duty to preserve the client's confidences and secrets. DR 4–101(B) of the Model Code provides that the lawyer shall not reveal confidences and secrets obtained in the course of representation. In addition, Rule 1.6 prohibits any use of the confidence that disadvantages the client. In the F–1 student example, the information about the student's employment is a client confidence or secret because it was obtained in the course of representing the client. Similarly, information regarding a client's fraudulent marriage received in the course of representing that client is also a client confidence or secret. In the former case, if the attorney informed the INS of the client's employment, the client could be deprived of the student visa and possibly removed. Likewise, if the attorney informed the INS of her/his client's fraudulent marriage, that client could be denied resident status, prosecuted, fined, and/or removed. Hence, it appears the lawyer cannot disclose the information to the INS without violating either the Model Code or the Model Rules.

The Model Rules, the Model Code, and the applicable C.F.R. provision, however, prohibit the lawyer from making false statements to the INS. According to the Model Rules, the lawyer shall not "knowingly ... make a false statement of material fact or law to a third person." Model Rules of Professional Conduct Rule 4.1(a)(1983). Likewise, according to DR 7–102(A) of the Model Code, the lawyer "shall not ... (3) conceal or knowingly fail to disclose that which he is required by law to reveal." The Code of Federal Regulations contains similar language. 8 C.F.R. § 292.3(a)(3). At times, the lawyer is required by law to reveal information about her/his client. For example, INS Form I–539, Application to Extend/Change Nonimmigrant Status, requires the lawyer to respond to questions concerning whether the client has worked. If the lawyer knowingly makes a false statement on these forms, s/he is subject to substantial penalties. *See, e.g., United States v. Lew* (9th Cir.1989) (immigration attorney convicted of making false statements to Department of Labor).

Attorneys who knowingly make false statements can also be criminally liable for their unethical conduct. In *United States v. Maniego*, the court affirmed the conviction of a lawyer whom a jury found to have knowingly prepared immigration documents that were based on fraudulent marriages in violation of 18 U.S.C.A. §§ 371 and 1546. *United States v. Maniego* (2d Cir.1983). Similarly in *United States v. Zalman*, the court affirmed the conviction of a lawyer who failed to disclose a fraudulent marriage in violation of 18 U.S.C.A. § 1001. *United States v. Zalman* (6th Cir.1989).

In such circumstances, a lawyer faces either violating the mandate regarding client confidences or violating the mandate regarding false statements. This immigration lawyer's dilemma, however, is not without resolution. The lawyer is charged with preserving client confidences only within the bounds of the law. Hence, while a lawyer cannot volunteer information about the client's activities to the INS, s/he must advise the client to answer truthfully. The lawyer does not impermissibly violate a client confidence when s/he truthfully answers a direct question because to make a false statement would violate the law.

§ 15–1.2 Advising the Client

Under the circumstances of this problem both the Model Rules and the Model Code apparently require the lawyer to discuss the probable consequences of the client's actions with the client. Rule 2.1 of the Model Rules requires the lawyer to render candid advice in her/his role as advisor to the client. In a comment to the rules, the Committee notes:

> (W)hen a lawyer knows that a client proposes a course of action that is likely to result in substantial adverse legal consequences to the client, duty to the client ... may require that the lawyer act [give advice]....

The ethical considerations of the Model Code contain essentially the same substance. EC 7–8 of the Model Code provides:

> A lawyer should exert his best efforts to insure that decisions of his client are made only after the client has been informed of relevant considerations. A lawyer ought to initiate this decision-making process if the client does not do so.

In addition, EC 7–5 of the Model Code notes that "[a] lawyer as advisor furthers the interest of his client by giving his professional opinion" about the consequences of her/his client's decision. In the case of the F–1 student, the client may suffer such adverse consequences as loss of visa and removal. If the client later qualifies for an immigrant visa, the client, at minimum, may be required to pursue immigrant status outside the United States.

The client may not have realized the adverse consequences of her/his decision to accept employment at the time it was made. Therefore, the lawyer's obligation to her/his client is to inform the client of the negative consequences of violating the visa conditions. The strength of the obligation may depend on whether the lawyer learns of the student's employment before or after the work commences. If the lawyer learns of the student's intention before the employment begins, the duty to act is stronger because the lawyer can prevent the adverse consequences by rendering the correct legal advice. If the lawyer learns afterwards, the duty to act is not as great because the legal consequences (loss of visa, removal, and ineligibility to adjust status in the United States) would have already become applicable. Nonetheless, a lawyer might advise the client against continued employment because the INS might take more severe enforcement action against a client who has been illegally employed for a longer period.

§ 15–2 Should the Lawyer Tell the Client About a Fixed Intent to Immigrate?

Different sorts of ethical problems are raised in advising the client regarding her/his fixed intent to immigrate to the United States. The problem arises when a client otherwise eligible for a nonimmigrant visa informs the lawyer that s/he wants to immigrate to the United States. The client would be ineligible for most nonimmigrant visas, however, if s/he has a present intent to immigrate. What should the lawyer tell the client to do? If the lawyer tells the client not to form a present intent to immigrate, would the lawyer be assisting the client in perpetrating a fraud?

Both the Model Rules and the Model Code have sections dealing with client fraud and the lawyer's duty, none of which provide any clear solutions to this problem. Rule 1.2(d) of the Model Rules refers most directly to this situation: "a lawyer shall not counsel a client to engage, or assist a client, in conduct that the lawyer knows is criminal or fraudulent.... " The Model Code contain similar prohibitions. According to DR 7–102(A) of the Model Code:

(A) ... a lawyer shall not:

...

(6) Participate in the Creation or Preservation of Evidence When He Knows or It Is Obvious That the Evidence Is False.

(7) Counsel or Assist His Client in Conduct That the Lawyer Knows to Be Illegal or Fraudulent.

In addition, EC 7–6 of the Model Code discusses the lawyer's position in assisting the client in developing state of mind evidence. It provides:

[The lawyer] may properly assist his client in the development and preservation of evidence of existing motive, intent, or desire; obviously, he may not do anything furthering the creation or preservation of false evidence.

See also the similar language in 8 C.F.R. § 292.3(a)(3). Those provisions, however, do not resolve whether the client commits a fraud in declaring that s/he has no present intent to immigrate. It is not clear that the lawyer would assist the client in committing a fraud or in preserving false evidence by discussing the effect of the client's intent on her/his immigration status. The situation is made more complex because only the client knows her/his own intent. An attorney, however, can advise the client as to the consequences of pursuing a specific course of conduct, which is separate from the question of the client's intent.

Other sections of the Model Rules and the Model Code imply that the lawyer has an obligation to discuss the probable consequences of alternate courses of action with the client. Rule 1.2 of the Model Rules prohibits the lawyer from assisting the client in fraudulent conduct, but "a lawyer may discuss the legal consequences of any proposed course of conduct with a client and may counsel or assist a client to make a good faith effort to determine the validity, scope, meaning or application of the law." Model Rule 1.2(d). EC 7–8 of the Model Code provides that "[a] lawyer should advise his client of the possible effect of each legal alternative." In this situation, the lawyer is not urging the client to adopt one course of action over another. Rather, s/he is merely discussing the client's two legal alternatives—to form a present intent to become an immigrant or a nonimmigrant—and the legal effects of each. The lawyer explains the consequences and the client makes the decision about her/his present intent. Such advice does not appear to be the kind of fraud contemplated by the drafters of the Model Code and the Model Rules.

In addition, one might draw inferences from the drafting history of the Model Rules. In an earlier discussion draft of the Model Rules, Rule 2.3(a)(2) mandated that a lawyer could not give advice that s/he "could reasonably foresee would ... aid the client in contriving false testimony." No counterpart to this draft Rule 2.3 appears in the Model Rules adopted in 1983. From this omission one could infer (1) that the drafting committee did not consider this advice an ethical violation, (2) that in a criminal law context this draft provision would be inappropriate, or (3) possibly that Rule 1.2 already covered this situation. In any case, even if draft Rule 2.3(a)(2) had appeared in the final version, the lawyer's advice would be unethical only in the unlikely event that it aided the client in contriving false testimony. Hence, the immigration lawyer probably can explain the consequences of the client's present intent to immigrate or her/his eligibility for a nonimmigrant visa without ethical violation, so long as the lawyer does not suggest which course of action the client should actually adopt.

The 1990 Act addressed this dilemma to an extent by recognizing the "dual intent" of many aliens seeking nonimmigrant visa status under the H and L categories. *See* §§ 6–8, 6–12, *supra*. Under the 1990 Act, a temporary worker with an H visa or a transferee with an L visa is not precluded from eventually seeking an adjustment of her/his status to that of a permanent resident. The problem still exists, however, with regard to several other nonimmigrant statuses, such as B, F, and J.

§ 15–3   Whom Does the Lawyer Represent?

Another problem concerns the lawyer who is retained by an employer to secure the proper work authorization for a present or prospective alien employee. For example, an engineering firm hires the lawyer to obtain an L–1 visa for an alien-engineer. In discussing the alien's ultimate career goals, the lawyer learns that the alien plans eventually to open her/his own engineering firm. When the alien's interest in the visa is adverse to the employer's interest, can the lawyer disclose the alien's intent to the employer?

Client confidences are protected under both the Model Rules and the Model Code. Rule 1.6 of the Model Rules provides that the "lawyer shall not reveal information relating to representation of a client" except in a limited number of circumstances such as to prevent the commission of a very serious crime. DR 4–101(B) of the Model Code provides:

[A] lawyer shall not knowingly:

(1) Reveal a Confidence or Secret of His Client.

(2) Use a Confidence or Secret of His Client to the Disadvantage of the Client.

The solution to this problem turns on whether the client is the employer company, the alien prospective employee, or, in the case of joint representation, both. In all situations, the governing principle is early disclosure on the part of the lawyer to avoid even potential conflict.

If the alien is regarded as unrepresented, the lawyer may not offer to the alien advice that is adverse to the employer-client's interests. If the alien/employee is the client, however, the attorney may not use information acquired from the alien to the alien's disadvantage by revealing that information to the employer. Furthermore, if the attorney has a continuing relationship with the employer, violating the alien's confidence may be equivalent to using information acquired from the client for the lawyer's own purposes. Both uses of client information are prohibited under the Model Rules in Rule 1.7:

A lawyer shall not represent a client if the representation of that client may be materially limited by the lawyer's responsibilities to another client or to a third person, or by the lawyer's own interests, ...

The Model Code adopts a similar position under EC 4–5:

A lawyer should not use information acquired in the course of the representation of a client to the disadvantage of the client and a lawyer should not use, except with the consent of his client after full disclosure, such information for his own purposes.

The Model Rules and the Model Code recognize the practical difficulties inherent when the client's interest is adverse to that of the fee-paying employer. The lawyer naturally feels a certain amount of loyalty to the company that retains her/him. Should the lawyer's loyalty to the company interfere with the effective representation of the client, both the Model Rules and the Model Code provide for the lawyer's withdrawal from the case. *See* Model Rules of Professional Conduct, Rule 1.16; Model Code of Professional Responsibility, EC 5–21. The lawyer must, however, recognize that in doing so, s/he may jeopardize the client confidence anyway, since the employer may become suspicious of the client when the lawyer seeks to withdraw.

Where the lawyer has a continuing professional relationship with the employer, the lawyer's responsibility to the employer cannot be readily dismissed. The employer, not the alien, has selected the lawyer and defined the scope of her/his duties, and probably must also be considered a client. If both the employer and the alien are clients, EC 4–5 of the Model Code requires that care be exercised by the lawyer "to prevent the disclosure of the confidences and secrets of one client to another, and no employment should be accepted that might require such disclosure."

The Model Rules provide more guidance than the Model Code in this dilemma. Rule 1.7 allows a lawyer to represent clients with conflicting interests if the lawyer reasonably believes that the representation of each client will not adversely affect the relationship with the other and that each client consents to the arrangement after consultation. According to the Comment to Rule 1.7, the lawyer should consider "the likelihood that a conflict will eventuate and, if it does, whether it will materially interfere with the lawyer's independent professional judgment in considering alternatives or foreclose courses of action that reasonably should be pursued on behalf of the client." The lawyer also should consider whether each client is willing to accommodate the other interest involved.

The alien and the employer may thus be co-clients. Because of their common interest in allowing the alien to work for the employer, each may be willing to accommodate the other's interests. With full and early disclosure of the potential for conflict and the consent of the parties to the lawyer's role in representing them both, the lawyer can represent the alien and the employer, sharing relevant information between the two. It may, however, be impossible to disclose the information necessary to obtain consent. If the alien refuses to disclose her/his ultimate career goals to the employer, the employer will be unable to make an informed decision as to whether it should consent to the arrangement. In this situation, the lawyer cannot properly ask the employer to consent. Comment, Rule 1.7.

Another possible solution under the Model Rules would be for the lawyer to regard the alien as s/he would regard an employee of the employer organization. The ethical responsibilities of a lawyer retained by an organization are outlined in Rule 1.13. Under this approach, the client is the organization. While the employees are not clients, communications between an employee and the organization's lawyer are protected by Rule 1.6. Comment, Rule 1.13. Under Rule 1.13, however, the lawyer has discretion to reveal confidential information to the employer organization when the lawyer knows that an employee intends to violate a legal obligation to the organization (or the employee's actions are in violation of law and might reasonably be imputed to the organization, resulting in substantial injury). Hence, under this interpretation, the alien's plans eventually to open a competing firm would be protected from disclosure to the employer company under Rule 1.6 unless the alien's plans are in violation of the alien's legal obligation to the company. Rule 1.13, however, requires that, in dealing with an employee of the organization, the lawyer explain the identity of the client when it is apparent that the organization's interests are adverse to those of the employee. When a conflict of interest arises, care must be taken to assure that the employee understands the lawyer cannot represent her/him and that s/he may wish to obtain independent representation. Comment, Rule 1.13.

Upjohn Co. v. United States (Sup.Ct.1981) is instructive as to the confidentiality of employee communications. Counsel for Upjohn learned of questionable payments to foreign officials and initiated an internal investigation, sending questionnaires to all foreign managers and pursuing the matter further with interviews. Based on the results of this investigation, the company made a voluntary disclosure to the Internal Revenue Service (IRS). The IRS then began its own investigation and sought to discover the questionnaires and interview notes. The lower court rejected Upjohn's work product defense because the communications to officers and agents of the company were not to the client under the "control group test," which labels as clients only those who have authority to make decisions based on the lawyer's advice. The Supreme Court, however, regarded these employees as clients and held that the attorney-client privilege applied. The Court noted that the employees understood they were being questioned so that the corporation could obtain legal advice.

Unlike the Model Rules, the Supreme Court regards the employees as clients. The applicability of *Upjohn* is also limited by the fact that the employer and employees did not have clearly adverse interests. The case remains instructive, however, because the Court extended to employees the protection of communications. This extension of the evidentiary privilege of confidentiality (including the work product doctrine) is significant because the ethical privilege of confidentiality is even broader in scope. The Comment to Rule 1.6 states:

> The principle of confidentiality is given effect in two related bodies of law, the attorney-client privilege (which includes the work product doctrine) in the law of evidence and the rule of confidentiality established in professional ethics.

The evidentiary privilege generally applies in judicial proceedings, while the ethical privilege applies "in situations other than those where evidence is sought from the lawyer through compulsion of law." Comment, Rule 1.6. EC 4–4 of the Model Code states:

> The attorney-client privilege is more limited than the ethical obligation of a lawyer to guard the confidences and secrets of his client. The ethical precept, unlike the evidentiary privilege, exists without regard to the nature or source of information or the fact that others share the knowledge.

Under *Upjohn,* employee communications with an attorney retained by the employer may be privileged under the work product doctrine and not subject to discovery by people outside the corporation. Under Model Rule 1.13, employee communications with the employer's counsel may be privileged from disclosure to the employer under the ethical obligation of a lawyer to guard the confidences of the employee. Under the Model Rules, however, the employee may not be regarded as a client and some information will not be protected, as described above.

Rule 1.13 has no direct counterpart in the Model Code. EC 5–18 of the Model Code states:

A lawyer employed or retained by a corporation or similar entity owes his allegiance to the entity and not to a stockholder, director, officer, employee, representative, or other person connected with the entity. In advising the entity, a lawyer should keep paramount its interests and his professional judgment should not be influenced by the personal desires of any person or organization. Occasionally, a lawyer for an entity is requested by a stockholder, director, officer, employee, representative, or other person connected with the entity to represent him in an individual capacity; in such a case the lawyer may serve the individual only if the lawyer is convinced that differing interests are not present.

DR 5–107(B) further provides that if a lawyer is hired by one person to render legal services for another, the lawyer must not permit the employer to direct or regulate her/his professional judgment in rendering such legal services for the other person.

As can be seen from the above discussion, there are several possible approaches to identifying the client and guarding the client's confidences. No simple consensus appears to be available for this problem.

CHAPTER 16

CONCLUSION

In reading through this volume, the student may get the impression that immigration law is comprised of a very stable set of administrative requirements for obtaining permission to enter and remain in this country. While that impression may be generally correct, the student should be aware that the immigration laws described in this Nutshell have changed significantly in the fourteen years since the publication of the first edition. Beyond landmark legislation like IRCA (1986), the 1990 Act, AEDPA (1996), and IIRIRA (1996), the INS and the judiciary continually update and clarify the regulations that form the foundation for practicing immigration law. Furthermore, almost everyone involved even tangentially in the immigration process is aware that the Immigration Service is overworked, understaffed, and nearly overwhelmed by its statutory duties. Congress and the Administration have undertaken reforms to modernize the procedures of the INS, to resolve at least partially the very difficult problems created by the thousands—if not millions—of aliens who wish to live in the United States, and to decide which aliens should be encouraged to immigrate. Population analysts have noted that the U.S. may suffer a severe shortage of workers in coming decades and that immigration will be an important way of supplying workers for the U.S. economy. During periods of high unemployment and economic distress, however, immigration becomes particularly unpopular and the long-term needs of the U.S. economy may be ignored.

Hence, students should be aware that the target at which they are shooting is, indeed, moving and will require continued attention.

It seems appropriate to conclude this Nutshell by making a general observation about the nature of immigration law practice. Faced with all the detailed requirements for visas and other immigration remedies about which this volume says so much, some advocates, including attorneys, and their clients devote most of their attention to gathering the minimum information necessary to fulfill the various requirements. Unfortunately, some lawyers and almost all unrepresented aliens do not view the immigration process as an appropriate place for intelligent advocacy. This tendency has been addressed by groups such as the American Immigration Lawyers Association (AILA) which, through seminars and publications, has sought to raise the level of expertise in the practice of immigration law.

Ultimately, it is the duty of immigration lawyers to muster the relevant facts in such a way as to convince Immigration Service officers that the lawyers' clients should receive the appropriate immigration status. One should never forget when submitting an application that one has the power to establish the record on which the client's case will be won or lost. In addition, lawyers should remember that immigration officers are administrative decision-makers who ought to receive the same sort of attention and polite, effective advocacy as judges. Certainly, immigration laws and the multitude of immigration forms about which the student has read are not invitations to forget all the advocacy skills used in other contexts.

CHAPTER 17

BIBLIOGRAPHY

This chapter suggests some principal references for research in immigration law. Items which are starred (*) might be found in the core immigration law library of an immigration practitioner or serious student.

§ 17-1 LAWS AND REGULATIONS

8 U.S.C.—Aliens and Nationality (Codification of the Immigration and Nationality Act, Pub. L. 414, ch. 477, 66 Stat. 163, June 27, 1952, and its subsequent amendments. This is the basic source of immigration law).*

22 U.S.C.—Foreign Affairs (Laws regulating the activities of U.S. consulates).*

8 C.F.R.—(Regulations governing immigration procedures).*

20 C.F.R.—(Labor Department regulations, including alien labor certification).*

22 C.F.R.—(Foreign relations regulations giving procedures and guidelines to U.S. consulates for issuing visas and passports).*

Antiterrorism and Effective Death Penalty Act of 1996, Pub. L. 104–132, 110 Stat. 1214, April 24, 1996.*

Bender's Immigration Regulations Service (New York, NY: Matthew Bender, 1994–) (2 vols. looseleaf updated bimonthly).

506

Bender's Immigration and Nationality Act Pamphlet (New York, NY: Matthew Bender, 1987–) (Immigration and Nationality Act, issued annually).

Extradition Laws and Treaties, United States (Igor I. Kavass & Adolf Sprudzs, comps., Buffalo, NY: W.S. Hein, 1980–) (4 vols. looseleaf).

Federal Immigration Laws and Regulations (St. Paul, MN: West Pub. Co., 1993–) (1 vol. containing the basic statutes and regulations, issued annually).*

Federal Register (daily newspaper-style publication that updates the C.F.R. and publishes proposed rules, regulations, and notices from federal administrative agencies).

Illegal Immigration Reform and Immigration Responsibility Act of 1996, Pub. L. 104–208, Div. C, 110 Stat. 3009, September 30, 1996.*

Immigration Act of 1990, Pub. L. 101–649, 104 Stat. 4978, November 29, 1990.

Immigration Act of 1990 (New York, NY: Matthew Bender, 1991) (special supplement to *Immigration Law and Procedures* which contains the text of the 1990 Act with explanation and analysis by Charles Gordon and Stanley Mailman).

The Immigration Act of 1990 Handbook: Complete Practice Guide to the 1990 Act (New York, NY: Clark, Boardman, Callaghan, 1990–annual).

The Immigration Marriage Fraud Amendments of 1986, Pub. L. 99–639, 100 Stat. 3537, November 10, 1986.

Immigration and Nationality Laws of the United States: Selected Statutes, Regulations, and Forms: As Amend-

ed to May 15, 1997 (T. Alexander Aleinikoff et al., St. Paul, MN: West Group, 1997).*

Immigration Law Service (Rochester, NY: Lawyers Cooperative Pub. Co., 1985–) (multivolume looseleaf service with statutes, regulations, and instructions).

Immigration Reform and Control Act of 1986, Pub. L. 99–603, 100 Stat. 3359, November 6, 1986.

Personal Responsibility and Work Opportunity Reconciliation Act, Pub. L. 104–193, 110 Stat. 2105, August 22, 1996.

United States Code Congressional and Administrative News (one of the first places to locate the text of new public laws and legislative history of public laws) (St. Paul, MN: West Pub. Co., 1953–).

United States Department of State, *Foreign Affairs Manual* (vol. 9 contains State Department interpretations and regulations on immigration and citizenship) (reproduced in *Immigration Law Service, supra,* and *Immigration Law and Procedure, infra*).

United States Immigration and Naturalization Service, *Code, Operations, Instructions, Regulations, and Interpretations* (Washington, DC: The INS, 1988–)(Internal policy guide covering the day-to-day operations of the INS).*

§ 17–2 CASES AND DECISIONS

BIA Index Decisions Reporter (Washington, DC: American Immigration Lawyers Assoc., 1986–) (4 issues/year; annual from 1986–89).

Federal Immigration Law Reporter (Washington, DC: Washington Service Bureau, 1983–) (contains selected court cases and administrative agency decisions).

Hein's Interim Decision Service (Buffalo, NY: W.S. Hein & Co., 1984–) (begins with #2951, Dec. 12, 1983).

Immigration Labor Certification Reporter (New York, NY: Matthew Bender & Co., 1981–1985) (contains selected court cases and administrative agency decisions).

Immigration Law and Procedure Reporter (New York, NY: Matthew Bender & Co., 1985–) (contains selected court cases and administrative agency decisions).

United States Board of Immigration Appeals, *Administrative Decisions Under Immigration and Nationality Laws* (20 vols., Washington, DC: U.S. Government Printing Office, 1940–).*

United States Board of Immigration Appeals, *Interim Decisions* (Washington, DC: U.S. Government Printing Office, irregular).

United States Department of Labor, Office of Administrative Law Judges, *Decisions of the Office of Administrative Law Judges and Office of Administrative Appeals* (Washington, DC: U.S. Government Printing Office, 1987–1993) (contains decisions concerning labor certification; this set was discontinued in 1993).

§ 17–3 HISTORY

Edward P. Hutchinson, *Legislative History of American Immigration Policy, 1798–1965* (Philadelphia, PA: University of Pennsylvania Press, 1981).

Nancy C. Montwieler, *The Immigration Reform Law of 1986: Analysis, Text, Legislative History* (Washington, DC: Bureau of National Affairs, 1987).

Edward E. Proper, *Colonial Immigration Laws* (New York, NY: AMS Press, Inc., 1967).

Selected Legislative History of the Immigration Act of 1990 (Washington, DC: American Immigration Lawyers Assoc., 1991) (including text of the 1990 Act).

Selected Legislative History of the Immigration Reform and Control Act of 1986 (Washington, DC: American Immigration Lawyers Assoc., 1987).

Oscar Trelles & James Bailey, *Immigration and Nationality Acts: Legislative Histories and Related Documents* (multivolume set with index; Buffalo, NY: W.S. Hein Co., 1979).

Voices from Ellis Island: An Oral History of American Immigration (Frederick, MD: University Publications of America, 1989).

Peter H. Wang, *Legislating Normalcy: The Immigration Act of 1924* (San Francisco, CA: R & E Research Associates, 1975).

§ 17–4 BOOKS, TREATISES, AND DIGESTS

1996–97 Immigration & Nationality Law Handbook (R. Patrick Murphy ed., Washington, D.C.: American Immigration Lawyers Assoc., 1996) (vol. 1 Immigration Basics; vol. 2 Advanced Practice).

AILA's Family Immigration Law Handbook (Lenni B. Bensen ed., Washington, DC: American Immigration Lawyers Assoc., 1994).

The AILA U.S. Consular Posts Handbook (Seymour Rosenberg ed., 7th ed., Washington, DC: American Immigration Lawyers Assoc., 1995).

Thomas Alexander Aleinikoff et al., *Immigration Process and Policy* (3d ed., St. Paul, MN: West Pub. Co., 1995; 1997 Supplement).

American Immigration Lawyers Assoc., *1996 AILA Annual Conference on Immigration Law* (Simi Valley, CA: Convention Seminar Cassettes, 1996) (sound cassettes).

American Immigration Lawyers Assoc., *1996 AILA Business Immigration Conference* (Simi Valley, CA: Convention Seminar Cassettes, 1996) (7 sound cassettes).

Deborah E. Anker, *The Law of Asylum in the United States* (3d ed., Washington, DC: American Immigration Lawyers Assoc., 1994–).

Annual Immigration and Naturalization Institute (New York, NY: Practising Law Institute, 1968–, annual).

Basic Immigration Law (New York, NY: Practising Law Institute, 1989–, annual).

Deskbook of the Board of Alien Labor Certification Appeals (James Guill & Todd R. Smyth, comps., 2d ed., Washington, DC: American Immigration Lawyers Assoc., 1992–) (1 vol. looseleaf).

Basic Guide to Naturalization and Citizenship (Washington, DC: U.S. Dept. of Justice, Immigration and Naturalization Service, Outreach Program, 1990).

Basic Law Manual: U.S. Law and INS Refugee/Asylum Adjudications (prepared by Asylum Division and Office of the General Counsel, Immigration and Naturalization Service, rev. and updated, Washington, DC: American Immigration Lawyers Assoc., 1995, updated irregularly).

M. Cherif Bassiouni, *International Extradition: United States Law & Practice* (3d ed., Dobbs Ferry, NY: Oceana, 1996).

Richard A. Boswell & Gilbert Paul Carrasco, *Immigration and Nationality Law: Cases and Materials* (3d ed., Durham, NC: Carolina Academic Press, 1997).

John L. Cable, *Decisive Decisions on United States Citizenship* (Charlottesville, VA: Michie Co., 1967).

David Carliner, *The Rights of Aliens and Refugees: the Basic ACLU Guide to Alien and Refugee Rights* (2d ed., Carbondale, IL: Southern Illinois University Press, 1990).

Robert C. Divine, *Immigration Practice* (Charlottesville, VA: Michie Co., 1997).

E Visa Form Book: Treaty Trader and Investor (E) Visa Questionnaires and Supplemental Information Forms Required by U.S. Consular Posts Abroad (Richard S. Goldstein ed., 2d ed., Washington, DC: American Immigration Lawyers Assoc., 1991).

Diana Elles, *International Provisions Protecting The Human Rights of Non–Citizens,* U.N. Doc. E/CN.4/Sub.2/392/Rev.1 (1980).

Federal Procedural Forms, Lawyers Edition (Rochester, NY: Lawyers Co-operative Pub. Co., 1975–) (contains sample immigration law forms and includes references to statutes, court rules, administrative regulations, cases, law review articles, legal encyclopedia sections, and ALR annotations related to the subject matter of the forms).

Austin T. Fragomen and Steven C. Bell, *H–1B Handbook* (Deerfield, IL: Clark Boardman Callaghan, 1995–).

Austin T. Fragomen and Steven C. Bell, *Immigration Fundamentals: A Guide to Law and Practice* (4th ed., New York, NY: Practicing Law Institute, 1996–).

Austin T. Fragomen et al., *Immigration Procedures Handbook: A How to Guide for Legal and Business Professionals* (New York, NY: Clark Boardman Callaghan, 1985–) (issued annually; 1997 is the most recent edition).

Austin T. Fragomen and Steven C. Bell, *1996 Immigration Legislation Handbook: Covering the Illegal Immigrant, Welfare and Antiterrorism Laws* (Deerfield, IL: Clark Boardman Callaghan, 1997–).

Hope M. Frye, & H. Ronald Klasko, *Employers' Immigration Compliance Guide* (New York, NY: Matthew Bender & Co., 1987–).

Guy S. Goodwin–Gill, *The Refugee in International Law* (2d ed., New York, NY: Oxford Univ. Press, 1996).

Charles Gordon & Stanley Mailman, *Immigration Law and Procedure* (2d rev. ed., New York, NY: Matthew Bender, 1988–) (formerly C. Gordon & S. Rosenfield) (multivolume looseleaf with case references, statutes, regulations, instructions, etc.).*

H–1B Toolbox: Samples for Representing Professional and Specialty Workers (Carlina Tapia–Ruano and Amy R. Novick eds., Washington, DC: American Immigration Lawyers Assoc., 1995).

Hurst Hannum, *The Right to Leave and Return in International Law and Practice* (Dordrecht, Neth.: Martinus Nijhoff Publishers, 1987).

Bill Ong Hing, *Handling Immigration Cases* (2d ed., New York, NY: Wiley Law Pubs., 1995 with 1997 pocket parts) (2 vols.).

Immigrant Investors: Creating Employment for U.S. Communities (Washington, DC: American Immigration Lawyers Assoc., 1991).

INS Forms for Applications and Petitions (Scott Borene et al. eds., 3d ed., Washington, DC: American Immigration Lawyers Assoc., 1995).

Introducing the 1996 Immigration Reform Act (R. Patrick Murphy ed., Washington, DC: American Immigration Lawyers Assoc., 1996).

David Jackson, *Immigration: Law and Practice* (London, U.K.: Sweet & Maxwell, Ltd., 1996).

Ira J. Kurzban, *Kurzban's Immigration Law Sourcebook: A Comprehensive Outline and Reference Tool* (5th ed., Washington, DC: American Immigration Law Foundation, 1995).

Stephen H. Legomsky, *Immigration Law and Refugee Law and Policy: A Coursebook* (2d ed., Westbury, NY: Foundation Press, Inc., 1997).

Richard Lillich, *The Human Rights of Aliens in Contemporary International Law* (Manchester, U.K.: Manchester University Press, 1984).

Karen Musalo, Jennifer Moore & Richard A. Boswell, *Refugee Law and Policy: Cases and Materials* (Durham, NC: Carolina Academic Press, 1997).

National Lawyers Guild, *Immigration Law and Defense* (3d ed., New York, NY: Clark Boardman Callaghan, 1988–) (2 vols. looseleaf).

Patel's Citations of Administrative Decisions Under Immigration and Nationality Laws (annual, New York, NY: Legal Research Bureau, 1988–).

Pravinchandra J. Patel, *Patel's Citations of Administrative Decisions Under Immigration and Nationality Laws* (New York, NY: Legal Research Bureau, 1982–).

Pravinchandra J. Patel, *Patel's Immigration Law Digest: Decisions from 1940* (Rochester, NY: Lawyers Co-operative Pub. Co., 1982–)(2 vols. looseleaf).

Juan Perea, *Immigrants Out!: The New Nativism and the Anti-Immigrant Impulse in the United States* (New York, NY: New York University Press, 1996).

Bill Piatt, *Immigration Law: Cases and Materials* (Charlottesville, VA: Michie Co., 1994).

Records of the Immigration and Naturalization Service (Alan M. Kraut, ed., Bethesda, MD: United Publications of America, 1991–) (microfilm).

"Redlined" Immigration and Nationality Act: Reflecting Amendments by the Illegal Immigration Reform and Immigrant Responsibility Act (IIAIRA) of 1996 (Washington, DC: American Immigration Lawyers Assoc., 1996).

Alan Edward Schorr, *Refugee and Immigrant Resource Directory* (3d ed., Juneau, AK: Denali Press, 1994).

Shepard's Immigration and Naturalization Citations (Colorado Springs, CO: Shepard's/McGraw–Hill, 2d. ed. 1991–) (also on WESTLAW).

United Nations High Commissioner For Refugees, *Collection of International Instruments & Other Legal Texts Concerning Refugees and Other Displaced Persons*, U.N. Doc. HCR/IP/1/Eng/Rev.1 (1996) (2 vols, vol. I Universal Instruments and vol. II Regional Instruments).

United Nations High Commissioner For Refugees, *Conclusions on the International Protection of Refugees*, HCR/IP/2/Eng/Rev.1994 (1994) (a new volume is issued every so often).

United Nations High Commissioner for Refugees, *Handbook on Procedures and Criteria for Determining Refugee Status,* U.N. Doc. HCR/IP/4/Eng/Rev.2 (1992). (the handbook is available in English, French, and Spanish on the World Wide Web/Internet at http://www.unhcr.ch/refworld/unhcr/unhcr.htm).

United Nations High Commissioner for Refugees, *United Nations Resolutions and Decisions relating to the Office of the United Nations High Commissioner for Refugees,* U.N. Doc. HCR/INF.49/Add.4 (1993) (this publication has been discontinued since all of the documents are available on REFWORLD, see below).

United States Department of Labor, *Dictionary of Occupational Titles* (4th ed. rev., Washington, DC: U.S. G.P.O., 1991). (the index is available on the World Wide Web/Internet at: http://www.wave.net/upg/immigration/dot_index.html). *

United States Immigration Commission, *Reports* (Washington, DC: U.S. Government Printing Office, 1911–)(41 vols.).

Visa Processing Guide: Process and Procedure at U.S. Consulates and Embassies (5th ed., Charles M. Miller et al. eds., Washington, DC: American Immigration Layers Assoc., 1997).

§ 17–5 PERIODICALS

For articles about immigration law, policy, and procedure, the *Index to Legal Periodicals* or *Current Law Index* should be consulted under the following headings: Emigration & Immigration; Deportation, Citizens & Citizenship; and Aliens. The following periodicals are of continuing interest in the area of immigration.

AILA Business Immigration News (Warren R. Leiden ed.) Washington, DC: American Immigration Lawyers Assoc., (1990–) (4 issues/year).

Annual Immigration and Naturalization Institute (New York, NY: Practicing Law Institute, 1967–).

Georgetown Immigration Law Journal (Washington, DC: Georgetown University Law Center, 1985–) (4 issues/year).

Immigration Briefings (Washington, DC: Federal Publications, 1988–) (monthly).

Immigration Law Advisory (Rochester, NY: Lawyers Cooperative Pub. Co.; Bancroft Whitney Pub. Co.; 1985–) (published 8 times per year as part of the *Immigration Law Service*).

Immigration Law Report (New York, NY: New Clark Boardman Co., 1981–) (11 issues/year).

Immigration and Nationality Law Review (Buffalo, NY: W.S. Hein & Co., 1977–) (annual).

INS Reporter (Washington, DC: Immigration and Naturalization Service, 1976–)(includes administrative decisions, C.F.R. changes, and statistics) (4 issues/year).

International Journal of Refugee Law (Oxford, U.K.: Oxford Univ. Press, 1989–) (4 issues/year).

International Migration Review (New York, NY: Center for Migration Studies, 1966–) (4 issues/year).

Interpreter Releases (New York, NY: American Council for Nationalities Service, 1924–) (weekly, good for articles and analysis of new rules and decisions, also available on the IRIS CD–ROM).*

Journal of Refugee Studies (Oxford, U.K.: Oxford Univ. Press, 1988–) (4 issues/year).

Refugee Abstracts (Geneva, Switz.: Centre for Documentation for Refugees, UNHCR, 1982–) (4 issues/year).

Refugees (Geneva, Switz.: Office of the United Nation's High Commissioner for Refugees, 1984–) (monthly).

San Diego Law Review Immigration Symposium (San Diego, CA: San Diego Law Review, 1975–(vol. 13)) (annual).

Transnational Immigration Law Reporter (Palo Alto, CA: Immigration Common Law Exchange Society, 1979–) (covers international immigration problems) (monthly).

United States Immigration and Naturalization Service, *Annual Report* (Washington, DC: Immigration and Naturalization Service, 1946/47–).

Visa Bulletin (Washington, DC: U.S. Dept. of State, Bureau of Consular Affairs, 1968–)(lists availability of visas by country) (monthly).*

§ 17–6 COUNTRY REPORTS

Listed below are the principal country materials for use with applications for political asylum. For further information, see section P "Country Situations" in David Weissbrodt and Marci Hoffman, *Bibliography for Research on International Human Rights Law*, 6 Minn. J. Global Trade 200, 315 (1996).

Amnesty International Report (London, U.K.: Amnesty International Publications, 1962–, annual).

Canadian Immigration and Refugee Board, Country Profiles (Ottawa, Can.: Research Directorate, Documentation, Information and Research Branch, Immigration and Refugee Board, 1990–, quarterly).

Country Reports on Human Rights Practices (Washington, DC: U.S. Government Printing Office, 1977–, annual).

Critique: Review of the Department of State's Country Reports on Human Rights Practices for ... (New York, NY: Lawyers Committee for Human Rights & formerly Human Rights Watch, 1983–, annual).

Human Rights Watch, World Report (New York, NY: Human Rights Watch, 1990–, annual).

§ 17–7 BIBLIOGRAPHIES AND RESEARCH GUIDES

Leah F. Chanin, Immigration Law in Specialized Legal Research, Chapter 8 (Boston, MA: Little, Brown and Co., 1987–).

Patricia G. Court, A Guide to Researching Immigration Law, 94 Immigration Briefings 1 (May 1994).

Claire M. Germain, Immigration Law in Germain's Transnational Law Research: A Guide for Attorneys (Ardsley-on-Hudson, NY: Transnational Juris Pubs., 1991–).

Daniel J. Jacobs, Immigration Reform and Control Act of 1986 and the Illegal Alien: A Selective Bibliography, 50 Record 246 (1995).

Daniel J. Jacobs, Political Asylum, Refuge and Sanctuary, (U.S., Foreign & International), A Selective Bibliography, 42 Record 561 (1987).

Donatella Luca, The 1951 Convention Relating to the Status of Refugees: A Selected Bibliography, 3 International Journal of Refugee Law 633 (1991).

Scott B. Pagel, *Research Guide to Immigration, Aliens, and the Law,* 77 Law Library Journal 465 (1984–85).

§ 17–8 ELECTRONIC SOURCES

Databases

IRIS (Immigration Resource and Information Service) CD–ROM (Washington, DC: Federal Publications, quarterly updates)(full-text immigration library including statutes, BIA decisions, and secondary sources).

LEGI–SLATE (database for proposed federal legislation).

LEXIS IMMIG Library (federal immigration statutes, court cases, administrative decisions, and regulations).

LEXIS IMMIG Library's BIA file (Board of Immigration Appeals decisions).

LEXIS IMMIG Library's REFORM file (text of Immigration Act of 1990).

LEXIS LEGIS Library (federal bills, bill tracking, Congressional Record, legislative histories, and other information related to the legislature).

REFWORLD on CD–ROM (UNHCR)(REFWORLD on CD–ROM is a collection of databases developed by the UNHCR Centre for Documentation and Research (CDR). REFWORLD contains authoritative information on refugees including current country reports, legal and policy-related documents and literature references. See the REFWORLD on the World Wide Web for more information at http://www.unhcr.ch/refworld/pub/refworld/refworld.htm).

WESTLAW FIM (federal immigration statutes, court cases, and regulations).

WESTLAW FIM–BIA (Board of Immigration Appeals decisions).

Web Sites

American Civil Liberties Union, Immigrants' Rights
http://www.aclu.org:80/issues/immigrant/hmir.html

> ACLU immigration materials and information on immigration and civil liberties information.

American Immigration Lawyers Association
http://aila.org/

> Background information on immigration and this organization. Provides information about legislation, AILA's publications, and links to other relevant sites.

Amnesty International On–Line
http://www.amnesty.org/

> Provides country reports from 1994 to present.

Dictionary of Occupational Titles Index (U.S. Dept. of Labor)
http://www.wave.net/upg/immigration/dot_index.html

Federal Register
http://www.gpo.gov/su_docs/aces/aces140.html

> Access to the Federal Register from 1995 to present. Provides for keyword searching.

Human Rights Watch
http://www.hrw.org/home.html

> Contains summaries of the reports done by HRW on the human rights situations in various countries.

Immigration Communique (Federal Publications, Inc.)
http://www.fedpub.com/immigration/communique/

Sign on to Immigration Communiqué for quick news tips and weekly updates on immigration issues from the editors of Interpreter Releases.

Immigration Forms

http://www.wave.net/upg/immigration/forms.html

A collection of immigration forms.

Immigration: A Practical Guide to Immigrating to the U.S.

http://websites.earthlink.net/visalaw/homepage.html

Lots of useful information on a variety of immigration topics (green cards, new laws, marriage, etc). The section called "Links with Other Immigration Sources" is very useful. The user can browse the Immigration and Nationality Act, search the CFR for relevant regulations, access federal appellate court decisions, and find links to other relevant sources on the web.

Immigration and Refugee Board of Canada

http://www.cisr.gc.ca/main_e.htm

This site has country of origin research information, other information on immigration and refugee issues in Canada, and find links to other Canadian immigration information.

Immigration Superhighway

http://www.immigration-usa.com/i_suphwy.html

Information on U.S. immigration laws as well as information on immigration and refugees in other countries.

REFWORLD (UNHCR)

http://www.unhcr.ch/refworld/refworld.htm

The databases of the United Nations High Commissioner for Refugees offer rapid access to reliable information in the public domain. The documents include a full range of law, country information, analysis, and comment on refugees and displacement. This site contains speeches of the United Nations High Commissioner for Refugees; UNHCR information; country information; legal information; and bibliographic information.

Siskind's Immigration Bulletin
http://www.visalaw.com/bulletin.html

Provides access to the Immigration Bulletin through an index and keyword searching.

Thomas Legislative Information on the Internet
http://thomas.loc.gov/home/thomas.html

Provides very timely access to pending legislation, status of bills, and recent enactments; prepared by the Library of Congress.

United States Department of Justice, Executive Office for Immigrantion Review, Precedent Decisions
http://www.usdoj.gov/eoir/efoia/bia/biaindx.htm

A collection of recent BIA decisions (3296 of October 4, 1996, to present).

United States Department of Labor, Office of Administrative Law Judges, Immigration Collection
http://www.oalj.dol.gov/libina.htm

Contains the full-text of recent BALCA en banc decisions, full-text of immigration decisions, the *Judges' Benchbook: Alien Labor Certification* (2d ed. with supplements), and selected labor-related immigration statutes and regulations.

United States Department of State, Visa Services
http://travel.state.gov/visa_services.html

   Provides information and notices on visas, the text of
   immigration legislation, and a variety of visa publications.

United States House of Representatives Internet Law
Library, Immigration, Nationality, and Citizenship Law
http://law.house.gov/104.htm

   A collection of foreign and U.S. law on immigration,
   nationality, and citizenship. Also provides links to other secondary sources.

United States Immigration and Naturalization Service
Home Page
http://www.ins.usdoj.gov/index.html

   This site contains information about the INS, statisti-
   cal information, immigration laws and regulations,
   forms, and other information.

United States, Department of State
http://www.state.gov/www/issues/human_rights/in-
dex.html

   The Human Rights Country Reports are available at
   this site for 1993—present.

United States Supreme Court (Cornell)
http://supct.law.cornell.edu/

   This site provides access to supreme court decisions.
   Keyword searching is available.

University of Minnesota Human Rights Library
http://www.umn.edu/humanrts

   This site provides access to the full text of the most
   important human rights instruments and documents

related to human rights. Documents from various international human rights organizations are available in full text. An extensive collection of human rights related links are also available. In addition, the site contains Immigration and Naturalization Service, Asylum Resource Information Center, Alert Series, Profile Series, and Perspective Series.

INDEX

References are to Pages

527

FEDERAL AUTHORITY OVER IMMIGRATION
See also Constitution
Delegated versus inherent power, 55–57
Executive authority, 53, 54, 73–75
Federal preemption of state regulations, 23, 61–65, 413–14
Foreign affairs, 53, 57
Foreign commerce, 4, 52
History, 3–4, 51–57
Inadmissibility (formerly "Exclusion"), 54–55
Judicial authority, 66–73
Legislative powers, 55–65, 92–108
National identity, 56–57
National sovereignty, 54–55
Presidential power, 53
Punishment of piracy, 53
Removal (formerly "Deportation"), 164
Rule of necessity, 56
Scope of federal power, 58–61
War power, 53–54

FINLAND, 138

FOREIGN MEDICAL GRADUATES, 20, 43

FORMS
Form ETA 750, pp. 127–28
Form FD–258, pp. 270, 281
Form G–325A, p. 281
Form G–325C, p. 270
Form I–20, pp. 155, 159–62, 168, 171
Form I–94, p. 157
Form I–104, p. 297
Form I–129B, pp. 147, 156
Form I–129F, pp. 149, 156
Form I–130, pp. 124–25
Form I–140, p. 126
Form I–151 ("Green Card"), 133–34
Form I–214, p. 202
Form I–263W, p. 297
Form I–328, p. 216
Form I–485, p. 157
Form I–538, pp. 162, 167
Form I–539, p. 491
Form I–590, p. 270
Form I–600, pp. 124, 126
Form I–765, p. 297
Form IAP–66, p. 156
Form N–400, p. 367
Form N–470, p. 346